THE SCARLET CABINET

A Compendium of Books

by

Alice Notley

and

Douglas Oliver

SCARLET EDITIONS

New York, 1992

Distributed by:

SMALL PRESS DISTRIBUTION, 1814 San Pablo Avenue, Berkeley, CA 94702.

INLAND BOOK COMPANY, P.O. Box 120261, 140 Commerce Street, East Haven, CT 06512.

BOOKSLINGER INC., 2402 University Avenue West, Suite 507, St. Paul, Minnesota 55114.

THE SEGUE FOUNDATION, 303 E. 8th Street, New York City, NY 10009.

Copyright © 1992 by Alice Notley and Douglas Oliver

All rights reserved.
Library of Congress Catalogue Card No. 92-80228
ISBN 0-9632219 0 6

Several of the books in *The Scarlet Cabinet* have had previous incarnations. *Penniless Politics* was published in a typescript facsimile edition by Hoarse Commerce (London, 1991). An early version of *Beginning With A Stain*, entitled *From A Work In Progress*, was published by the DIA Art Foundation (New York, 1988). *Homer's Art* was published for the Institute of Further Studies by Glover Publishing, Canton, NY, in 1990. Selections from the above and other works herein have appeared in the following publications: *Bombay Gin, Talisman, Poetica, Assemblage, Broadway 2, Brooklyn Review, o.blek, Ploughshares, Shiny, Avec, On the Ledge, Hambone, New Directions 55, Mudfish, dark ages clasp the daisy root, The Best American Poetry, 1990*, and, of course, SCARLET.

First Edition, March 1992

Cover art and design by Yvonne Jacquette

With special thanks to Joel Lewis

>Scarlet Editions
>101 St. Mark's Place #12A
>New York City, NY 10009
>U.S.A.

```
810.80054 N913s

Notley, Alice, 1945-

The scarlet cabinet
```

Contents

Introduction	v
Penniless Politics, by Douglas Oliver	1
The Descent of Alette, by Alice Notley	61
Sophia Scarlett, by Douglas Oliver	213
Beginning With A Stain, by Alice Notley	349
Twelve Poems Without Mask, by Alice Notley	381
Homer's *Art*, by Alice Notley	397
Nava Sūtra, by Douglas Oliver	419

Introduction

THERE is too much of human material now everywhere: the world is covered with "the man-made." None of our problems can be solved by making more of it, more of the material, including books. Shiny-covered, same-looking books everywhere. To go into a bookstore & be made sick by all the books there, is almost the same as to be made sick by all the dead cars in New Jersey, seen from the train window, early in the morning. All achievement, writerly & poetic achievement included, must become more invisible. The notion of "soul," of the Invisible, must be taken up again, as the world becomes more & more a piece of bricabrac, with books the same as everything else — detritus, anybody's effusions made tangible then quickly discarded. Many of the world's great achievements *have* been invisible in the past. The entire achievement of the Australian aborigines, for example, 40 to 50 thousand years worth of invisible spiritual wealth possessed by a people who wore no clothes, had no possessions, & lived in the desert. One is no longer entitled to write down every thought, rush it straight into print. Things must be thought out & saved in the air, in order to do less harm to the world. Obviously only the most memorable will be saved; obviously things will not be saved that only the author can remember.

To come at the issue from another place, if you were a woman amid the bombs in the 1991 Gulf War, your only sense of comfort would have come from the inside, not from the outside. Not from physiology or biology. Is such comfort an illusion? When people die who are close to one, comfort comes from a very much deepening widening sense of self — eternal, invisible something — mysterious, suprasensory something. It helps no one suffering now, right now, only to want to remake material structures in societies. That is the future that never comes — *they* are suffering *now*. The only help there ever is *now* comes from the invisible. And we cannot continue to fill this world with the man-made. We need a sky, we need a river, we need the outskirts of town & the mysterious lives of animals nearby. We can no longer tolerate seeing ourselves everywhere, for we are ugly & dirty & tasteless, because we have become so self-absorbed that we care for nothing but staying alive, staying material. The spaces within us are empty with words from books, images from screens, the day's boring routines: very much empty with the most superficial kinds of reasoning — from newspapers & politicians, & from academies which mass-produce trains of thought. We are the same as this ugly outer world we've made, we are outside entirely outside, but the world is no longer beautiful & original.

Poetry (including prose that is poetry, novels, stories that are poems) could be a force for the re-establishment of the invisible, for making people's inner lives more important than this constant assertion of substance. For poetry is not about words, or how one thinks, or making things. It is about essence — the secret inside the material. It uses rhythmic speech to tell what it knows, because measure helps the defining of essence, because whatever is done should be done attractively, because rhythm is bound up with living. Poetry aims at truth. But the truth is not intellectual, it is the truth: that fact poetry knows, & academic disciplines do not. For example, a mythic assay at the truth is probably better than a run of polysyllables or equations, because figurative outlines & bright colors are easier to see & understand — & paradoxes are better resolved, & used, when they are not named paradoxes but are named Coyote or Athena. Poetry has had many uses in the past which are denied it now. It told stories, for example, often more quickly & more *essentially* than prose does — & taking up less bulk of pages, less of the physical & psychic space of the outer world. Movies, & most novels, are simply more dominating than poems are. They *impose* their stories, they impose minds upon us. Poetry's involvement with music formalizes it, beautifies, its aesthetics are more like nature's, less like a human's. What is made becomes mysterious, instantly, itself, even if what it tells is tragic.

Poetry, of course, has increasingly become an expression of the individual self, at least in this culture. Or an imposition of self, if you will. Partly people have become isolated from each other (& so one does say "I" instead of "we"); unifying beliefs have dissipated; one would like to protest against being one of the so many bodies there are (Science, ever the villain, having made humans so pervasive, beyond all reason). One feels that this personal "I" is too well known by now. Those who use it well will continue to bear important witness, but poetry cannot be brought out of isolation with the use of this isolated "I". The poet must prophesy the future, speak to it, educate it. A Whitmanic "I" might do that again — but then, that's been done. On the other hand one must not make poetry boring by reasoning the human figure, the poet with mouth & tongue, out of it — leaving only the mannered tracings of a mind which, by constantly denying its own existence as "someone," becomes of interest only to translators of difficult discourse, to critics. *Someone*, at this point, must take in hand the task of being everyone, & no one, as the first poets did. Someone must pay attention to the real spiritual needs of both her neighbors (not her poetic peers) & the future. We must find our voice, we must find a story — something that reproduces itself in the aether, not necessarily in bookstores. There must be a holy story, that is told again & again, that is known in the air, that satisfies without the temporality of successive pages, the terrible linearity of all these successive books.

The problem with changing — our ability to change — would seem to be that we can only change in ways that are implicated in prior ways of doing things. There *is* no revolution; nothing ever changes enough. By the logic of what I've been saying, (for it really is an "I" who has been speaking), Douglas Oliver & I shouldn't publish this book at all. By my same logic, though, we *should* be writing or making poetry. What should we do as it's made — merely read our work, at readings attended by people who already know it? Or should we keep trying to reach more people? We present *The Scarlet Cabinet* as a *different* book, an *economical* book, a *slightly less* self-aggrandizing book in the sense that two selves are sharing the same space. All the works herein are themselves dedicated to the re-establishment of the spiritual, the invisible, human world. We hope that they are better than us & better than the object this volume is.

Alice Notley, January 25, 1992, New York City

(...and a word more...)

Given what Alice Notley has just written, let me add: so we thought we'd put a publication together which made less of a fuss about being any one particular author's precious book designed to further an equally precious poetic "career". No-one has expressed better what it means to be a Reagan-Bush era poet than David Smith and David Bottoms as editors of *The Morrow Anthology of Younger American Poets* (New York, Quill, 1985) as they characterize their contributors:

> He, frequently she, is born between 1940, at the onset of World War II, and 1955, the third of Eisenhower's smiling presidential years. A child of suburban parents, television, and the nuclear nightmare, he is often the first in his family to complete college and escape a life of physical labor, the first to fight in or publicly oppose an unpopular national war, and among the first writers for whom intimate and personal revelation would not result in obscenity prosecution. He is also young enough to think of Vietnam as the war of the older brothers, of Haight-Ashbury as the scene of curious movies, of Martin Luther King, Jr., as a day off from school. He has one or more graduate degrees in literature or writing and teaches both in a college. Yet he is sometimes a lawyer, a psychotherapist, a businessman, a librarian, a filmmaker, a rock musician, or a sheepherder. On the average, he is thirty-seven years old, married with children, has been or is an editor of a literary magazine, has published widely, frequently translates poems from the Spanish, French, Hebrew, Swedish, Polish, and Italian, has been awarded a grant from the National Endowment for the Arts or the Guggenheim Foundation, or both, and rarely lives where he grew up.

I won't scatter that with (*sic*)s. This, with its conscious and unconscious irony, has become a favorite piece of prose for me. It catches very well how powerful the US academy and writing schools such as Iowa have become in determining the most respected styles of poetry. Much worse, it shows that influence at work in imposing a cautious, conservative, middle-class, career-seeking *life-style* upon the poets of the academic cliques, even upon the radical ones. (As for rock stars, sheepherders, etc., we can count about one each in the Morrow anthology's 100+ choice.) Of course, this is just one -- the most socially pernicious and aesthetically narrow -- of U.S. poetic power-bases. Acquired fame as a mainstream "Giant", a Beat, a leader of ethnic or sex/gender causes, a performance/song poet, a fast-rapper, a language poet, a regional or city-based poet... allows you to join other cliques, which foster other poetic styles. We, with our own power bases, can't get free of these modern "careers" but we think they betray the poetic, spiritual, and political assumptions of our own work. What you can't do in the orthodoxies of present-day publishing is be too unusual within your clique, or publish what you think is important *just because* it's not in currently favored genre "A" or "B" ("Quotation marks? What's *that*?") or, even, is regarded as played-out ("*Dialect* romance?").

Why not, we thought, publish a book rather like a chance collection of Medieval manuscripts bound into one volume, a book which thumbs its nose at all this? We only care about the spirit of what we write anyway: we don't care about the business-suited poetic world, or the NEA -- any of that. So why not have some fun?

Douglas Oliver, January 25, 1992, New York City

PENNILESS
POLITICS

a satirical poem

by

Douglas Oliver

Penniless Politics

All politics the same crux: to define humankind richly.
No-one non-populist or penniless can found a viable party
though most religions have such saints. She was his Haitian
saint Emen — Emen for Marie-Noelle — for non-Christian
Mary-Christmas. In New York with him, her husband, Will Penniless,
they'll found their party in a poem. Black with White nation,
Voodoo-Haitian with immigrant Anglo-Scots, hairy-chesty,
penniless, Mrs. Penniless, with him, Will Penniless.

To begin with everything missing. Emen set aside contempt
for extreme right or left, mein kampf or ill-kempt
politicians, or for middle-roaders. She held fire. "If we got married
all might be overcome," said Will hopefully, knowing their road
had to start absolutely from rough ground, not a track behind them,
just doves crowding trees black with starlings, white bird
between each black one. Their first steps aimed to pre-empt
mimicry of the past, to enter silence, then put it behind them.

Their poet has a white male face just as mean as each face
of rich white males in today's *Post*: the New York Mayor race.
So though he may tell he may not star in the story, outlawed
from penniless power. He (Will) tells how that day, bored,
Emen asked Will, "Do we have to get married?" Who replied, "For you,
power may grow by separation. But we whites are so flawed
that we must change sexually too. You decide." "For your race
I'll marry this once. And for love I'll make Voodoo for you."

As Will and Emen tumble down through their love, he'll
keep telling their story impersonally. Sex needs such tact. They'll
always know she opened Will's eyes one morning in Brooklyn,
Utica Avenue; on their marital bed she, the Haitian,
changed his skin sympathies, unshackled his stiff pelvis
by mounting him, squirting black womanly sperm into him,
remaking his mind and his tongue while he was still
asleep, new conceptions warm and liquid in his pelvis.

The opening of eyes, changing of person, exchange of sexes,
Black for White, We for They, Woman on Top, all this is
not merely antithesis: lying on his back, Will gazed
up at Emen's eyes browsing as if he were a book while she grazed
his lips with Haitian lips, her hips working
at his hips, on his chest her breasts drifting cloudily sideways.
He felt male, white, but so much gave up his penis
to Emen that it could have been hers in him, working.

She sat above him on her altar there. Finished. Like her mother
once, a U.S, voodoo mambo retired to Ouanaminthe, crooning to Legba:
"*Attibon Legba, ouvri bayé pour moin,*" open the wicket
to the spirit world. "*Ago! Ou wé,*" you see me at the gate,
open it for me. "*Ouvri bayé pour moin, ouvri bayé.*" Hear
the call to Legba, Will, "*M'apé rentre lo ma tourné.*" Will wait,
"I will enter when I return". Praise him, Will, "*Ma salut loa
yo!*". In origin male or female, red clay, Legba's old phallus here.

They talked of a Haitian memory: rare rains had caked the savannah
plateau as they travelled south from seeing maman
at Ouanaminthe on the Dom Rep border; they sat, stranded, shaken
by truck rides, beside the few huts, the Belgian mission
of St. Raphael, crossroads in flatlands, their rice and beans
bought from a householder; in the backdrop each black mountain
patched with erosion's tarpaulins; this for Will a true Legba-
like moment, recalling Port-au-Prince slums, the kids lacking beans.

Under Nature's blind eyes, on Earth's body, Emen drew the congo cross
of souls circling criss-cross of living and dead. Heterodox,
Emen took a political vow with Will there, since maman mambo,
orthodox, had scorned their wedding, and had added: "I told you no:
I lived there: I was a *boat people* in a land of baseballs.
Her religion's Yankee politics. Mine's true to *noirisme*, voodoo.
My poor *pays terrifié*, suffered so bad from Papa Doc's
pouvoir baroniel, and now our poor make your country's baseballs!

"What matters," maman had snarled, rounding the mid-pole of her *hounfor*
by the Massacre River, "is how wide (*large*) you're thinking before
you begin." Emen had made an oath: "Let us live on the margin
of life and death, world citizens before our national origin,
unsexed before sexed, poor before rich. A great bowl fills a bucket
through a hole in the bottom, the world fills the domestic, women
fill men, magic fills the rational." This became what they swore
by the St. Raphael huts where "wealth" was pink and slimy in a bucket.

Dawn there. Worrying burble of dawn chorus quietening. Dull.
A cloudy nowhere. Yet political. No sound now. Already political.
Pink light behind closed eyelids. In Will's blindness her brown hand
drawing a *vévé*, the sacred figure, drawing with flour on to sand,
a simple cross on a St. Raphael path, white on brown, Legba
the Voodoo crossroads loa; in silence they were going beyond
pantheons and had trod out that single path to the simple
cross-stroke, first political choice, sign of Legba.

The *vévé* scintillated at its cross-point, a glint of fire
issuing from an ant-hole in the inert silicon, a power
that transcends naming by priestcraft, not Allah's oneness,
nor Guatama's enlightenment, nor unity of trinity, nor singleness
at the heart of any four-fold-truth or of four ends of humans,
nor therefore finally Legba's own fire, not a loa's prowess
but something obvious to all, a grand cliche: higher
knowing includes birth of action; at crossroads we become humans.

In the tiny flame's center the idea of their party was found.
Exactly in, not round it. They stepped inside there. Flames around
their embrace. Brotherly...sisterly...but also the sexual
flame inaugurates the political. Sweeted by flame they fell
down a chute of memory, partly personal but also transforming
the personal into memory held by whole peoples; central, central,
get central and you'll fall down that chute, flames, a dark
descent into conception, blindness of ideas transforming.

Under Brooklyn's pale windows they reaffirmed Haiti, their apartment
a telephone receiver shape. Up on Utica, the brick tenement
looked downhill long past Carib cafes, bodegas, the Santeria
botanica where Emen bought plaster saints, down to shadier
Prospect Park; wind swept white doves off branches; starlings:
black dice thrown a moment. Trembling as if Legba possessed her;
"You've got to join my spirits before we talk of government."
White doves skirting out in fear then flocking to the starlings.

Naked brown and whitey-pink, they walked through their apartment
on Utica and, arm round her, Will warned: "You can't make government
from religious spirit." The room full of charms, a St. John
statue at his knee, thunder loa stone, wall blankets, the Oshun
chiming bracelets beside steaming coffee. "Political theory,"
she smiled, "splits the world one way, and religion
splits it the other. We'll not mean more than we know and we'll invent
the unexpected, free of priestcraft, messianism, masculine theory."

That morning they drafted their first manifesto, not in verse.
They looked in the jar: twenty dollars, a few cents, worse,
the phone cut off and a pizza to buy for lunch. Will put carbon-
layered sheets into his Olivetti and typed a little. *"Ah bon!"*
exclaimed Emen. "Now add this, oh and this, and this,"
as the keys rattled and a fuzzy document emerged from the ribbon.
"Chain letters!" blurted Will. "That will get over the curse
of poverty!" After retyping, the document read like this:

Dear Dolores:

The U.S. has room for a political party twice the size of the tired old Republicans and Democrats. Less than half the American people vote — easily the lowest turnout of any major Western democracy. Just add it up: 40 million missing voters or many more if everyone registered. A new political party could swamp an election. And it's going to be simpler to start one than you ever believed, so simple we're doing it by chain letter.

Photocopy this and send it to three of your friends — preferably ones who don't normally vote. Then come to the Memorial Day Center, 13th Street, on September 14. All questions about the new party will be answered then. We, the undiscovered political America, will make sure it's something we *can* vote for.

Sincerely,

Emen and Will

Take that prose and I'll... Let music take the prose and I'll
tell some real thing, giving the fictional melody and muscle
as 20 Hispanic and Black women bunch underneath the day center's stage,
13th Street, and a massive Afro-Cuban who may
not stay, being the only male besides Will, and somehow does.
Emen at the mike says: "Some of you think there's not so many
of us, but we only wanted 20 and thought probably female,
and here's a second man. Look at his size! He's tremendous!"

Emen sparked like static in her store-bought dress, gleaming brown
in buttercup yellow, hips perched on gold-painted pumps, downtown
strut across stage light shining from fierce excitement tight
and controlled. "Yes, Mr. Magnifico Cuban, *gwo neg*, you a right-
wing refugee? All *my* brothers sent back at sea. You get resident
status easy?" The man grinned like a bison. "Just wanted to fight
for money, Ma'am. Ain't no professional fights on Cuba. I come aroun'
tonight to hear how you're goin' to give us our next pee-resident."

Emen: "I'll name you now... name you High John, a long and knotty tap root.
Yessan my thoughts tie up in knots, my words'll untie the knot.
Listen to me girls, listen to me John, listen to me Will,
we're starting way in our minds behind the politicians. What'll
they do for us? D'you see East River swirling chemical
past our lives? White man sells a normal, sells a normal
condo: we're gonna drum a normal, drum a normal congo.
How does the song go? We all learnt it long ago
the hard way: ses sold on the corner, crack at Prospect Park.
Gonna drive through, senator? Don't stroll there in the dark,
shadow over neighborhoods, your cartop movie
of clouds wiped black by bridges; coasting along, Senator, groovy, poverty
only half visible, but evil all around. Do you get the vibes?
Car phone rings, another builder offering bribes.
In the toy war of your politics it's who has that ringing tone
who gets stuck in craters sleeping on their own.
Behooold this Brooklyn school, just trying to advance,
dirty feet itchy in old socks shuffling into the Regents
exam; and the school board dubious...
Does that make you furious?
Those politico horsemouths open and swallow the wind
while their high-rise projects suck our children
into elevators pungent with poverty. We're gonna put our sex
into estate management and City Hall won't guess what happens next.
You ought to see my new mind
new children alive there from microsecond to microsecond
and the wider winds rise in fury
us, us, supremely now the jury
sitting down in judgment on a loss of nationhood
we women with our bodies of light and blood
no longer on the doorstep making what we scrub
clean rise in price, no longer the soft-shelled crab
creeping into their kneeling buses, victims of the soft sell,
the hardness power of an exploding city. Well,
no law against making half a city highly moneyed
but we're going to make it spiritually honeyed
for behooooold the grim order reaper waiting for our lives
while lawyers and medicos store our honey in their hives.
Race, race, race, prunes supposed to hate the milk,
milk souring, greed, graft, greed, white talk
souring. We're going to eat Black food, my honeys, taste the snake;
we'll be Ayida-Weda's daughters; we'll take a trick
or two from Legba the trickster, even if you're Catholics
or whatever your sense of the sacred, you Hispanics,
or godless like Will, my husband dear, who tries so hard
to have dark consciousness though dressed in his leopard

spotty skin. As yet, don't ask me, we don't have a *program*.
Who d'you think I am? An economist, a law-maker? Don't be absurd,
High John. Let's put the serpent back in the sky. Politics
will come once we recreate spirit; then we'll talk *program*."

High John thrust fist in air, captivated by the active haunches
of the buttercup Haitian striding there; he rode her vocal punches
with "Awwight!"; otherwise grinned like a bear now, mute.
Fat and busy Dolores, at 50 unable to pay for her first heart
pacemaker, got irritated at male-ficarum and climbed the stage.
She fluttered black mackerel hue of Hispanic eyelids, her salute
fist contra fist to the Cuban, meaning "You're out to many lunches",
as she said... but I'll enter her mind not her words at this stage.

I come over from Morrisania section, South Bronx, a bit
of Santeria here, Catholic there, great danger this room gets lit
up by flimflam. Don't be too smart: fool sees corruption
and hates the whole thing; police bad: hate policing; politician
bad: hate governing; monopoly stores bad: steal their produce;
until we live among and are thieves. City housing departments? I mention
"honest" up there I'm called naive. I been pitching it
to them a hundred years; no result for puertorriqueno, can't produce

the *quid pro quo*, they say. D'you think my *barrio* don't know
'bout powerlessness? Morrisania, just tops for living below
the poverty line with income support, public assistance, 46 per cent.
plus... medicaid, supplemental security: citywide only 17 per cent.
Vacant lots 39.1 per cent.; citywide 7.5... "Verna Lee Judge,
70, clearing wine bottles from the sidewalk." The per cent.
of AIDS deaths double the city's... Dolores spoke: "You
gonna do a little *brujo*, little spell here or somping? Judge

for yourself, Emen. Who gonna listen? Sure, you look right pretty
up here, but try being dumpy, hunchback, chipmunk-eyed in this city
like me..." She grinned wide and whirled round to show her plump rump.
"You gonna take out full page ads like billionaire Donald Trump?
I tell you how to go to work. First we tell plenty lies, make trouble
until everyone say 'Hey! Whass going on?' We gotta bump
up the action, start us a little newspaper, get publicity,
dream a little trouble, make more, keep on troubling, no end to trouble."

From the floor, Will: "Our friend Dolores is celebrated
for championing her, er, *barrio*, Morrisania. But let's not get hated
like the city bureaucracy. We have to spread out from the, er, Tao
of immediate neighborhood, of ourselves doing good, into

an honest politics engaged in the wider good. How can lies
be the best beginning?" Emen answered him: "Put these two
views together, call the lies cheap tricks to get the poor started;
later appoint party honesty-functionaries to see where truth lies."

Dolores again: "It will need a few bucks to succeed with my plan,
for first this center's custodian needs a bribe; and then
you'll all go out tonight, infesting the neighborhood with rumor
invented by me. Next, find me some trashy block newspaper
too local to know me, too small to check a freelance story—
and Will, you can rewrite my English. *The Brooklyn Blazer?*
Just right: only other editors read it!" It was the Cuban
who came up with cash; they got busy; so now read their story:

VOODOO'D VOTERS SWARM TO NEW U.S. PARTY

POLS WHO WORK BY MAGIC

The leaders of Spirit, a new political party, denied today that a Voodoo spell brought the public flocking to their first open meeting.

A surprise turnout of 900 packed a small day care center in Brooklyn after attractive Haitian, Mrs. Emen Penniless, daughter of a Voodoo priestess, sent out a single chain letter only two weeks before the meeting. The letter urged recipients to send further letters asking friends and strangers to go to the event.

Bronx Hispanic radical, Dolores Esteves, charged that Mrs. Penniless, well-known for her Voodoo practices, could only have raised such support by casting a spell.

"My envelope had herbs in it, and Emen's husband admitted that there were certain rites performed, though he wouldn't tell me what."

Emen retorted that Dolores was miffed because her own years of activism had failed to draw the crowds. "It's just plain tomfoolery," she claimed.

She added: "We are not a Voodoo party; but we respect the spiritual aspirations of ordinary people and think this respect is the missing element in modern politics."

Spirit is aiming for the much sought-after "third party" in the U.S. — the vast army of non-voters, whose numbers are double those of either the Republicans or Democrats.

Meanwhile, day center custodian, Giorgio Jacopucci, was grumbling: "I wish they'd told me to expect so many — we nearly had a riot."

The old chain letters would say, "A woman in Syracuse
refused to participate and her house burnt down: don't you refuse."
Despite your grin, some fear would seep in. To disturb
Spirit's electorate, the next letters had some harmless herb
dust in the envelope corner; and the chain began as before,
spreading links outward, down Long Island's great curve,
spattering into the Bronx, and to the Birth of the Blues
in NY, that's Harlem; and meetings were staged as before.

This went along with scandalous irruptions
into official occasions, such as the famous interruption
of the Nuyorican festival one August in Central Park,
when Emen, Dolores, and a horde of Hispanic women, stark
naked, leapt onto the bandstand and invited all men
to strip the secrecy off their masculine pride and mark
the festival with a vow to end male domination
of politics, reviving an ancient spirit between men and women.

Will himself, poet of the poem, was still the first non-American
convert, a non-franchised alien, a BBC-speaking Scotsman
who'd seen a bit of the world. He told them all
at a party gathering in Brooklyn that he had a call
as a Bard to charter their progress: he had a scheme
— since occasional arrests and constant publicity put them on
Page Three so often — that he thought would appeal to more intellectual
audiences: and NYCU were planning a lecture. Thus went the scheme:

A great writer from Africa was warming on sherry in the wings,
a voice they admired, the hall packed, when Emen and her sisterlings
mounted to the mike. "We're the Student's Party for Internal
Righteousness and International Tolerance," she lied, but with a kernel
of truth, for it spelt SPIRIT. Because she was so black
no Uni official dared stop her: a photog from some journal
snap-snapped as Will joined her. "Now listen to the things
this white man has written for those who aren't black."

Will declaimed this:

WHITE CROSSROADS

*"Ah'm to suck your asshole, stomp it,
ain't mah style. You tell it, baby,
you tell it, John, okay?
This is the play-off boy, you know it, I know it."*

All the propertied amusements, whether
Leona promised Trump to sell her lump
of land, or whether Wall Street crashes
only temporary within the lifetime
of the dispossessed, it's psychological poverty
of tired whites with lots of balls
pretending to speak for heterogeneous nations,
sadly moral faces of governors, wizened
with the humor of getting their own way.
Even if their millionaire bridges are breaking up
already thin smoke lines
of the new bridges arc above falling girders
and Catherine wheel firework tires
of phantom buses whisk across from City Hall.

*"Ah'm to suck your asshole, stomp it,
ain't mah style. You tell it, baby,
you tell it, John, okay?
This is the play-off boy, you know it, I know it."*

At crossroads mental crossroads multiply
down by City Hall of Cities Going Wrong.
So white Manhattan manwoman white of sick tongue,
my white, my white shirtskirt, white of eyes,
newly arrived at crossroads of choice, as
white owner, leather attache box with locks
moral owner manwoman me never could manage
Black bab bab voices crossing
smoked tarnish of tar of crossroads,
while Iyou white cross
to squash courts of whitened stainless steel,
fuckwords rising round us from legs
stretching out from walls. Me this
in other ways. Give up my plummy fucker voice.
Learn situation. Having left an English dream
half-finished, come abroad
seeking a voice change
to find that my voice must
crack open like a snake's egg for,

being its old self, whole and ineffectual,
it takes part in the real only by irony.

*"Ah'm to suck your asshole, stomp it,
ain't mah style. You tell it, baby,
you fucking tell it, John, okay?
This is the play-off boy, you know it, I know it."*

My white life learns till middle age and stops.
Ask the white elderly what per cent
of their fellow world they've ignored.
Not too late in middle age to open out
to the Dahomey snakeloa, Damballah
the Voodoo-Santeria ordainer
whose red body wriggles along rainbows
whose venom spills yellow like egg purity,
the white skin of my life a container
of snaky kindship, moving in my moving limbs
across the crossroads, woman in me snaking,
my regard for myself priapic,
me, only a stranger, without right,
willingly drinking righteous venom
until white face becomes suddenly spotty,
along my lily forearm a white wart,
my eyes discoloring and seeing new colors,
vomit on the street like a yellow ochre city
seen from a satellite, not without beauty
in these Cities Going Wrong.
On a stoop a bar of soap, white barges Blacks
a dropped neon tube explodes into argument.

*"Ah'm to suck your asshole, stomp it,
ain't mah style. You tell it, baby,
you fucking tell it, John, okay?
This is the play-off boy, you know it, I know it."*

Voodoo's loa Attibon Legba
cannot rule my crossroads of white indecisions
but protects in my dreams the black crossroads
and protects threshholds of new lives
writhing with the principle of the snake.

12   THE SCARLET CABINET

Below Will the hall seemed a tray and the audience its sweetmeats
in ranks: their silence another of poetry's defeats.
But the African writer swirled out in her highly-hued dress
from the wings, beaming and gently applauding. Quite shameless,
the intellectuals awoke to clap. Alas the stewards were already onstage
and Will and Emen spent the night in jail. Their arrests
reached the *Post*, page 3 again, "Caught clambering over the seats".
Though Spirit, as party, was mounting, no-one guessed the next stage.

For with first success came first danger. They got too busy,
forgot spirit, spent on stunts, mailings, had the hypocrisy
to trade on their "Voodoo Party" label, in *Post* headlines
became "The Hex", while Dolores fed the *News* other lines:
"Non-Voters Anon", "The Stunt Pols", "The Slaughtered Chickens",
"The Spellbound", "The Underdogs", and they always met deadlines,
until in the party inner circle Emen spoke out: "We're the Non-Policy
Party with a party machine. That's not how the spirit quickens.

The students have printed Will's poem; it's drawn in some scholars,"
Emen said, "bibliophiles of the asshole, linguists of the followers
of the dollar. But you see my eye bruise?" (Badly swollen temple.)
"I earned this recruiting in crack tenements: it's all too simple —
with middle class white faces now joining our variegated force,
and their Press seeking copy — to become some Aime Semple
Macpherson phenomenon and forget we're the party for non-voters."
At that, the silent Cuban, High John, revealed his own force.

Spirit'd had no suspicions of High John, monosyllabic, statuesque,
once a bit battered, baggy in suits like the dispossessed
he seemed to be. Maybe if he'd been more flamboyant a bruiser,
a notorious heavyweight, not a quiet cruiser,
the members of Spirit, mostly women, would have pierced the pseudonym
given by Emen. Instead, they'd written him off as a loser.
Anyway he'd been absent three weeks. But now a sudden unrest
by the door revealed him, Conqueroo, fists high to suit his pseudonym.

He came from the shadows to show them he too had an eye bruise
and a swollen chin. "I don't s'pose many you women read the *News*
sports page today," he said with his usual grin. "And none you scholars
did's for sure. But this here's a cheque for 3 million dollars,
'cos I'm the new light-heavy champ of the whole freaking world!"
Pandemonium, rustle, newspaper sharing, until the Cuban's gappy molars
stared out from the back page. "You've never asked for my views,"
said High John, "but I can help your non-voters to win over the world."

"Don't make me scales of laughter in this room," said Dolores.
"What we going to do with this money? You, boxer, it sure is
everything we fight against you bring here." But the Cuban replied:
"Okay. Capitalism. My big fist. Thump, thump. Right,
I read you, Dolores. But I have a little Capitalist housing plan,
mostly it is for the inner circle. And allow me this: we hide
the 3 million from the media. Can't fight slam-bam if the story is
you fight for charity. And I take a few risks in a hidden plan."

The plan led to tragedy later with the party under attack:
the inner circle of Spirit were involved not with the crack
dealers, said a Channel 9 special, but with *Behemoth*, the new Ecstasy.
Emen didn't waver, for she strongly admired the Cuban, and I...
that's the poet... Will... suspected... that is, he had suspicions...
well never mind... For love of Emen and of Spirit, he swallowed a lie
in her loyalty and, liking the plan, fell not far behind
in backing the Cuban, even when fighting the most public suspicions.

For the time we'll keep the plan hush-hush, but High John staged
strict auditions for some kind of play. Even Will plunged
those with his rendition of "White Crossroads". "Good, but not enough
courage," chuckled his wife. But though she might laugh
a sadness invaded her during the secret rehearsals: the cast
seemed to play various ghosts, an old crone, a rough
Columbian with stereotype Uzi, cops, and some part the Cuban upstaged
them all with; he looked reckless, as if his die were cast.

One day there could be other Cities of Spirit, and the model
for action will constantly change; but we'll tell of the ritual
that first made the party famous. Emen asked Will for love to dress
her one night as she lay down. He placed a finger vertical to bless
the wet rind of her glistening pubis, so's to seal in the love,
locate the political in the personal and spiritual, her breasts kissed,
a pallid mood lifting, nipples caressed, a radical
pair of panties covered with hearts slipped up with his hands of love,

twin-heart sex shop strapless brassiere, a dress golden
and red with more hearts, symbols of the loa of love in the olden
religion, the jet ringlets gleaming on her black skull,
his male lips in the hairy perfume, the final kiss from Will
and then she dressed him with the same care. That night,
he rose high on stage in his cowboy boots and told a thousand people
that they would now see someone lovely to behold in
his eyes, the mother-like, the loa-like, Erzulie that night.

"We are the gods," Emen told them. It was her new thing. "Who are
the gods? We, we, we are. We are in train—" (a rare
grammatical lapse in her oracular excitement) "—We are in train
of creating a ritual, yes a ritual for a politics beginning again
in the breath of spirit. There will be a tunnel, there will be a mirror;
we shall pass through; there will be an altar: we shall attain
mercy before it; there will be a book: we shall write our
deepest thought in that book, over a cross, glassy as a mirror.

The cross will be on a tomb — Christian enough for you Christians?
I'll be thinking of the Voodoo family Ghéde, and you Buddhist nations
can think of the great beyond; and you atheists can just shiver;
but one thing we'll all learn by the ever-flowing river:
you can't speak true politics unless you keep knowing you're dying.
We'll resolve conflicts, yes, but that creates others. I believe a
tremulous sense of the sacred, a goodness that frightens,
wins our hearts fully when a friend lies to rest by that river.

And that's how we'll create policy, and they will call us the gods,
the founders, the neglected people who against all odds
will bequeath their spirits to the future and become the loas.
Now, I know that only I and some others have Voodoo, that most
have no religion or have other dogmas; this is not the issue,
for our nature is half spirit and this must speak so as
to touch the deeply inter-communal in humans, the lightning rods
of sympathy which should flash in each political issue."

For a moment she sobbed softly at the beauty of thoughts
none can share with another, Erzulie, loa, in her courts
of love, perfumed with flowers, coquettish in a dance,
spinning round, showing brown thighs, wooing the audience
to the spirit of love, poignant. "D'you tell me of the homeless?"
she sighed. "I tell you of homes in your soul, a residence
there for everyone: that's where we build first.
No creation of policy if it's our souls which are homeless.

We'll plunder religions for their best, make off with spoils
— deadliest ceremonies, altar paraphernalia, and sacred symbols —
we'll set up wide arenas, travelling temples made of wood
and canvas, rituals of the dead turning to good
in white tents enclosing night on darkening river meadows.
They'll be 'art shows' to the park authorities but we'll be understood
by people of spirit, meditating there until the mind fails
and the soul speaks of policy in the tents by river meadows."

By F.D. Roosevelt Drive, bordering the ungentrified
Alphabet City of Avenues C and D, the Lower East Side
has its playing fields. New York's Parks Department,
told of a "performance art work" — though "art" meant
here the art of creating politics — left them alone.
Each non-voter would meditate in a tiny compartment
then pass through a tunnel to a tent, there, ritually, to decide
what Spirit should choose were it to have one policy alone.

And so the party referendum began. At first it seemed absurd:
down by the river on grassy wasteland at dusk (the word
already spread by the correspondence network, funds upcoming
from the Cuban), flatbed trucks arrived amid a murmuring
crowd, a line of Portacabins went up, with a white tent central
and a wooden tunnel creakily winding towards it. Voodoo drumming
muffled on tambours. All on hire. Night fallen. Traffic heard
far-off. Otherwise silence. Non-voters in the cabins. The tent central.

Spirits sat down in darkness with their private mind,
these were party members squatting on stools, behind
doors saying "Occupied": they'd hired converted lavatories.
Lavatory, *hounfor*, cave, rushing water, wind through trees...
in isolation you can shed selfishness; shed
the pell-mell mind of self-interests until you find
your truest interest which you and others share. Rousseauist,
perhaps, but his citizens never squatted down in such a shed.

The faint urine smell was desirable; it anchored down
wandering thoughts; but as Mama Johnson for example hunkered down
in her shawl, on her stool, she, like all others, saw
a photo of cemetery crosses glimmering on the cabin wall,
and, like all others, heard a memory of voices in her head:
"Go be hard with men, chile, doan go be any more
hard with me, right? Liable pregnant her. Sank herself down
on ma sofa, stoned and risk of AIDS, just shit in her head.

"Shit, this place smellin of it. Did I tell you to watch the big guys
or what? I ain't talking to no Voodoo gods, but my eyes
shut all right, right? Praying into the heart of gold,
just like Emen told me, and I'm finding what? Old
Mr. Pappy Man O' Mine, this heart finds you, this place
smells of piss. What's this? I see the urine trickling from cold
old bums in doorways, their blue black skin, slitty eyes
and damaged voices. My own old mama in that hospital place

"puffin at that oxygen tube, urinating in hospital, bare
black half moon ass, nurses wiping her drool, you doan care
'bout no politicky at the bed of death's for sure. Deep
things hover round her, come in your soul, doan quite weep
in your heart but get weepy for others' pain. I feel their power
in me now, working, that infected white baby next door, sleep
the last sleep, baby, with horrible blue black round your ear
spreadin' down your shoulders, I wan' you to take my power."

Mama began a travail of spirit, the eyes of her own dead
mother looking at her. This poet leaves aside as sacred
her hatred of wrongs to her race, but all other hates
flicked mothy wings at her mother's blank stare, twin agates
which still saw *her*, and the moth wings departed.
Still, male street talk bothered her ears. "Jessie states
this, Sharpton that..." but her dead mother's face shuddered
with underworld breath, and finally all street-smart departed.

"These death things in me working. Oh, we can't put none that
right, right? Not the death things. But death's what we got
for to purify life with. Now *that's* politics.
Good protestant me, none them juju tricks.
Just this soundless dagger of death stuck in my soul
and this piss leaking from old men's pricks,
old women's pussies makes me feel alive. Thrilled. I've sat
long enough now. I'm clear, clear right to my daggered soul."

A half hour in darkness. Mama Johnson lived close to suffering,
but other non-voters sat for hours, their culture buffering
them from such clarity: that politics begins with the knowledge of death,
at a moment of birth, a moment of marriage, mid-breath
in the death of minds, birth of minds, sharing of minds,
measure for measure. They sat until there was nothing left
in their thinking but the mid-moment, no false toughening
of attitude or wise cynicism, nothing but the sharing of minds.

A West-side lawyer came, scornful, and so spent two nights
encabined, wrestling with his demons, whereas three minutes
sufficed a Baptist minister, who opened his night's door and cried
"Hallelujah!" and so on, only to be mortified
when made to re-enter that darkness until he got kinder;
fast-thinking gays, closer than anyone to those who had died,
emerged weeping; and many failed and some started fights
when asked to retire; but those who voted had nearly all become kinder.

And we shall live in Ma Johnson's body, feel our stomach's weight,
breasts couched on it like elbows, troubled frown, heavy gait
swollen buttocks behind us under a print dress, an ache behind
our varicose knees as, feeling sombre, unusually kind
we climb out of our hut and tread damp, silvered grass to the tunnel,
where silently our people guard the entrance, a perfect mind
among us all, not our own. The wooden tunnel has a wooden gate;
the river gleaming across to Brooklyn; drumming in the tunnel.

Not yet a mass revival, this referendum, police car
flashing by the baseball diamond where a bonfire
lit the dancing, a line forming for the meditation,
a Haitian possessed by Ghede — one form of elation,
the old East River in this spiritual, just a-rolling,
and Ma Johnson just a-strolling to the tunnel, proud in her nation
and in her body. "I've got to keep my heaviness, my ugliness, entire:
that will light my fire, set the spirit rock and rolling."

"Ouvway biyaay poor mwon," was her password; they opened the wicket.
She mounted a ramp up to flat-bed trucks, set
at angles with others, bearing a "tunnel" of rail wagon
bodies, gutted and linked together. Puffing, Ma Johnson
peered around in the close dark, smelt old food, but saw nothing
in the tunnel's first leg until a low lamp came on
in an alcove, where sat a fat black man, top-hatted,
a dead cigar in gap-teeth, bright smile full of nothing

except banquet: plump cummerbunded stomach, gold-
rimmed shades, lawyer-striped trousers, and old-
fashioned spats above spit and polish toe caps. "Ouvway
biyaay?" Ma repeated hesitantly. No reply.
He sat on, cross-legged, obviously a party member
taking part in a fun house charade, with nothing to say
as the lamp went out, the floor creaked like ice, cold
futures ahead, warmth in the past she'd begun to remember.

In a present of many choices, a hand tapping her shoulder
made her spin round in the tunnel. A bright diorama
like a florist's window lit up to one side
a vista of real roses, but after a second they started to slide
sideways as stage machinery rumbled and were nudged out the way
by a panorama photo of graves. And who it was that had died —
whether her husband, her mother — she felt no-one had told her,
and it would be herself one day, treading her graveyard way.

The short journey brought her to a final corridor
with a side table, two leathern chairs: an abandoned Pullman car,
a woman in white satin sitting there; she had a blue
stole, a sort of black Virgin Mary look, and she beckoned to
Ma Johnson to join her as she wolfed some wedding cake
beside a brass table lamp, her lips covered with goo
and her body breathing flower scents. Taking her place, Ma
nibbled, as directed, the sickly-sweet wedding cake

and found it falsely-happy opposite this wedded "Mary"
who waited till she'd finished, then nodded, glanced away,
implying "Now go". (Unaware, Ma had passed an assessment:
anyone not solemn, any wrecker, anyone who offered harassment
in that car would by a trick of the doors be ushered
outside and calmed down by counselors. Ma Johnson's embarrassment
was acceptable.) She rose and walked on, remembering the day
of her own wedding but wrongly: she a burlesque bride ushered

along a deserted aisle to marry that woman,
call her Mary, Emen, Erzulie, someone not quite human
but large like her own soul. Down the corridor ahead
the exit now glimmered grey as all other lights cut dead
and walking towards the grey screen she saw an image
of herself approaching, waddling the way she had, a dead
spitting image in the same clothes, mimicking her every movement.
She passed straight through the screen, straight through her own image

as a curtain of silvered threads, that is, the "screen", drifted
over her face and a whirring video camera clicked and stopped.
Suddenly fit for the occasion, Ma Johnson danced down a steep ramp
that led to a wide space of trampled grass, a damp
temple: overhead swooped shadowy wings of canvas
falling, skirting into walls; the dark air glistened, for an arc lamp
in the roof lit up a large mass on the ground, solid
wood that rose in black ledges; Spirit planned to canvass

political opinions on an altar. Now, this wasn't Voodoo
or the "phenomenology of the transcendent self" — just a trick or two
for freshening up the normal, and Ma Johnson felt quite normal,
though she confronted a coffin sticking out of the altar: a funeral
despair and a hope of spiritual meaning transcending the religious.
The squared arches of many ledges formed a stepped mantle
over the coffin and each shelf bore icons, the Buddhas, the Hindu
figurines, a Koran, a minorah, a Toltec calendar, and not just religious

objects: a Humanist lapel badge, a philosophy book, "The Sovereignty
of the Good" (for its title), activist posters, the rich plenty
of Civil Rights buttons. Above the coffin, dazzling on the altar,
lay a book whose pages were boldly handwritten. She felt a
fleck of water on her cheek as someone flashed out of the
shadows and sprinkled the grass with libations. They'd taught her
what to do next; so, whispering an oath to write down truth, and empty-
minded otherwise, she stepped forward, straddled the top of the

coffin and saw in its surface an embedded hologram: a white cross
seemingly swimming on blue waters, and at the criss-cross
was a hole like a mirror of waters, a depth we can sink
into, or from it dead souls may ascend if we think
of them as sunken. She moved till her knees were each side
of the cross, now under her crotch in the darkness; she was a link
between upper and lower worlds; the book lay just across
from her on the ledge arching over the coffin, which from the side

formed the tongue of an altar-mouth, embedded with the hologram
on which Ma squatted. ("Must write. Rest my goddam mouth,"
she muttered. "Momma up my middle. Or is it Jesus who is the Angel Mary?
Or my ancestors rising from some underwater island? Scary
feelings in my hand. Must write the three things Spirit must do.")
She wrote: "I never wanted much, just goodness. I wish we'd been happy.
Oh but we can be." ("Is that a thing? Okay then...") "Make wealth,"
she wrote and added, "for others, for the children, anything we do

has to help the future and make our dead mommas and daddies proud."
("Is that two or three? Well...") "Stop the garbage." She spoke aloud
as she wrote: "'STOP ALL THIS GARBAGE, MA JOHNSON HAS SPOKEN'..."
It seemed so trivial, yet she felt the whole world had awoken
as she looked at the book's instructions: "Write the three
things that Spirit must do. Turn to a clean page in this book and
write the very first things in your mind. Don't be a coward
about this." Now Ma had done so; and these were her three.

And *Newsday* made it all clear:

VOODOO PARTY CASTS SPELL -- OF AGREEMENT

Spirit, the political party rumored to act through Voodoo, claimed today that they'd found incredible agreement among the faithful about what party policy should be.

In a secret two-month referendum, Spirit set up a fun house on meadows bordering New York's East River.

At night, party members meditated in cabins, then walked through bizarre tunnels before entering a tent arranged like a temple. There, they straddled a coffin, and in a book resting on an altar wrote down their recommendations for policy.

"Call it supernatural or what, of the 1,000 members we had time to ask, 98% came up with an identical policy program," said Spirit spokesperson Will Penniless.

"It's amazing. Once everyone's in the right frame of mind, we all know what a political program should look like."

This was the program:

- Make material wealth for other people, spiritual wealth for ourselves. (Some, mostly men, specified that "other people" meant the "third world" or the "homeless". Some, mostly women, specified, "Help our neighborhood first.")

- The only qualification for party membership should be goodness and respect for the history and future of the people's individual families.

- Long-term earth environment issues must have first consideration to save resources that our children's children should inherit.

Mr. Penniless said this meant: "Evidently not an end to the making of wealth. We can't help anyone without listening to the business lobby."

The point was to make greed go out of style, so that more desirable ways of using wealth result and that individual fortunes should not be amassed.

"Following one suggestion, we shall hand out year's suspensions -- in a kindly way -- to members who use normal political manoeuvers to destroy party happiness and decency."

As for environmental issues, Spirit wants to confront popular opinion by cutting down on private car use, domestic trash and industrial waste. One voter just wrote: "Stop this garbage."

What about drugs and crime, and, if there's less of hydrocarbon pollution, unemployment? Policing, rehabs, housing, international relations even -- no real change in practical policies can come until the moral climate has changed, the party claims.

The Era of Dispute began. Marxists and anarchists, observing
the rise of the party, infiltrated meetings, noisily swerving
every debate into a grab for power. "Power! Power! --
Pyuuhh! Pyuuhh!" Emen would reply, pointing a pistol finger.
Church persons, too, sought to color all talk with their god. Spirit
politely asked some of these serpents to retire for a year:
then the slithery could come back on their own feet, deserving
to pass through the gate if they'd open their doctrines to Spirit.

Some non-voting students joined up and the agency newsman Peter Belia
(or "Belly" Belia, pronounced "Memorabilia"),
brilliant, Blakeian, Zoa-like, jowls full of politics, T-shirt
of bottlegreen vinyl formed as if from leaves, pert
eyes with arched brows meeting in hooks. Leftist cliches
dazzled like coins on his lips: ozone, brokers hitting paydirt,
greenhouse effect, endangered forests, Nicaragony, Cubaphilia,
constitutional change, freeze on Wall Street dealings... But the cliches

made more than one eye gleam, for the great belly had swallowed
up Pentagon strengths on this missile, what House rules allowed,
who was deputy foreign minister in Boukina Fasa -- the Belly
had met him -- who were Haiti's more notorious torturers, naturally
he'd met them, which made Emen shudder; above all he was expert in
the failure of American third parties, being himself a revolutionary
totalitarian who believed in the schizoid as authentic: few followed
him there, but some were impressed by all he was expert in.

He fell in the Purges for decency, which gilded the party with fame
for the first time, as the Voodoo label dropped limply off and the name
became simply: pure Spirit. Belia and his kind were a venomous
enemy if we're still talking Paradise. The worse enemy was
this influx of white liberalism, of those whose own nation
did not live under day-to-day threat, and even your poet must
repeat that he lacks right to speak, yet must speak all the same
in honor of what he is not, of all that Baraka calls "nation".

For decency may also be dangerous: it opens the door for the brutal;
and while the deprived rage, it's there smiling, utterly futile
in its wish to be liked, to do right, to avoid discord, unease.
Yes, it rots the union of races it seeks; it's often a social disease
because it can't tolerate strangeness and mystery in others and secretly
it, too, seeks for power: as if the unengaged self, wishing to please
everyone, might also dominate them. Yes, nothing more subtle
than this enemy, which could survive these purges -- but secretly --

-- but secretly." The line's lame. The plot simultaneously sticks.
A poem gets stuck at a point; you can find it; the music is
always faulty there. Step back in the dance of the verse
and you see that the thought had already flagged, or, worse,
couldn't solve its problems. We were warned of this from the start:
"No-one penniless can found a political party"; the poem stutters
to a halt at that point; the party not fully political, the public's
attention not fully caught. Go back; find the music; restart.

The music begins in each point over again, the beats that unite
the flow of melody into infinitesimal perceptions. And within each beat
the overall form is anticipated; so the past is caught up in the present:
the future breathes in the point. Here is the clue to the decent
founding of politics in a poem: that the future comes alive
now: that the neighborhood is to the world as the moment
is to the whole; unlike the politicos, poets get their world right
if the point and the flow of the whole are united in beats: all alive

now and thrilling with the future. And so I look for the singer
who will sing the next part of the song truly. And I find her
making love: any woman. "Our world," she dreams, "is shining with promise,"
and she spreads her labia for the pearled and purpling head of the penis,
while the man thinks: "Point, point, penetrate right to the source
of time," and she: "Keep it moist with the promise, for this
is our whole world weeping with joy, a gaseous planet, a voyager
through the ethereal to time's borders, pulsing out from the source."

PART 2

Yuhwa Lee, Lee Yuhwa also, in Queens, at 4 a.m.,
or are you one of the thousand Kims? So different from Emen
but now our standard-bearer, engaged in the same sexual act
as she, you on top: your husband, Juan, Hispanic. Only through mixed
marriage of minds can Spirit come into full being,
for Korean-Chinese-Japanese stand apart, wanting only an intact
economy in which to practice their aggressive capitalism.
Not to be racist, Spirit must be full, "full" being

difficult to describe, when the stores run by other people
are threatened by square-shouldered Korean work ethics. Yuhwa Lee
had tossed aside a students' weekly from Seoul: its "wits"
had written: "Oh, EHWA Women's University recruits
male students: I may take the admissions exam. Better choose
the Home Economics. After graduation...perhaps it's
a man I should marry" — to Yuhwa, this reminiscent of Seoul,
its sexism still alive in her new community, much as she'd choose

her own people above others. But Juan, one of the new Hispanics,
had joined with her in reformed sexual politics,
and now wanted her to join Spirit. She with her bright
Republican mind: in its darkness an electrically lit
honeycomb, an America of rooms, each clean as a Korean restaurant:
inside each room, a neat capitalism, orders in place, no get-out
from unceasing hard work, a Confucian familism, business
ethics that begin in a Christian church or a Korean restaurant.

She and Juan were joking, with tags from that magazine,
as they gyrated on the bed: on top, she felt obscene
in a nice way. "Oh, I am hurting for money," she said with feeling,
feeling quite different really. Juan sighed at the ceiling,
"How about practicing the alcohol reaction?" "No more thought
of drinking," she trilled scornfully. "Let's play at see-sawing."
He picked up on the script: "The top person is like a stock concern
whose 60% profit left investors bankrupted." "No more thought,"

she grunted, "let's do away with such a non-productive math."
And pinching his glans, she disclosed the slit -- one path
to the human unity of number, then furtively, like shop-lifting,
stuffed it under her, settling back, buttocks uplifting
and down-posing, while she still talked, chirpy as a bird in Korean
sing-song. "Yankee politics—it lost its way, Europe shifting
all its power balances, East no longer enemy so much, don't laugh
when I'm UP talking please: I'm being DOWN to earth, very Korean.

24   THE SCARLET CABINET

'Yankee politics brain-dead,' said Representative Obey, *Times* today.
No-one can make speeches no more: consultants tell them: 'Okay
sentiments but too *risky* for say in public. Got
question for you, Pol, what kind of 30-second spot
they going to make TV out of that?' asks consultant.
No debate left in Congress. Three election issues: What
money in bank? Who your media adviser? Can they take away
your mustache? It's con, con, con, con-sultant

all the way." With mustacheoed dreamy smile, Juan came beneath
her in political unity and rhythm. She grimaced through her teeth
and continued: "No wonder your people lose all respect. Respect
me, I respect you. Simple. Crawl to me, give me money, then expect
me to think you slime. A cynical people, a cynical no-show vote.
Listen, in Seoul we got terrible politicos, graft, spies, select
your opponents, rough 'em up. And still we got some kinda belief
in government. Everyone's gotto vote, vote, vote

or there's no aaah!, life." Her turn. She rose in dignity
like a mare rising. Her bedroom displayed a Christian civility:
wall photo of Seoul, its mountains topped with huge TV mast
surrounding the plunge of white skyscrapers, all the past
her family had lived. Her ink-stones in obsidian, white
writing-brushes, wood lanterns, kiss curls on pink-faced
figurines: yellow and red panels, thick calligraphy: in a pretty
picture, Jesus, Korean speech balloon but he Jewish-White.

"Thing is, you can't draw the liver out of a flea," she said,
dressing. "I join your party I gotto organize some trade
for you, small business lines, we Koreans know well. Now don't
get worried, no grasping capitalism, we work for party. I won't
do no thing your Emen don't agree. But you can make each neighborhood
finance center for Spirit. You come along with me to Hunt's Point
market, right now Juan, I show you how to make a bed
of roses out of fresh produce, a Spirit shop in a neighborhood."

As cabbage leaves drift on the sidewalk, and cherries, squashed, bleep
their stones, ice sparkles under broccoli, the washed beans seep
water through slats of wood out at Hunt's Point, and it's only 6.30,
the wholesale market already almost done, the rest of the city
barely waking as the dawn gleams on unsold boxes of onions,
the trucks in circles like cowboy wagons, the gutter clogged with dirty
produce—a cab draws up from Woodside. Juan and Yuhwa step
out, staring at these early risers who return, squeeze the onions,

in case they've missed a dollar. And beauty curls its lip, and Spirit
turns away. For this is trade, whose only merit
in poetry is to fund sentiment and bourgeois drama and treacle
family life, steady ascensions above poverty; trade's vehicle
like a heavenly car, bears the business soul up to the clouds
of international enterprise. Juan, like Will a poet, had little
taste for buying and selling. While Yuhwa, lithe as a ferret,
slipped from stall to stall, his head was lost in clouds

of romance: revive neighborhoods, yes, but day to day labor,
no romance there. His eye caught suddenly a Korean neighbor
from Woodside, a grandfather, squatting by the kerb, in his palm
a translucent plastic box, misting, as he packed in farm
raspberries for the store, the compound-eyed seeding of the fruit
weeping and the speckled crimson cushions kept from harm
in his cupped hand, a careful installation, like a favor
paid, a nestling in richness as plastic closed over fruit.

Juan knelt. "May I buy that?" he said. "Here's 10 dollars"—
so badly he wanted it. Box and money changed hands, the oldster's
eyes black anemone blobs under grey hair waves.
At four or so, the child plays with money purchase, saves
real cash at five; so, in civilization's childhood, money
comes in early and is not ugly: someone craves
the beauty of the fruit, a way is found that answers
that need: the berries glow: the dullness is just money,

and represents absence. When humans exalt this absence into holiness,
not "value" but "profit, price, trade", then ugliness
begins its necessary rule...Well, Yuhwa got a loan
in a Woodside basement, another member of her Korean
church rotating the credit that had got him started; and a store
was bought in Morrisania. "See?" she said, "For Emen
and Spirit to take over one day. D'you think Her Holiness
Emen" (this, jealousy) "will bow down and consider our store?"

Now celebrated, the project, "Buying back the Neighborhood",
dates from this time, though Dolores and her sisterhood objected
at Yuhwa's Opening Feast. "Having fun, are we? Look, we have Af-Am
and Hispanic peoples, the Caribbeans, a few whites, not many Jews—am
I just racist if I ask what of Chinese and Koreans?" Don't they stand
apart? Will Spirit just switch on, switch off, if the Asian
communities aren't with us? Getta a capitalist, getta hood,
lissenan where do we stop? Or, rather, where do we stand?

In Morrisania? Your store in my neighborhood, where I radicalize
the people? Dirt money from Seoul's going to open our little Bronx eyes?
Huh!" A speedy-gay, lawyer-rasp voice broke in—Lou Levinson—
joined up with the journalist Peter Belia but stayed—"Listen
to the Korean, Dolores: afterwards radicalize. I gave my youth
to law—hundreds of corporate paydirt deals and then some.
We've got multi-national input here: with all you guys
we'll turn Capitalism about-face, give Morrisania back its youth."

Dolores spat back: "Hear of one Ramon Rueda, with his Mao Ze-dong
cap, an' his People's Development gangers? Squatted a Washington
Ave block, Bronx, in the 70s, homesteaded it with city loans,
made it a showplace. In came a President to Carterize Ramon's
dreams of a model village for the poor, Ramon's pay rising
to 30 grand as he hit stardom. Then came the fights and arson's
charred visit to PDC offices. Ramon disappeared, all the ranting
finally amounting to little. Ha! Morrisania not rising."

Emen eased her breasts on the table top: "Dolores, you left-wing, honey,
me Haitian, Juan from Puerto Rico, Yuhwa with her money
from Seoul, Will with his WASPISH *paw-try*, Mr. High John,
Cuban capitalist *de la quint' essence* — cash from K.O.s — and Ma Johnson,
with her Harlem wisdom, are talking true together: aim to join us?
You and Lou Levinson? While we buy up this whole section our intention
can't be public, has to be *petit-à-petit*, act a little funny,
be a little dense, and house to house get residents to join us."

High John had arrived in a chauffered Merc: he was taking an airing
before the next day's championship bout. His trainer, despairing,
skulked behind smoked glass and the boxer had entered, tired,
perhaps of training: his politics were suspect but most admired
his generosity though Emen worried that he lacked center. "Soon enough
Dolores," he said, "a little drama in your *barrio*. Look, I haven't retired
yet: 'nother win tomorrow, with my purse and a little bit daring,
'*Vinceremo!*' iffn I get that money working fast enough."

Some sat round the long table, some round the noodle table with its side
dishes of baked, raw and broiled meats, fried
vegetables, kimchi, soup. "Korean cookery's a marriage
of two dominating ideas, say China and Japan, having the courage
to make a third new thing, leaner, fitter for the nation," orated Will.
Long table: rice, bun soup, raw fish, more kimchi. "Not to disparage,
the Korean," he added. "Now New York's like a nation, whose died-
in-the-dish politics has lacked *cuisine*: watch and we'll

"put new ingredients in the recipe," Will said. "The wealthier Japanese
let's set aside — and the up-town Chinese, but we need a down-town Chinese
member." They found a waiter, Peter Sung, and added one of the calmer
homeless people who hung around their meetings, Georg, a peasant farmer
from Mittle Europe who'd hit the bottle in New York, but had a lifetime
knowledge of greens. Then Peter pierced through their radical armor:
"All profits ploughed back, all work very low pay. You get happiness,
if you your own boss. No unions. Experience of lifetime."

Members of Spirit honored the Wobblies and the early heroical
unions; like them, this poem is scandalized at Peter's unradical
approach to wages. Pay low pay! A squabble broke out
between Dolores on the Marxist edge and Koreans standing out
for family advancement. But Peter just said, "Low pay
means good life. Capitalism powerless. See? All talk about
greed, waste, environment — all depend on paying people
more than real need. S'great, S'great on low pay

providing you pay yourselves." An over-heated Dolores,
(husband dead, you gossip mongers), who had rather liberal mores,
took Peter to bed that night. She blinked telephone switchboard eyes
at his thin ribs, his penis grey-wigged, at the peasant-wise
face-lines taking her round and round many smiles. He, half
his life womanless ("a Kwang Tung ancient, a historical prize,"
Dolores was thinking), experimentally poked her thick forest
and cupped her curdling buttocks, dividing them gently in half.

Dolores, her mind boiling with argument, enflamed by Puertorriqueno
radical rhetoric, now divided herself; she opened the "O"
at the center of mood. To describe aging lovers at work
seems intrusion. But we forget Legba and the unvarying fork
upon fork of his crossroads. Two paths cross. The center is sucked
down and up into the divine. At a liquid point, at a rhythmic jerk
of a naked penis, Dolores formed her full lips into an "Oh!"
full of good humor and spitty remarks; then she set to and sucked,

and this was the idea she sucked in: though Peter's orgasm was feeble
(low pay), Spirit grew warm between them, a church without steeple.
Low pay had divided her right and her left thigh. Marxism:
give us high high pay, the workers' just share. Capitalism:
give them high pay to a point, for exports are built on home
sales, and the cash coming in from abroad is the jissom
that signals the standard of living has risen all round. An inescapable
logic either way. "But what if we took less pay home?"

wondered that dyed-in-the-wool radical, Dolores. Home sales
would fall, but if we didn't *mind* that, made ourselves
Third World workers almost, exporting generously from the self outward,
the bigshots would be delighted at first: competitiveness restored!
More pay for them! Exports would increase, the bosses get richer,
while unions howl; and then one day a nation restored
would cry, "Enough!" Low pay has brought back our spirit; the scales
shall be balanced: we simply take the wealth of those who got richer

while we were learning the lessons of spirit and use it for national
purpose, limiting personal wealth by a ceiling, the only rational
polity. (By extension of logic, the spread of cheap exports would cut
world demand, lessen Third World tensions, tend to even out
international incomes, and do wonders for the environment.)
Pure idealism, of course, But this is a poem; and it's not
not going to happen. Readers may try but can't become cynical:
the poem has decreed the penniless will win: it's a closed environment.

The story of Spirit and the drug, Behemoth (it made you walk tall,
the biggest beast in the world — citizens kept to the wall
when anyone BM'd walked by)... that story of Bad Mind
has its place here, as the party set out to refind
Spirit in Morrisania section, the Bronx. Secret rehearsals
have earlier been mentioned, as if a drama were being refined
for public performance. If so, it concerned drugs, property, real
dangers run by the actors, and death foreshadowed even in rehearsals.

The Cuban, through a front company, bought a condo infested with rats
and Behemoth dealers: "Dirt cheap," he grinned. "It's the dirt that's
costing the money." His next fight, well he bought him another.
Condo A he refurbished — not too much — every brother
and sister of Spirit gave their labor, their civic virtue,
as they would in this Bronx, Dolores's section. However,
condo B: he let the druggies in. Lawful families from B found welcome mats
when they moved out to A, a comfy haven of civic virtue.

Each apartment in B had roaches, sure, but microphone bugs
in the walls too; the wiring ran down to the basement where, under rugs,
an ancient Hispanic lady, Madre Hubbard, kept miniature recorders
sunk below floorboards. Madre Hubbard was really Dolores
in disguise, acting as spy, willing to stash Behemoth
for short spells if the guys on her stoop gave the orders.
The Cuban kept the attic. He was absentee, covert, one of the cogs
in high-level dealing. In his attic he also stored Behemoth.

The Fat Men, the major Columbians, thought they'd the mystery man
over a barrel. On the take but careless, in possession
of the stash, he'd get landed out front if a crash came,
while they'd disappear. Strangely, right then, in the fight game
High John reached his peak, fighting almost for joy,
feeding off risk, conscious of purpose, a boxing Hall of Fame
slot secure; but the joy secret — that the druggy population
who bought the Behemoth would only enjoy

its heady delights for a moment; and some were members of Spirit,
their funds recycled for use in false buying. A demerit
of the scheme (low pay) was depletion of High John's income;
but he didn't mind. In an intimate moment he told Emen
how he'd lost a brother to Behemoth, after dabbling himself, a debt
he now was repaying. The main thing he worried
about was that real addicts bought from the dealers. "When we come
to defeat this evil," he said, "I can never repay *that* debt."

Oh cynical New York, everyone so smart: riots, marches answering
corruption and bad government. Citizens cynical or despairing
cause this: constantly blaming party machines that are voted
for. It only needs a burying of precise platform, voters devoted
to the one end: their city and its cleanliness of heart. An end,
then, to that pride of the breakfast table or the street corner, the toted
solutions with scornful citation of newspaper stories, everything
smart-answered, the means questioned, questioned without end.

Oh New York, remember the Cuban and Dolores who suffered! Simultaneously
five schemes were put into action: the Drug Bust, the Drug Rehab, the
Bank Scam, the Store Score, and the Yuppie Cream. When the Behemoth
dealers and users filled every apartment in Block B, sloth
and crazed violence marked its corridors and environs. Block A
now had a ground level store, run by Yuhwa and some tough
Spirit Party members, working to Korean discipline; and gradually
the neighbors shopped there only, in the store called "Block A".

Store profits siphoned up to the attic of B, to the "unknown" owner;
rumor said he was running an illicit bank and that a loaner
could get top interest, plus laundering of any soiled dollars.
The attic door was of steel, with a grille, and Peter Sung's molars
greeted the callers: even the drug lords did their "laundry"
there. Yet no-one saw cash leave the building. (A lift on oiled rollers
ran down the old chimney to Dolores — Madre Hubbard — that "loner"
in the basement, and *she* took it out.) Not trusting so sudsy a "laundry",

the drug lords mounted a guard. One dawn, old Mo
Hubbard bundled off with her bags, unremarked. Later, a limo
with smoked windows drew up close and the drug guards thought
that Peter had climbed in as the car drove off — at least, they'd caught
a glimpse, but a crowd of women apparently gossiping had obscured
Peter's escape back through a basement window; so the guards bought
the feint; and their bosses, over the walkie-talkies said, "Follow
that car", and it went, empty, back to its garage, which obscured

the trail. The guard's remnant rushed upstairs to the steel door,
now labeled: "This bank has failed and was outside the law."
(Legitimate debtors got their bills in the mail.) Cars
raced off to the front company's offices. Shut. The drug czars
couldn't believe the nerve of this classic bucket shop act
and started detective work, you'd better believe, in the bars
and stores of the neighborhood. That same day, all the poor
users and rich dealers in B got a message, "Clean up your act

and your neighbors will help. If not, get out." But who was the landlord?
They looked out the window: the building was surrounded by a silent horde
of women, five deep in a circle. They were besieged. Now the police
appeared, drawn by the crowd, and it became a national news piece:
the women who wouldn't allow drugs in or out, although food
was sent in. After two days, the desperate users gave up in peace,
leaving the dealers inside, unable to shoot, starved
now, abandoned by their bosses, surrendering at last for food.

Newsday reported Day 1 like this:

WALL OF WOMEN FOILS DRUG SHOOTOUT

An iron wall of women, five deep, encircled a tenement block and foiled a drug-related shootout in Morrisania yesterday, after a sting operation by persons unknown ripped off hundreds of thousands of dollars from Behemoth gangster Bigs.

Police were called to the tenement at 778 Miramont when the silent women assembled for no apparent reason about 8 a.m.

It turned out that an illegal bank plus a Behemoth supply depot had been established in the penthouse. Drug lords, wooed by high interest rates and profit laundering, had cautiously lent the "bank" money, thinking their own fire power would deter any sting by the bank's proprietors.

While they took quick advantage of the interest rates, they mounted a guard across the street to make sure banked money was not whistled away from the building which is full of Behemoth addicts and dealers.

But by an elevator concealed in an old chimney route down the walls, both drugs and money had been conveyed to a ground-floor apartment. At dawn yesterday, Sting Day, the ground floor tenant, Madre Hubbard, a 75-year-old Hispanic, escaped with the loot past the drug guards' eyes. She is still on the run.

Behemoth Bigs figured that the concealed elevator meant involvement of the tenement's owners, Part Meant Estates, and planned a mid-morning raid on the company's Spring Street offices. Another slap in the face awaited them: the company had done a moonlight flit, leaving the Bigs hundreds of thousands of dollars out of pocket.

Back at the tenement block, the gangster guard got walkie talkie orders to invade the building. As two of the armed guards crossed the street, they ran against a wall of women confident that they couldn't use their guns.

While the gangsters dithered, the police arrived, and the gunmen fled. So far no-one knows:

- Who owns the tenement

- Who really lived in the penthouse

- Who was the Chinese man who acted as bank teller

- Where Madre Hubbard has gone with the cash and drugs

Red-faced drug lords have gangster-detectives combing the streets, competing with police to find the answers.

Today the women are still besieging the building, trying to force the dealers and addicts to leave by refusing to let food or drugs in or out. One woman said: "Everything's on the grapevine, so no-one can get picked off as a leader or for knowing too much or anything."

She added: "There's a new feeling in this neighborhood. That's what we're responding to."

Police spokesman, Lt. George Keeley, says: "We'll leave this siege in place. It's a force for peace and without it who knows what would happen?"

They'd smoked out Behemoth by Day 30. (Taped evidence
of major supply lines had been handed on to the cops, but since
that's not a Spirit story, we'll leave it.) Building B
became a co-op — not a yuppie paradise, of course, with enormously
inflated values, but something more modest: nevertheless, a profit
was made, and now with two buildings renovated and a lot of money
both licit and illicit freed for further buying, a new confidence
trick was played upon capitalist forces, creating yet more profit.

Property C was bought. Now the party store run by Yuhwa and Juan
with neighborhood help was booming; it had leaked out to everyone
that profits for Spirit bought buildings: almost a boycott operated
on shops which lacked party blessing — not that they intimidated
customers: it was just the buyers' choice. Then they sold the store
at its peak of success to a capitalist chain, which over-rated
its prospects, since the contract banned Spirit from opening another one
in competition. But because the capitalists set all their store

by contracts, they under-rated neighborhood networks. Extra-legally,
a store promptly opened in property C and all the
customers transferred. This shop was owned by a consortium of residents
(on secret "laundry bank" funds). The first store slumped and the incensed
capitalists were without comeback: no law had been broken, except that
the neighborhood gave its profits to Spirit, just as presidents
of capitalist corporations support the Republicans. Property C
rose in value and the party was gaining in power, except that

protection was given to *all* local firms, many of whom paid
dues to the party willingly. So it went on: mutual aid
for renovation, in the fight against drugs, all increase in value
kept in the residents' control, some co-ops, gradually new
small shops receiving neighborhood loyalty: we may leave
the detail: the struggle bitter, violence rife — soon a few
Italians and Irish lent aid. A financial basis was laid.
Order advances, neighbor helps neighbor, and criminals leave.

Meanwhile, in Manhattan, a meaty bone had been left beside
that sleeping dog, the City Council — in fact, more a great side
of beef. The Estimates Board had been dissolved; now, the Mayor,
seeking budget approval, went to a council become bull-terrier.
In a bad move for the party machines, they'd added a third
more Council districts — and Spirit, pointing like a lurcher
at the scent, had realized that ethnic minorities had
this moment to increase their members on Council by that third.

Of the 51 seats in a poll, Spirit candidates mopped up
20, giving them the sway of the balance and the invite to sup
with a long spoon at the devil's banquets of politics. Patronage
from the pols was refused. Came news from an upstate village
that a Spirit party had formed, then in LA, and Seattle awoke,
and Washington realized at last that this was part of the slippage
of Congress from voter affection: Spirit, a jester, had its lip
at the cup of power: the FBI turned an eye as Washington awoke.

Morrisania, a play within the play of Spirit's success,
now reached its tragic denouement. Remember Peter Belia, the memorious
journalist, who was ousted during the Decency Purge? He'd saved
his revenge for two TV one-shots. The first asked, "Is Spirit depraved?"
and revived the old "Voodoo Party" label. A headless goat,
the remains of a sheep, sundry chickens, and a white dove had
been found in a New Jersey rail siding. "Obviously a Spirit sacrifice,"
claimed Mr. Belia, thinking privately, "This'll get Emen's goat."

"Pamphlets from Spirit were found in a nearby boxcar," he intoned.
"Does Spirit only gain power from magic and blood? Stay tuned
for reactions from Christians Fighting Satanic Crime — after this break."
The fade-out paused on the wretched goat. Belia and his fake
outrage returned to the screen with a really damaging charge.
"Spirit pretends to be radical. Where's its support from the Black
activists?" Appearing beside him, a virulent Marxist, a little stoned,
accused Emen of appeasement, of pacifism, of abandoning her charge.

Yes, Belia's Shot Two, "compiled with the help of anonymous sources",
exposed High John the boxer as the laundry bank banker and Dolores as
Madre Hubbard. Belia re-ran the clips of their cash heist,
showed how the ring of women stopped them all getting iced,
and asked, "Where's that money now?" (His sources were criminal,
and they wanted to know too.) "Was this High John's highest
paid fight, a fight against drugs, to add to his boxing resources?"
Belia asked. "What's the difference between this hero and a criminal?"

Even today, Emen wears on her breast a pendant of jet,
for Belia caught them in an impasse and she kept silent. The profit
had gone to the store scam, and High John refused to clear
his name by endangering the party. "I'll get on with my fightin' career,"
he said. "No-one's goin' to touch the champ: don't get soft:
the cops loved us!" The night of a title defence drew near
and High John became strangely withdrawn as he trained. He kept fit
but the snap went out of his sparring; he was the one going soft.

Making a thin trail through a stormy forest, the champ and his team
entered the stadium that night, a tangle of arms, a victorious beam
in High John's eyes as he wrassled through his fans. Distant trumpet
fanfares far away from the forest from some mountain parapet
out of sight in this dark and furious tunnel; and the blue ring
the red ropes and brilliant lights drew them on. A shot. A bullet
blasted the boxer's forehead wide open. A frightening scream
from elsewhere. The boxer slumped in the aisle and lay shuddering.

The gunman escaped in the melee; the fighter was stilling in death;
and the stadium quietened, shocked: open mouths, held breath.
And again the frightening scream pierced the silence. Oh, it was Dolores
at ringside, her hands to her ruined eyes. As deep in that forest
the boxer had fallen from the assassin's bullet, a flask of vitriol
had been hurled into Dolores's face. There was an arrest...
two little crowds within the vast fight crowd... but let us leave
in sorrow this boxer dying and Dolores scarred by vitriol.

PART 3

The boxing world, bitter against Spirit for "ruining a fighter's career"
("sport comes first"), grabbed on to the funeral. They draped the bier
in blue satins surmounted with vermillion gloves and hired seven black
horses with sooty pompoms. In the coffin, of jet shellac,
High John lay low in his ring strip. Past and present champions
headed the cortege, TV cameras were high in apartments, a crack
brass band started up... but then other crowds began to appear
along the route — whole neighborhoods — to honor a different champion

from that of the fight fans: not just Morrisanians, but any in New York
who could give their hearts to a martyr: they flocked to the sidewalk
as High John passed by, and boxing made way for the real world.
The sober air grew full of cheering, Spirit's flags unfurled
over thousands of heads, the procession swelled with High John's joy.
From Madison Square Gardens it turned down Sixth Avenue, whirled
into Fifth, Emen at the head, the promoters engulfed. A cork
had flown from bottled up sentiment; and the people released their joy.

Mid-town, a motorcade took over the burden, sweeping out of Manhattan,
the boxing "fraternity" escaping with the dead hero draped in his satin.
Their route lay to Queens, graveyard of New York, but Spirit members
jumped into yellow cabs and followed, over East River, under the girders
of the Williamsburg Bridge, and down to the cemetery. This was the scene:
two TV vans, a fanfare of trumpets as if from the ring, "Boxers remember
The Champ" on a banner, cabs screaming up — and a strange pattern
of rainbow-robed people, squatting by graves, some distance from the scene.

Feet first, High John had traveled to these smart suburbs of Queens,
feet first to the blinding white tombs and the lawn-smooth greens
of the cemetery, the fight crowd muscling in, walling round
the grave, blocking out Spirit, hogging publicity for the pound-
for-pound best fighter of his era, protecting that last ditch
and its false glory. A promoter began a round-by-round
summary of a "great career" (oh, fights ennoble, ordinariness demeans
"the Hero"). But a fat little man, who was making a last ditch

attempt to get in on the action, came wiggling through. Black activist,
Islamic preacher, a Holy Book held high in his fist
(High John had been no believer), knowing he could rely on
everyone else's decorum, he began his familiar oration:
poverty caused crime; white racism caused poverty in the Black
or Hispanic sections. "Has no-one caught the real lesson
of High John's war against drugs?" he bellowed. "Each white racist
has created these hoods — I mean neighborhoods *and* Columbian or Black

gangsters—" The boxers were ready to punch him out, but a veiled
woman in black appeared in their midst, a dumpy person, who railed
at the "preacher": "D'you suppose Spirit doesn't believe anythin'
you can say about racism? You got divine truth or somepin'?"
(Of course, this was Dolores and she was half-weeping.) "You dare face
me and tell me what you done, 'cept shout your goddam fuckin'
mouth off? We go buying back a whole hood, High John bailed
us out for the cash, ok fuckin' activist, tell me to my face

what you done?" Dolores whipped off her veil. Her face was grained
like wood by the vitriol, scars and tributaries, eye corners stained,
skin flat-planed, roughened, a whorl, and a little knotted stuff,
the voice, once shrill and perky, now basso, turned a little gruff.
"I gotta letter here, you flaky big boxing promoters in your sable fur
collared overcoats, says, 'Hi, from High John.;' This is enough
to shut you boxers up for ever." Her eye-corners rained
down tears as she took out the letter. "What d'you think he fought for,

you money junkies? Listen: 'Hi, from High John. They're gonna get me,
sure. And I'll have a burial, sure. You'll all forget me,
sure — a line in the fight encyclopedias, maybe. Well, it's my funeral,
so here's what. I started out fighting the world, while that mortal
brother of mine began his fight with the needle. Well I won
and he lost. Emen changed all that — pardon me Will,
for I admire meekness and she will always be yours — but let me
place my murder at the party's *service*, till we've won

each goddam election we're boxing for. And shaddap, you tight
ass boxers at my burial. Only one thing I want. All you, unite,
left-wing African-Americans, Spirit, the good whites, Koreans,
Muslims, Rastas, Peter Sung and his Chinese, you all discuss what it means
to have spirit, there, right by my graveside, so I can lie upwards
and stare at you above, smile on my face. Dolores, queen of queens,
you tell them in Queens that High John's fighting his last fight
on his back, dead and full of Spirit, his Spirit rising upwards.'"

Like a crane grab, Dolores sprang down and straddled the coffin, her feet
braced against earth. The afternoon light fell dead-beat
on her damaged face; and it was a witch-doctor's mask with dark
eye sockets and cheeks decorated by strips of whitened bark.
She squatted over High John as if his soul could pass into
her crotch — Ma Johnson had squatted like that once, though the shellac
here had no cross hologram, just an invisible, dead heart
below. And the TV cameras zoomed so that viewers could look into

the shaman mask of her ruined face. "I'll tell you High John's
meaning for us," came that growly voice, speaking Ma Johnson's
words to the viewers: "Make wealth, for others. Don't imagine
that if you live selfish, somehow wealth will grow generous in
your land. First, comes the change in your spirit. Don't you go
to the Right. They say: the rest of humanity lives in sin;
so keep *our* taxes low, crack down on crime, fill the prisons,
take the babies of the wicked and put them in camps.' Don't you go

to the Centrists. They say: 'We're all in this together, but...
with a social service boost, things as they are, better budget
management... our society works, dammit, this is a great country.'
Don't you go to the Liberals. They say: 'Raise taxes from the wealthy. Don't
lavish it on the poor — those the "inadequate, idle" poor!'
Don't you go to Revolutionaries, minds full of hell. They say:
'We, we are pure!' — mouth full of righteousness, gut
full of cruelty! Don't fall for Single Issues: Feminists, the Poor

even. Gays, Abortion Rightists. They say: 'Solve this one issue
and the world will be transformed.' No doubt. But it's a tissue
of lies to think one issue will do it. Don't you go
to Anarchists: self-will ain't no social ethic. No,
all solutions are false when the spirit is wrong: the biggest mistake
of our age is to think politics will cure our lives. I know
High John fought this one evil" — and she wept — "How we miss you,
High John — you never believed your wealth was your own, that mistake

the rest of this goddammed nation makes daily. We — I say we —
spent multi-billions bailing out white-run, Congress-friendly
savings and loans banks, while the Freedom Bank of Harlem (which fed
new firms into *that* heartland) needed six million but was left for dead—
'The Feds will pay half' — does that make you laugh? A white cloud
fogs the national mind, 'spite what the national mouth has said,
in all its prudent pity... Whatcha burnin' bout, Bush? Tellin' me
some god-father trooths from yr White White White House smoke-cloud?"

Like a whitened oasis of light in the cemetery gloom, the debate
took place amid spreadeagled crowds, half of whom sat
on funerary slabs, the TV trolleys a Martian incursion
to and fro. The audience at home heard clearest — their version
came with a Peter Belia voice-over: indeed "the Belly"
idled, mike in hand, by a tombstone, his angle mere subversion
of all that the party stood for: "Spirit is politically isolate
during its greatest tragedy, its martyrdom," broadcast "the Belly".

"We know these things," came a Robeson voice from a cloud of rainbow
robes now alongside Dolores. Lifting her gently by the elbow,
the man helped her from the grave — call him Mr. Rainbow, a coalition-
minded pol from Flatbush, strong on tradition, but who was wishin',
despite all that Peter Belia had claimed, for alliance with Spirit
at this cross-point of martyrdom. "We have Muslims, Marxists, Christian
salvationists down in Flatbush," Rainbow said; "but below
the high-flying rap, we're working hard, not so unlike Spirit."

"Mr. Rainbow," spat the preacherman, "You're just too darned amicable
for anyone's good. Spirit now faces *us* — its Islamic radical
alternative." Will, hand in hand with Emen, came to the graveside
where High John, lying still, still was the motion beneath each side
of debate. Rainbow stood aside while their Islamic opponent,
sharp-eyed, no taller than Dolores, charged: "That Belia hasn't lied.
Your movement hasn't gone deep: think you've got City Hall
worried? Drug lords! Ha! Come down to earth, we's your real opponent.

For you're just new immigrants, some whiteys, some quiet-living oldsters,
like Ma Johnson from Harlem, some Asians, ain't no guns in them holsters
that I can see. You got nuttin' to say to the Black activists,
no Day of Outrage among your thinking, don't see no Marxists,
or one of our lawyers or reverends to fan the flames into heat.
You certain you got angry enough? Or 're you just quietists
of the usual kind, wondering what the next day's opinion pollsters
are going to say of your party? Sure, Dolores here got the heat—

we honor you, Dolores — but you can't run politics on morals. You need
political theory, Black religion, history, anger, and a new breed
of citizen, something of a swagger in yos walk." "Yeah, yeah, you talk,"
returned Dolores, "but 's two hunnered thousand businesses in New York
only fifteen hunnered black-owned: where *theory*, where religion,
where anger in that? Gonna boycott another Korean grocery? Walk
how you like, but if you not gonna buy back your city from the greed
of whites, you not talking real: so don't trust to no creepy religion,

Mister." "Listen, sister," intervened Mr. Rainbow, with a frown,
"You've never heard of GIFT — that's Garvey Income For Tomorrow — down
in Flatbush, where they've bought 74 Kenilworth Place by pooling
Black *resources*, taking out shares? So they're not fooling
around like you say; they're gonna open up stores one at a time,
cost so far's three hundred thou'. They don't need any schooling
from you — didn't Marcus Garvey get 'em buying factories, and one
time a steamship line in the twenties?" At last, Emen's long time

PENNILESS POLITICS 39

of mournful silence ended, though her voice stayed throaty, as she
lifted her own black veil: "We'd give gift for gift, as long as the
males haven't any *fixed solutions* to impose on the rest of us.
You going to be that humble in politics or religion? Don't bother us
if not. And what are these robes — the rainbow coalition?
Few too many male politicians in that for us
to cohabit with happily! Everyone staying in fixed tracks: that's fantasy
politics, hard edges to stripes in your 'rainbow coalition'".

Deadlock. A TV technician switched out a light and, bored,
rejoined his producer — the camera panning over that graveyard
of non-consensus: rainbow robes swirled amidst tombstones, while masculine
pride wanted — not that there be a *solution*, but to be the *politician*
that knew it. So radical warred with peacemaker — the boxers left,
other details inessential — for now a man took up the feminine
cause, the one man without right; it was Will who came forward,
white, new immigrant, poet not politician. "Now they've left,"

he said, "I am going to speak on matters I am debarred from
by every sacred rule of justice, for I represent the problem,
the evil one, the oppressor, in his weakest form: I'm the penniless
envoy of moneyed power, a poet now utterly poem-less
to hear this buzz of counter-dialectics: racial-universal,
majority-minority, minority-minority, creed-creedless,
patriarchy-matriarchy: all's trapped in a web. Where is the poem
that High John's spirit can inspire with the truly Universal?"

Poetry? And not even Black poetry? And on such a subject!
A huge and derisive laugh swept the cemetery at this abject
white male whom Emen, too, was grinning at. Undeterred, Will
continued: "Without a yielding white voice — and that a male
one — we shall not achieve the uproarious incantation
which alone will rouse Spirit. I bow to your honors, as I tell
you that only a transcendent, angelic spirit can unite dialectic
without outright war. It comes! Ah, at last! This is my incantation:

Will's Incantation

I see the Jewish Christess rise with black Judaic skin
thick lips of a Sicilian, and she speaks Islamic Puerto Rican words
in an Irish brogue, her cheeks and eyebrows plumped out
in Koreanesque-Japanesoid narrowness, and she fingers
her fortune-cookie testicles as she speaks,
the prick rising like that of a messiahness,
a lion prick in a lioness
more ambiguous in sex than Voodoo's Legba
more thunderous than the Yoruban Shango
her peace palm in air,
mutated seven fingers like branches
of a minorah, or like a Buddha's enlightened palm,
or the fingers of Shiva,
and she is also atheist,
and she is rising in a stable of origin.

Oh Lord — Who is Lord? — Oh Lordess
you are the bridegroom to Justess,
which is female, a black mare of night,
arise in your stable, Christess,
in your groom's leather leggings arise:
provide the stirrup that burns
under the instep of the jockeys of night
riding the black night mares
shadows racing down the lost perspectives of street lamps
past burning automobiles of darkness
fires in the streets of lost civil rights
the race of invisibles down lanes alternative to the fast lanes
dearborn angel in black
angel more than us arise from politics of contest
not to end contest, but to add spurs and stirrups
to the one, true race of our time,
Come to this stable, Judaic Christess,
from your Italo-Irish Protestant cathedrals,
take at last the white wafers of guilt from my mouth
my tongue coated as if with thrush
in my sorrow-song at those we have outlawed
who die on the margins, in garishly-lit hospices
or in African countries stricken with plagues;
come and saddle my stallion of justice
with the female; let the dead ancestors, feminine/
masculine, rise from the straw and fill me
with their strange coffin energies, till

bestride my mare at the stable's very door
I sense the spirits of past lives,

arise and mount their saddled stallions
or saddled mares
and the groom, the Christess, rising,
mounts her own ambi-sexual mare
to head us out in processional
under the startling readiness of stars
to move and alter heavenly pattern.

Inhabitants ride out from side streets,
in readiness to join us and change their fates,
leaving the overturned automobiles
which make the air stink with vanquished power.
Until at a crossroads the horse of the Christess
leading us, rears, paws the ground, impatient
to start down the last straight
of this race towards human-ness and meaning of lives
this almost possible track directly ahead
beyond Western horizons,
where we would be jockeyesses
our pricks frotted on our feminine animals
turning their wild black heads as if to suck at our shuddering breasts.

When I come there may my mare, too,
paw and rear at those crossroads of choice,
for the true cross unites all religions;
it is the entirely free choice, the zen moment of spirit,
the darkness of center-non-center in all metaphysics,
and atheist astrophysics.
Right there in the non-mid-point, rear, my mare of night
saddled by the Christess, your dark groom,
and then light out for dead ahead,
the air crackling with spirits around,
my stirrups in flames round my shoe soles,
everything suddenly obvious:
the crabby males
that run nations, wrongly voted in,
wrongly voted in —
left behind in the ruin of their cities.
Here, over the horizon rim in a darker darkness.
a new world out of the western old one
riders hugging the neck of animals running,
black flanks flickering with lights.

He finished, turned to the one TV camera still operating, and despite
the producer's reluctance to keep filming, gave a great shout,
in Latin — Marlowe's Ovidian tag, "Slowly, slowly,
ride, you horses of the night", but changing this to "swiftly":
Celeriter, celeriter, currite noctis equi! . . .
                                           . . .Silence
followed! What happened next has entered the annals of party
history. Emen, changed from her widow's weeds, came out
of the crowd her face rapt — possessed, some said. Silence!

She had donned fancy clothes, male clothes, out of spaghetti East-
ern tradition: fly-away leather riding coat, a vest
of red velvet, plump leather jeans, platform boots, and over
her ears was hooked a false beard — the full chest coverer
kind of Karl Marx. Her head, by means of a bisected pink
balloon was made white-man hairy-bald, a buffoon above her
black cheeks, and the whites of her eyes were showing. Impressed,
the TV team zoomed in on the balloon, so that viewers saw pink.

Now changes of clothes are common in Voodoo possession, and Will
and Emen had planned this charade. But there came an electronic wail
from the feminine lips of the black grandee, deliciously shiversome
a wail in what Voodoo calls *langage*, a speak known to no-one,
the words of possession. Waiting with his mike, Belia was grinning
impishly. "Pardon me," he began, "but do I address you as someone
with a definite sex, or is that question, er-hum, best left well
alone?" A high cheekbone in her face caught a gleam, and, grinning

back at Belia, the figure disclosed under its chin
an electronic voicebox, whose grille bleated in feminine
tone of an Indian, a Japanese, a Spaniard — or some other:
"Mis amigos han obrado con poco tino y con menos politica..."
it said. *"No es verdad?"* asked Belia, and added: *"Véro?"*
because a Sicilian shrug had followed the Spanish phrase.
*"Il senso più comune di 'che' non e il piu véro... — Hélas,
il serait bien nécessaire de souligner... Excusez-moi..."* *"Véro?"*

asked Belia, falling one Panurgian language behind. *"Nga nsibidi
adohe — aku natongena wud nsibidi... Excusez-moi. Sthiti-
prabhāvasukhadyutileśyāviśuddhīndriyā-
vadhiviṣayato adhikāh."* Like all the new born, the figure
had trouble beginning to speak. *"Strobodi nkta homongas katit
kordovi plan"* (East European, say Siberian, dialect?) "I'd rather
we spoke English for the viewers," chuckled Belia. "Weren't we
discussing what sex you were?" "My rider in me is complicated,"

PENNILESS POLITICS   43

came a *femina perturba* voice in English — rider being a usual
Voodoo term for the loa. "I'm not bisexual, but all-sexual,
he-she-she-he originating together in unique desires. Not African
desires, or Waspy ones, or Asian, or Hispanic, or Amerindian:
I contains all of esh, differences held separately, separate in unity,
held in each flash of personality like facets of the one
personality: think of a painting whose colors are individual
but simultaneously perceived, separate in brilliance, formal in unity."

"Esh?" queried Belia. "Ms. Rider, is that your name?" "I am Hooman."
"So is 'esh' one of those feminist pronouns?" "My nominative pronoun
is Esh — pronounce it not carefully like a name, but careless-
ly as in 'h'does this' — 'Sh'does this' — or with Esh — ' 'shdoes this'.
I am Esh from out of the Yoruban Eshu-Ellegbara, cognate
with Voodoo's Legba, a nimble she in reverse. Objective case:
Em — it suggests mE backwards and also my horse, Emen.
The possessive nominal's Eshine (for the nominal must become cognate

with shining — the self-possession that shines). Possessive attributive,
Sher (in generous possession Esh shares what is Eshine). To give
me a name, as a Hooman, I am Thus Spirit, "Thus" being my equivalent
for Mr. or Ms. Or call me Hoo." "Well," ironized Belia, "that's ambivalent
enough for anyone! And you seem a rational spirit! There are things
going on I don't understand." "Some things can't be understood in virulent
moods, Mr. Belia," Hooman's voice suddenly said. Belia paled as if
a steel blade had cleaved through his soul. It was one of those things

that can't be explained: entire authority exercised without force.
"Suppose you become yourself, Mr. Belia," said this courteous,
possessed woman, face eshining, so that viewers saw the Good there,
transcendental in Emen's own skin — "yourself but also your neighbor
humans on Earth imagined vividly — vividness, the vital quality
of a mind that unites with goodness in a rush of warm feeling, a quiver
of warmth stabbing like fear. In that instant, your sex or your race
is both sexes, all races, yet one and your own — heightened in quality.

Je suis comme ça! And how can I tolerate another's poverty or exclusion
when I see it so vividly as my own in them? This is ur-dimension
empathy I'm talking about, a possibility you fourth dimensional creatures
are powerless against." Emen's changes of physical features
were rapid, a confusing of forms in the beholder's eye, yet a stable
identity both frightened the heart and warmed it. No speech is
adequate to say this truth firmly enough: when Emen's Good became vision
vividly enough, it was blindingly obvious; the most detestable

of humanity's failing is refusal to open the iris to that Good,
and Hoo emself was that vision, riding Emen who had humbly stood
aside while Will chanted, until her gaze dimmed and the loa's weight
descended on her back, and she'd writhed, and spoken in the inchoate
synthesized words of her voice-box. Then gathering around Hooman
came the Black activists — cameras still whirring, the program was running
late — but back in the studios the program chief, enchanted, could
not cut it short: for Emen was so photogenic, ridden by Hooman.

"Yes, I invoked you, Hooman," Will called. "You are us collectively
speaking: the Present, the Voodooed Present, but even more lively
than spirit possession, esh's the dance of the Present in space-time
Esh's the Presidance, the Presidente, the President al dente, the sublime
moment when hard becomes soft, sexually, socially, politically, open.
Pardon me, I'm a poet, I got carried away with the beauty of rhyme."
Belia, the memorious, blurted out: "But there's something here olden time.
Isn't Esh like Gouverneur Morris, whose revolutionary aristo pen

framed the final draft of our Constitution? (Morrisania's first notable
oddly transnational, transsexual, viewers.)" Tripping on his cable
he lurched into camera; so as the studio grumbles, "I don't know why,
we're doing this segment", we leave the cemetery and enter some family
lounge with the TV on and the face of Hoo looming, the kids bellowing
to change channels but, oddly, that doesn't happen. And the sides
of the set frame the face stagily, the pale crowd in the shadowy
background like secondary actors, and the night like tent walls billowing.

At Emen's throat, the voice-box spat and took over again:

"DECLARATION,

"When in the Course of Hooman events it becomes necessary for one people to dissolve the political bands which have connected them with another, and to assume among the powers of the earth, the separate and equal station to which the Laws of Nature and of Nature's Godd-ess entitle them, a decent respect to the opinions of Hoomankind requires that they should declare the causes which impel them to the separation.— We hold these truths to be self-evident, that all Hoomans are created equal, that they are endowed by their Creator with certain unalienable Rights, that among these are Life, Liberty and the pursuit of Happiness.— That to secure these rights, Governments are instituted among Hoomans, deriving their just powers from the consent of the governed,— That whenever any Form of Government becomes destructive of these ends, it is the Right of the People to alter or to abolish it, and to institute new Government, laying its foundation on such principles and organizing its powers in such form, as to them shall seem most likely to effect their Safety and Happiness. Prudence, indeed, will dictate that Governments long established should not be changed for light and transient causes. But when a long rain of abuses and usurpations of the democratic processes, in which the powerful and wealthy pursuing invariably the same Object evince a design to reduce any considerable number of people under absolute Despotism, it is their right, it is their duty, to modify such Government, and to provide new Guards for their future security.

Such has been the patient sufferance of the A1 Congressional District, New York State, of these United States; and, though despotism has disguised itself in the cloak of democracy, yet it has condemned us to the meanest conditions of survival, and has refused to acknowledge in Congress the interests of this District, judged in recent times the poorest of all Congressional Districts in these States. And this great evil has arisen partly out of historical circumstance of immigration, but more particularly out of the establishment of absolute Tyranny over the electoral processes of these States by: two powerful political groupings; what has been called the military-industrial complex; and the seizure of the nation's financial resources into the private hands of impersonal corporations, of greedy and ambitious families, and of financial entrepreneurs. That Government should not stand long, for which the majority of an electorate, in its disgust at the briberies and the toadying time-serving of its alleged representatives, has ceased to vote at all. In this desertion of a people from its electoral duty, elites may lead whole nations into immoral behavior. We declare that President effectually a tyrant who, voted in by 20% of an electorate, supported in policy by Congressional majority representing little more than one third of the electorate, and — scantly heeding even that popular mandate but swaying a nation by lies and political manipulation — enters into a cabal with a few nearest friends, his own appointees, to commit our own hands to the bloody sacrifice of soldiers and civilians in foreign nations. Meanwhile, the powerful have made themselves secure in their local and national offices, ensuring through clumsy laws that the uneducated will be deterred from electoral registration and that only those faithful to party elites, or to the military complex, or to the private wealth of corporations or individuals, may succeed in presenting a political platform fully before any electorate. Particularly, we would protest at the overweening size of these United States, measured not only in land mass but also in population, so that any individual voice crying for justice in the wastelands of urban deprivation cries utterly in vain; any larger group cries in vain; knowing that Congress has ceased to represent the needs of the poor and disadvantaged.

Such great evil may not persist without the opposition of all honorable Hoomans. It is to address the effectual tyranny of elites and of all political Machiavellianism that we reluctantly combine to change, unilaterally, our allegiance to the laws under which we are governed. We are yet gravely mindful of the dangers of civil warfare that may result from acts of secession, and so we voluntarily rescind our natural right to rebel absolutely against all absolute tyranny; and still we, the disenfranchised of District A1, New York State, United States of America, act to save ourselves from remaining the *de facto* slaves of that richer nation comprised of the whole United States themselves. We have determined to live by the dictates of a new Constitution, so to be an exemplar for our nation, how a peaceful people composed of many races can live harmoniously together on much smaller a scale, denying money for militaristic causes, denying the runaway reign of greed, and electing our own President and Congress out of new laws existing, as it were, in parenthesis to the old ones. All legal consequences of our actions incurred by us under the provisions of the original, broader Constitution will be suffered by us peacefully and patiently, for we would be model citizens. We have confidence that Justice itself is self-evident in its Truthfulness; and that a nation brought up from its earliest days to respect Democracy and Justice will hardly look unfavorably upon this Little Nation within the Larger Nation, since our whole wish is a return to those ideals now perverted into financial considerations, and into a permission for slavery, by the original framers of our liberties.

We hereby proclaim our own governing Constitution:

At the throat, the black voice-box crackled, and bled a last
phrase: "The new Constitution's been stored on disks, which we'll pass
around now." Then, like one who'd been stabbed in the jugular,
Emen went rigid, with stretched chin; suddenly her regalia
looked ridiculous, and she shivered white eyed, tongue pushed
out, her knees knocking; her hands in jerky irregular
gestures produced from her clothes and scattered all over the grass
a slew of computer disks; and she fell as if brutally pushed.

Lou Levinson, the lawyer, rushed to her: in a second, he'd found
a piece of paper tucked in her breasts. "Let me lie on the ground
while my loa leaves me," he read out. "The rest of you stand back.
These disks will be sent to the Press. Load them into a Mac
Classic computer, but expect no screen display; everything's on audio,
synthesized through the sound system. Don't try to back
up the disk or you'll lose everything. To capture the sound,
take an ordinary acoustic recorder and record it direct on audio."

The TVs faded in each living room, as the transfixed producer
at last threw the switch and, hastily calm, the studio announcer
excused the length of the funeral segment. But the switchboard reported
a significant number of callers who asked that the aborted
coverage of Esh and Emen be resumed; the 11 p.m. news
only referred to High John's boxing career, so, thwarted,
the callers turned on their local newspapers to produce a
full story on the new Constitution as front-page news.

The callers were soothed to be told that by cross-national Express
Mail similar disks had been sent already to the Press,
who had set up their Macs. And this is what happened. Once in its drive,
the disk caused the computers to speak (screens blank). Anyone who tried
to copy the disk would see this message: "Warning: a virus
will attack your hard drive if you continue." So only the "live"
recording survived, because, once the voice finished, a new message appeared. "Disk being initialized (rubbed out) thanks to our virus."

(Spirit would later claim that Emen's "rider", the Legba
composite, in a move of surprising modernity for a Voodoo loa,
had projected the program on to the disks, but the Supreme Court
was to throw this claim out with great scorn.) Only a brief report
of what the voice said may follow: for the whole new U.S. Constitution,
as spoken through the computers, can't be relayed in the short
span of these verses. So we'll confine ourselves to the changes, to a
stripped-down account of Spirit's new U.S. Constitution:

CONSTITUTION OF DISTRICT A1, NEW YORK CITY, UNITED STATES OF AMERICA

PREAMBLE

We, the people of District A1, New York State, in the United States of America, having come to understand that the original Union of these United States has outgrown the Constitution of its setting out, do ordain and establish a newly reformed Constitution. We do so not in disrespect to our forebears, who wished to create a great union out of the diverse peoples of the Earth but who could not have foreseen the vast growth of an oversized nation; rather we act in culmination of their wishes, aware that no set of words is so utterly sacred that it can endure for ever or subsist in truthfulness merely through addition and amendment.

Beginning again in small compass, we proclaim the setting up of a more perfect union and a more equitable Justice. We shall insure an end to Corrupt Ways, make different provision for the common defence, promote the general Welfare through smaller groupings of peoples, and thus secure domestic Tranquillity and renew the Blessings of Liberty to ourselves and our Posterity."

(And these are the main changes):

Section

1. The Constitution first adopted by District A1 (a pro-tem Congressional District of New York State), eventually to be changed for adoption by the necessary majority of the whole United States electorate;

2. Establishment of Congresses at three levels: old Congressional Districts, State, and National (with special arrangements for major urban centers).

3. All executive power, save that of signing Bills of National Congress into Law, to be stripped from President and Vice-President of the United States, who become ceremonial heads of the Nation.

4. An end to the easily corruptible system of primary and full elections for Presidential and Congressional offices, to the multiplicity of elections for local administrative offices, and to the Presidential power to appoint any but sher own advisory and office staff, who shall have no other powers. Replacing such systems is a single series of elections through popular plebiscite at each level, beginning with that for District President, Vice-President, Representatives, and Senators (chosen from among Representatives). Only those holding such District offices will be eligible for election to the same offices at State level. Only those holding such State offices will be eligible for election to the same offices at National level. Candidates' campaigns to be limited to means provided by District, State, and National government as appropriate. Some weeding-out of candidates may be necessary by popularly elected Boards, but within strict limits. All candidates for administrative offices to be appointed after public advertisement of the posts by Boards selected by the appropriate Congress.

5. Where the original Constitution reads "life, liberty, and possessions" this be modified to "life, liberty, and those possessions which do not create egregious hoardings of individual wealth expressed as proportions of the national average wealth as elsewhere defined in this Present Constitution."

6. All Bills shall originate in either the House of Representatives or the Senate, or by vote of the Electorate through plebiscite. Plebiscites shall be limited to not more than one each year and a two-thirds majority of the electorate shall be necessary before a Bill originating in such a fashion be presented to the Congress of this District. (Save only that the words "he" shall read "esh", "his" shall read "sher", and "him" shall read "em", and being made applicable to this District, this Section follows the wording of Article I, Section 6, of the Original Constitution and is taken as read.)

7. Powers of the National Congress will include:

(a) To concentrate by whatever legal means necessary the main interest of the United States upon the concerns of other nations in the world to achieve a better Planet Earth and a fairer and more conservative use of global resources. It has the Duty to take such legislative action even against the narrower national interests of the United States, whose citizens henceforth regard themselves as world citizens before they are national citizens.

(b) (To raise Armies, a Navy, an Airforce, a Militia, etc. as in the Original Constitution, but limited as stated in the provisions of the Present Constitution.)

(c) To lay and collect Taxes, Duties, Imposts and Excises, to pay the Debts and provide for the common Defense and general Welfare of the United States; but all Duties, Imposts and Excises shall be uniform throughout the United States. All levying for military expenditure will be submitted to national plebiscite every two years in six alternative, itemized lists bearing the following proportions to each other expressed as percentages of total cost: 5%, 20%, 40%, 60%, 80%, 100%.

(d) To enforce phasing out of all nuclear-based armaments. To ban all sale or use of armaments outside the geographical borders of the United States, except where essential to national defense when War has been Declared by National Congress.

(e) To ally the United States of America absolutely with all peaceful decisions of the United Nations, where passed by due process of the Laws of the United Nations. Any decisions of the United Nations involving wars to be subject to the National Laws relating to warfare, as outlined herein.

(f) To define and to punish any scientific experiments or commercial activities that are judged by Committee of the National Administration inhumane or detrimental to the interests of Citizens of the Planet Earth, its Atmosphere, or to the Regions of Outer Space.

(g) To limit monopolies and to curb any expenditure of money by private individuals, or by private, public, or foreign clubs, firms, organizations, or corporations, or by foreign nations designed to influence unfairly the governmental, political, or democratic processes of the United Sates or to interfere with its elections.

(h) To declare a state of Official Dispute with multinational clubs, firms, corporations, or foreign governments if they engage in activities detrimental to United States interests, and to press for the strengthening of international legal means to settle such disputes.

(i) To borrow Money on the credit of the United States, provided that these sums when added to total present borrowings do not exceed half the previous year's gross national product. These provisions shall take no account of borrowings already made at the time this Constitution may be adopted for the whole of the United States.

(j) To establish an Administration of Incomes Estimates (A.I.E.) to define and measure the wealth of individuals and of private firms and corporations and to report the results to the Nation at least every three years. To levy such taxation that will ensure that no private individual shall earn an average annual income of more than eight times the national average, as most recently measured by the A.I.E. While existing holdings of private wealth may not be immediately attacked, it is understood that Congress will endeavor within such time as is consonant with sufficient national prosperity to reduce all holdings of private wealth to no more than ten times the national average holdings, as most recently measured by the A.I.E., while firms, organizations, and corporations will be rigorously controlled and if necessary their officers punished to prevent all attempts to evade these aforesaid restrictions upon private wealth.

(k) To decree what forms of transport are allowable in the United States and to regulate and facilitate such transports as may be needful while suppressing those forms which may not be needful having due regard to the prosperity and happiness of citizens of the United States and of the planet Earth.

(l) To review the distribution of happiness, opportunity, and prosperity throughout the United States and, not tolerating any notorious injustice between Congressional Districts in any such distribution, to undertake such measures as may be necessary to restore a more equitable balance and to create favorable environments for the health, and educational and moral development of the young people of the United States.

8. Where any of the foregoing provisions in Sections 1-7 are in conflict with provisions of the Original Constitution of the United States of America the foregoing provisions are deemed to be the higher authority.

(Otherwise, the Original Constitution will be modified to accord its detailed provisions with any discordances it presents to the Present Constitution.)

To those Amendments to the Original Constitution known as the Human Rights Amendments the following shall be added:

(a) Notwithstanding Section 7(b) of the Present Constitution, any United States Citizen shall have the right to withhold such measure of sher taxes as may be assigned to the creation of armaments or to the maintenance of armies. The right of self-defense being unalienable and natural to every Hooman, in all matters regarding the raising of armies or militias or regarding the Declaration of Wars for the common Defense of the whole United States, it shall lie within the authority of each individual member of the electorate of this District to agree or not to agree to participate in such armies, militias, or wars, without let or hindrance from any fellow citizen or any group, organization, or governmental body whatsoever. Where this provision of the present paragraph creates a contradiction under Law with the Original Constitution of the United States, this same paragraph of the Present Constitution shall be deemed the higher authority under Law.

(b) Article II of the Amendments to the Original Constitution (right of the people to keep and bear arms) is hereby annulled.

On a dull news day six factors held sway: High John's career,
his martyrdom, the successes of Spirit, a whiff of Voodoo, the sheer
weirdness of Emen's "voice" and fancy dress, and, a bit,
the novelty of the Constitution — what would the Feds do about it,
since it ranked as an act of secession, albeit only by one
Congressional District? Oh, and anyway, what District? Spirit
had said "A1", which didn't exist. Columnists thought it near
the Bronx neighborhood; but: "Spirit's HQ is Brooklyn," said one.

The Feds sneered and sent their most Ancient of Days, Joe Fedora,
to check the Bronx. His car on idle, Joe groaned when he saw a
huge wall billboard: "District A1 secedes from the Union by a hundred
per cent majority. The new U.S.A. starts here!" He wondered
if that was the only poster; so before taking action he continued
towards Brooklyn Bridge, already hungry for lunch, but he blundered
into a score of posters West Side — East Side many more, a
white plague of them Downtown. *Dio mio!* What next?" He continued

to a precinct where cops were asking the question: how'd they succeeded
in posting those posters unnoticed? What district had seceded
and in what voting session, where? Joe Fedora found it all worse
than investigating the Teamsters: no-one would mutter more than a terse
"Ask at Spirit's headquarters on Utica, Brooklyn." And at that HQ
the bosses were missing — just more citizens. Yes, worse than the Mafia's
silence, because thousands of people seemed involved. Though hope receded
of finding out more, Joe set up surveillance 'cross the street from HQ.

The Feds had a stroke of luck. Ma Johnson moved in next door
to Joe's surveillance post. "Af-am — FBI? You're
kidding if those became friends!" Well, we're not. No sex though, for Joe
was a closet gay from the Hoover era of gays. And lo
and behold, Ma proved voluble but vague. She implied that something
was going down in the Bronx — Morrisania on some Wednesday, scenario
fuzzy — a waste plot, an election for President — "Ah don' know mo':
A huge votin' session on some hot ballotin' machines, or sump'in'—,

load o' nonsense, if you aks me." The Feds staked out Morrisania
and Washington gave Joe a back-up team. What was even zanier
for the Feds, a tacit agreement had somehow been struck by numerous
taxpayers across the U.S. not to pay taxes for defense.
The Treasury raised a fuss but thought that the threat of prison
would bring most protesters to heel. More worrying was the anonymous
way the movement had spread, though Spirit was certainly a
prime suspect for conspiracy to hide crime. A charge of misprision

was laid against Emen, who simply replied that the loa had spoken
through her while she'd been unconscious, and that when she'd awoken
the disk that had created the voice at her throat — initialized
on the funeral day to be clean for the voice that surprised
a nation of viewers — had auto-destructed like those they had sent
to the Press. "Listen, Man," said her cheeky letter to the wise-
guy Treasury lawyer, "our party's called Spirit: by that token
we mean we invoke it. We have no control on when it is present."

In New York, the drivers of cars would report to the cops that a wall
of women — now famous as Spirit's main tactic — had stopped all
traffic from entering such and such a district. But no rhyme
or reason connected these incidents which lasted for such a short time
that the police on arrival found the streets empty, with the local squad
car blocked in on all sides so the doors wouldn't open — no crime
really involved. This was a puzzle. Then there'd follow a call
to the precinct to say that easy arrests awaited the drug squad,

as some dealers were locked in their crack pads — the locals had instant
devices to bar doors and windows; they could seal up a basement
from round corners so the crackheads couldn't get off a shot. The police
called these areas "the Brigadoon No-Gos", but whether designed to decrease
drug traffic or the ordinary motorists' waste of world fuel
resources was unclear. Assembling a case was hard. In the first place
many had worn masks; second, a locksmith who'd obviously lent
the bars said he'd turned a blind eye — been a bit of a fool.

At last someone brighter on the Mayor's staff said, "Listen: these assholes
are laying their plans; they're not moral crusaders — they're pols
just like us. All this war on gasoline is just their asshole routine
and so are the drug busts. We'll go wrong if we think they don't mean
what they say: this is Constitutional, Secessional, a little more serious
than we supposed. I'd guess that when they wall off a street they convene
a planning meeting — a no-go area so's to leave no loopholes
for us to spy on them: we should now tell Capitol Hill this is serious."

PENNILESS POLITICS 53

So the Feds got leant on again. Now how does a Fed know how to act
like a Fed? From his colleagues? Well, how do they? In fact,
part of their manners and lingo they learn from the movies, and part
from organized crime, which also learns from the movies; so art
without spirit has an effect on real life. The FBI
buzzed warnings to all agents to step up surveillance, to get dirt
on Spirit's leaders, to check their crime records, to contact
the local IRS, try for sex scandals — yes, this, the Hollywood FBI.

"Well, I am aksing *you*, Ma," parodied Joe one day, very frustrated,
for he was taking a lot of heat. "I'm a Fed —
should've told you that before." "Oh no!" wailed Ma Johnson throwing
a stage fit. "What's all that I've bin tellin' you 'bout what's goin'
down in stolen ballot machines? 'Taint none of it true, d'you hear?
I'm not saying nothing more to a Fed: you check Charlotte Street,
won't find no thing there till the day — but what am ah sayin'?
None of it's true. We'll ballot away just in thin air, d'you hear?"

The FBI told Joe: "Check it." So, while a partner glued
his eyes to the binocs, he went to a bar where he met a lewd
eye contact from the gay Jewish lawyer, Lou Levinson, who invited
him to his table and eventually back to his pad. "Don't get excited,"
said Joe, "I haven't yet said who I am." "Yes you have," said the lawyer,
"without meaning to. You're the Fed on surveillance. Really, I'm delighted
to meet you... just doing your job and so forth. And I shan't be crude,
sweetie, I see you're too old for me" — added that gay lawyer.

"I'm speaking little difficulties, Lou," said Joe, all pinpoint-
eyed. "We found a yellow notepad on your desk — get the point?
Yes, a draft of this Constitution thing — shall we say 'sedition'
or 'treason', or 'conspiracy to avoid defense tax?' Now I mention
tax, Lou, shall I refer to the undervalued stock sale
on your '87 return? Yes, we raided your offices — I had a notion
we might find something — huh! wuz no need to turn the joint
over — wuz all in plain view. Now what you got for sale

in return for a plea bargain, I wonder, 'cos *we* got *you* in a squeeze!"
And squeezed Lou did look, his cheeks gone pale. "I'll talk, but please
understand my loyalties here to Spirit," said the stoolie, with unctuous
morality up for offer. And Joe understood all too well with a gracious
and ironical nod. "What I want," said the Fed, "ain't too hard to give.
Jest a date an' a time for this cockamamie Constitutional caucus,
convention, whatever, that's comin' up. Don't spill the whole beanz,
no names or nuffin', jest a date, I say: that ain't hard to give."

Lou stared at Joe's tie-pin: "I bet you've a bug; you're all wired,"
and he laughed nervously. Then he rose, dragged down by newly-acquired
disloyalty, went to a wall calendar, pointed silently to a date;
next to a map of New York where he showed Joe a waste plot
in the Bronx, shot a cuff and swivelled the hands on his watch
to 11 a.m., finishing off with a little playlet
of a voter voting at a ballot machine, glancing sideways, scared.
Lou gave the shrug of bad faith, sat again, and watched Joe watch

him with those narrowed eyes. The lack of sex in this scene will be
remarked. Nothing here of "Lou on top," or of "Joe willingly
accepting the masculine sperm", here where Federal and District
stayed at loggerheads, symptom of a national failure to conscript
the local into a wider, fairer political process — a failure of law
and of justice, so it seemed. We'll let Joe leave and phone his transcript
of these proceedings to Washington, where the powers that be
sent agents into Morrisania, and studied their Constitutional law.

On the eve of the poll, they called Joe in for debriefing: the assistant
under-deputy chief Fed, an administration deputy head of department,
a police superintendent from the Bronx, and a Treasury official
halfway up the hierarchy — Spirit was a problem but not a huge social
issue. "Zeze guys ain't doin' nuttin' hefty yet," Joe agreed
with the Admin man. "But jeeze organized, yes. An' that Haitian'll
charm the pants off a peacock. They're going to lead us on a dance,
election day, take us the wrong way. It's been agreed

by hundreds maybe thousands of 'em to take the wrong subway outto
Brooklyn, throw us off the scent; then at 11 a.m. double back to
Morrisania for the poll. This checks out three, four times,
I tellya." "So what've we got?" asked Treasury. "We got names, seems
we got date, time, place, we got stake-out by that plot
in Morrisania, agents on the subways ready, and major league teams
o' cops. We got the lot." It all broke up with "Well done, Joe,"
and a call to New York's Mayor, with full details of the plot.

That Wednesday morning, Ma Johnson opened her door a crack
at 6 a.m., and Joe was listening; he softly followed her out the back
of the block and on to the subway platform, packed with people going
to Seventh Avenue, Brooklyn, he guessed gleefully, his face glowing
with pride at a job well done. "You ain't foolin' me," he secretly
told those crowds. While Ma waited, he huddled by a newsstand and knowing
what to expect put a walkie-talkie to his ear. Great! A large shack
had appeared overnight on the Morrisania waste plot, and secretly,

the Black Activist allies like emergency medics carrying stretchers
had imported long packages in brown paper wrappings. Stretches
of ground were being cleared and marked in white tape for the voting
lines. O.K. Joe back in Brooklyn watched Ma and the others entering
the F train then climbed in a bulging car: out at Seventh
and a walk uphill with a large enough crowd for the Yankees trying
for the World Series. He admired, as a pro, these nice touches
in Spirit's plans, everyone idling before rushing back to Seventh

and taking the subway to the Bronx. As the morning was still quite dark
it took him a while to get uneasy. Not till they neared Prospect Park
did he notice everyone changing direction, the approach roads
become blocked by people lying down and the rest in hordes
entering the park. At least 10,000 and probably more.
His beeper sounded — the Brooklyn cops were trying to make inroads
across the bodies of peaceful citizens — sounded again and he barked
to the Bronx agents, "Call off the Sting — Round 'em up, any more

come your way arrest 'em. We got problems." (To finish the Bronx story,
they raided the shack to find the activists mocking an effigy
many feet high of the President — the real president, we should say —
though if wealth decides who is real, there's the devil to pay.)
Suddenly, in Brooklyn, 7.55, everyone started running
from side roads uphill to the park, cops among them, as the first ray
of the sun broke over the trees. No crime committed, just a mystery
that Joe had to fathom. Hand on shoulder holster, he began running.

Behind the windows of morning two bodies, brown and white,
pass through a curtained apartment, slanted with light.
In parks greying into dawn, the pigeons crowd trees black
with starlings, white bird between each black one. Looking back
over her shoulder, Emen stared down at the immense crowd
gathering by the empty band shell and she smiled. At her back
Will smiled too and checked his watch. The cops with their light
automatics surrounded the foot of the stage along with the crowd.

Through curtained apartments linking their naked arms, our hopes
of union pass in their poverty; they gaze down at the lightening slopes
of the park, at this moment's assembly, this vaporous moment caught
between night and day, where goodness might rein in mid-thought,
in the voodooed mid-thought, if we could only get it, something primitive
to our sophistications, a susurrus in the peoples, an instant taut
with knowledge of poverty: our hopes gaze down as the popes
gaze down at Vatican Square, not in majesty, something more primitive

in the soul. Emen knew they could never get it for more than this
moment: too much at stake in ordinary lives -- a child is
a future to pay for continently, a morality to hand on, and it *seems*
that an income measures hard work and sobriety. These are dreams
masquerading as real, the only real, and we vote for them, despite
their final cost to global peace — make no mistake, the extremes
of war and pollution stem from the most ordinary moralities:
decency, wanting to be prosperous, builds hell in heaven's despite.

In the park everything hung on a thread, the hour thunderous,
the thread extending heavenwards from the bandshell to dark clouds,
the stage empty except for some public address speakers, relic
it seemed from a previous Sunday's festival. And then on the tic
of eight, the speakers crackled and out came the electronic voice
of Hooman, piercingly artificial. (Emen had gone suddenly frantic
up in her apartment and, loa-ridden, swooned.) In the park the vast crowds
pressed Joe on all sides; he had nothing to shoot but a voice.

"District A1," came that sing-song, inhuman tone of Hooman,
"in your secret assemblies you have chosen the names of two women
to bear high office in the new-formed Union of States, this gathering
being its commencement, a reform of a nation's corruption to the furthering
of international sanity. Your task this morning is to say 'Amen'
to the reading of names, if you so will it." At that a feathering
of doves flew from branches of trees, and the starlings joined them
on the lawns of Prospect Park, and the poem restarts: "Amen!

and Amen!" for here came the reading of names. "As your President,"
said Hooman's voice, "you have chosen one name only, but consent
must now be given. Emen Penniless is that name." And "Amen!"
came a huge roar. "For Vice-President, you chose Dolores—" And "Amen!"
came that roar at the very Christian name. The voice finished,
— Esteves." "Amen!" came once more, followed by a cheer. And then
everyone turned and ran for it, the cops gazing in amazement
and Joe himself spun round by racing bodies. It had finished

in seconds. A muffled boom from under the band stage indicated
the equipment had auto-destructed in Spirit fashion: what is stated
lasts for a breath, but Spirit endures for ever. By 8 oh 5
the park was cleared, whole families hurrying along streets alive
with laughter, and twenty or so of the ordinary voters held
by the cops — but who had shouted what? No-one could ever prove
anything. Spirit's leaders had been absent; the crowd had created
a new U.S.A. in a park: that was the district their "Union" now held.

CODA

What was promised has been performed. The Penniless couple have begun
a new path on rough ground. Emen is president of the one
district fit to be united, to be a state. All has happened in a breath
and now it has ended, not a trace left behind. Why this death
of the so-newly-born? Well, follow the brief sequel and you'll understand.
The Feds tried to find charges, but so little had happened; they had weft
without woof; the evidence unraveled, everything came undone.
Lou on tax crimes: small, a fine — as I expect you'll understand,

he'd sort of confessed by leaving the clues for Joe's Spiritgate
team. The others, a day or two in jug, an attempt to slate
Emen for that misprision charge — fizzled out. The reader has been had,
evidently, by the poet (by Will?). Well, it's who's has had
who? The story built nationally for a month — most racist headline:
"The Black Confederates of District A1". "The Secession of the Hundred
Thousand" read the *Post* in the usual media attempt to inflate
collapsing news. Is that what it comes to? A mere headline?

It all flickered on for a year. Lightning elections were staged
in other states like old-time prize fights while authorities raged
to see evidence vanish away. The wall of women became
world famous as a political tactic; versions of the drug scam
cropped up; neighborhoods were being bought up somewhat more than before;
High John was a legend; national election turnouts — already a shame-
ful statistic — worsened. All too soon, Spirit seemed to have aged.
As it does: doesn't breathe for more than a moment before

the poem is finished. What did you expect? You, hypocrite reader,
et cetera? You want some opiate, a poetic abracadabra
so your ordinary responsibility for our ordinary political failure
can be charmed away? No. America, that jackass soiled with its ordure,
its continued braying of freedom, knows half its own people
block their ears and don't vote. Take case. Suppose a peculiar
political wind blew, and a plebiscite — to decide whether a
new Constitution like Spirit's was acceptable to the people —

should be nationally staged by some worst U.S. president — Johnson
or Nixon or Reagan or Bush or Kennedy, all of them poison
and stained with death. Just the one proposal, to prevent the waste
of world oil by cutting out private cars, would suffice for the rest
of the changes not to be listened to, for it scarcely requires astute
judgment to see the consequent recession, massive job loss, the unrest
in manufacturing industry, the crash on Wall Street, and so on.
Not to mention the other proposals whose drawbacks those scarcely astute

minds can equally easily plumb: the leveling of income
("theft"), a Great Power fallen powerless when war has become
an individual matter of choice in its people. The people don't vote,
agreed. The people don't vote, all right. They let dangerous men float
into office on a flotsam tide of neglect — themselves still decent,
unresponsible for genocide and globicide. "Free." So suppose a turnout
of 70% — virtually unprecedented this century — everyone from the bum
to the wealthiest GOP, from Mafia riff-raff to the sober and decent,

voting whether to enter national poverty. We imagine it turned down
overwhelmingly. Ah! Search the past for the most ancient wisdom
in the world: that too much possession, too great a seeking of thrill,
harms the soul! Are all the saints and saintesses who fill
the sacred pages of myth simply wrong? Can science, another jackass,
be braying Final Truth? We walk, 20th-century-blind, towards burial,
pretending that all will come right in some personal heavenly kingdom.
We wouldn't know Spirit if, Spirit on top, it fucked us up the ass.

The Descent of Alette

by

Alice Notley

For Albert Edward Notley, Sr.

"One day, I awoke" "& found myself on" "a subway, endlessly"
"I didn't know" "how I'd arrived there or" "who I was" "exactly"
"But I knew the train" "knew riding it" "knew the look of"
"those about me" "I gradually became aware—" "though it seemed

as that happened" "that I'd always" "known it too—" "that there was"
"a tyrant" "a man in charge of" "the fact" "that we were"
"below the ground" "endlessly riding" "our trains, never surfacing"
"A man who" "would make you pay" "so much" "to leave the subway"

"that you don't" "ever ask" "how much it is" "It is, in effect,"
"all of you, & more" "Most of which you already" "pay to
live below" "But he would literally" "take your soul" "Which is
what you are" "below the ground" "Your soul" "your soul rides"

"this subway" "I saw" "on the subway a" "world of souls"

"On the subway" "we rode the trains" "Got on, got off" "Sat & watched, sat" "& slept" "Walked from car to car" "Stood in stations" "We were caught up" "in movement" "in ongoingness" "& in ongoingness" "of voices," "for example" "Which of us spoke? did" "it matter?" "Who

saw what" "was being seen," "knew what" "was known?" "Gradually what was seen" "became what I saw," "to me" "Despair & outrage" "became mine too" "Sorrow" "became mine—" "To ride a" "mechanical" "contrivance" "in the darkness" "To be steeped in" "the authority"

"of" "another's mind" "the tyrant's mind" "Life of bits & pieces" "cars & scenes" "disconnected" "little dreams" "False continuum" "mechanical time:" "What do we miss?" "What do we miss?" "Was there once" "something else?" "There are animals" "in the subway" "But they"

"are mute & sad" "There are singers" "There are corpses" "There is substance" "of darkness" "And emotion" "strong emotion" "The air" "is all emotion"

"A woman entered" "a car I rode," "had a misshapen" "slowing foot; &"
"she wore" "thick-lensed glasses" ("her eyes were small," "over-focused")
"She carried a cup, announced," "'I need" "enough money—" "the amount is
eighteen dollars—" "to take my daughter above the ground" "for one
night" "just one night" "I promised her a night" "above the ground'"

"'Money will not" "be enough,'" "a woman said to her," "'Not just money,"
"he wants your things," "your small things," "your emblems," "all your
trappings" "You must give up" "to the tyrant" "all your flowers"
"all your carnations" "Or your cut hair" "Give him your hair"
"You must give him your jokes" "your best jokes," "he takes whatever—"

"Makes fun of it," "but uses it" "Give him your only" "silk scarf"
"your tiny" "turquoise pendant" "Your old-fashioned watch" "your copper
barrette" "& your nail polish" "Give him your lotion, your gardenia"
"perfume" "Give him your coat too" "But keep your sweater" "Let him take"
"what he wants" "from your wallet" "red leatherette coin purse" "& then

he'll let you" "go upstairs" "& walk around in" "our times" "He will smile"
"his boyish smile" "& let you go up there awhile'"

"There was a woman," "in a station," "with a guitar &"
"amplifier," "who sang" "sang a song" "that said this:"

"'As the old man lies dying" "in his bishop's robe & gown"
"surrounded" "by museum cases full of jewels" "& gold"
"shards of Venuses" "oldest potteries" "He" "is on exhibit"
"too" "as he is dying" "As we watch him," "the women,"

"we receive our" "emerald rings" "They grow"
"begin to grow" "around our fingers," "as we watch him"
"Because" "we're his loyal" "secretaries" "as we
watch him" "on exhibit" "always governing" "always ruling

as he lies dying" "He" "could die forever" "On exhibit"
"in his mansion" "in his Vatican" "in his Parthenon" "in his"
"admini-" "strative offices" "See" "in the emeralds"
("which can get murkier" "uglier") "an endless" "endless male

will" "But the tyrant" "is a mild man" "Look in our emeralds"
"& see shadows" "We are those" "against the green" "green
lush light" "We are weightless" "Left with rings,"
"we will be old &" "left with rings" "By the time the"

"lakes thaw the" "green lakes" "of the great cities"
"of the North" "We will be dead" "with emerald rings"
"Green stones upon our" "fingerbones" "That is our love"
"Must be our love" "That we" "will be dead &" "he"

"will live forever," "on exhibit" "in his museum'"

"I was standing up," "on the subway," "holding onto" "a metal
strap" "A man in" "an army jacket" "sat in front of" "me, eating"
"eating a piece of meat" "which he held" "in his hand," "a piece of
cold steak rimmed with fat" "& with black dots of pepper on it—"

"He gnawed the meat" "awhile, then" "looked up & said to me,"
"'I need to find" "our father" "our fathers...'" "'But what about"
"our mother?'" "I said auto-" "matically," "'the one mother"
"first mother" "of all?'" "He said nothing," "finished eating,"

"leaned back into" "his seat." "He was young," "familiar-looking
to me" "He fell asleep then" "his chin doubling" "as his head"
"fell forward" "He was brown-haired" ("brown-eyed, I'd seen")
"moustached &" "straight-nosed" "He spoke" "in his sleep—"

"'I need a dolor" "a few more dolors" "Then after that" "I'll see
our father'" "Another time" "he spoke & said," "'I'll give him
floral rocks" "floral rocks'" "After awhile" "he awoke" "& said"
"to me, 'Shall we look for them?" "Or I'll" "look for him,"

"you" "look for her...'" "'Then yours" "would be easier" "much easier,'"
"I said with anger" "'But I am agonized,' he said" "'I killed for him,"
"I was a soldier'" "The train stopped" "He abruptly" "left the car"
"Disappeared" "disappeared"

"We couldn't find" "our fathers—" "there were several" "of us"
"We were walking through subway cars" "looking" "for our fathers" "Endless
train" "It seemed the longest" "train there is" "as if it circled"
"the world—" "& we walked it, we were searching" "for our fathers,"

"when we entered" "a car of" "suited...animals—" "men, actually,"
"in business suits," "clean shirts" "Charcoal suits, &" "navy-blue"
"ties (crimson stripes")" "—beautiful suits—" "And the men all" "had
animal" "heads." "It was a dimly" "lit car" "the lights" "on occasion"

"would go completely:" "Darkness" "Silent" "Animal" "Faces" "Shaggy"
"or Sleek:" "He is a falcon, a gyrfalcon" "his head cocked toward his"
"business-suited" "wing-arm" "His eyes," "clear-dark-round," "stare"
"Or he's a lemur" "a reddish lemur" "reddish eyes" "fur, tipped in orange,

glows orange" "above his grey suit" "He's a panther, black sleek hair"
"You want to touch" "above his nose" "feel his short hair plush face,"
"black velvet" "He's an owl" "His face is feathers, it is ruffed,"
"his eyes are critical, a" "grey owl:" "Were these our fathers?" "And

if so, which" "was which," "who" "was my father" "your father?"
("And the men" "couldn't speak to us" "made no sound" "made no sign")
"Can you" "find your father?" "Mine is probably" "an owl" "He stared"
"He stared at me" "But owls stare" "And then he looked away"

"'An animal-mother'" "'is crying,'" "a voice said" "to another (I" "couldn't see them," "I was sitting—" "a crowded car:" "bodies" "pressed together" "Braid of voices" "& machine noise") "'Animals don't cry,'" "the second" "voice said" "'She has large, furry forearms,'

the first continued," "'Can you see her" "over there? She is showing" "such sorrow'" "'They don't do that,' the other said," "'& don't have" "things like sorrow'" "'You mean emotions?' said the first" "'I see her,'" "said the second," "'Why" "is she wearing" "a dress? What"

"animal is she?'" "'She is one,'" "said the first voice," "'of the large cats—" "a long-haired, large cat" "The species" "is thought to be" "mostly" "extinct" "& for a long time—the grey-eyed" "brown-haired silky" "cat of the—" "I can't remember where, exactly—" "with a

musical—" "it's not a roar," "a softer sound" "It would blur" "into the wind" "from high up on" "rocks & hills" "There were" "rocks & hills" "where the cats lived" "where they once lived" "A dress was put on her" "in the subway" "You can't ride this train" "without clothes" "Unless

you're crazy" "really crazy" "She has no one" "See her sorrow?'" "The second" "voice replied," "'They must be" "the only" "cats that cry," "what" "happened to them?'" "The first said, 'We don't know" "They don't tell" "But we think" "her children—" "the children of" "her

generation—" "are suicidal," "eat datura," "have no real mates'" "'Animals,'" "said the second voice," "'are not" "suicidal'" "'I'll bet she carries things,'" "the first said," "'They carry things" "in their pockets" "I'll bet she has" "a bit of snake bone" "a bit of creosote"

"a bit of tiny" "yellow blossom" "or other blossom" "A pebble" "2 pebbles maybe" "A rusted bottlecap" "A piece of paper," "a scrap of it" "A lock of fur" "clump of fur'" "'I don't believe you,' said the second voice," "'She's an animal'"

"A mother" "& child" "were both on fire, continuously"
"The fire" "was contained in them" "sealed them off
from others" "But you could see the flame" "halo
of short flame all about the" "conjoined bodies, who

sat" "they sat apart" "on a seat for two" "at end of car" "The
ghost" "of the father" "sat in flames" "beside them"
"paler flames" "sat straight ahead" "looking
straight ahead, not" "moving." "A woman"

"another woman" "in a uniform" "from above the ground"
"entered" "the train" "She was fireproof" "She was gloves, & she"
"took" "the baby" "took the baby" "away from the"
"mother" "Extracted" "the burning baby" "from the fire" "they

made together" "But the baby" "still burned"
("But not yours" "It didn't happen" "to you")
"'We don't know yet" "if it will" "stop burning,'"
"said the uniformed" "woman" "The burning woman" "was crying"

"she made a form" "in her mind" "an imaginary" "form" "to
settle" "in her arms where" "the baby" "had been" "We saw
her fiery arms" "cradle air" "She cradled air" ("They take your
children" "away" "if you're on fire")

"In the air that" "she cradled" "it seemed to us there" "floated"
"a flower-like" "a red flower" "its petals" "curling flames"
"She cradled" "seemed to cradle" "the burning flower of" "herself gone"
"her life" ("She saw" "whatever she saw, but what we saw" "was that flower")

"A woman came into" "a car I rode" "about thirty-seven" "maybe
forty" "Face" "a harsh response to" "what she did" "had to do"
"face rigid" "but she was beautiful" "Was," "we could see,"
"one of the ones who" "strip for coins" "on the subway—"

"They simply" "very quickly" ("illegally") "remove all their
clothes" "Stand, for a moment" "Turning to face" "each end"
"of the car" "Then dress quickly," "pass quickly" "the cup."
"But she—this one—" "face of hating to so much that" "as she

took off her blouse," "her face" "began to change" "Grew
feathers, a small beak" "& by the time she was naked," "she wore the
head" "of an eagle" "a crowned eagle" "a raptor" "herself—"
"And as she stood" "& faced the car" "her body" "was changing"

"was becoming entirely" "that bird" "those wings," "she shrank to
become the bird" "but grew wings that" "were wider" "than she had been
tall" "Instantly," "instantly, a man caught her" "A cop came"
"As if ready" "as if they knew" "Her wings were clipped,"

"talons cut" "as if as quickly" "as possible" "She was released
then, to the car" "to the subway" "Perched" "on the bar the
straps hang from"

"I entered" "a car" "in which I seemed" "to see double"
"Each person I" "looked at seemed" "spread out" "as if doubled"
"Gradually" "I perceived that" "each person" "was surrounded by
a ghostly" "second image" "was encased in it" "& each"

"of those images," "those encasings," "was exactly the same"
"each was in fact" "the tyrant" "Though colorless," "a grey
ghost of him" "But he bent & swayed" "& walked with" "every
person, his" "expression" "always" "the same:" "mild &

benign" "And he encased many" "men not so" "uncomfortably"
"But others," "especially women," "looked as if they" "suffered from"
"trying" "to fit inside" "this other" "As if his form" "squeezed
theirs," "their breasts & hips," "very painfully—" "his long

thin streamlined form" "One woman" "tried to cast him off,"
"shake him off" "Writhed & jumped" "Then I felt him" "begin to
encase *me*" "He sank down" "into my head" "into my thoughts,"
"which instantly" "separated" "assumed a terrifying" "strict

order" "unfamiliar" "to me" "Each felt distinct" "from each,"
"arranged" "in a progression" "My head" "contained an
army" "of separate" "same-shape thoughts" "Soldiers"
"soldiers marching" "never touching each" "other" "It wasn't"

"wasn't" "like a mind" "No thought felt true" "Thoughts felt
efficient" "He squeezed on me" "would squeeze away" "my shape"
"I cast him off" "& ran" "from the car"

"At a subway stop, crowds of people" "some sleeping" "on the
platform &" "Behind them," "caveish stores," "a row of stalls niched
in the walls" "A snake" "lives in this stop," "lies there" "on the
platform" "before a door—" "which is an exit—" "lies large

coiled & sleeping" "Women" "vaguely whorish" "come & go here,"
"they are ant-faced—" "smooth carnelian" "carapaces" "above bright-
colored" "cotton blouses" "There are men" "large-handed furry"
"They are round-eyed" "grey spiders" "But the snake sleeps" "before the

door that's" "an exit" "to the tyrant's world" "She is black,"
"gold, & brown" "Sleeps because" "she is sad" "is drugged by"
"melancholy" "Corpse-souls" "from the cemetery" "wander here" "near her
coils," "disturbed &" "white-dusty" "Too many of us" "underground"

"But we think" "the snake is growing" "She is growing; here's an
example:" "A woman" "who is standing," "waiting" "for the train,"
"is someone who" "will be allowed" "to exit—" "wears a business suit
big shoulders" "Her animal familiarity" "to us is" "powdered over,"

"pearlized" "She's attractive," "is suffused with" "her powers"
"a sense of" "her own powers" "But she" "is surrounded by" "a pale gel"
"a thick light" "a viscous" "transparency" "It sets her apart from us"
"Some other" "kind of will" "It is substance of" "the tyrant's thought"

"She belongs to" "the tyrant," "though she thinks she's" "her own"
"Now this is" "what happens:" "There is a figure" "in her body"
"another one, it" "steps out of it" "Leaves her body" "It is brown,"
"& naked" "Both humorous" "& shadowed" "of face—" "A spirit leaves her"

"& lies down by" "the snake" "Becomes ghostly" "brown coils"
"Disappears into" "the snake"

"A woman" "a crazed woman—" "seems crazy" "crouches naked, in a corner" "of the car" "Seems to try" "to stand up, it's as if her legs" "won't work" "won't quite" "Or as if" "she can't remember" "if it's okay" "to be naked," "if you're wearing a" "shawl" "an ugly shawl" "It's the color of"

"a dirty pale kitchen wall" "Now stands up" "She stands" "even though she is naked" "Assumes a place here," "anyway" "How old is she?" "maybe, in her fifties" "She is speaking" "Is it to us?" "Lips are moving," "speaks softly," "but urgently:" "'No place no" "place" "except me" "No place"

"except under" "this shawl" "I can have" "this place" "I don't want you" "Don't want it" "Please don't" "give me anything" "Money, clothes...ideas" "What you think are" "yours'" ("Says to me,") "'It's all made by" "a man" "You were made by" "men, made out of man-thought" "All women now,

all of this here," "man-made—" "Under" "my shawl" "I try to be, I" "am" "another world" "a woman's world—" "Why I may be" "the only one" "the first one" "since before" "the tyrant's history" "So you must leave me alone...'" "And then she left us" "unsteadily, walked away" "afraid of us"

"afraid" "we would corrupt her" "corrupt her world"

"'When I was born,'" "'I was born now'" "'fully grown,'" "'on heroin'" "'When I was born'" "'fully grown'" "'in the universe'" "'of no change'" "'nothing'" "'grows up from'" ("Who sings this, whose voice?" "This person" "is in a shadow" "down at the end of" "the platform" "I can't see him" "at all" "He continues

his song:") "'When I was born,'" "'I was now'" "'When I was born,'" "'I'm not allowed'" "'to remember when I was'" "'the little baby'" "'in a darkness, joy of darkness'" "'Was I the cub'" "'for an instant?'" "'if so'" "'only an instant,'" "'before I'" "'was a soldier'" "'before I'" "'was a soldier...'" ("Where is the

battlefield?" "At a station" "no longer" "in use" "Train goes right past it" "But veterans" "know how" "to get in" "In that station" "is kept a piece of" "a battlefield" "of the old war" "In that station" "grow white flowers" "large blossoms" "that are faces," "with eyes closed" "lashes

closed white" "White skin white hair" "Soldiers go there" "Call to" "the victim-flowers" "They don't answer but" "seem to grow" "The soldiers water them" "water the flowers" "which were" "their own victims:") "'When I was born,'" "'I was born now'" "'When I was born,'" "'I'm not allowed'"

"'to remember if I was'" "'the little baby'" "'the little boy'" "'Was I the cub'" "'for an instant?'" "'Or was I'" "'already'" "'a soldier...'"

"When the train" "goes under water" "the close tunnel" "is transparent"
"Murky water" "full of papery" "full of shapelessness" "Some fish" "but
also things" "Are they made by humans?" "Have no shape," "like rags"
"like soggy papers" "like frayed thrown-away wash cloths" "black"

"& encrusted with" "dirt & scum" "The fish" "move among them" "& weeds which"
"grow black," "dirty in" "blackened water" "A fish, an" "immense fish"
"approaches" "our window" "A face as if" "to be recognized" "nuanced,"
"full of pain" "A face" "as of a man" "wide-eyed," "of course," "& gulping

but" "a face of" "a man" "No it's a fish face," "slime-encrusted" "Is
it a man" "or a fish?" "Someone stares," "stares back at him" "& cries"
"just a little" "She says, 'He's so sad-looking'" "His face changes"
"often changes" "as if we have him" "out of focus" "He blurs" "The

woman says," "'It makes me" "so uncomfortable," "that I can't"
"see him right'" "And the fish, too" "seems to weep" "moist blackish beads"
"He can't keep up" "with the window" "& is left behind" "Then the
woman says," "'He looked" "so familiar" "to me...'"

"There is a car" "that is nothing but" "garbage" "Shit &
spittle" "dropped food" "frayed brownness" "dirty matter"
"pressed down & flattened" "Paper piled" "piled on the floor"
"heaped on the benches" "Napkins yellowed" "tampons bloody"

"paper twisted" "torn & sodden" "Ashes &" "grey rags &"
"old skin & nails" "Old hair" "old bones" "& a Corpse"
"a skeleton corpse" "a skeleton in a" "dress, some sort of
old" "native dress" "of tattered skins" "animal skins"

"animal skins now brown-black," "coral beads now greasy" "She
lies against" "a mound of garbage" "at one end of" "the car"
"She has a small skull small finger bones" "a small woman"
"elegant skull" "The only ones" "who ride in this car" "are

those who" "take drugs" "So it's left this way—" "They"
"don't mind the smell" "They say" "she protects them"
"protects them from fearfulness," "by being" "the gentle fearful"
"herself" "They don't" "touch her though" "They say she hums"

"like a motor" "Or something does" "in the garbage"
"Something" "is still alive in there," "has power"

"I walked" "into a car" "No one there" "There was no one" "But there were voices" "I heard voices" "All of these voices" "were like beggars" "beggars' voices" "the voices crowded" "together" "intoning" "like beggars:" "'Spare? Spare any?" "Spare any mothers?" "fathers?" "Spare any, I won't" "hurt you," "lady," "My body" "Spare a new" "new body?" "body?" "Today" "is my old" "baby's birth-

day, do you have" "any change?" "My old baby" "is gone but" "Change" "Spare any" "Old babies" "Young fathers" "Spare any" "generations" "of mine, Can you" "spare" "my mother" "a mother" "Spare any...?'" "And on louder" "& the phrases" "more crowded" "together" "The car seemed empty" "but I" "was afraid" "to sit down" "Gradually," "as I stood there, still afraid" "to move" "too afraid of" "bumping into" "an invisible"

"person," "somehow I" "began to see" "the voices," "or their locations" "A window" "black window, both" "rigid, &" "rushing" "A grey bench place, dirty" ("the usual, sharpened" "by sound") "A space" "in the middle of" "the car" "through which you looked" "at a picture" "of a tropical" "Island" "& words:" *Fly to Heaven* "'Spare," "spare" "a spare heaven" "spare a city'" "'Look at me,'

said a voice," "'I am dying.'" "I looked" "at his voice &" "saw another" "silver pole" "'I'm dying,'" "he said" "fiercely" "rather proudly" "'Look at me I'm dying'" "I couldn't see him, I still" "couldn't see him" "'Look at me I'm dying'" "Give me change" "Give me change'" "I couldn't see him"

"In one car people work" "seem to work there" "It's their office"
"But when you enter it you" "see them" "perform actions" "without objects"
"As if in pantomime" "Without papers" "without machines" "Most of
these are women" "They wear dresses," "pantyhose," "grownup shoes,"

"& makeup" "They carry" "leather pocketbooks" "And they do things"
"continuously" "with their hands" "Perform motions" "of working"
"Work invisible" "keyboards" "carry invisible" "files," "invisible
papers" "Hold up airy" "phone receivers" "against hairdos"

"& move their lips" "say silent words" "They are working, working"
"Then a man" "in a suit" "enters" "& they hand him" "all their
invisible work" "He goes through it" "as if page by page" "& scrutinizes
air" "with a grave," "lined face" "Sometimes smiles with" "mild

approval" "Appears to think" "hard" "Goes quiet" "They watch him as"
"he picks up" "the invisible" "phone receiver" "His lips" "begin to
move" "He motions" "the women" "to resume their work"

"At a station" "there's a mirror" "a black mirror" "Just a mirror" "on the platform" "where the train stops" "But it's solid black" "When you look in it, you" "see a mask" "your mask" "It's your present mask," "I guess" "I looked in it" "& saw" "...a benign

plain wooden mask" "plain mask" "nothing special" "just a brown mask" "Another woman" "standing near me" "looked" "& saw a mask with a" "snake-like face" "fangs" "& thin tongue" "golden eyes" "flat head (eyes had cut out" "dead pupils" "of a mask)" "'I had a dream,' she said" "'last

night" "I was angry," "& then" "was a snake" "Armless, legs together, into one, I" "drew myself up" "snakelike" "to my full height—" "all length & head—" "& lunged at" "a tall man," "like the tyrant," "who was impassive" "who watched me," "watched my anger," "as if I were" "a

small child" "I don't know why" "I was so angry" "in the dream" "What had happened, but" "my striking" "out at him" "had no effect" "He only looked at me" "kept looking," "calmly" "I had become" "unreason" "And I had become" "despair" 'He was reason" "I was despair,"

"it was as if with" "my moment" "of anger" "with him I had" "ruined my life" "had shown myself" "estranged from" "the world" "I was anger" "I was other" "I was now nothing but" "lost" "He didn't care" "I was nothing" "nothing" "to him, & I" "continued to" "strike at him"

"unsuccessfully'"

"'I once" "found an exit" "from the subway'" ("the woman told me")
"'I once" "found a staircase" "that led to" "an exit" "temporarily
unlocked" "I opened the door to—" "It was an" "Antarctic"
"light, up there" "As if dawn or dusk, but" "neither" "Everyone

wore black" "black cashmere" "discreet diamonds" "had guarded,
dark eyes" "Was it" "the winter holidays?" "I saw" "crushed-red lights"
"reflected" "in snowy puddles" "White lights" "in naked trees"
"For me it" "was frozen time," "from past pain," "from a time"

"when I was young," "before I came beneath," "came down here—" "before
I'd willingly" "walked away from" "that upper world," "had left"
"a university—" "I then remembered from" "long before" ("as I stood"
"near the exit") "a library I'd entered" "in that partial light, in

Spring" "There was grass," "there were blossoms" "Huge windows"
"looking out on grass" "And shelves" "of books" "all the books there
were:" "The books were decayed matter," "black & moldy" "Came apart"
"in my hands" "All the books were" "black rot" "Were like mummies"

"More body of" "the tyrant" "It is all his body" "The world is" "his
mummy" "Up there, up there" "Down here it is" "a more desperate"
"decay," "as if" "rich emotion," "pain," "could still transform us"
"despite him" "despite his power, &" "tyrannical" "…ignorance,"

"passing as" "knowledge—" "And so of course I" "re-entered" "re-
entered" "the subway—" "I can't leave it" "ever" "unless"
"we all leave—'"

"'Once,' she continued," "'years ago, the tyrant" "was shot"
"We saw it happen" "onscreen" "He was shot by" "a masked
assassin" "at close range—" "Blood spurted" "from his chest & head"
"A mother," "someone's mother" "came & cradled" "his head in

her lap" "There was wind & rain," "wind &
black rain" "His flesh colorless," "he seemed dead"
"Blood—" "his blood—" "was smeared onto" "the camera lens—"
"He didn't die." "A few weeks later, he" "reappeared onscreen"

"Announced he'd been" "in a coma," "then had recovered" "His
white hair was" "strangely reddish" "He said he'd been" "near death"
"He said he'd seen" "a white light" "forgiving" "all embracing"
"He said he'd shed" "his blood for us" "But it was worth it" "worth it"

"for that," "that light" "which would, he now knew," "embrace us all"
"Which does" "include all" "That's when I knew,' she said," "'light
meant lie" "That's when I knew that" "the Light" "was a lie,"
"& that" "I would never" "seek light" "I will never" "seek light,'"

"she repeated" "before she boarded" "her train"

"Awhile before" "I entered" "the subway," "all money
underground" "became diseased" "It seared your skin," "when you
touched it" "& poisoned" "your bloodstream" "Within days,"
"you would die" "Thus all money" "was taken" "by people in"

"special suits &" "burned" "No more was issued" "here below—"
"So money" "became invisible" "Invisible money" "began to
change hands" "Paid" "in invisible" "Things paid for"
"by invisible…" "Everyone knows," "everyone knows"

"if you have it or not" "if you have enough or not" "All is
exactly as" "before" "when there was money," "except"
"it isn't printed" "isn't seen" "But it is money"
"just the same" "Thus," "there was a woman" "who kept trying"

"to leave the subway" "She was pointed" "out to me" "at a
station," "in process of" "trying to leave us" "A young woman,"
"curly-headed" "with a slightly" "loony look," "encased"
"in a large" "plastic container" ("people wear them" "when they

leave here") "She passed through" "the turnstile" "The other
side of" "the turnstile" "being obscured to us, as if" "everything on
that side" "were somehow" "blurred for us," "were viewed by us
myopically—" "I couldn't see" "exactly" "what happened:"

"movement of figures," "then" "she was" "returned to us,"
"sent back through in" "the plastic" "'They *never*" "let me leave"
"I get my plastic," "I get my money" "but they always" "turn me
back" "There's always" "something wrong with" "my money" "Usually

they say," "it's not enough" ("though" "it always is") "This time they
said it was" "too old" "I must have saved it too long" "Old money"
"isn't used" "any more" "above the ground'" "'Why do you want"
"so much to go there?' I asked" "'Anyone does,'" "she said fiercely"

"I surprised myself" "by saying" "with conviction," "'I *don't*'"

THE DESCENT OF ALETTE 85

"A man" "in a suit" "in the first car the" "front car of the train—"
"This older" "distinguished man" "asked me to" "ride with him"
"join him" "I declined &" "moved back" "far back, I" "joined a
car" "that contained" "women &" "girl children" "women in skirts"

"girls in dresses" "I wondered" "who the man was, why he wasn't"
"above the ground" "He must work for" "the tyrant" "But I forgot him
among our flags—" "we had a multitude" "of flags" "Some were red"
"red & wildly torn" "Some were silken" "almost flimsy" "Some were

spangled" "Some were lacy" "One girl carried one" "with a snake"
"appliquéd on it" "And one woman had" "the largest flag" "It said—"
"in gold letters" "that were burning," "in gold that showed through
flame" "which followed" "the letters' shapes—" "on white unburning

silk—" "said *Presence*" "*Presence*" "But the burning" "letters
shifted" "when the man entered" "our car" "the distinguished man in a
suit" "He sat down" "Did he only" "want to look at us?" "For he was
sitting" "there, staring" "And the letters" "the burning letters"

"shifted" "& changed" "to spell *Poverty*" "instead of *Presence*"
"He didn't need" "to ride the train" "He'd made us poor" "in an instant"
"They walk by" "& make you poor" "They look at you & make you poor"
"Surreptitiously I began" "to remove my" "bits of jewelry" "my earrings"

"with small citrines" "my ring of" "mismatched garnets" "I put them"
"in my pocket" "They weren't" "good enough"

"In a station" "I saw" "a woman crying" "She stood against"
"the wall" "looking dirty" "& exhausted," "crying quietly"
"I asked her who she was" "& why" "she was crying" "She
said: 'I" "am a painter" "I have been trying" "to find"

"a form the tyrant" "doesn't own—" "something" "he doesn't
know about" "hasn't invented, hasn't" "mastered" "hasn't
made his own" "in his mind" "Not rectangular," "not a
sculpture" "Not a thing at all—" "he owns all things,"

"doesn't he?" "He's invented" "all the shapes" "I'm afraid he's"
"invented mine," "my very own" "body'" ("she was hysterical")
"'Did he invent me?" "I want" "to do something like
paint air" "Perhaps" "I even want to" "invent air" "I've

painted" "thin transparent" "pieces" "of plastic" "They—"
"the pictures on them—" "always turn" "rectangular," "circular"
"I once painted" "on bat's wings" "I caught a bat" "painted
colors on" 'let it loose &" "watched the air change…"

"He owns form," "doesn't he?" "The tyrant" "owns form'"

"A beautiful" "gaunt woman, a" "bird-like" "dark woman"
"Large tall, erect" "in a white dress a" "long robe"
"Head in profile, cowled head" "& she cradles" "a baby"
"dead baby" "Its spirit," "which seems a grown man," "rises"

"into black" "We are at" "a large, black-ceilinged"
"station" "Has a baby" "or a man died?" "She cradles"
"a dead baby" "But a man has died, he is rising" into the air"
"It isn't" "isn't night sky up there, it's a black" "black

ceiling" "He will not" "continue" "to rise to" "the sky"
"We are confined below" "confined" "He sinks again" "Stands
on the floor" "while his mother, unseeing" "still cradles"
"the baby" "he once was" "They are near a decaying wall"

"crumbling, full of holes" "Another landscape" "shows beyond it"
"Seems to light up" "to appear to us" "A large, unbounded
space" "full of a throng of" "the Recent Dead" "Spirits,
all spirits" "A forest a city" "of white" "transparent

shimmering" "spirits" "close together" "And one" "one
disengages" "Comes toward the man" "Raises thin arms, has an
open" "dark mouth hole, says," "'Welcome" "to you dead man"
"we cannot rise, as we should" "We cannot pass through"

"the tyrant's world's" "new fabrics" "the materials
of his world" "He has changed" "the chemical" "composition"
"of everything" "but spirit" "but our souls" "but us—"
"We" "who are nature" "when nothing else is," "we are all

trapped below" "We can only go" "down" "further down—"
"Down" "is now the only way" "to rise" "Come & wait with us"
"wait with us" "to descend'"

88   THE SCARLET CABINET

"A car" "awash with blood" "Blood at our feet" "& I
& others" "have small springs" "of blood from our"
"feet & knees" "There is an inch or two" "of blood"
"all over" "the car floor" "Replenished" "Periodically"

"by our body springs" "of blood" "And trickling out"
"the door," "when it opens" "at stations." "The
tyrant" "sends a hologram" "a life-sized hologram" "of
himself" "into our car" "He stands mid-car" "& says:"

"'The blood at our" "feet" "has cost me" "so much"
"The blood" "at our feet" "has cost us so" "much"
"To clean" "the blood" "is difficult" "to clean the
car.'" "There is a litter" "of things" "in the

wash of blood" "I see sanitary" "pads," "kleenex,"
"black-blood encrusted" "old bandages" "An old black
suitcase" "spills out" "torn men's clothes" "& frayed towels"
"The hologram tyrant" "says, 'Here" "are my tears'" "Holds

up his palm" "His tears are" "small drops of jade"
"Red" "& white jade" "His tears have turned to jade"
"They will be placed in" "a National" "Museum" "There is
something in" "my ear" "I pull it out a" "white cord"

"a long" "silk cord" "I pull it out &" "hear our blood"
"It hums" "a unison one" "note loud a" "sheet of sound"
"It hangs there" "sad insect noise" "insect-like"
"Our blood."

"Two people fucking" "behind the stairs" "that led" "to other
trains" "The woman & man," "fucking," "had grown wings" "grey
feathered," "Subway grey, and" "the wings" "would beat the air"
"or stir the air, slightly" "Pause" "then encircle" "the back of"

"the other lover," "as arms" "grey wing arms" "The two lovers"
"were not naked" "They had feathers" "they had greyness" "Though they
had" "pink genitals" "in the midst of" "grey feathers, and"
"heads" "of dark hair" "Had dark hair," "dark

heads touching" "There's no place to" "make love"
"down here" "in the subway" "except near others"
"near all the others" "Like animals" "elegant animals"
"As in the days" "when there were animals" "animals in

the world" "Before the tyrant" "became everything" "before the tyrant"

"I saw" "a black flower" "growing" "from the platform"
"It was" "a small flower" "petunia-like" "black,"
"growing up from" "grey cement" "dirty" "bespattered non-earth"
"Small black" "like black blood" "like crushed-velvet black blood"

"As I looked at it" "it seemed" "to enlarge" "As I came nearer,"
"as if" "by my attention" "it enlarged more" "& I entered it,"
"I was it, for a time" "was that black blood crushed velvet" "velvet
womb, I guessed" "womb of Hell" "I was womb" ("was I

also dead?") "& inside it" "inside me" "In the center"
"was a seed that was" "an eye" "a small eye" "a blue eye"
"pale blue" "And smaller," "its black pupil" "Look"
"inside the pupil" "Inside the pupil's the" "black flower," "again"

"enormous" "crushed velvet" "black blood" "But
whose eye" "whose" "would it be?" "If it was mine," "whose
was that," "who" "would I be?" "Did it matter" "to me?" "Since really I"
"was womb?" "blood-black." "And would always" "again"

"become that"

"I walked" "into a car where" "everything was membrane-
like" "thin-membrane petal-like" "& veined"
"Fetus-like" "fetus flesh like" "In shades of pink" "purple black &"
"brown" "Thin" "reddish veins" "Fetal flower" "soaked in

subway light" "The car walls were translucent" "orchid-
flesh" "The seats were & the floor—" "All was naked flesh"
"We were naked" "A fetus" "delicate" "tiny faced," "eyes closed,
concentrating" "curled" "almost spiralling," "floated high" "in the

air." "We sat naked on our" "membrane-like" "tan benches"
"All of us" "smooth & wrinkled" "brownish, or"
"darker," "or paler," "palest" "were as if" "within a flower"
"as if" "within us" "This" "This is" "simultaneous," "I understood"

"Uncontrolled by" "the tyrant" "Someone else"
"in all of us" "is this lovely" "fetal flesh," "flower skin"
"We are being this" "this flower" "And then" "the flower
vanished" "I was clothed, there was" "no fetus" "Grey subway car

of people" "riding quietly some sleeping" "Someone's earphones"
"turned up too loud" "buzzing wire" "vaguely song"

"Eyeball" "single eye" "a lashed eye" "funny eye"
"looking all around" "from the floor of a" "subway car"
"It's self-propelled" "moves in scurries" "near my foot"
"What's it looking for?" "It's so funny" "Its eye-

lashes" "are black" "demarcated" "They have wit, it has"
"wit" "This eyeball's funny" "on the grey floor"
"among round stains" "& ashes" "Looks all over"
"the car" "Expressive" "only looking, but" "stretching, in a"

"struggle" "to see" "Rolls about in" "itself," "& looks"
"I guess it's blue-eyed" "dark-blue" "No eyebrows, of
course" "Doesn't blink much" "Intent" "intent on looking"
"What's it looking for?" "I guess, whatever"

"In a large" "subway station" "a non-descript man tells us,"
"'We'd like you" "to meet the tyrant—" "The real tyrant is not"
"the tall man in a dark suit" "That man is" "his representative"
"*This* man" "is the real" "tyrant...'" "He presents to us" "a large

man, pale—" "oh yes he's ghoulish" "As if he's what we'd" "expect,"
"really" "expect" "He smiles sheepishly at us" "He has a large face,"
"longish white hair" "Dark" "blue eyes" "all iris no white,"
"like cracked" "sapphires" "like jewel inserts" "in skull sockets"

"And his jaw" "is decaying" "pulpy soft" "oozy jaw" "His jaw"
"is decomposing" "That must be right for" "a figure" "of evil?"
"They want us" "to hate *him*," "if the tyrant" "must be hated"
"I say," "'He's a substitute" "He's not the tyrant" "He's a simple

ghoul" "The tyrant" "is a mild-" "looking man" "He does not show"
"his decay" "He has no such grace," "you might say" "His sense of"
"his own knowledge" "presumed rightness" "preserves him" "forever"
"He could have never" "have never" "been that wrong:" "That thousands"

"upon thousands" "of years" "of enslavements" "so many different kinds"
"be integral to" "the solid" "& beautiful" "structures" "cathedrals"
"museums" "& mansions" "& temples" "he has built" "above the ground?"
"How could that be?'" "The non-descript man" "missed my irony" "& led"

"the ghoul away" "to meet another" "small group in" "the subway"

"I was standing" "in a room" "in a station—" "Had found a
place like" "a room," "an abandoned" "shop, perhaps" "I was en-
closed," "a private space" "The room was dark" "with a pale
whitish light" "resembling moonlight" "that shone in through"

"a burntout" "glassless window" "A man I knew"
"had joined me" "We stood talking" "in dark rubble," "I"
"near the window," "when the man" "assumed a look of"
"calm alarm" "on his face" "& pointed to" "something" "be-

hind me" "I turned & saw a" "head" "upsidedown" "in the
window" "An old man's face" "vaguely" "familiar—"
"old," "& white-haired," "looking friendly" "upsidedown"
"drooling" "just a little—" "old man who" "can't help that"

"I wanted" "to show" "my companion" "that I wasn't"
"afraid of" "this old man," "this familiar" "sudden old man, so I
patted" "his cheek" "his upsidedown" "cheek" "He smiled,"
"& disappeared" "I gasped & said," "'That was the?'" "'tyrant,'"

"the man finished" "He looked annoyed" "'You hypocrite'" "Or is it
sucker?'" "'Both,' I said" "But in one way" "he is just" "an
old man'" "The man said," "'You've just patted" "the cheek of"
"the man" "you must confront" "& vanquish'"

"A car" "I was in" "became filled with" "an owl"
"A huge owl" "huge wings spread out" "huge owl face" "The owl was"
"a great" "horned owl" "a strange color" "of blue"
"a midnight blue" "as if an owl who" "was a night sky somehow,"

"a piece of night sky" "The owl's eyes" "were intent, intense"
"the beak dangerous" "But I was" "entranced" "'How
are you here?' I asked him" "He said, 'I am" "a projection"
"from another place" "am not so large" "Am a simple" "owl"

"I've come here" "to say" "that when you finally" "meet with
the tyrant—" "do you know yet" "you must confront him?—'"
"I said nothing" "'Well, anyway,' he continued," "'when you
meet him," "I will help you" "I will help you, that is,"

"if you don't" "hurt anyone—" "anyone except" "the tyrant'"
"'What must I do to him?' I asked" "What" "the situation" "'will
require,' he said," "'but I think he" "must die'" "Die?"
"I can't kill someone" "I can't kill," "I have no right'" "'You

are an animal,' said the owl," "'an animal" "as I am" "Act like
an animal" "when you kill him" "As little" "as possible"
"must happen" "It must be clean'" "'I have no prowess,' I said"
"'I will help you" "as I said'" "Then he left," "disappeared"

"I thought, 'That" "was my father," "I think" "that that owl"
"is probably" "my dead father'"

96 THE SCARLET CABINET

"I changed cars, on a train" "I felt distraught" "& had to move around"
"There was something" "trying," "in my head, to" "swim up," "a bad
dream" "Then I screamed—" "it was leaving" "my head" "I screamed"
"before everyone" "in the car" "It had burst out of me," "& we could

see it" "It was a dreamed man" "a man I'd never" "seen before"
"He was young I guess" "handsome" "dark-haired brown eyes" "He
had a knife" "& he killed himself" "before us" "With a knife he"
"stabbed his own neck" "deeply" "There was a jet of blood dark" "purple"

"across the car" "There was blood on me" "He vanished" "But there was
blood" "real blood" "on my leg & on no one else" "Though some had stood"
"just as close" "Everyone" "came to comfort me" "A youngish" "brown-
skinned woman" "in a cotton flower print" "took a handkerchief from her

purse" "& wiped the blood off" "my leg" "'It's as if I killed *him*,'"
"I said" "'Will I always'" "feel guilty?'" "'It's not your fault,' someone
said" "Then voices" "surrounded me" "with comfort" "caressing shadows:"
"'*You didn't do it*'" "'As if,'" "I said," "'I didn't love him" "enough'"

"They were somber" "for a moment" "Then one man said—" "in jeans" "& a
handkerchief" "tied round his head," "brown-skinned—" "said, 'The key"
"isn't always" "the word 'love'" "The key is literal" "A key'" "He held
a key in" "his hand" "then put it back into" "his pocket" "Literal

key" "literal blood" "'What is" "literal love?'" "I asked him" "'It is
this,'" "he said" "He took a pen knife" "from his pocket" "a small knife
but sharp" "'Hold very still'" "He made a cut on—" "'Hold still'" "He
cut my chest," "above the breast" "a small incision &" "it bled" "down my

blouse" "'Only your own blood" "is on you now" "is on you now,'"
"he said" "'It washes'" "his away'"

"I stood again" "on the platform" "of the station" "where the snake sleeps" "Stood near" "the snake herself," "in the shadows there," "thinking" "I felt poised" "to be decisive" "be decisive in some way" "But only knew" "the same decision:" "Get on the next train" "or not"

"The snake" "the sad snake" "opened bleary dark" "gold-ringed eyes—" "crusty sticky" "around their edges" "Opened eyes" "& opened mouth" ("I'd never seen her" "awake") "Extended" "a black tongue" "& said in" "a woman's whisper:" "'When I was" "the train," "when I was" "the train,"

"flesh & blood" "flesh & blood" "took you to your" "destination" "to your life" "to your life" "carried you through your life" "Flesh & blood were" "your life" "Flesh & blood were" "your time" "A soul" "was not so naked," "so pained &" "denied" "abused &" "denied,"

"when I was" "the train...'" "'You're not big enough,'" "I said to her," "'not big enough to'" "be a train'" "She ignored me" "& repeated" "over" "& over," "'When I was" "the train" "When I was" "the train" "When I was" "the train...'" "until she" "finally" "fell asleep again"

"On a train, I" "fell asleep" "& dreamed I turned away" "from light:"
"I was reading" "I was reading" "an old book brown leather" "I
walked" "as I read" "I was reading" "& walking" "On a grassy"
"path that led" "to a small house" "up to its door" "I opened

the door—" "The house was filled with" "filled with white light"
"The tyrant stood there" "white-haired, round-blue-eyed" "black-suited,"
"& slim," "light" "all about him" "I turned & ran." "I awoke then"
"& thought," "'He owns enlightenment" "all enlightenment" "that we

know about" "He owns" "the light" "I must resist it'" "I slept again"
"My head" "fell against" "someone's shoulder, I" "jerked awake,"
"peered at a car of" "quiet men," "sleeper's mask each" "the smooth
eyelids," "the subtle modeling" "near each line of mouth" "I slept"

"& dreamed again:" "The tyrant floated" "in a blue sky" "He had
frayed edges" "all about himself," "became tatter-like" "His hair &
face," "his suit & hands" "were like rags blown" "on a clothesline"
"his eyes" "were bulging," "his mouth open" "His tatter-arms

stretched out" "his white thin hair blowing" "He became" "pieces of
cloth; sky" "appeared" "between the pieces" "which scattered" "He
blew away" "Where he had been was" "a chaos" "cave-like," "cave-
shaped a" "blue-black" "cell of winds" "The cave stretched backwards"

"into the blue sky a" "black" "snakelike tunnel"

"I was in a car" "with huge holes" "in the floor," "& in the
walls" "Each time I" "looked at them" "they seemed larger"
"There was hardly" "any floor to" "stand on" "I pressed myself"
"against a pole" "At my feet" "through the floor" "the tracks

gleamed," "slid by in darkness" "& the walls" "let in darkness"
"through spaces" "shaped like missing slats" "There was less & less"
"car there" "It became" "its own skeleton" "When the train"
"finally stopped I" "inched my way" "around the edges" "of where the

floor had been" "& out the door" "The station" "had a sign"
"hung above it" "which said" *"Tyrant's Head"* "It was dimly lit,"
"almost dark" "Strange clouds hung" "in front of it" "like eyes,
nose, & mouth:" "I walked through them" "into the semi-dark" "There was

a dress dummy to my right" "dressed up queen-like" "in a long dress,"
"jewels," "sash & crown" ("ragged hemline," "diamonds sooty")
There were masks" "on the wall" "made out of garbage:" "old news-
papers & rags" "& grey" "cotton wadding" "There was a button" "on a

pedestal" "to be pressed &" "when I pressed it," "lights went on"
"The queen's jaws moved" "She smiled & said, 'Our" "stripper"
"will now give a" "command performance'" "The lights dimmed again"
"into a spotlight" "on a woman" "in a black dress" "a long dress"

"She began" "to undress:" "everything she wore" "was black"
"When she dropped her skirt, she said," "'This is my love'" "When she
unbuttoned" "her blouse &" "slid it off she" "said, 'This is my vision'"
"When she removed" "her bra" "she said," "'This is my life'" "She

stood before me" "in a black" "thong G-string" "& high heels"
"She slid" "the G-string off" "'No one is sure,'" "she said," "'if this
is positive or negative,'" "it just is'" "She slid the G-string on & off"
"repeatedly" "& repeated" "what she'd said," "'No one is sure'" "if this is

positive or negative,'" "it just is'" "Finally" "the queen said,"
"'Thank you, that's enough'" "'I must" "finish stripping,'" "said the
stripper" "She began" "to masturbate with" "her finger" "saying
over" "& over,'" "'Invent the world'" "'Invent the world'" "so I can

come again'" "After" "she had come—" "in a seconds-long" "weak spasm—"
"she turned into" "the tyrant" "The queen" "took his arm" "They both
bowed &" "the station" "became pitch-dark"

100   THE SCARLET CABINET

"There is a car in" "two worlds," "both worlds, the upper" "&
lower" "It is here" "in the lower" "every" "other second &"
"in the upper" "every other," "thus flickers as if" "strobe-light-
lit" "I can't enter it" "I can only" "look in" "at a window" "be-
tween the cars:" "I had been told to" "go look at"

"the man" "who wants to change things" "He is a large man in
fatigues," "vaguely round-faced" "& dark-haired—" "flickering—"
"Others—" "a few are women—" "similarly dressed," "flash"
"between the two worlds" "Hard to focus" "So hard to see them" "They
have various" "guns," "cartridge belts" "Converse" ("though I can't

hear them" "Such a roar in" "my ears" "between the cars")
"The man who" "wants to change things" "has a creature" "a small
creature" "on his shoulder" "At first I think it's a" "monkey"
"but gradually (they flicker so)" "I perceive that it's a"
"woman" "a tiny woman" "naked, & brown, with a" "chain" "that extends"

"from her neck—" "a small collar—to" "his belt" "He strokes her
head" "as he speaks" "Something" "is making him" "sad" "He
weeps" "His tears are hard, like" "the tyrant's," "small jewels"
"blue crystals" "A man picks them up" "from the floor" "& collects
them in a" "leather pouch" "The woman," "tiny woman," "has

aboriginal" "features, a" "wide nose a wide mouth" "eyes are wide
apart" "wiry hair" "face of knowing" "face of humor—" "sad
humor now—" "shiny-souled, she" "is perfect" "But her eyes" "I
gradually realize" "are grey" "look like mine" "look" "just like
mine" "And on the walls there are posters" "of men" "hero-leaders,"

"I guess, of" "rebel armies," "revolutions" "flickering, vibrating"
"& there floating," "flickering" "in space as if" "detaching, are"
"two eyes" "two grey spots" "two eyes that look like mine"

"'What have we" "to do" "with the tyrant?'" "said a woman" "'He somehow keeps us here" "but in my life I'" "must have my life," "must squeeze my life out of" "being here" "Must be here" "since I am" "She was crying" "A dark woman" "large-

faced" "comfortably fleshed-out" "Her eyes" "shut the tears in" "then opened" "again,'" "A life gets closer to" "being over" "You've only done what" "he makes you do—" "because he says" "what a life is" "And yet something else goes on" "For example" "when I curve" "my arms"

"just so,'" "I am a grotto" "of diamonds'" "I looked & saw that" "she was" "was a curved" "rock wall" "studded" "with black" "faceted jewels" "She curved towards me" "a dark shining" "I wanted" "to stand enclosed by" "As if you could" "stand upright en-" "veloped" "by a

geode—'" "'But no one knows," "no one sees," "I said" "'His great failure—'" "the tyrant's failure—" "& yours too?' she said,'" "'is to think that" "achievement" "must be evident," "in the light—'" "The black gems spoke now" "There were purple-black"

"amethysts" "among them" "small purple lights—" "'What you make" "is nothing" "unless it's dark" "Darker than this" "And in the dark" "in the great dark'" "'What do you mean?'" "'In the dark" "Made in the dark" "Reflecting darkness" "Only darkness'"

"As I stood" "in a station" "looking into" "the tunnel,"
"I saw" "disembodied" "lights" "coming toward us" "Then I realized"
"a black train" "a solid black train" "was arriving" "at the station"
"It stopped" "The doors opened" "I entered, & sat down" "& then"

"a voice announced:" "'This particular" "train" "will leave the subway"
"for another," "deeper," "unilluminated place," "where all is"
"uncharted" "If you want" "to travel with us," "listen first:"
"The sides" "of the train," "the train's form will" "fall away"

"All will" "become a darkness" "in which each of you" "will also
lose form" "We can't say" "what happens then" "We don't know how
you'll return" ("It has been done—" "Stories vary" "as to what
happens...") "But you will" "descend" "into an unknown" "unlit world"

"Decide" "to stay or leave" "within the next" "sixty seconds'"
"I didn't move" "The doors closed" "The lights dimmed &" "went out"
"There was no light" "within the train" "except from" "the station"
"We looked shadowy," "shadowy" "Then I felt" "my flesh tingle"

"I looked down & saw" "that my flesh" "was starting to" "disappear"
"I was becoming—" "I became—" "a shadow, literal shadow" "We"
"inside the train" "were all shadows" "But with eyes bright" "still
bright" "And then our eyes too" "became shaded" "Their moistness"

"became matte" "their whites grey" "The train began" "to pull away"

"As we pulled out" "from the platform" "there was opaqueness" "of a tunnel" "And then a last thing," "perhaps" "a power station" "A litup" "power station—" "all lightbulbs," "an erector set" "of lightbulbs—" "it lit up little," "a few feet" "of the dark"

"The starkness" "the powerlessness" "of the electric light" "terrified me" "Was this" "the outermost edge of" "the subway?" "These are last lights," "we are leaving" "Train pulls away" "Where" "are we going?" "Will I be there?" "Who am I now?"

"Going into" "true night" "endless night" "And the train," "has it dissolved?" "Its sides fall away" "I am floating" "There is nothing" "but the dark" "everywhere" "around me" "And my mind" "is still there somehow" "suddenly weightless" "I am weightless"

"Set free" "And my bit of mind" "seems to drift" "drifts in blackness" "as on a small—" "obscurely green—" "basil leaf" "On a leaf" "or a petal" "a piece" "of black lettuce" "Like a temple" "tiny, & nearly" "transparent" "My mind floats" "my mind floats but"

"ever downward"

BOOK 2

"I floated" "down in darkness" "among" "the other bodiless"
"people" "from the black train" "Heard" "their whispers:" "'I feel"
"so light so empty" "of heavy thought,' they said" "'I feel" "so
unbounded'" "So we rode" "soft air" "like leaves falling" "but with

no notion" "of any" "ground to fall to—" "Then" "an old man"
"an old man's voice began" "to sing:" "'When the snake" "was the train,"
"when the snake" "was the subway, we" "entered her walking over"
"her long tongue" "her long tongue" "And inside her" "was red & white"

"& we looked out" "through clear scales" "Inside her" "was red plush,"
"was bone white" "was safe; and we" "rode her" "as she slithered"
"through the earth &" "its darkness" "through the earth &" "its dark smell"
"We let" "the snake swallow us, take us into" "her self" "She had no"

"arms to hug us," "she gave us" "her whole body" "We were in"
"her whole self" "Safe in her whole self" "When a snake was" "our
mother" "When a snake was" "our train'"

"When the old man" "stopped singing" "all fell quiet," "no voices sounded" "I lost sense of other presences," "felt nearly" "non-existent" "Later" "I saw that" "there was a mountain," "down &" "at a distance" "It was cone-shaped" "& shiny" "barely visible, in the

dark," "looked onyx-like" "or obsidian" "with the texture the surface" "of a chipped-out arrowhead" "I seemed to be," "of no power of" "my own," "headed for it" "I regretted" "having to" "arrive somewhere:" "My smallness" "in this darkness" "had been relief &" "happiness"

"But I headed" "for the mountain" "in a gradual" "downward arc—" "It was set in" "the most vague of" "terrains, some black flatness" "And as I" "approached it closely," "a large eye appeared" "on the air, an" "outline drawn in white—" "as if in scratchy" "white ink—"

"many times" "the size of" "a whole body" "There were" "lines of character," "of humor," "beneath it" "& at its corner" "Then I flew through" "its pupil" "And suddenly" "I had limbs again," "felt bodied" "I landed" "before the mountain" "in a pool of" "yellow

light:" "there was a lightbulb" "in a fixture" "that projected" "from the mountain" "Then the mountain" "shook a little," "gravel fell from it" "The mountain opened" "in a vertical" "chasm" "A man" "was there inside of it" "dressed like a main-" "tenance man" "He thrust out his

arm" "& pulled me inside" "Quiet, cool there, the" "smell of earth" "protective" "& intimate—" "The wall closed" "I was within" "a cave-like place that" "was well-lit" "I sat down on" "a boulder" "& for no reason" "wept"

"I stood in" "a cave that was" "a sort of" "antechamber" "Its walls
were smooth, bland" "& brown" "There was a door," "a rough archway,"
"which seemed to lead towards other caves" "But I talked now" "with
the maintenance man" "He wore a navy-blue uniform" "with words embroidered"

"in red" "on his pocket—" "they were illegible" "But what was
strangest" "was that his skin looked" "like rock like" "grey granite"
"I asked him" "what eye I" "had passed through" "in the air" "'Why
yours,'" "he said" "'Where are" "my companions?'" "'You are" "your

companions—'" "your companions" "have temporarily" "become you'"
"I saw that" "my hands' outlines" "were several" "& seemed blurred"
"Likewise" "my arms & legs—" "I looked plural" "'But my eyes are"
"unified,' I said," "'my vision single," "my mind single" "Inside I

feel like" "one person'" "'Of course,'" "he said" "'That is the only way"
"to know & see," "through one person's" "mind & senses" "But in this
place," "in these depths—" "a cave network, as you will find—"
"what you see" "pertains to everyone'" "'Can you tell me" "more clearly"

"what these caves are?' I asked" "'I can't be that clear:" "But they are
something like" "our middle depths" "or middle psyche, if you prefer"
"You must pass through them" ("though not through all of them—" "by
any means") "on your way to" "your deepest origin" "Now get on with"

"your journey'" "He turned to leave me—" "I could now read" "the words"
"on his uniform" "They said, *In Use*" "'Wait a minute,' I said,"
"'can't you give me" "some directions?" "How do I" "begin?'" "'You will
simply" "begin" "through that door there—'" "he pointed" "to the

archway—'" "'& pass through" "the dreams" "that are enacted" "in the
rooms...'" "'Now I really must leave'" "He walked out quickly,"
"disappeared"

THE DESCENT OF ALETTE   109

"I stepped through" "the archway" "& there was" "another door"
"immediately" "before me," "another round entrance" "It led"
"into a cavern" "which was walled with" "gears & clockwork—"
"a large room," "with a rock floor," "whose walls were" "composed of"

"large round gears," "with toothed edges," "turning" "in semi-darkness—"
"the room was lit to" "twilight level:" "the gears were colored"
"blue & grey" "The round disks' surfaces" "as I looked at them" "began to
change" "to change" "Images" "appeared on them" "soon becoming" "other

images:" "patterns of small circles," "of squares &" "triangles,"
"appeared" "& dissolved" "Once" "they looked like tree-trunks, like"
"gnarled" "turning bluish wood" "Once" "they looked like flesh—"
"you could see the" "pores of skin," "which changed to" "rippled ocean,"

"then" "to dotted starry sky" "Then" "the gears were finally" "metal"
"gears again" "One gear—" "I now stood facing it—" "was larger"
"than the others" "It seemed" "to be turning" "in the center" "of my
chest" "& the enmeshing" "of its teeth" "with those of" "adjacent

gears" "produced" "sensations in me" "of deepest" "satisfaction"
"As I watched the gears" "I felt stronger," "better" "I stood there"
"a long while;" "finally I" "turned to leave" "through" "another door"

"As I went on," "a next cave" "a next entrance would" "be in front of
me" "a few footsteps" "from the last one—" "But I would exit through"
"a second opening" "This was the case" "throughout the caves" "Therefore"
"I now entered" "without real transition," "after the room full" "of

gears," "a small cave" "in which a woman sat" "on a wooden" "folding
chair—" "the room was other-" "wise empty" "She had shoulder-length
dark hair," "wore a full-" "skirted cotton dress," "beige—" "'I'm a
scroll-" "swallower,'" "she said to me," "'I take scripture" "on

scroll" "& hold it," "keep it in my throat—" "I've got two" "in there
now but" "there's no room for" "this third one—'" "she showed me"
"a roll of paper," "a small scroll—" "'What scriptures are they?'"
"I asked her" "'Past, Present,'" "& Future—'" "Oh I've got the third

one down—'" "she swallowed it—" "'Good,' she said" "'Otherwise'"
"'I'm imperfect,'" "you know the way" "a baby's crazy'" "I said I
didn't know" "what she meant" "'Yes,'" "you do,' she said" "'Once
they're all down,'" "I wake up'" "She smiled" "& disappeared" "into the

air"

"I next approached" "a large cavern" "above the door of which" "was written" ("carved in rock") "the words, *Mother Ship*" "Inside the cavern" "was a clipper ship" "its sails folded" "But the ship had" "soft-edged outlines" "& began to" "shrink & change:" "As I

came closer" "I saw that" "it was now a" "small house" "with no door on" "the hinges," "no glass, no slats in" "the windows—" "those were dark" "empty places" ("though the cave outside" "was well-lit") "They looked like two eyes" "& a nose-mouth" "'Perhaps,'" "I thought," "'it is"

"someone's head'" "Then I entered" "that dark house" "& began to" "speak aloud:" "'If this is" "the Mother Ship," "does the Mother" "have a voice?" "I call on you" "to speak to me'" "The door" "became soft &" "slightly rounded" "like gums" "The windows softened,"

"looked like flesh" "I waited" "But she couldn't seem" "to speak" "right away" "Made a sound first" "like a low wheeze" "Then the door—" "the mouth--moved" "to form" "these words" "in a whisper" "The words came slowly," "'My real voice" "is further" "further down, in"

"another place" "Keep walking" "keep walking" "I hope you finally" "get to me...'" "Then" "the doors & windows" "became hard-edged" "again" "The house was dirty" "inside" "There were black ants on the floor" "There was no furniture," "it was a bare" "single room" "of un-

painted" "old boards" "It made me sad," "it made me sad" "I walked out slowly"

"I entered a cave" "in which a wall" "opened back," "limitlessly—"
"like a painting" "of a landscape" "but this landscape" "was somehow
real" "It was an un-" "ending field" "that was a battleground"
"of corpses," "sometimes" "single-layered," "sometimes piled up" "in

pyramids" "The eyes" "of all the corpses" "were open" "A white
substance" "dead-white sticky," "as if spilled" "in a great spill,
was everywhere," "erratically," "dripped over" "the corpses,"
"standing in the field" "in pools," "like white blood, like a thickened"

"chalky lotion" "Between myself" "& the vista—" "where the cave
wall would have been—" "was a screen" "of thinnest gauze," "almost
airy" "It was daubed" "here & there" "with the white substance"
"And there were drops of it—" "just a small trail—" "on the floor on"

"my side of" "the screen," "leading to me, it seemed," "to my feet"
"I looked down at" "my hand" "A small drop of" "this evil" "this
white substance," "oozed" "from my palm" "'I've never" "killed,'
I thought," "'I've never" "been to war" "I've never" "been allowed"

"to participate" "in the decision to go to war—'" "I then" "said
aloud," "'Who has done this to me?'" "How dare he" "implicate me"
"in such evil?'" "Another white drop" "appeared" "in my hand,"
"& another" "'I've done nothing,' I said" "'Has someone" "such power"

"as to make his sin" "ooze from my pores?'" "All was quiet" "I fled
the room" "& then" "the white substance" "dried up" "disappeared from"
"my hand"

"There came to be" "a voice in" "my head" "always a faint voice"
"that ordered me" "to keep walking" "from room to room" "'Keep walking,"
"keep walking,'" "it whispered" "as I approached" "what appeared to be"
"a monstrous snake" "with a wide" "open mouth" "The snake,"

"a black snake," "which I took to be" "a female—" "she wore"
"a gold fillet" "the shape of" "delicate grasses" "& tiny flowers—"
"had black eyes" "that appeared blind," "eyes that were solid" "black
membrane," "but a pink" "flower-like mouth" "'Keep walking,'"

"the voice said," "& I entered" "her mouth," "walked among its
moist parts" "on through into" "her body's" "long dark corridor"
"Her bones were silver," "barely visible" "Made a soft noise" "like
wind chimes," "as I brushed by" "Midway" "through her body"

"I came upon" "a small alcove" "with a chair, & a lamp" "On the
chair," "chin spread" "across" "the chair's arms," "was an enormous"
"head" "of a man," "quite alive" "He had long" "shaggy hair,"
"light brown skin," "& feverish" "bloodshot eyes" "I tried" "to rush by"

"'Stop!' he said" "'You can't make me' "stop,' I said" "'But you're
inside me!'" "His voice grew louder" "'This snake is female,'" "I
answered" "'Then inside us'" "He grinned at me" "'Now worship me,"
"I am a great man!'" "'Sorry,' I said," "'I can't worship" "anything'"

"Then he squeezed" "his brows together" "angrily, &" "blew"
"a great wind at me" "I" "was carried backwards" "& blown out"
"of the snake's mouth" "I stood" "before her head again" "But she had
turned white" "all over" "Her eyes white, & her mouth" "cotton-white"

"dry &" "white as" "her fangs"

"I came upon" "a cave which" "contained" "a giant woman" "who was
lying" "on the floor" "She was ten" "or eleven" "feet tall"
"Large" "but not fat" "In a shapeless tan shift" "Normal-"
"sized people" "entered" "with clothes & trappings:" "a lace blouse,"

"flowers," "a necklace," "a red" "velvet skirt" "They helped her"
"slip the clothes on—" "she was slow," "inattentive" "The flowers
were a" "crown" "for her head of" "matted dark hair" "Then someone
crowned her" "& said," "'She is now made," "she can give birth'"

"The giantess" "remained impassive" "Then they left the room"
"She reached" "beneath her skirt," "between her legs," "& pulled out"
"the baby" "As she cradled it" "& cradled it" "the trappings"
"fell from her" "The chaplet" "of flowers" "disappeared" "Her clothes

dissolved" "She could be seen" "to be alternately" "herself & a"
"blurred naked man" "who was also" "the mother—" "he was" "the
same mother" "the same body" "as she," "cradling" "the baby"
"His face" "became clearer" "It was round;" "his mouth was wide"

"He had cropped hair," "distant eyes—" "a pale-grey to her"
"raisin-dark ones" "Suddenly" "he separated" "himself from" "the
giantess" "Stood" "apart from her" "from her &" "the baby"
"And she had shrunk" "had shrunk instantly" "to a normal-" "sized

woman" "'Now,' he said," "'that we are separate," "I am the larger"
"I am the taller" "Now that I" "am separate," "I can be stronger"
"I am clear'" "Then the man" "& the woman" "both turned to me"
"& asked," "'Is this true?" "Is this what happened" "a long time

ago?'" "'I don't know,'" "I said" "Then the room filled" "with a
dark mist" "a cold mist" "They were gone" "I was alone"

THE DESCENT OF ALETTE 115

"There was a cave in which," "when I entered it," "I rose up in air"
"to hover" "against the ceiling" "looking down at" "the floor"
"The floor was" "a movie screen" "on which was shown" "a desert"
"in daytime, sandy white" "with bare cactus trees," "leafless tree forms"

"light brown & faintest green" "There were" "distant mountains,"
"a pale sky" "above them" "But there were hundreds" "of these trees,"
"close together," "at regular intervals" "They were short &"
"all alike" "But one—" "just one—" "which I felt I" "was meant to

look at—" "was larger," "that was all," "somewhat larger"
"Indifference," "sadness," "a perfunctory" "sort of interest" "were"
"what I felt" "A dark" "male presence," "a rather bodiless" "man,"
"came & hovered" "beside me" "'If the larger tree,' he said," "'were

you say,' "or I," "would it make" "any difference?'" "'Not really,'
I said" "'Or it would,' he said," "'change the landscape," "a little,"
"the way it looks'" "'But to whom?' I said" "'To those who hover"
"above it?'" "Larger of same" "in that landscape" "is nothing anyway'"

"'Forget it,' he said," "'it's just something" "to look at'"

"I came upon" "a group of people," "ten or so," "relaxed &
sitting" "on boulders," "in a cave" "They had red eyes," "entirely
red—" "red pupils, red whites—" "red-light red," "stained-glass
red" "A man whose profile" "seemed familiar" "turned to face me,

& said," "'We are waiting" "to cross the river," "are you the pilot"
"of the boat?'" "'No,' I said, 'but" "why are" "your eyes so red?'"
"'We're dead; we're demon-saints;" "it is hard for us" "to get across"
"the river'" "'What river?'" "'We don't" "exactly know yet'" "'What

is a demon-saint?' I asked" "'Drink from this paper cup" "& find out'"
"It contained" "a black liquor that" "had a hint of red" "phosphorescence"
"'It will make you be like us," "temporarily," "make your eyes red
for a time'" "I began to see" "through a red film" "& to feel strange"

"sensations:" "as if" "I had killed," "killed many people," "the way a
soldier has," "has fought & killed" "for others" "Sadness" "& hysteria"
"made my heart expand" "into an" "immense" "sick flower" "grotesque
blossom" "huge red orchid," "with an attenuated thin" "yellow stem"

"which couldn't drink in" "enough moisture" "I danced I ran" "about the
room" "as if to make the" "flower smaller" "'That is a strange dance,'"
"the man said," "'which I recognize'" "I danced until" "the drug
wore off:" "my feet had beat" "a curving line," "a narrow trench into"

"the rock floor" "'It will hold water,'" "the man said," "'it will be
deep enough,'" "when the water comes" "'We will be able" "to cross'"
"I fell asleep," "exhausted" "& when I woke up" "the red-eyed people"
"were gone &" "the narrow trench" "was also gone," "the floor was"

"smooth again"

"A large cavern contained" "the skeleton of a" "colossal woman"
"On the skull was" "a wig & crown," "the wig" "long & coarse brown—"
"& not ancient;" "the shiny crown—" "also" "new-looking—"
"set with" "flat blue lapis" "I stepped into" "the skeleton's

huge ribcage," "stood where" "the heart had been" "'Going further,"
"going further,'" "I heard a faint" "woman's voice say," "'Going
backwards," "going backwards" "in time'" "'Am I closer?' I asked"
"'Can you speak yet?" "Are you our mother?" "A firefly appeared"

"in the center" "of the ribcage" "It floated vibrantly" "before me"
"& seemed to be" "the source of" "her voice:" "'I was" "a queen,'
she said," "before they banished me" "beneath the earth" "made me"
"a serpent...'" "'I'm not looking for" "a queen,' I said" "'A

queen is not" "my origin" "Our mother would not" "be a mother"
"of others' poverty," "a mother" "of the subway—" "You are
not her" "are not her'" "The firefly's" "light went out;" "I
left the cave"

"I entered" "a soft cave," "soft to the touch, like flesh"
"Inside this room" "my clothes evaporated" "from my body—" "I was
now" "all flesh," "soft as the walls" "The air" "in this room was"
"peculiarly soft too" "There was a bed against one wall" "I sat

down on it" "A naked man appeared," "suddenly," "to sit beside me"
"He smiled" "& said," "'I wonder" "what it's like" "not" "to have
a sex'" "'I believe that in this room" "we can find out,' I said"
"'Let's give" "our sex organs" "to these" "fleshy walls'" "'How

can we do that?' he asked" "'I believe,' I said," "'they will disattach,"
"though I don't know" "how I know this'" "We disattached them then—"
"my vagina," "his penis" "Pulled them out of" "our bodies" "like
rocks stuck into clay—" "& inserted them" "shallowly" "in the

cave walls," "where they stayed fast" "And then all at once" 'I
couldn't see," "see anything" "except vaguely" "a brown-pink flesh tint"
"I seemed to swim in it," "ride waves of it" "uncontrollably"
"I couldn't think" "at all" "Was formless," "was in chaos" "The man

cried, 'I've become lost'" "And I too" "shrieked out to him" "somehow,"
"that my mind was becoming lost," "unfocused," "stretched out & thin—"
"I saw it as" "black water" "oily black" "a slimy puddle" "hung in air &"
"spreading vertically" "thinly" "over the brown-pink tint..." "'I want

"my sex back!' I screamed" "My sex" "was then replaced" "between my
legs," "instantly back" "The man's" "was too;" "& we were then
delineated," "formed," "ourselves again"

"I saw a tree" "in blackness" "a leafless tree hung with" "grinning heads" "The faces" "were dead-white," "made up clown-like," "with white face paint" "& red lipstick smiles" "I knew instantly" "these were the heads of" "the soon-to-die" "I seemed to recognize" "one or

two" "from somewhere," "from the subway," "& know them" "to be suffering" "from slow" "self-destruction" "or extreme lives:" "drugs," "danger," "aftermath" "of war," "emotional" "extremity" "Their smiles were huge," "on the trees, their" "humanity all gone in"

"the bizarre paint" "I thought to run to" "another room, then" "stood still instead" "Stood & stared back at the heads" "hung on a wintry" "black tree" "in a black cave" "One of the heads" "began to speak to me" "It was a man with" "long orange hair" "His mouth grinned

as he spoke:" "'If you are frightened" "if you are frightened," "then stand &" "be frightened" "For you will die too," "you will die," "if not so garishly" "as I'" "Then fear came" "in electric waves," "fear of losing" "my 'I'," "fear of personal" "extinction" "I

fell to" "the floor," "moaned a little," "hugged myself" "The tree remained" "The heads remained" "The tree would not change" "or go away" "There was nothing" "to do" "but gain control of" "myself" "I stood up," "stared at the tree" "of death" "once more" "Then I left"

"I stood before" "3 paintings" "painted onto cave walls," "faded,"
"partly effaced" "One was a portrait" "of the tyrant" "in white,"
"pink, & blue—" "white-haired pale man" "He looked noble," "deeply
serious" "Swaths of rock showed" "across his face & chest" "through

the worn-" "away paint" "Close by" "was a nude" "standing woman"
"She had no face" "but where her face should be," "was a black hole"
"which tunneled back" "behind the wall" "The third painting" "was the
face of" "an animal," "a mountain lion," "yellow-brown—" "its paint

fading" "overall" "The paintings" "were disappearing" "as I
stood there" "Paint dissolving," "rock encroaching" "faster & faster,"
"as if time were" "speeded up in" "this room" "I began to weep—"
"a pressure" "from this speeding-up" "of time" "seemed to squeeze

tears" "from my eyes" "I wasn't" "sad inside," "but I wept & wept"
"A roaring" "sucking wind" "began blowing" "all around me" "The room
darkened;" "I stood suddenly" "inside the" "painted woman,"
"stood nude inside" "her dark facelessness:" "I had" "become her,"

"& the tunnel" "behind her face" "was now life-size," "was what I
stood in" "just behind the" "wall of paintings" "The tyrant's portrait"
"came alive & spoke" "'Don't walk through" "the tunnel" "At the end of
it" "you will die" "Look at me," "see how I'm truly" "afraid for you'"

"'But I can't see you,'" "I said viciously," "'I have" "no face'"
"I did" "have sight, but" "where I stood was" "very dark" "I began"
"to walk further" "into the tunnel" "'This tunnel" "represents"
"my whole journey, doesn't it?'" "—I called back to" "the tyrant—"

"'Well I'm going to" "see it through'" "Then I saw floating" "in air,"
"coming towards me," "a real lion's face," "bristly, moist-eyed—"
"I feared it might" "attack me:" "instead it fastened" "itself" "onto
the blackness above my neck—" "it gave me its face" "I took several"

"more steps forward," "but at that point" "the tunnel vanished"
"I stood outside" "the cave of paintings" "I touched my face:" "it was
my own" "& I was" "clothed again," "was back in" "my real journey"
"In front of me" "lay the next door" "I must pass through"

THE DESCENT OF ALETTE   121

"I entered" "a cave" "in which I instantly" "divided into three"
"separate" "figures," "chained together" "in single file"
"I was most the one" "in the middle" "A man stood watching us,"
"professorial," "in glasses, bearded," "dressed in suit & tie"

"'Why are there three of me" "in here?' I—we—asked him," "our voices
separate," "out of sync" "'You are your" "Past, Present," "& Future,'
he said" "'You divide into" "those components" "in this room'"
"But I do not have" "components!'" "our three voices said," "'My

secret name—'" "'Time's secret name—'" "'is Oneness," "'is One Thing'"
"As I—the one" "in the middle—spoke," "the one of us in front—"
"who was the Past—" "had already" "finished speaking" "& was awaiting"
"his reply" "He said," "'Don't we seem" "to experience" "things

somewhat this way?" "There is past, present" "& future'" "The Future
then cried out," "'Where is my life?'" "'Where is my life?' 'You have
stolen" "my life!'" "There was a silence" "The man" "reached out &"
"pressed a button" "on the cave wall—" "we three united" "into

one again" "while he wrote words on" "a clipboard" "Then he looked up
& said," "'Going forward?" "Going on?" "Death lies ahead, you know'"
"Any woman" "may already" "be dead," "I said" "'What do you mean?'
he asked" "I opened" "my lips, but" "someone else seemed" "to speak,"

"'No remembrance" "No remembrance." "No remembrance" "of our mother"
"No remembrance" "of who we really are" "Thus a woman" "may be"
"already dead" "born dead'"

"I entered" "a cave" "whose walls closed up" "around me," "until"
"it became" "exactly my size, my body's size" "I stood & stood there"
"stood forever" "A small" "blue salamander" "came out from" "beneath a
rock" "He was turquoise blue," "clear like jelly" "I couldn't move well"

"move freely;" "but he climbed up to" "my shoulder," "sometimes peered into"
"my face" "He had a tiny face" "with a black-line mouth," "tiny black"
"eyes with whites" "Occasionally" "as I stood there" "I would feel"
"something like" "an orgasmic" "sensation," "a hollow shiver—"

"not exactly from" "the salamander," "but from no one," "from nowhere"
"The sensation" "had a visual" "manifestation" "as thin frond shapes"
"etched in grey," "trembling in the air" "in front of me" "While I was
in this space," "when I looked down" "at my arms & hands" "they weren't

plural" "Instead," "a clear single edge" "delineated them" "I
became sad" "sadder..." "Until" "I fell asleep" "& dreamed of falling"
"from a mountain" "high as an airplane" "to a blue map" "in darkness"
"I fell onto—" "the map became—" "a field of" "snow at night"

"cold & cleansing" "pure & cold" "When I woke up" "my room was larger,"
"had a door &" "I was plural," "was others," "was my companions" "again"

"In a dark cave, I saw" "an apparition:" "almost real, almost there—"
"a human-sized" "hooded snake," "which looked as if" "it had arms"
"wing arms" "cape arms" "The snake" "had a smiling" "womanly face"
"Reared up taller than I" "Seemed to hold towards me arms" "Then

vanished" "the cave lightened" "grew full of light—" "but also" "seemed
curiously" "buoyant" "I felt light-footed;" "the air itself" "was
balmy" "Other" "people entered now" "who were naked or" "half-clad"
"Then I saw" "a black line" "begin extending in air—" "in the center"

"of the room—" "made an" "airy drawing," "rectangular," "six feet tall"
"'That is *The Senses*,'" "a woman said," "'Step through it, it's a door'"
"I stepped through the" "rectangle" "& immediately the walls" "of the
cave" "looked different" "They were covered" "with jewels" "But the

jewels were" "cartoon jewels—" "as if from" "an animated" "cartoon—
& more beautiful" "than real jewels" "Larger," "the colors clearer,"
"brighter," "more transparent" "Everything" "about them was" "magical"
"Their colors were" "white-glinty violet" "bright orange" "magenta"

"blood red" "fierce blue" "green-spotted black..." "'These are the ones,'"
"a voice said," "'We've always wanted" "to be near'" "It was" "a man
who spoke" "We sat down together" "on the cave floor," "in shadows,"
"bright jewels" "all about us," "& began to make love" "Part of me"

"seemed to float above" "our bodies" "& I saw that" "we looked like
cartoons," "outlined in black," "drawn & painted" "But as we made love"
"we changed to" "thick velvety black air" "Blackness" "flowing out,"
"rayed from" "a small center," "another jewel," "clear yellow—"

"which was" "the point" "where our" "sexes met..." "Afterwards,"
"the man fell asleep" "I left the room," "resumed walking" "'Keep
walking,'" "'keep walking,'" "the voice was saying" "in my head"

"I entered" "a cavern" "in which a queen sat" "on a throne—"
"a golden woman," "metallic woman, in" "black-yarn wig" "& gold crown,"
"kohl-outlined eyes" "The queen" "was being bowed to" "by white-robed
figures;" "the floor before the throne" "was strewn with" "plastic

petals" "As I watched her" "she grew larger," "grew taller" "& also
fatter—" "expanded like" "a balloon" "Until" "with a loud bang" "she
exploded," "disappeared" "Her courtiers" "vanished into air" "& Where"
"the throne had been," "sat a woman, on the ground," "weaving straw into"

"a basket" "I approached her & sat down" "She was dark-robed" "& dark-
eyed" "She lifted towards me" "the half-made basket," "& I pressed my"
"cheek to it" "It was smooth & tight" "& tan" "It gave off" "a dull
light" "whose very muteness" "was its beauty" "I sat quietly"

"there a long time," "as she resumed" "her weaving" "Watched her
hands weave" "the straw" "Until I realized" "I had become" "the basket"
"in her hands—" "looked out" "from where the basket was:" "no one
sat now" "where I had sat" "I had no wish to be" "otherwise" "A creek

was running" "in the cave, & I" "listened" "to the water" "as she
handled me" "as she wove me" "When the basket" "was completed"
"I became my" "human self," "sat across from her" "again, but" "the
basket" "now had a stripe" "broad, single stripe" "of red" "It was

my blood, thick" "& caked" "Dull red," "drying red," "it was"
"my own blood"

"I entered" "a dark cave" "stood in a lightless cave room"
"Could see nothing" "at all" "Then my body" "dissolved," "until
I was" "a single small thing" "a cell of 'I' afloat" "on the
dark air" "Am I still" "the others," "my companions?' I asked aloud"

"'You are us still,'" "I heard voices say" "'This I,'" "I thought,"
"'isn't so small'" "I felt curious," "humorous," "quite poised"
"despite my size" "And those feelings" "seemed to work a change"
"on the darkness:" "a jagged" "turquoise line" "shot out from me"

"& unfurled downward" "into a sheet of" "white light" "like an airy"
"movie screen" "& then I saw" "on that quasi-screen" "this scene:"
"A group of people stood" "naked crowded" "on a small island"
"in the ocean" "All was early blue" "blue sky & water" "White flesh was

bluish," "dark flesh had blue glints" "I saw that" "I was one of"
"those people—" "& now I entered" "that scene," "my reality"
"was on the island" "And one of us" "was a murderer" "He held a gun"
"down by his side," "his face was desolate," "made old" "I walked to"

"the water's edge" "& looked down into" "the water" "I saw there"
"a strange mermaid a" "girl child" "with tangled black hair" "who had a
man's" "hairy chest" "& a fish's" "lower body" "Her scales were dark,"
"emerald-black" "I poked my head beneath" "the water," "'Who are you?'

"I asked in a" "bubbling" "underwater way" "She answered quite clearly,"
"in a slightly" "childish voice," "'A forgotten" "possibility" "You,"
"you yourself," "don't want my" "hairy chest now" "Your people" "have
divided" "themselves in two:" "have made" "domination" "your principle:"

"why have you done this?'" "'I don't know,' I said," "'how it happened"
"What I like of yours" "is your streamlined" "leglessness" "Your human
qualities" "make me sad'" "'But you must not,' she said," "'hate
creation…'" "must not…" "You must begin again," "create again"

"each moment…'" "Suddenly" "I couldn't breathe, I was" "drowning"
"I fought to rise" "to the surface" "When I finally did" "I stood again"
"in a dark empty cave" "I had my body" "I was back" "I left the room"

"I opened" "a door to" "a dark desert," "nighttime-like desert,"
"in a cave:" "It was both there &" "depicted" "Both reality—"
"vast—" "& a movie" "on the walls of" "a room" "Its colors"
"were dark & red," "brown & black," "harsh" "Sometimes" "glaring

light" "poured in to open up" "the darkness" "Soon the edges"
"of the room" "began to" "team with figures" "Dark-clothed people"
"swathed in cloth" "walking" "beside horses—" "I sensed horses"
"in the shadows" "And then I was" "one of those people" "It was the

past or" "the future" "We were" "a horde of nomads" "of migrants"
"after a war or" "revolution" 'Our hearts—" "my heart—" "I could
see into" "my own chest" "as if from" "a distance—" "contained a
picture of" "forest stubble," "blackened tree stumps" "Our babies"

"cried dirty tears" "Our leaders" "were all men;" "our women's
hands" "worked with" "meal & water" "I was imprisoned in" "my heart &
clothes" "I walked with" "greater" "& greater difficulty..."
"Till my entire" "my entire" "body" "burst open" "like a seam"

"seam splitting" "from screaming mouth" "to crotch" "Blood burst
out of me" "in slow motion—" "I watched this" "as it happened—"
"& also" "from inside me" "came a black sprite" "small winged thing"
"Winged," "but couldn't leave them," "winged" "but stayed & hovered"

"about the nomads," "flew near them" "as they continued on" "after
burying" "my body"

"I found," "in a cavern," "a huge black crystal" "shot with red;"
"the size of" "a cubicle," "hollowed out &" "with a door"
"As I neared the door" "I saw that" "a figure stood inside" "this
darkly" "red place" "this immense" "black-red garnet—" "she stood"

"in its center," "with a low sink" "in front of her—" "a woman,"
"a dark-skinned woman," "with eyes closed," "working with" "something
clay-like" "She seemed both clothed" "& naked," "for I could see through"
"her clothes" "Her genitals" "were blank, were not there—" "As her

eyes were" "large smooth eyelids," "did not open," "in fact" "Her hands
were working," "were engaged in" "a making, a" "shaping," "a playing
with a" "dark" "oozing moist mass in the sink" "She squeezed & kneaded it,"
"let it slip through" "her fingers" "Let it drip down like mud—"

"All" "the while she hummed" "a song with" "an always-changing" "shape,
un-" "repeatable:" "Suddenly" "she held up a" "statue," "small,"
"powerfully simple," "a hairless," "sexless figure" "Just as quickly"
"it wasn't there, was mud again—" "She laughed &" "continued" "to work:"

"Had she" "somehow seen it?" "I" "couldn't tell; but she knew"
"that I stood there" "& she said to me:" "'Staying'" "is the making,"
"the real making'" "Then after" "awhile" "she held up something else:"
"a globe, a" "mappemunde" "with mud continents but" "blue seas"

"of literal" "water:" "it sloshed about" "on the globe—" "which she
held carefully," "by the poles, with fingertips—" "'Does it look like it?'"
"'I guess,' I said" "'What's'" "the point?' she said" "'I was about to
ask you'" "'That's the last thing" "a god would know,' she said"

"'Are you" "a god?' I asked" "'I don't know, I'" "don't know'" "She
laughed again" "& then she" "& the whole jewel" "dissolved"

"In a cavern" "there was a small stream" "& I sat down" "beside it
tired" "I saw across the stream," "cut into the wall," "a door that"
"was a slab of rock" "It opened—" "bright yellow light" "streamed from
behind it," "& a man whom" "at first I couldn't see" "emerged"

"Then he stepped closer," "focused on me" "I saw that" "he was the
tyrant" "He had curl today" "in his white hair," "smiled boyishly at me,"
"'Would you like" "to come inside" "& rest" "on a real bed?'" "I saw
a bed" "beyond the door," "with clean bedding" "& big pillows" "'No

thank you,' I said" "He smiled again," "then a small image" "of the
door—" "three inches high—" "appeared" "before my feet,"
"& leaped up" "onto my forehead" "I was now" "as if dreaming,"
"was in a fantasy" "in my own mind" "I uncontrollably approached the

door—" "the tyrant" "was no longer near—" "& entered" "the room"
"It was full of" "food & drink:" "wine & apples," "bread & cheeses,"
"berries," "unbruised lettuce," "pink ham &" "thin-sliced beef"
"But there was something" "already" "in the bed, a" "strange form:"

"Human" "without facial features," "without eyes," "nose or mouth"
"Nude & reddish-colored," "wizening" "wizening before my eyes—"
"its unsensed face shrinking," "its emaciated" "torso shrinking,"
"changing," "rotting..." "'He is a corpse" "from a battlefield,'

a voice said," "'He's just" "a dead soldier" "We will remove him
from your bed'" "The man who spoke—" "an attendant" "to the tyrant—"
"now approached" "with a shovel" "But I left" "left the room"
"& tried to" "cross the stream" ("It was only" "about a foot wide) I"

"couldn't" "move my legs" "except a little" "just a little..." "I
awoke then" "where I had been," "on the other side" "of the stream,"
"weeping" "for the man," "the dead soldier," "in the bed"

THE DESCENT OF ALETTE   129

"I entered" "a cave" "where a woman sat" "who looked made of rock—"
"had grey granite-like skin," "though her eyes" "were lucid grey-green"
"She was clearly" "grieving for" "a man," "lifeless near her,"
"lying on the ground" "Tears ran over her rock face" "'Your son?' I asked—"

"his face was like hers—" "though not rock-like" "She nodded"
"'How shall" "we celebrate this?' I said," "not knowing" "exactly why"
"I said 'celebrate'—" "I seemed meant to" "'We'll carve" "his name,'
she said," "'into a wall" "where there are so" "many names" "that

none" "remains legible" "for very long" "All the carved names" "together"
"make a texture" "much more beautiful" "& mysterious" "than even"
"stone itself" 'Then we'll" "commit his body" "to" "the deeper
darkness," "deepest darkness'" "'And what of you?' I asked," "'how will

you be?'" "She smiled" "& said," "'I am" "of course rock" "I'm
afraid" "I have" "turned to rock'"

"I entered a cave" "which was all white inside" "& smooth & round in"
"a regular way" "I was beneath" "a white dome," "& on the white floor"
"were scores of" "what seemed to be" "serpentine" "shadows—" "small,
black," "& nebulous," "a mass of almost-snakes" "A voice," "disembodied,"

"spoke to me:" "'This cave,' it said—" "or she said," "a female voice—"
"'is like a snake egg" "Lie down on" "the floor" "among these ghostly
snake babies'" "Then I lay down" "& wriggled with them:" "pressed my arms to"
"my side," "my legs together—" "I laughed doing so" "'Now close your eyes,'

the voice said" "I closed my eyes" "& was no longer" "playing snake in"
"a cave:" "I was" "a snakelike line" "on an ocean somewhere," "but was
not even" "quite a line" "I was a ripple," "not quite defined" "I was
a line that would not" "quite form," "that floated," "flowed out"

"Below me" "the ocean" "was ab-" "solutely empty," "full of light but
lifeless" "Its floor was bare & flat" "Peaceful," "it was peaceful,"
"to be almost" "a line" "Soon the voice said," "'You must open"
"your eyes" "Resume your journey" "Keep walking" "keep walking" "You do"

"have legs" "Time for you" "proceeds step-by-step," "yet there is"
"something snakelike" "in your journey's" "movement" "You have not
lost her," "you have not lost her" "You bring things with you" "much
faster" "than step" "by step" "But keep walking" "Keep walking'"

"I entered, this time," "a long corridor," "in which I soon felt"
"that I" "was being followed" "I turned" "to look behind—" "a figure
vanished" "whom I just glimpsed," "a woman" "darkly robed"
"A minute later" "I saw her" "ahead of me," "where the path turned"

"& rose higher," "led to a door with" "a torch outside" "She
went in there" "& I soon followed" "I" "was now inside" "a great
chamber," "empty dark" "She sat alone" "in its center" "beside a fire"
"She was the woman" "who had woven me" "into a basket," "had decorated"

"a basket" "with my blood:" "She had olive skin," "a thin-lipped"
"smiling" "knowing mouth—" "the lines" "on her face" "of a woman"
"in her forties" "I approached her" "'What is your story?' I asked"
"'I made you,' she answered" "'I know that you" "are my history,"

"but why" "do you follow me?'" "'To tell you this:" "There are few
books" "by us," "by women," "because it wasn't" "to be books"
"It was to be" "something else:" "the same instant" "of life forever"
("Perhaps like" "an insect's" "bright being," "or an animal's")

"Books" "books ruined us" "Scrolls & tablets" "created time," "created"
"keeping track" "Distanced us from the" "perpetuation" "of our
beautiful" "beginning moment..." "only moment" "Created death" "created
death," "death being" "the child of men" "'You are too" "well spoken,'

I said," "'& so" "I can't believe you," "exactly'" "Then she" "appeared
angry" "& changed suddenly" "into a crow" "with red & blue gleams"
"in black feathers" "& a yellow" "beak that glowed" "in the firelight:"
"'However,' she said," "'it may have happened," "we all lost" "our

moment" "Our moment" "of life" "No one" "has lived" "for thousands"
"of years'" "She flew up" "into the shadows" "of the ceiling &"
"disappeared" "I myself" "was shaken" "I didn't" "believe her" "Not
exactly—" "but I was shaken"

132   THE SCARLET CABINET

"I entered a cave" "full of women in" "black clothes, long-skirted,"
"their heads covered" "They surrounded" "a woman" "in a light
shapeless shift—" "who stood weeping" "'What has happened?'" "I
asked one of them" "in a whisper" "'She is a widow,' was the answer,"

"'Her husband has just died:" "watch & see" "what happens now'"
"Slowly, the woman" "sank to the floor," "as if sorrowfully" "dancing"
"As if the air were" "a weight which" "pressed" "her body down"
"First she sat" "with her knees up" "& as she sat, her skin" "began to

turn grey" "grey & grainy" "It turned" "into rock," "though her eyes"
"were still moist" "Then she—" "again, slowly—" "lay down on her side,"
"her back curved," "her legs drawn up," "her knees close to" "her breasts"
"She laid one arm" "on the floor" "encircling her head—" "the other

made a" "semi-circle" "in front of" "her breasts" "All curves"
"& hills, she" "became" "herself cave-like" "She froze" "into a model of"
"caves like the caves" "we stood in" "Her facial features disappeared"
"Her garment turned to rock" "She was caves" "she was caves" "I was

now afraid I stood" "exactly" "inside of" "women's bodies:" "Was"
"the human psyche" "made of women" "turned to stone?..."

"In a cave I saw" "a film projected" "onto a rock wall," "which showed a naked" "woman & man" "moving slowly" "among greenness," "trees & shrubs" "Others like them" "soon appeared," "& these words were superimposed" "upon the scene: *The First Ones*" "I understood

by that" "that these were the first" "people ever" "Then I forgot" "which two I'd seen first," "tried to remember," "but I couldn't" "Nor could I" "remember" "the faces" "of any others, from moment" "to moment—" "I would try" "but I'd forget" "I'd think, 'Ah this one,'

"I'm fixing this one" "in memory'" "A moment later" "I wouldn't know" "which one that" "had been" "They were" "as alike for me" "as leaves on" "a tree;" "their movements leisurely," "pure & beautiful" "They often" "fell into twos, into couples" "Children" "appeared among them" "Had they

been there" "from the beginning?" "I couldn't" "quite recall" "Then a woman" "laid down" "on the ground &" "fell asleep" "Her dream appeared" "above her head," "that there was" "a blue shape," "vertical," "amoeboid—" "a pool" "of blue" "Nearby" "a thick brown line" "began

extending" "from a point in air—" "to the left of" "the blue shape," "but in a plane" "in front of it" "It moved straight towards" "the blue shape," "approached it & pierced it through" "Extended out from it" "on the other side" "The dream dissolved" "The woman" "had blood on"

"her chest" "She was dead," "killed by the dream," "as far as" "I could tell" "The words," "*First Murder*," "appeared" "onscreen" "Then a rectangle" "of light" "which disappeared"

"I found" "a room of voices" "It was a cave of" "small containers"
"urns" "glass bottles" "rusted coffee cans" "old alembics—"
"each" "contained a voice" "which emerged in" "a line of white smoke"
"& spoke" "in mid-air" "When I entered" "the cave," "the air was

voices" "entangled," "a snarl a blur of" "white smoke" "They seemed"
"to be voices" "of direction to action" "or even," "to emotion:"
"'eat some meat'" "'you can cry now'" "'the pain'" "is overwhelming'"
"'if you make love,' "you will find it'" "'in two days'" "you will

find it'" "'Go to sleep'" "'Sing a funny song'" "'Find something'"
"you can worship'" "'Cross the room'" "'Lie down'" "'Kill the tyrant'"
"'Cross the river...'" "Phrases" "were repeated," "almost sung,
chorus-like" "I stood still in their midst" "while they noised" "all

around me" "There was a larger" "container" "sunk into" "the ground"
"like a well" "It was a black urn" "& its voice arose" "in a greyer
smoke" "It spoke" "in a rich" "female whisper:" "'Don't guard'
"your footsteps" "Don't guard" "your footsteps" "I will protect you"

"I always do" "Don't" "protect yourself, I" "will protect you"
"while you pay me" "no mind'" "There were gold sparks" "in the grey
smoke" "I tried" "to catch one," "like an insect," "between my thumb &"
"middle finger" "but it instantly" "became invisible—" "Whose voices

are you?'" "I asked them all" "'Voices'" "voices of" "whoever's here"
"voices here" "You are the mind of" "our voices" "What else would"
"you like us" "to say?" "Tell us the next thing" "to say'" "I said,
'I want you" "to say,'" "'*Whatever*" "*is frozen*" "*will now melt*'"

"'It will melt'" "it will melt now" "will melt,' they" "began to chorus"
"'Whatever's frozen'" "will now melt...'" "I slipped out of" "the room"

"I entered" "a vast cavern—" "barely lit by flickering" "lights"
"like stars" "in the black of the" "unseen ceiling" "The cavern's
central floor" "was ice," "a frozen pond" "I stepped out onto"
"its middle area" "The ice was" "like a diamond," "hard & shiny—"

"clear" "You could see into it" "& inside it" "I saw a"
"frozen face" "Was it perhaps" "my own?" "A face of" "a woman"
"who was suspended" "in the ice" "Light eyes & dark hair," "hair fanning
outward" "like a fresh-" "water weed" "Her eyes were" "imploring,"

"stared at me" "frozen grey" "I was fascinated" "by the clarity"
"of the outline" "of her body:" "dark hair & eyelash" "grey iris"
"ragged fingernails" "bulge of wristbone—" "she held her hands up"
"as if trying" "to push out of" "the ice" "I heard footsteps" "on the

pond" "A man joined me" "& said," "'The ice will melt now" "The
switch is on'" "Instantly" "the ice was water," "except for"
"floes we stood on" "The woman beneath the ice" "rushed upwards"
"to the surface" "She climbed atop a" "third floe," "wet & panting,"

"long hair streaming" "We three floated" "to the pond's edge &"
"stepped onto" "a still-hard surface," "which extended around" "the room's
periphery" "'Who are you?'" "I asked her" "She said, lips trembling,"
"'...frozen soul," "was dormant soul...'" "I cannot yet" "speak well,"

"I'm still cold'" "She vanished" "through the exit door" "'Does she
look like me?'" "I asked the man" "'Yes,'" "he said," "'I think she's
very much like you" "I think she" "might be you'"

"I entered" "a cavern" "& immediately" "felt a fluttering"
"of something inside my shirt—" "a sinister" "tickling:"
"A small" "moth-like bat" "flew out of" "my shirt," "up my
back &" "out the shirt's neck" "I felt" "other bats now" "My

back was brushed by" "their fleshy wings" "I was panicked:" "saw
vaguely" "at one end of" "the cavern," "& as high as it," "some
sort of" "black & red" "mask," "floating" "before a darkness—"
"no rock wall" "behind it" "The bats—" "there were several—"

"struggled out of my shirt," "flew towards the mask" "& into its"
"black sense holes—" "disappeared" "I approached" "the mask then,"
"sank to the floor" "before it" "Its material" "seemed to be"
"brocade-like:" "It consisted of" "red roses" "embossed on"

"transparent plastic," "through which was visible" "the vibrant
darkness" "behind the mask" "The mask thus" "appeared to be"
"composed of roses" ("themselves the size of" "human faces")
"floating" "on a face shape" "made of air," "made of black night"

"The roses" "were sumptuous," "soft, & yet," "slightly waxen"
"as if red paraffin" "had been lightly—" "almost" "imperceptibly—"
"brushed over them" "The darkness behind the mask" "was an emptiness"
"I could see nothing in" "Yet all of this—" "mask & voice behind—"

"seemed alive," "electric," "the mask a" "sort of deity—" "some
divine" "neuter principle" "I felt love &" "awe for it"
"Or rather" "its lush roses" "seemed to" "become" "my feelings of
love & awe" "And then, of course," "it dissolved," "the mask

dissolved" "A brown rock panel" "slid over the" "airy void"
"I was returned to" "the plainness" "of the cavern," "stood up
again" "to go &" "find another"

"I entered" "a cave" "which was empty" "except for" "a rather
small snake" "on the floor," "perhaps a foot long," "brown"
"& plain" "It slid towards me," "lifted up its head—" "it had
spare black friendly features," "dot eyes & linear mouth—" "& said"

"in a high-pitched" "but sexless, amusing voice:" "'A snake is"
"just a snake" "A snake has snake toys," "knows snake songs," "& is"
"a snake...'" "'May I ask you" "a question?" "since you are here,'
I said" " "The snake nodded" "'What is" "the divine" "neutral

principle?" "do you know?—" "since what these caves do" "is know;"
"& you are in one'" "'Well,' the snake said," "'a snake" "has a
snake god" "Not neutral," "it is scaly," "though I guess it has no
sex" "& that's all I know'" "'Then are you,' I asked," "'a clue to"

"the woman" "I'm looking for?" "A lost" "first mother," "an Eve
unlike Eve," "or anyone" "whose name we know'" "'A depiction"
"of me,' the snake said," "'will help you find her," "when the time comes"
"Oracularly speaking," "my symbol will mark her place" "And some

may say" "I am her—" "Obviously I'm not" "Remember me here,"
"when you can, when" "you want to laugh" "Humor" "is closer" "to the
divine than" "you might think" "The trouble is" "when you're laughing"
"you don't always" "bother with" "anything" "else," "like thinking,"

"like helping" "Excuse me I have to go" "I must return to" "the
snake world...'" "It then" "disappeared," "leaving behind a" "molted
snakeskin" "that evaporated into" "a pile of dust" "with a faint"
"stinky odor" "which made" "me laugh"

138   THE SCARLET CABINET

"I entered a cave in which" "there was a mirror" "across one wall"
"A man stood" "before it—" "I saw the back of his" "dark-haired head"
"But in the mirror" "his image" "was a shapeless" "grey substance,"
"thin sticky-looking," "gummy" "As I came towards" "the mirror"

"a similar image" "appeared beside his" "that was obviously mine"
"'What does this mirror show?' I asked" "'I'm not sure,' he said"
"In the act of" "conversing" "we seemed to" "have made" "the two
images" "slide close together" "& merge, in one place," "their

irregular" "borders" "I then walked away from him" "to see what"
"would happen" "The substance" "was so sticky," "that when my image"
"pulled away from his," "bits of my" "grey substance" "stayed attached to"
"his grey substance;" "& mine took on" "a frayed look" "where I"

"had broken loose" "'I suppose,' I said," "'we exchange it" "with
others" "all the time'" "'It doesn't seem to be" "individualized,'
he said" "Then he left the room," "his grey substance" "receding"
"in the mirror" "I began" "to stare intently" "at my own, &"

"its center changed" "A face" "appeared in it," "a face of mine, but"
"idealized—" "not old, not young—" "though my hair was" "quite dark,"
"with no grey in it" "whatsoever" "But it wasn't" "like young hair,"
"it was like" "the name 'hair':" "a place" "around the face" "Line of

jaw & brow" "& nose" "was" "pure line" "I could have been" "ten or
sixty" "for my skin" "was not there" "Something like thin paint" "stood
in for it" "But the eyes" "between the lids—" "the lines of lids—"
"were mine," "exactly," "& exactly" "alive" "I stared at" "this

image" "long moments" "till the sticky" "grey substance" "encroached
upon it" "& slowly" "closed over it" "over my face" "Then I left"

"I entered" "a dark cavern" "that had a marked-off" "rear area"
"a little like" "a stage" "but not elevated," "demarcated"
"by four stalactitish boulders" "at the corners" "of its rectangle—"
"The front part" "of the cavern" "was filled with people"

"who blended in" "with its darkness" "so much that" "I couldn't
tell" "if they were dark-skinned" "or just shadowed" "I looked down &
saw" "that my own skin" "now looked dusky" "I felt" "strangely
blissful," "as if my substance," "my flesh," "were permeated" "with

air" "A small transparent" "silver disc appeared" "before my eyes"
"I seemed" "to be seeing" "& hearing" "through it" "Between the
area" "where we were, & the area" "set apart" "was an almost"
"invisible" "veil, perhaps" "of grey air" "And then a man" "walked

through it" "& disappeared" "entirely" "I began to see" "strange
figures" "dim figures" "in that space" "Like moving" "grey line
drawings" "But I couldn't" "make them out, what" "they were, what"
"they were doing" "After a while" "the man emerged" "'I dissolved in

there,'" "he said to us" "'And I seem to" "have had a dream:"
"Instead" "of a body" "I was an object," "a drinking vessel" "of red"
"cut glass" "with figures" "carved around me:" "scenes" "from my
life—" "being a baby," "a boy," "being married," "being old" "I

revolved in space" "being all at once," "all of them, but" "actually"
"being glass" "red glass" "in a world" "of light" "Then someone
filled me" "with water" "& drank from me...'" "I laughed at that"
"He said" "to me," "'The water" "was crystalline" "It tasted"

"of herbs" "& river air..." "The glass could" "taste the water'"

"I entered" "a cavern" "crowded with" "shadowy people"
"I stood feeling drowsy," "then thought to myself," "'I am now"
"asleep,'" "though I functioned" "as if awake" "Most of"
"the people" "I stood among were men" "I noticed one man" "by his

shirt, a" "dirty red" "Another wore" "a billed hat; &" "many"
"carried bags" "round" "shaped like heads" "There was a
blanket" "spread among them" "of a dirty" "baby blue" "I
knew that" "it was mine," "my bed & house," "my place" "& I

lay down on it" "The floor" "of this cave" "was dirty"
"Brown bugs crawled on it" "A grey-haired woman," "lank-haired
chipmunk-jowled," "speaking to herself, came" "towards me—"
"she smelled of urine—" "hands stretched out, she" "stooped down

towards me" ("her face" "was very mean;" "her hair so shapeless")
"I handed" "her something:" "I discovered" "that it was"
"a sickly" "greenish orchid," "yellow-green" "that looked like
plastic" "As she took it," "as she held it" "I realized"

"it was real" "'I always knew" "it was real,'" "I said—" "was
I lying?" "She vanished" "& I looked up" "at all this"
"crowd of others" "There was a covered" "bowl of food" "at one
corner" "of my blanket" "They stood crowded" "foodless,

blanketless" "I tried" "to will my blanket" "to grow larger"
"'I've been told,' I said," "'that it will grow'" "But I knew I"
"was being false," "& those around me" "were silent" "Then"
"I took the blanket" "picked up my blanket," "stood up &"

"made a shape of it" "a com-" "plicated bundle—" "I acted"
"as if I knew" "what I was doing," "though I didn't" "didn't
really;" "I made it" "into a sort of" "lumpy sphere &" "held it
up for" "all to see" "It was still dirty" "A torn-off satin edge"

"trailed down to" "the floor" "'Will someone take this?' I said"
"A man took it" "& thanked me for it," "not disarranging" "its
shape" "Then I left the cave—" "& woke up," "seemed to wake up"
"as if I had" "been dreaming"

"I entered a cave" "& found a half-mask on the floor" "made of
thin cellophane" "of the sort" "a candy-wrapper's made of"
"Adhering" "to the cellophane" "were black" "paper shapes,"
"geometrical," "spheres & oblongs" "I put the mask on & said"

"to those in" "the cave—" "they had just entered," "a group of
four or five—" "'We must tear down" "the old structures—"
"the subway" "& other buildings—" "& build beds for" "all the
living'" "'But we have to do" "one hard thing first,'" "a man said,"

"One thing" "holds us back...'" "There was" "too much noise then,"
"everyone spoke" "at once &" "I couldn't hear" "what he said,"
"but knew somehow he was right" "'Someone must do it,' he continued"
"'We will draw cards,' I said," "'for who does it" "The one who

draws" "the highest card" "performs the act'" "The man handed me"
"a deck of cards" "It contained" "the two suits of" "roses"
"& panthers" "Red roses &" "black panthers" "'Which is the
higher suit?'" "someone asked" "'The highest suit" "is a third suit"

"always,' I said," "'& this deck" "contains that suit:" "the
composite suit," "roses/panthers," "half & half'" "Then I myself
"drew the highest card," "the ace of" "roses/panthers" "'I will
do it,' I said" "'You want me, don't you," "to kill the tyrant?"

"I will kill him" "but it won't happen" "quite yet" "I have to
journey first" "further down" "into this darkness'"

"I entered" "a small cave" "above the door of which" "was written:"
"A Piece Of" *"The Tyrant"* "The cave contained" "a table" "over"
"which hovered, like fireflies" "five or six" "constant lights"
"As I came nearer" "I saw that" "there lay on" "the table" "a small

polished stone," "egg-shaped, of lapis," "deep blue" "Whatever
of him it was," "its presence here" "meant, I knew," "that
something of him may be" "indigenous" "to any one of us" "The lights"
"seemed to be guarding it" "I reached for it" "& one" "dipped

suddenly" "& seared my hand" "before I even" "touched the stone"
"The lights now clustered" "close to the stone" "A woman entered"
"the cave" "with a bucket" "full of water" "'They can be" "doused,'
she said" "I took the bucket," "hurled water at them" "Their lights

were quenched, &" "they fell—" "several" "tiny men," "rather
pallid," "green-&-silver winged" "'You mustn't" "harm the angels,'"
"one said in a" "small angry voice" "I laughed & turned to" "the
woman," "'What is this" "blue stone?'" "'A bit of" "the tyrant's

heart,' she said—" "'What do you" "want with it?'" "'I think I'll"
"return it to him'" "I scized it" "from amid" "the little wet-winged
men" "lying helpless" "on the table" "Then I left" "the cave"

"I exited" "from the previous" "cave into" "a corridor"
"which stretched ahead" "as far as" "I could see"
"'Keep walking,'" "that voice still said to me" "I walked,"
"surmising" "that I was about" "to exit" "this whole system"

"of caves" "The corridor was straight," "the walls & floor"
"quite smooth" "My shoes" "echoed quietly," "I saw no one"
"no one" "I walked for perhaps a mile" "Then I saw" "what I
thought at first" "was a dead end—" "a wall" "As I neared the

wall," "an opening" "in the ground in" "front of it" "became
apparent—" "which turned out to be" "finally" "a staircase"
"descending deeply" "below the level" "of the caves" "I
hesitated briefly—" "the corridor, the" "staircase" "were

so plain &" "so empty" "Then I began to" "descend the staircase"
"I couldn't see" "to the bottom" "of it" "at all" "Somehow the
staircase was lit" "so that only" "those steps were visible"
"that fell directly" "in front of me" "I descended" "& descended,"

"winding round & round," "became" "wobbly-legged," "sometimes
proceeded" "very slowly" "But then" "there was" "a scent in"
"the air" "It was the smell of" "a river," "a smell of water &
weed" "A piece of white down" "drifted past me:" "tule fuzz"

"on a breeze," "a real breeze" "Suddenly I stepped down"
"onto" "earth again" "& passed through a door" "into night air"
"I stood" "on a riverbank," "water flickering" "yellow-white"
"in the electric light" "cast by the bulb at" "this exit" "I wondered"

"if I hadn't" "somehow been here" "before" "A river at night:"
"No," "all rivers at night," "I thought," "are the same—"
"that's all..." "Then the voice said," "'Keep walking'" "I walked to"
"the river's edge," "took off my shoes," "left them there"

"Began to wade" "into the water"

BOOK 3

"The water" "of the river" "was mild-temperatured," "the current
gentle" "I soon began" "to swim—" "in a moonless," "starless darkness"
"The sky held no clouds—" "no luminous" "spheres existed here"
"Yet the sky was" "a sky;" "for the river air" "was fresh & sweet"

"Then," "as I swam," "the others I contained—" "my companions
from the subway—" "weightlessly" "emerged from me," "looking
shadow-like," "& quickly" "solid-bodied" "began to swim with me"
"I never really" "saw their faces" "We swam quietly," "concentrating,"

"our motions almost synchronized" "In the distance sat" "small yellow
lights" "where presumably" "the other shore lay" "Partway across"
"the river," "something else, a substance," "a state of being,"
"a thick noxious" "distress" "in the form of" "a grey cloud,"

"welled up within me" "& left my body" "from a point along" "my spine"
"The cloud" "hovered near us" "& so we turned onto" "our backs to
watch it" "It was full of" "ghoulish faces," "phosphorescent" "death's
heads;" "one skull grew large" "& open-mouthed" "It had long" "glowing

hair," "screamed as if" "in terror," "then spoke" "to me:"
"'We are dying' 'You are killing us' 'killing us'" "The cloud exploded"
"into greenish flame" "which was soon consumed" "by darkness"
"We turned over" "& resumed" "our swimming"

"Presently" "we neared a pale beach," "narrow" "with trees behind it" "thick & blue-black," "& lights" "many lights" "deep inside the" "wooded land" "I touched bottom" "& walked ashore" "Then I saw" "a final entity," "airy image, pass" "out of my body—" "from my

forehead" "A small shape," "perhaps brain-shaped," "that seemed to" "contain in miniature" "the cave network" "where I had been" "I saw the rooms—" "the caverns—" "streaked with color," "dotted with lights," "but all tiny" "as in a honeycomb" "The image" "receded,"

"gently floated" "away" "on the wind," "like a flower" "a hibiscus—" "all reds & darks" "& yellow glow—" "Or like a lantern," "paper lantern" "Then was gone." "The others" "other swimmers" "had not walked ashore" "with me" "I turned to find them" "I thought they

must be" "still floating" "in the water" "But they had vanished," "I was alone" "Myself &" "alone" "Yet emptied" "of much, it seemed" "I felt unburdened" "& even buoyant"

"I walked into" "the forest;" "for the woods were lit" "by yellow
street lamps" "along various" "dirt pathways" "I paused a moment"
"to absorb" "the texture" "of bark & needles" "The wind carried"
"with a pine scent" "the river's aura—" "delicious air" "Then a

figure" "appeared before me—" "a woman" "in a long dress" "standing
featureless" "in a dark space" "'Welcome,' she said," "& stepped into"
"the light" "She was dark-haired" "but very pale" "I stared hard at her,
realizing" "that her flesh was" "translucent," "& tremulous," "a

whitish gel" "She was protoplasmic-" "looking—" "But rather beautiful,"
"violet-eyed" "'What is this place?'" "I asked her" "'It would be
paradise,' she said," "'but, as you see,'" "it's very dark,'" "& always
dark" "You will find that" "those who live here" "are changed"

"enough" "from creation's first intent" "as to be deeply" "upset..."
"But you must really" "keep going now'" "'Are those tents" "over there?'
I asked" "I saw small pyramids" "at a distance" "'Yes, these woods are"
"full of beings," "primal beings," "hard to see—" "because it's"

"always dark here" "Most of them" "need not concern you now" "But
wait here," "someone is coming" "to show you your way'" "She stepped
back into" "the shadows," "turned & left me"

"I stood waiting" "for some minutes" "in this very" "alive darkness—" "the air so vibrant," "the trees awake" "There were flowers," "mixed grasses," "growing lower" "in the dark," "& I was relieved" "to be near them" "after so much time" "where nothing grew" "Then" "I heard a

song" "faint & blurred," "a slow song" "I heard it" "as if through walls" "As if" "there were a room" "next to where I stood" "& someone," "a man," "sang inside of it" "The tune was sad," "& attracting" "I approached it—" "where its source seemed to be—" "& it moved away

from me" "just a" "short distance" "This happened twice" "Then I understood" "I was to follow it:" "& so it led me—" "through deep woods" "& clearings," "for" "a long while" "The voice sang" "the same melody" "over" "& over" "mournful" "& intimate" "in a language"

"I didn't recognize—" "or didn't think I did:" "it was hard to" "hear the words—" "Till at last we" "reached a meadow" "where the song" "ceased to sound," "pale & empty" "with trees around it" "Then I sank to" "the ground" "& fell asleep for" "a long time" "But when I

awoke" "of course" "it was dark"

"I saw, on awakening," "what I had not" "seen before:" "at the
meadow's edge" "etched into the grass" "fine white lines which formed"
"a large curving shape" "I stepped closer" "to see the shape:" "it was
a coiled snake—" "head erect," "tongue extended," "itself thin & long"

"& snakelike," "a snake from" "within a snake's mouth" "I knelt to"
"examine" "the nature of" "the etched lines," "when a powerful"
"gust of wind" "rushed through me" "& stayed blowing" "a gale" "where
I knelt" "It grew stronger" "& more howling" "I fell over" "& thought I

saw" "my head," "my own head," "having been blown" "off my body"
"rolling" "on the grass" "But I also knew" "I was still intact" "Then"
"the wind subsided" "& I saw" "sitting near me," "on a log," "a
headless body," "in a light dress, the" "bloody neck" "black & deep"

"I didn't" "want to look" "but" "of course I had to:" "this headless"
"woman" "was a living personage," "whose hands moved slightly,"
"whose feet shifted" "As I looked at her" "I was filled with" "an oceanic"
"sorrow," "staring at her gruesome neck," "its black well" "I knew she was"

"the one I sought," "our mother," "first woman" "I gripped the earth with"
"my hands" "to stay composed" "And then I heard a voice," "a woman's
voice," "a rich changing voice—" "capable of both" "high & low tones—"
"begin to speak:" "'...finally arrived" "You are very" "very late"

"I've been waiting—" "We've been waiting...'" "I realized" "that the
voice" "issued from the throat" "of this headless" "body"

"'I'm late," "am I?' I said" "'What time" is it here," "that I"
"can be late?'" "'It is,' she said," "'the long moment" "after my"
"decapitation" "It is a kind of" "forever:" "nearly since" "the world
began" "The holy men," "the wise men," "are frivolous" "& cruel"

"They have invented" "eternities" "but left me here" "for one—"
"They call their visions" "transcendent" "Call me" "accounted for"
"in heaven," "or nirvana," "or wherever," "in extinction—"
"The blessed selflessness" "They were wrong," "I am the same:"

"in time, headless self, &" "suffering" "I have never" "gone to
heaven" "Never died," "never changed" "The truth of us," "the real
truth of us," "is here" "in this darkness," "*is* my decapitation"
"History *is* eternity" "until this" "is righted—" "No wrong has"

"so long endured" "There can be no truth" "elsewhere," "until"
"this is changed" "The holy men," "the saints," "the wise men," "the
heroes," "the poets" "are ignorant," "are like" "simple drunks'"

"'I thought" "you would be" "intact here,' I said" "'I thought"
"there was a place" "where everything was intact" "& this was that place'"
"'Perhaps you" "are intact somewhere," "but I am not,' she said"
"'Tell me" "what happened,'" "I said" "'I'll try,' she said"

"In the beginning" "of the world" "there was a whole" "edgeless
entity," "sea of dreaming," "of floating" "changeable shape"
"After awhile" "was differ-" "entiation," "as if pieces of sea,"
"of water," "became fish" "As if air" "became birds—" "I can't remember"

"It keeps escaping me" "But the sexes came to be" "in pleasure," "in
glee" "There was much of" "what you'd call" "obscenity" "at the
beginning" "Much orgasmic" "sensation" "permeated" "the primal entity;"
"& when there came to be" "two human sexes," "that was a sharpening,"

"a clarifying" "of the pleasures" "of existing" "The edges" "of our
forms" "made us shiver & gasp—" "This sounds so" "vague, I guess"
"Then something happened" "to the male—" "perhaps because he"
"didn't give birth" "He lost his" "connection" "to the beginning"

"of the world," "to freshness" "of sensation" "To sensation's"
"being soul" "Became a fetishist" "A thinker" "A war-maker" "& ruler"
"Made me dance naked alone" "before all men—" "any man—" "on a
stage, a" "spotlit stage" "Made lewdness" "lose its" "mutuality,"

"its holy aura" "The scales of" "a serpent" "were painted on" "my
body—" "I was stippled" "with diamond shapes" "And as I" "was thus
degraded—" "as all" "went astray—" "I was yet" "the only memory"
"or sign of" "the creation" "I was all there was" "of that" "And so

I endured" "that dance" "I danced" "& I danced" "Nothing" "but sex"
"My head gradually" "over ages" "disattached from" "my body" "as if
by the will" "of everyone" "My body" "still danced then—" "but my
head" "played audience" "to the achievements" "of males" "See it there?'"

"She pointed suddenly" "A head sat" "several feet from us" "with open eyes,"
"frozen eyes," "& fixed" "frozen smile" "Brown skin lifeless," "dark
hair windblown" "'I learned to speak from" "my throat," "from darkness,"
"not from behind the eyes" "Made up stories to tell myself" "through

centuries" "Then one day" "I walked carrying" "my own head" "down through
darkness below the earth," "to this place" "And was forgotten,"
"mostly forgotten," "above the ground"

"We were silent" "a long moment" "of sadness" "Then I asked her,"
"How" "can you see?'" "'I see,' she said," "'with my voice," "as I talk"
"I see you" "as we converse" "But I see things" "within myself—"
"pictures, & stories—" "that you might not see" "ordinarily" "I have the

power," "as I speak" "to enable you" "to see them too," "to forget that"
"I'm speaking them" "They take on" "their own life then," "before us,
around us" "I cease to speak" "as they exist;" "though they do" "soon
dissolve," "are never permanent" "For example," "I see this now" "I

see this whole scene:" "A little" "girl's father" "is a corpse in"
"a coffin" "He has swallowed" "a vial of chemicals" "so he will come"
"to life again" "as a ghoul," "a soulless ghoul'" "As the voice spoke"
"I saw before me," "as if in a dream," "the open coffin," "in a house"

"The corpse was handsome," "sapphire-eyed" "Young" "& still alive"
"The vial made him live," "grow facial hair & fangs" "The little girl"
"was very young: five or six" ("The voice still rendered this") "& then"
"slightly older'" ("The voice seemed" "to cease now") "She stands"

"in a forest," "looking" "like a girl from" "an antique greeting card,"
"small mouth soft hair," "remote eyes" "conceived by art" "Something"
"she carries" "slowly comes" "into focus:" "a silvery broad axe"
"on a long" "wooden handle," "leaning" "upon her shoulder—" "But the

scene now" "dissolved," "the dream was over" "already" "'The axe,'"
"said the headless woman," "'is real now" "& is nearby" "You have brought"
"new power here" "I have never before" "seen an object" "made real
this way" "But the axe" "must become" "a long cloth, I think," "to tie"

"my head back on'" "'What about" "the ghoul?' I asked" "'Forget"
"the ghoul for now" "We must tie my" "head back on" "But first" "I will
tell you" "some more of what" "only a throat," "only a headless"
"body knows" "Only your first" "mother knows'"

"'What" "was it like" "before we first became?' I asked" "'Can't you
remember" "any more of" "our beginnings—" "that primal entity"
"or how we" "emerged from it?'" "'How can I" "explain it?" *"Before"*
"life on earth" "I remember" "a surround of" "faces" "in a heaven"

"smiling welcoming" "me" "to exist" "among them—" "Who were they"
"if I" "was to be" "the first woman?" "There is no first, then,"
"only always" "They were the company" "of existence" "Co-angels"
"Co-spirits" "The unborn" "the dead—" "all the same—" "& had I"

"always already" "known them?" "But they were welcoming me" "to this
knowing" "that was existing," "where everything that was to be"
"seemed to exist at once" "Objects" "& events" "in a swirling" "present
moment" "were like bright-colored" "liquid circles," "small light-

streaked galaxies" "Each wheeled" "forever" "& it seemed as if"
"I could know each" "in perfect present pleasure—" "Did I?" "I don't
remember" "For history" "began:" "I was never" "outside of time again:"
"There was the sky now" "& the sea" "A man & I" "stood knee-deep"

"in calm pale sea water" "peering down at" "bright fishes," "red &
orange—" "in flat seaweed—" "& strange sweet" "sea horses" "There was
one of those," "seemingly," "beneath my navel," "deep within me"
"I remember" "no more than that" "of before humans" "became" "I must

honor" "my predicament" "& take you forward" "into history" "Show
you something else'"

THE DESCENT OF ALETTE 155

"'My voice" "will show you now,' she said," "'an early woman, prehistoric—'" "This time" "you will be" "in the story'" "I saw before me" "a naked woman" "in a tawny plain" "She was brown-skinned," "& small," "with tangled hair," "gentle eyes" "'What happens now?'

I asked" "The woman suddenly" "held a baby" "who fingered" "her hair" "'Merge" "with the woman,'" "the voice said to me," "& I walked towards her" "until we merged &" "I was her" "I held the" "baby closer" "'You see,'" "said the voice," "'you are not" "that much different'"

"'I can see" *"the phantoms,"'* "I said with" "great certainty" "For I saw shadowy" "masked figures" "but at a distance" "I felt afraid" "'Where are the males?' I asked her" "'The males &" "their phantoms" "do something to me," "don't they?'" "The voice said nothing" "Then I

saw the men" "herding the phantoms" "from behind" "with long sticks & spears" "& I saw that" "the phantoms—" "as the whole horde" "came closer—" "were like men" "Had ghostly" "human bodies," "but wore dark" "painted masks" "with geometric" "designs in white lines:" "crude

grimacing" "faces" "Sometimes they walked on all fours" "Sometimes they" "walked upright" "'The males,'" "the voice said," "'periodically" "are attacked by them" "Sometimes a" "man is killed'" "As she said this" "I saw the phantoms" "turn back upon" "their herders—" "who quickly

fought them down" "But one was injured," "one man walked now" "with blood streaming" "from his shoulder" "The men drove the" "phantoms faster" "Towards me" "Exactly towards me" "I gripped" "the baby hard, but" "the phantoms" "rushed straight towards us—" "Darkness," "all went

black—" "& when I was" "revived again," "my babe was gone" "The herders" "had disappeared with him" "I wept with" "grief & rage" "Some men remained," "tried to comfort me" "with food &" "caresses" "Said, 'Your child will" "become a man" "He will be taught to" "herd the phantoms'"

"'But they are phantoms," "only phantoms!' I cried" "'They can kill now,' said the men" "'We have created them" "& they are real" "They can harm now" "They can harm now" "We can do nothing" "but herd them—" "Or they" "will turn on us'"

"I became," "perhaps too suddenly," "myself again," "in the meadow,"
"drained & shaken" "as if awakening" "from a nightmare" "My arms
felt painfully" "empty" "of the early" "woman's baby" "'Did I really"
"need to live this?" "Must I know this?' I asked" "'It is" "a true

version,'" "the headless" "woman said" "'A true version" "of what
happened" "long ago" "Though I can't" "remember" *exactly* "what happened"
"I" "am only headless," "a headless voice" "Watch my voice now:'"
"Colored lights," "bright pure colors—" "already seemingly" "wordlessly—"

"rose up from" "her throat" "& danced against" "the darkness"
"Turquoise & yellow" "& red spheres," "glowing spheres" "Their dance
relieved my" "grief, somewhat" "There were many" "& they approached me"
"& touched me," "warm" "but not intemperate" "They didn't burn" "my skin"

"The lights cajoled me" "Teased me" "Rubbed my cheek, brushed" "my arm"
"Rested lightly" "on my shoulder" "Then I heard" "the voice say,"
"'...The past is shadows" "We'll make" "another child...'" "The lights,"
"the lights settled" "in my arms &" "made a shape of" "a glowing baby"

"with a phos-" "phorescent smile" "It was a symbol" "of the future"
"I held it" "Held it" "for a moment" "of peace, till" "it dissolved"

"'Who" "is the father" "of the baby?'" "I asked her"
"A new stream" "of orange light" "arose from" "her throat"
"& shaped itself into" "a fiery face" "against" "the black night"
"But its outlines" "were sketchy, its character" "unformed:"

"It was simply" "a crude drawing," "large & high," "in front of us"
"Where are his sufferings?' I said" "The face" "became more lined then;"
"almost real eyes" "seemed to look at us," "& with interest"
"But how is it" "a person," "a man?'" "The face smiled," "became

fleshed with," "successively," "different textures" "of the planet:"
"earth, rock, leaf, water, cloud—" "each was his skin" "a moment"
"And then real flesh," "a human texture" "It seemed miraculous"
"to see flesh on him" "I wanted to" "touch his face" "I felt love for him"

"because" "he had" "my skin" "I loved him for sharing" "my skin"

"But the man's face" "changed" "It gradually became sad—"
"as I stood there," "marvelling" "at its nuance, its" "expressiveness—"
"The eyes sank," "their sockets darkening" "Eyes reflecting"
"disappointment," "pain," "only the smallest" "spark of life"

"His eyes were light brown" "but bloodshot" "His wide mouth turned
down" "The night" "seemed to get darker" "& creep into" "his face"
"To change from magical" "to death-like" "Finally" "he spoke:"
"'We must" "have the child soon—" "must make a" "new future"

"I am dead you know" "I am *dead*" "Years ago I died" "in my suit & tie,"
"in my coffin" "Let me tell you more as we fly...'" "His face diminished to"
"normal size" "He became" "a whole person," "had a body—" "wore a dark"
"business suit" "He lifted me in his arms" "& flew straight up carrying me"

"We rose high above" "the meadow" "& then drifted" "over the forest"
"black & green" "with the rare shining" "yellow jewels" "that were the
streetlamps" "'I must,'" "the man continued," "'be the father—"
"of this baby that's not a baby" "Is some sort of" "a future—"

"And as the babe" "is not a babe," "I will father it" "without
fathering it...'" "'I think you're babbling,' I said" "'I must,' he said,"
"'bequeath my heart" "The love in it was" "pure & true" "many times,"
"many times" "As this flight is pure flight:" "for most intrinsically"

"it is that" "You cannot" "discount my essence" "I must leave something"
"of myself'" "'Your essence" "has prevailed,' I said," "'for centuries'"
"'Not my *essence*,' he said" "'Something in me" "is only pure" "Does not
dominate" "Will not hurt anyone...'" "anyone...'" "I realized he was drunk"

"Now we spiralled" "back downward" "'You must use" "my heart somehow'"
"He handed me" "something pulpy," "a red organ" "'You must" "accept
a heart" "I must be part of" "what happens'" "The instant" "we landed"
"in the meadow" "he was gone" "I still" "held his heart" "My hands were

red with" "its blood" "'What do I do now?" "What do I do with this?'"
"I asked the" "headless woman"

"'Lay his heart down" "for the moment,' she said," "her voice trembling"
"'Lay it on" "the grass" "& wipe your hands clean there too—'"
"I did—" "'Then let's sit" "for a minute" "enjoying this night"
"before we change" "Change forever'" "We sat quietly" "a short while,"

"a mist" "about us now" "that softened" "her headlessness,"
"obscured" "her body slightly," "hid the horror" "of her neck—"
"'I'm afraid,'" "she said," "'to take my head back'" "'Why?' I asked"
"'I'm afraid" "I'll lose my power" "to speak from" "deep inside of me"

"Lose my power" "to make visions..." "But we must put it back on" "anyway'"
"'How do we do it?' I asked" "'Please bring my head here'" "I lifted it—"
"it felt dry," "the face looked chalky" "Place it on my neck—"
"I will hold" "very still—" "Now find the heart in" "the grass'"

"I brought" "the heart close" "to the newly" "headed creature"
"Smear blood from" "the heart" "on the line of" "separation'"
"I daubed" "a ring of sticky red" "all around" "her neck, like a
necklace" "of liquid ruby" "'Now find" "the axe," "the girl's axe—"

"Over there somewhere'" "Her voice issued now" "from a pale mouth"
"though the lips" "didn't move yet" "I found" "& brought the axe"
"'Smear blood on" "the blade's edge,'" "she said" "Which I did"
"The axe went limp" "became a white scarf" "'Tie the scarf around"

"my wound'" "When I had done so," "her face" "began to change"
"Color" "poured into it:" "Her skin was golden brown" "Her eyes
deep-set & brown," "tender" "beneath fierce eyebrows" "She was young"
"Younger than I" "& yet she was, I felt," "truly" "our mother..."

"Wide nostrils, wide lips..." "She smiled at me" "warmly" "'I'm not
afraid" "any more,' she said" "'My voice has not lost" "its power'"

"'My voice has power,' she repeated" "'More power" "than before"
"For as I'm speaking—" "as I speak now," "look above us:'" "she
pointed" "to the sky, where" "tiny stars" "were coming out"
"just here & there" "in that blackness" "They formed no patterns"

"that I recognized," "were not at all" "my own stars" "'As I
say a word,' she said—" "'As - I - say - a - word,'" "she said again"
"but in a" "staccato way," "'a - new - star - appears'" "And at"
"each word she said" "a point" "of light appeared" "Meanwhile she"

"touched her own face," "stroked" "her cheek lightly," "ran fingers
through" "coarse tousled hair" "'These stars,' she said," "'do not
disappear…" "They are permanent…" "My voice is making them" "Truly
making them" "As many stars" "as this sky needs" "are as many"

"as I say tonight" "Life is changing" "I have much to do" "And you too"
"have much to do" "You must continue" "your journey'" "'Where do I
go now?' I asked" "'Simply walk towards" "that tall tree,' she said
pointing" "to a hill in" "the distance," "just visible" "through a

road's opening" "in the pines that" "ringed the meadow" "'There is
someone" "waiting there for you'" "'But I don't want to" "leave you yet,'
I said" "'I thought my journey" "might end with you" "I feel that"
"I need you'" "'You must take action elsewhere" "& I will be" "with you

really'" "Her face glowed" "I awaited" "some sort of" "transmission
from her," "some sort of" "final miracle," "final vision" "She merely
handed me" "a small leaf" "'to remember by' she said—" "& set me"
"on my path" "saying gently," "'Goodbye'"

"I began walking" "towards the hill—" "it seemed to be" "a few miles away—" "on which small from here," "a sketchy mark," "a tree rose twistingly," "& disappeared" "into low-lying clouds:" "rose up above" "the pines, with their intermittent" "lights" "matched now by"

"the new stars..." "I walked awhile," "then sat down to rest" "Fell asleep & dreamed..." "The formerly" "headless woman" "materialized" "as a small form" "from the tiny leaf she'd" "given me" ("it now rested" "in my pocket") "Materialized" "as a spirit" "with a snake's"

"lower body" "& entered me through my mouth," "down my throat" "She tasted" "sharp & spicy—" "thymish..." "I awoke" "for a moment," "then fell helplessly back asleep" "I now dreamed" "I was lifted up" "& lay floating in air" "amid wings," "many wings" 'They were brown"

"& composed of" "softest feathers" "I was in" "a black space" "with wings & nothing else" "No faced being" "was there" "I felt comfortable," "protected" "'I am flying,' I thought" "Then I flew through," "or I & wings flew," "through" "a sort of barrier" "A blackness"

"ripped open" "like fabric" "or paper..." "Then I awoke, but" "I was no longer" "Where I'd fallen asleep" "I was in" "a new clearing," "brightly lit" "I saw the tall tree close by," "among pines & several lamps" "The clearing held" "wooden tables" "with benches—"

"And on one of them," "before me," "perched an owl"

"The owl was brown," "had huge stern eyes," "clear, yellow" "&
staring" "There were countless" "feathers" "on the breast & wings,"
"on its facial disk" "So many," "so many," "that I was" "made dizzy"
"by fixing on them:" "They seemed to ripple" "& multiply" "before my eyes"

"Such a density," "a concentration of" "shifting..." "physicality"
"I'd never seen, as on" "this owl's body—" "It *was*" "a small being,"
"though large for" "an owl," "& would be wide-winged, I supposed"
"Away from us, in the trees," "people—" "shadowy people—" "moved

about &" "I saw tents," "green canvas tents there:" "voices blended,"
"laughed a little," "feathered into" "the wind" "I turned back"
"to the owl" "whose gaze had been & was" "on me," "continuously"
"I sensed goodness" "in the creature" "But its sternness" "was forbidding"

"so I waited" "for a sign from it" "Then finally" "our silence broke"
"for the owl spoke—" "though almost" "without moving" "its beak"
"The voice" "seemed to emanate" "from the whole owl—" "a man's voice,"
"measured," "rather gentle," "a lower register of tenor"

"'Your neck" "is healing,'" "the owl said" "'My neck?'"
"I touched" "my neck" "& felt a clean thin" "scabbed line"
"all around it" "like a thread—" "'You have her" "in you now,'
he said" "He turned his whole head" "to the side" "for some moments"

"Then looked back at me" "'We have" "work to do" "Plans to make'"
"'What have we" "to do together?'" "'We must prepare for"
"your confrontation" "with the tyrant'" "He turned his head"
"to the other side" "but continued" "to converse with me" ("From

then on" "he did this constantly" "For he really was" "an owl"
"Always startlingly" "an owl") "'You have a man's voice,' I said,"
"'which is familiar" "to me—" "Can you explain this?'" "For
from his voice I" "believed he was" "my father" "'If I once was"

"a man,' he said," "'I no longer remember who" "Have forgotten"
"those particulars" "Remember only" "a little" "about being" "a man—"
"Perhaps I knew you?" "Or was your relative?" "That is not relevant"
"to our purpose," "our urgency'" "'How did you" "become an owl?'

I asked" "'When I died,' he said," "'my spirit was released" "& grew
feathers" "one by one:" "an ecstasy" "of finding" "another way"
"of being;" "to become" "another..." "material—" "It was so"
"entrapping—" "before I was" "an owl" "Such pain to *think*"

"continually," "of what I'd done" "& would do" "It was too thoughtful
to be a man," "my head full of" "ghosts of acts," "of scenes"
"Full of ghosts of truths—" "do you understand?'" "'I think so,'
I said" "'When I" "became an owl" "my feathers" "were what"

"my personality" "became" "Each nuance" "a feather," ("that had been"
"formed in pain") "& I" "became light," "feathery light" "My mind,
my brain," "became these eyes" "I see & hear," "I fly" "I don't
remember" "the past much," "or foresee" "the future" "Excuse me,'

he said abruptly" "He suddenly" "flew up" "on great wide brown wings—"
"Turned to me" "a moment" "in a lovely" "twist of wing" "'I am
beautiful" "now," "the way a man can't be" ("I will be back"
"shortly'")

164   THE SCARLET CABINET

"I waited" "on a bench," "drinking in" "the voices"
"of those I" "couldn't see" "among the trees &" "the tents—"
"Intonations" "of informality," "activity—I" "didn't," "couldn't
make out" "any subjects" "of conversation" "It was simply"

"the music," "the vocal texture" "of beings" "free together"
"I sat enwrapped in—" "unaware" "of how much time passed—"
"The voices murmured, laughed," "shrieked & dropped," "paired &
soloed" "& chorused," "speeded up," "hesitated," "in female,

male &" "childish registers" "All their being" "seemed externalized"
"& hearing them," "mine was too" "Sometimes they seemed to be"
"much closer than" "they were" "Or I myself" "was elsewhere" "than
the bench," "floating" "among them," "bodiless," "lost in voices"

"Bodiless" "in patchy yellow light" "'Perhaps heaven" "is voices,'
I thought," "'speaking voices," "not singing voices" "Perhaps
paradise" "is just like this'" "Someone said" "a slow 'ohhh'"
"Then one of" "the voices" "was an owl's" "hoo hoo hoo hoo"

"For he suddenly" "rejoined me" "Swooped down upon" "the table"
"with a dead" "grey mouse" "in his beak"

"The mouse—" "the mouse's face" "had much beauty" "in its stillness"
"its pink" "front paws" "touched each other, its" "long"
"pink tail" "hung down" "There was" "an air of gravity"
"all about its" "weak body" "The owl" "laid it down"

"on the table" "before me" "& settled" "next to it—"
"'We shall eat now,' he said" "'I can't eat a mouse,' I
said" "'I don't mind" "if you eat it," "but I can't'"
"'You are" "carnivorous," "try this flesh,' he said,"

"his yellow eyes" "relentlessly" "staring at me"
"'It is too freshly killed,' I said" "'My food is killed"
"by others'" ""But he only" "kept on staring" "Everything"
"I was saying" "was naked" "& wrong'" "'I don't eat" "my own

prey;" "I mean I" "don't have prey" "Though I eat meat—"
"perhaps I shouldn't" "I shouldn't" "Of course" "all of the world"
"feeds on itself," "doesn't it?" "I mean one form of life"
"on another—" "it's somehow part of" "our unity?" "our union?"

"isn't it?'" "He still stared at me" "'Of course" "there are
rules" "& I," "I can't kill—" "Oh I'm just babbling'"
"'Will you eat some?'" "'Yes,' I whispered" "For I now knew"
"I must" "'I'll give you" "just a small bit,'" "he said, &"

"with his beak" "he quickly cut off" "a leg & thigh"
"'Put it in your mouth" "& chew" "for as long as" "you can"
"Swallow" "what you can" "Spit the rest out'" "I thrust it"
"in my mouth" "& began to chew" "before I" "could taste it, its"

"hair & blood," "bone & claw—" "Then it tasted—" "the words
came to me—" "'like myself," "like myself'" "'Are you
crying" "for the mouse?' he said" "'The mouse's" "life"
"takes care of it—" "the life" "takes care of" "the mouse..."

"in our case" "that's what happens—'" "'I'm crying,' I said,"
"because I was" "so hungry'" "'Do you want more?'" "'No, it's
enough'" "Then he swallowed" "the rest of" "the mouse whole"
"before my eyes" "& I" "I spat out" "what was left of mine"

166   THE SCARLET CABINET

"'It's time to go,' he said" "'Go where?'" "'You'll see'" "He
perched on" "my shoulder," "& directed" " me down" "the other side of
the hill" "on top of which" "the camp lay" "I saw a lake below,"
"black & flat," "almost perfectly" "round" "We proceeded to" "a gazebo,"

"an old open" "wooden structure," "with a peaked roof," "at the
water's edge" "'We will stand here,' he said" "'What is this lake?'
I asked him" "'It is the center...' he began" "'I find it difficult'
"to define" "It is the center" "of the deep..." "Of this underworld,

I guess" "But you must" "look into it" "Look into" "the lake.'"
"Though the trees" "around the lake" "contained among them many lights,"
"none shone directly" "on the lake:" "it was very" "very black"
"'How deep is it?' I asked" "'Infinitely" "deep,' he said" "'It

connects with" "the great darkness," "connects with" "one's death—'"
"'Is it—" "can it be—" "really" "water, then?'" "'Put your hand
in it'" "I did" "& felt nothing" "at all" "'There is nothing there,'
I said," "but it does" "look like water" "'Look into it,' the owl

repeated" "'Don't you see" "something there?'" "'I see eyes,"
"pairs of eyes...'" "darkness" "with fish-like" "pairs of eyes'"

"As I stared down" "into the black lake" "I saw more & more"
"pairs of eyes" "The eyes were" "flat yellow" "fish-body shapes,"
"two-dimensional," "with irises suggested by" "drawn-on black lines"
"The eyes were bright," "seemed lit up" "They unpaired," "mixed

together," "swarmed like fish," "yellow fish" "I tried"
"to concentrate" "on the blackness between eyes—" "for hadn't"
"the owl just said" "that the darkness in the lake" "was the great
darkness," "the essence" "of death?" "Wasn't it" "extinction,"

"my own end?" "But the yellow eyes" "multiplied," "became so numerous"
"that the blackness" "was covered over" "by them" "All was eyes,"
"lit eyes," "fish-bodied" "lantern eyes" "'What do you see now?'
said the owl" "& when I" "told him, said," "'Keep trying" "to see

between them'" "And then I" "concentrated" "on a place" "between
eyes," "a thread-thin black line" "As I frowned & stared" "a space
widened" "The expanse of eyes" "was drawn back" "like curtains"
"revealing darkness" "On this darkness I saw" "a person appear"

"composed of more eyes," "composed of tiny eyes," "minute eyes"
"As if the smallest" "constituents" "of matter were" "somehow eyes"
"The person died—" "died then—" "She lay down on black air"
("as if there were" "a bed there") "Air now interspersed," "here &

there, with the" "minute eyes," "to show that air too" "is eyes—"
"Her head rolled" "to the side" "& she was still" "Her face partook of"
"the stillness of" "the mouse that" "we'd eaten" "Then she"
"began to decompose" "She decomposed, she changed:" "all of the eyes"

"that had been her" "floated" "away in air" "Her mass of eyes"
"became dispersed eyes," "dispersed everywhere" "'Is there nothing that"
"isn't eyes," "that isn't eyes?' I cried" "'Was she—" "is she only"
"eyes," "all eyes?'"

"The horizontal" "black void" "where the woman" "had lain—"
"defined by dispersed eyes" "as corpse shape" "but empty
black space—" "slowly" "became a play of" "new" "con-
figurations" "Haphazard-" "seeming lines" "of white light"

"began to fill it" "Many lines" "of several thicknesses"
"spread themselves" "throughout the woman's shape," "organizing
themselves" "into an" "apparent system" "like veins" "or nerves—"
"And all the eyes," "all the eyes," "completely" "disappeared"

"All around" "the woman's form" "was even" "blackness now"
"'What does this mean?'" "I asked the owl" "'Who is" "she now?'"
"'She has entered" "the other world," "the simultaneous" "one"
"As when" "you dream" "But it is" "no one's dream" "It is the

other" "being," "free of the body's" "time, its heaviness,"
"the body's slowness compared to mind—" "It is" "as when you
dream," "nowhere" "& everywhere" "She has entered there" "Is
there now" "You must enter" "it too" "before you go back"

"to the tyrant's world" "You must enter that world'" "'How can I
do that?'" "'You will die" "a little death now—'" "He flew
up at me" "Talons thrust at" "my neck" "Pierced me" "And he
pulled me" "into the lake"

"Talons tore me," "tore my flesh," "as I was dragged" "into the darkness" "The pain was fire in" "spreading pools," "quick-opening flowers," "fiery blossoms" "with torn" "pecked centers" "Till all I was was fire" "Fire &" "my screaming" "But soon" "there was

no pain" "There was a numbness" "& an eating" "An eating of" "my body" "Sometimes" "I was eaten" "Sometimes I watched" "I was watching" "a woman pecked at by an owl" "Her face was eyeless," "pocked with red holes" "Sometimes while I" "was being eaten"

"I was inside" "the owl:" "he would swallow me" "I would float" "into a warmth," "a dark warmth," "that was his body" "The noise of" "the eating" "was mutedly" "deafening," "a low crunching" "gulping noise," "that filled my senses," "myself," "now scattered," "chaotic,"

"dissipated" "into his body," "& also hovering" "outside of it," "outside of her" "Then finally" "I coalesced," "was unified" "again" "somewhere outside in air" "I looked down at her," "my body" "She was still," "a still lump" "Though strangely" "she was intact now"

"Not eaten," "not even pecked at" "But I was sure she" "was dead" "I hovered over her quiet face" "tenderly," "recognizing" "this & that" "idiosyncrasy" "of brow & nose," "of hairline," "of earlobe" "The owl had vanished," "we were alone" "And then I fell into"

"unconsciousness"

"When I awoke I" "was in darkness" "& could see nothing" "at all"
"I was surrounded" "by voices:" "'She's come to'" "'She's ready'"
"'Please stand up,' one said gently" "I moved" "as if standing up"
"But I seemed to have no form," "seemed to move nothing" "as I made

motions" "'Very good,'" "the voice said" "'Have I stood up?'" "'Yes,'
it said" "'I can't see anything:" "am I blind?' I asked" "'There is
nothing here" "to see,'" "one of the voices" "answered" "'But also"
"you have no senses here—" "you are hearing us" "without ears'"

"'You don't have" "bodies either?'" "One voice laughed" "a low laugh—"
"'I couldn't" "identify" "any voice by sex—" "& said, 'Walk this way'"
"I thought of where" "my legs should be" "& tried to move that," "move
them" "'Good, good,'" "the voice said" "'What am I walking on?' I asked"

"'On nothing,'" "another voice replied" "'Stop here now" "Someone is
joining us'" "A voice neared us," "somewhat more" "authoritative-
sounding," "saying, 'What" "do you wish here?" "You are not really one"
"of the dead'" "The voice was" "before me now" "'I must,' I said,"

"'probe being's depth...'" "Before I try to" "change its surface—"
"But how can I" "not be wholly dead?" "An owl tore me" "apart & ate me'"
"'That is only" "what you perceived" "The owl is" "very powerful'"
"The voice fell silent" "a moment," "then continued:" "'Some of your

body parts—" "your *death* body parts—" "parts of your insubstantial
body—" "have been" "replaced" "The owl replaced them" "They will stay
functional" "within your so-called" "real body'" "'Which parts are
different?'" "'Your sex is now bone'" "'My sex?'" "'Your vagina is

white bone" "& your eyes," "your eyes," "are now like" "an owl's eyes"
"Though they seem more like" "two black flowers—" "two black hollyhock"
"flowers" "They are black flowery" "craters" "You are now equipped"
"to experience" "what you need'"

"'We will be silent" "& wait,'" "the voice said" "Then we were truly quiet" "& being that," "were nothing" "Really nothing" "but the darkness" "This moment was very long," "very long &" "very wide" "It had a" "vast diameter" "I felt as if" "I could be" "falling

asleep forever" "Then I saw it" "coming towards me—" "so stately," "so stately—" "a light," "a white light" "A radiant" "small sphere, I guessed" "Diameter" "of but a few feet" "It was seeking" "me out," "this light so" "unexpected" "'What is this light I see?'" "I asked the

voices" "'You are blind,'" "the voices whispered" "'You are blind'" "You do not *see* it'" "'You have no senses'" "'You are effectively" "dead'" "'I see it,' I said" "'It is a small light—" "It lights up nothing" "There is obviously" "nothing here" "But it is beautiful"

"Beautiful'" "'It is is not a light,'" "the voices said" "'It is yourself'" "'It is something like" "yourself'" "Then the authoritative" "voice said," "'We are going to" "leave you now'"

"I looked into the light" "directly" "with what I knew to be black eyes"
"Light streamed down through" "my eyes" "into myself" "And"
"as if inside me" "were only mirrors" "which faced each other" "I
felt myself" "light up within," "entirely," "the length of me"

"I was sight," "pure sight" "Was being," "was seeing," "with no object"
"whatsoever" "Nothing to see," "nothing to be:" "There was" "an other
though—" "the light which lit me" "& I loved it" "most purely"
"though I" "was also it" "'Is this" "the deepest darkness?'" "I

asked it" "'It is,'" "it said," "in no voice at all" "'It's what you've
always" "suspected" "It's nothing but" "what you've always known,"
"always been" "For you've always" "been being" "It's simple" "Simple'"
"'This light,' I said," "'our light,'" "is the same as the" "surrounding

darkness'" "'Of course,'" "said the light" "'Both" "are being"
"There is no darkness" "or light, here" "But when I leave you" "you
will be lit—" "even if the light" "does diminish'" "We were silent"
"awhile;" "then I spoke again:" "'I'm at peace with" "being" "In

this moment" "I've become" "all that" "I am" "I'm ready" "to
go back'"

"Slowly" "the sphere receded" "& disappeared" "into darkness,"
"retreated backwards" "to a pinpoint" "& vanished—"
"My light shone brightly" "for some time," "then its intensity"
"diminished" "to a moonlight-like" "pearlescence," "a consistent"

"soft glow" "Then I saw" "that nearby" "was a skeleton," "my
skeleton," "sent close to me" "by whatever" "agency" "of this
so-called lake—" "My face was gone" "My flesh was gone"
"I recognized" "my own bones" "only" "by instinct" "I wondered"

"what the purpose" "of my body" "had been:" "I felt" "affection
for it" "but its individualities," "recollected," "seemed
small & tame," "its capabilities so mild," "its sorrows" "too intense"
"I sat beside" "my skeleton" "I knew that" "I had to" "somehow"

"reinhabit it," "reinhabit it & return" "It lay" "on its back:"
"so I stretched out" "on top of it—" "on my back—" "& slowly"
"sank down within," "sank down & stretched around" "I inhabited it"
"somewhat now," "almost being" "my own bones" "My bones" "were full

of knowledge," "the history" "of the planet" "As I put them on"
"I saw shapes" "in the darkness" "before my eyes—" "dreamy figures
& scenes" "I saw amoebas" "swell & divide" "Saw apes die" "& be mourned"
"I saw a king" "in blood-soaked velvet" "standing" "in a puddle,"

"a small puddle" "of blood" "The blood smelled" "like rotted orchids"
"All the trapped light" "of creatures" "seemed so dirty" "& scuffed,"
"so neutralized," "debilitated" "So obscured"

"I felt skin" "begin to grow on me," "grow on me" "again" "Felt organs, within," "swell & flower, blood flow" "The I" "that had just been—" "that had been light," "pure light—" "now shivered" "with pleasure" "to be entrapped" "by flesh" "My senses" "were

delectable;" "my mouth gasped" "at its own moistness" "But the tyrant's" "body," "dream-image of it," "now appeared" "floating stretched-out" "above me," "face down," "face near mine—" "dressed in his dark suit & tie" "As if" "to enter me too,"

"mingle with" "my flesh & organs" "Dwell within me until I died" "I caught his large blue smiling eye" "His right eye swelled" "& enlarged" "Enlarged, disattached" "& came closer" "It was full of type," "of letters," "slightly raised &" "in a spiral"

"All the excess light" "that hovered" "about the outside" "of my body—" "that had not been" "enclosed by it—" "was sucked up into" "those letters," "till the letters" "glowed white" "His eye" "was replaced" "within his face" "His smile grew larger" "'It all"

"becomes yours" "Becomes yours,' I whispered" "The tyrant's" "image vanished" "by sinking down into me" "Yet I felt my" "flowered owl eyes," "my bone vagina," "in place beneath" "my flesh" "& I heard" "a voice whisper—" "the authoritative" "voice—"

"'Do you feel" "a tightness" "about your mouth & nose?'" "'Yes,' underneath,' I said" "'Underneath as if" "within the bone'" "'You have grown" "a hidden beak,' it said," "'an owl's beak—" "Don't forget" "that you have it" "for you will use it'"

"I must have slept then," "long & deeply" "Hours passed," "perhaps days" "I dreamed" "at one point," "as I had" "once before," "that I was carried in flight" "through the darkness" "among wings" "When I awoke" "the owl's face" "was above me" "And I" "was at the

campground" "in the forest" "'You brought me back" "from the lake,' I said" "'Do I really" "have a beak?'" "The owl nodded" "He pressed liquid" "to my lips" "brushed my face with" "his wing"

"The owl" "held a wooden cup" "of broth to" "my lips—"
"it smelled of mice," "smelled of warm fur" "& meek blood"
"People stood round," "human figures," "bending over me in a blur"
"The owl motioned" "them away" "with his long soft brown wing"

"Brown, dark" "& light" "Scalloped" "with finger shapes"
"It was beautiful—" "his wing—" "as I awakened," "alive" "in the
forest" "'I think" "you can sit up,' he said" "I slowly pulled"
"myself up" "He perched next to me" "'You are ready,' he said"

"'Ready" "for the tyrant—'" "except for one thing—'" "He drew his
left claw to his beak" "& in an instant" "extracted a"
"long talon" "His claw bled" "'Give me your right hand'" "I
extended it" "He cut it quickly," "painlessly" "an incision"

"on the back of it—" "with his right" "middle talon" "& then
inside the" "incision" "he inserted" "the extracted one"
"'You now have" "a talon," "your own talon,' he said" "You have
weapons—" "& your travail—" "with which to face him" "Your

weapons" "are moral" "They were given you" "by an animal"
"Manufactured" "by nature," "were made by nature" "Not by"
"the human mind" "Not a rational" "device," "not a vicious" "device"
"You are now part owl'" "He flew up" "& hovered" "before my face"

"Extended" "his bleeding claw" "& smeared" "a drop of blood"
"on my forehead" "'When the time comes,'" "think like me,' he said"
"'Not like" "a human woman" "but like an owl'"

"'How will I return" "to the tyrant's world?' I asked" "'That tall tree,' the owl said," "'leads upwards" "to a doorway" "beneath" "the tyrant's house" "I will now take you there myself'" "Then people came" "& crowded round me" "They were human" "yet ethereal" "They were

like motion" "of humans" "For they were always" "moving, talking," "laughing" "or singing" "Were busy" "& also airy" "& when someone, say, moved her arm," "an afterimage" "of that motion" "lingered" "in the air" "One of them—" "a man," "with a face both" "old & youthful,"

"said, 'Don't let" "the tyrant fool you" "He can fool you into" "despair &" "submission'" "Then a woman" "tied a cloth," "a clear red sash," "around my waist" "Kissed me lightly" "on the cheek" "The owl said," "'It's time to go'"

"The owl" "held a wooden cup" "of broth to" "my lips—"
"it smelled of mice," "smelled of warm fur" "& meek blood"
"People stood round," "human figures," "bending over me in a blur"
"The owl motioned" "them away" "with his long soft brown wing"

"Brown, dark" "& light" "Scalloped" "with finger shapes"
"It was beautiful—" "his wing—" "as I awakened," "alive" "in the
forest" "'I think" "you can sit up,' he said" "I slowly pulled"
"myself up" "He perched next to me" "'You are ready,' he said"

"'Ready" "for the tyrant—'" "except for one thing—" "He drew his
left claw to his beak" "& in an instant" "extracted a"
"long talon" "His claw bled" "'Give me your right hand'" "I
extended it" "He cut it quickly," "painlessly" "an incision"

"on the back of it—" "with his right" "middle talon" "& then
inside the" "incision" "he inserted" "the extracted one"
"'You now have" "a talon," "your own talon,' he said" "'You have
weapons—" "& your travail—" "with which to face him" "Your

weapons" "are moral" "They were given you" "by an animal"
"Manufactured" "by nature," "were made by nature" "Not by"
"the human mind" "Not a rational" "device," "not a vicious" "device"
"You are now part owl'" "He flew up" "& hovered" "before my face"

"Extended" "his bleeding claw" "& smeared" "a drop of blood"
"on my forehead" "'When the time comes," "think like me,' he said"
"'Not like" "a human woman" "but like an owl'"

"'How will I return" "to the tyrant's world?' I asked" "'That tall tree,' the owl said," "'leads upwards" "to a doorway" "beneath" "the tyrant's house" "I will now take you there myself'" "Then people came" "& crowded round me" "They were human" "yet ethereal" "They were

like motion" "of humans" "For they were always" "moving, talking," "laughing" "or singing" "Were busy" "& also airy" "& when someone, say, moved her arm," "an afterimage" "of that motion" "lingered" "in the air" "One of them—" "a man," "with a face both" "old & youthful,"

"said, 'Don't let" "the tyrant fool you" "He can fool you into" "despair &" "submission'" "Then a woman" "tied a cloth," "a clear red sash," "around my waist" "Kissed me lightly" "on the cheek" "The owl said," "'It's time to go'"

"The owl" "led me, flying," "towards the thick black tall tree"
"It was obscure," "swathed in mist" "Had no visible" "leaves or branches"
"It was a long naked tree trunk" "as far as" "I could tell"
"'You have something,' said the owl," "'that belongs to" "the tyrant,"

"something" "in your pocket'" "I remembered" "I had a piece of"
"the tyrant's blue lapis heart" "My hand" "closed around it" "'You will
use it" "when you arrive" "to draw the tyrant" "to the door—"
"He must unlock it" "& admit you" "And now" "we will fly upwards"

"I'll be your wings" "My wings behind you" "will elevate" "& guide you"
"But in the tyrant's world," "you must fly alone'" "'I will fly?'
I asked" "'You are owl,' he said," "& then darted" "behind me"
"'Lift your arms out," "straight out" "from your sides'" "He spread

his wings out" "behind my outstretched arms" "& we began to" "ascend"
"Rode the air up" "I rode the air" "through much mist" "& darkness"
"The new stars glinted sometimes" "through foggy patches" "like mica pieces"
"Soon we entered" "an opaque darkness" "& the air became" "stale & close"

"'We are in a" "vertical tunnel" "piercing the caves &" "subway system"
"It encloses" "the tree" "The tree's few branches—" "at its very top—"
"are embedded in" "the foundation" "of the tyrant's house...'"
"Presently" "he said, 'There it is," "the tyrant's basement" "& there's

an opening" "the years have made," "that ages" "have made'" "It was
a small" "jagged black hole—" "we were illuminated" "murkily"
"by an electric bulb" "somewhere above" "'Squeeze on through it now,'
he said" "'...through the hole—" "climb up—" "there!'" "I knelt on"

"the floor" "peering down at" "the owl" "'A stupid place,' I said,"
"'for goodbyes'" "'I have only" "one expression" "for my face,' he said"
"'I can't smile" "I can't cry" "I have my owl look—" "Goodbye, my dear'"
"Immediately" "he began" "to descend"

BOOK 4

"I stood before" "a dismal door," "an old paint-eroded" "wooden door"
"I took from" "my pocket" "the fragment of" "the tyrant's heart"
"& held it," "just held it," "standing there in" "murky brown light"
"The lapis" "now had" "a pulse in it:" "one place throbbed rhythmically,"

"as if the stone were," "really, blue flesh" "The lapis soon" "became
luminous," "haloed" "Proximity" "to its owner" "was making it
come alive—" "& I felt it" "exert" "a pull outwards" "into the
building" "It grew heavier" "& more vibrant," "as I stood there,"

"reflecting" "on my recent" "ordeal," "my death into" "the lake"
"I felt joyous" "but knew" "that I must subdue" "my joy" "I searched
my depths for" "another character," "a self appropriate" "to what I
must do—" "to what I must do now" "My face changed—" "I felt the change—"

"into a former" "mask of sorrow" "Lines deepened in" "my cheeks,"
"deepened near" "my eyes" "Then I heard footsteps beyond the door—"
"heard the lock turn" "Abruptly" "the tyrant" "stood before me"
"Grey-haired, blue-eyed" "Very tall" "Charged up" "with anger" "He said,"

"'You are presumptuous" "Only" "presumptuous" "That is all that"
"you are" "There must be little else" "in your soul...'" "He snatched
the lapis" "from my hand," "then said sarcastically," "'Won't you"
"come in?'"

"I didn't move" "at all," "stared at the tyrant," "at first seeing"
"only a" "remembered face," "recalled from" "screens & pictures"
"White-haired" "round-eyed image," "thin lined cheeks—" "his
photograph" "Then in the glare of" "his intensity" "for a moment"

"I thought" "I might perversely" "become drowsy" "become sluggish"
"or still..." "The moment lengthened..." "'Come this way *please*!'"
"The tyrant grabbed me" "by an elbow," "led me" "down a hallway,"
"up a staircase—" "I stole sideways" "looks at him—" "boyish,

lanky" "in his dark suit" "But was there something" "slightly in-"
"substantial" "about his being?" "It seemed to me" "that his body"
"was..." "not all there" "His limbs looked" "slightly airy,"
"slightly marbled" "with air," "slightly streaked" "with absences"

"Small, very small" "pieces of" "his face," "patches" "of his hands"
"weren't there" "And yet he had" "all force & presence" "His grip on"
"my elbow" "was very" "very strong &" "his opaque" "blue eyes"
"were whole" "& disconcerting" "He led me into" "an immense" "tiered

room—" "museum hall—" "with a central" "open space," "& many levels"
"of balconies" "lining" "the walls" "On each level" "were cases"
"full of animal" "& plant specimens," "full of artifacts" "& dioramas"
"The whole was lit by" "a domed skylight" "But the light from it"

"was not bright, &" "suspended" "near the ceiling," "partly blocking"
"the light," "causing shadows everywhere," "was a large" "plaster brain,"
"apparent model" "of a brain" "The tyrant led me" "to the court"
"in the middle of" "the ground floor" "'So,' he said," "'so,"

"Miss Owlfeathers," "you're here without" "appointment" "returning
a piece" "of my heart" "to me'" "He tossed it up" "& caught it"
"Then he grinned—" "his mouth was very wide" "He looked" "almost zany—"
"He dropped the stone in" "his jacket pocket"

"'You are casual" "with your heart,' I said" "'This piece,' he said,"
"'is all that's left of'" "my personal" "heart" "It belongs in"
"the caves" "as a reassuring" "symbol'" "'Have you no real heart?"
I asked" "'A heart" "has grown to be,' he said," "'superfluous" "to me"

"in as much as" "I have become" "reality, itself" "I am reality,
itself" "My 'heart' is" "probably everywhere..." "anywhere...'"
"I felt that" "he was lying" "& didn't know why" "he might be doing so"
"'In the subway,' I said," "'is it there?" "Is your heart there?'"

"'The subway" "is surely" "the same as" "my heart,'" "he said with"
"sudden intensity" "'Then:" "'I understand you've" "come to kill me'"
"His large blue eyes," "round blue eyes," "unblinking," "fixed on me"
"So kill me," "so kill me,'" "he said" "I was" "disconcerted" "I had"

"at that instant" "neither impulse" "nor ability—" "felt no directive"
"whatsoever—" "to kill" "this person" "standing next to me"
"I wanted merely" "to be there," "like myself in" "most moments,"
"fairly comfortable," "& not taking" "drastic action..." "'We'll see,'"

"I said" "'But I'm not vulnerable," "not vulnerable" "at all,'"
"he said" "'I'm not even" "a real person'" "'Not" "a real person?'"
"Why else" "do you think" "bits of my body" "are airy," "seem to be
missing?" "You didn't" "really think" "you could kill me," "just

kill me?" "Kill me & change the world?'" "He laughed" "& laughed some more"
"I half believed him," "half didn't" "'Come tour" "my house with me,'
he said" "'You can't kill me;" "so join me" "for now'"

"We walked past displays" "of dead animals" "behind glass" "Climbed
from balcony" "to balcony" "in the erratic" "weak light" "It was the
first" "natural light" "I'd seen in years—" "it seemed nothing,"
"meant nothing" "I had a grievous" "impression" "of a hallful" "of eyes:"

"monkeys' eyes," "fishes' eyes" "Eyes of tigers" "& rhinos" "Eyes of
falcons," "of ospreys" "The eyes, even" "of owls:" "a case of owls,"
"all dead-alive" "& affecting" "Were owls' eyes" "not my own eyes?"
"or the eyes of" "my own—" "my own," "my owl?" "It was the same look."

"the one owl look," "as when he'd" "said goodbye" "But I also" "saw
human eyes:" "there were" "dioramas" "of groups of humans—" "models,
not real—" "but with lifelike" "glassine eyes," "lucid," "lucid as"
"the outer domes of" "cats' eyes" "The humans" "were in ethnic"

"& historical" "environments" "In various robes," "veils & turbans"
"In tents or houses" "of laquer, bamboo," "hides or wood" "But one"
"diorama" "was of a subway car," "in darkness," "as if in motion"
"Through the windows" "one saw stiff figures" "standing," "holding poles"

"Or sitting" "on metal benches..." "Still, they were" "so still"
"with those grave" "glassine eyes" "And on one bench" "head framed—"
"head framed by" "a window—" "sat..." "it was myself," "an exact figure"
"of myself," "unsmiling," "somber, shadowed—" "mentally shadowed"

"I winced" "& glanced up" "Looked up at" "the tyrant" "He smiled"
"a small smile," "the smile of" "the self-pleased" "Then directed"
"my attention," "with a motion" "of head & hand," "toward another"
"diorama:" "a bedouin-" "like woman" "who sat weaving" "a basket"

"Draped in" "rich black robes" "Weaving" "a tan basket" "with a single"
"red stripe" "I was sure" "she was the woman—" "the one from" "the caves—"
"who had woven" "me," "who had called herself" "my history" "She was
as still as" "all else here—" "'How did you know?'" "I whispered"

"'I told you" "I told you" "I am reality,' he said" "'No you aren't,'"
"I said fiercely," "but I wasn't sure" "'Were you with me" "when I died?"
"When I died into" "the dark lake?'" "'Yes,' he said," "'yes, I was'"
"in a slightly stiff," "slightly false" "intonation" "He was lying"

186   THE SCARLET CABINET

"'Would you like to see" "my government?'" "he said, obviously"
"to change the subject" "He led me" "toward miniature" "dioramas,"
"scenes that sat on" "waist-high pillars—" "involving" "tiny figures"
"an inch," "two inches high" "Some showed" "men in suits & ties"

"in conference" "around tables" "One showed" "a large assembly of
such men," "most seated," "one standing" "as if orating," "one
presiding" "at a desk" "The figures" "had painted faces" "& were
each alike" "The rooms themselves," "the little rooms," "were built of

rich brown wood pieces" "with deep green & red" "rugs & curtains"
"Exquisite small-paned" "louvered windows" "minute golden" "light
fixtures" "As I looked at" "the legislature," "the body" "of men in
session," "I saw that" "the orator's mouth" "seemed to move"

"His hand moved too," "up & down" "in a short" "repetitive gesture"
"'Clockwork?' I asked" "'This *is*" "my legislature," "real legislature,'
he replied" "He lifted" "the glass" "that enclosed this petite scene"
"& I heard" "a soft squeaking sound" "continuous" "& undulant"

"'That is his voice,' he said" "He replaced the transparent hood"
"'I keep telling you," "I keep telling you:" "all" "exists in me'"

"The tyrant" "next led me" "away from the" "tiered balconies"
"through a door" "& into" "a high-ceilinged" "darkened hall—"
"full of visages," "full of masks—" "a room of faces" "with holes
in them" "Eye- nose- & mouth-holes" "'What are these masks of?' I asked"

"'Oh I suppose…'" "'Well *these* are" "masks of principles," "essences"
"For example," "this is a mask of" "vegetation'" "It had a grain-"
"of-wood face," "with leaves for hair" "'This one's a mask,' he said,"
"'of cities'" "It was painted" "to look composed of" "red bricks with"

"white mortar" "'Mask of… sexuality!'" "He laughed at it" "It had a
penis nose," "vagina mouth," "nipple eyes" "'Mask of childishness!'"
"A bifurcated" "baby's face," "one-half laughing," "one-half bawling"
"'These masks" "are not all" "of the same type,' I said" "What

are those" "demonic faces?'" "For the far wall" "was hung with crudely"
"caricatured" "expressions of" "ferocity" "& viciousness," "unclear,
shadowed" "from where I stood" "'Those are—'" "we approached them—"
"'the literal faces," "real faces," "of warriors," "conquerors…'"

"I could see now" "that they were that—" "beneath thick red &" "black
lines" "were stretched dead faces," "real skin" "Coarse brown-discolored"
"dead-hide skin," "eyes shut," "sewn shut" "Mouths sewn shut" "The
grotesque" "caricatures" "were an overlay" "in lipstick" "& greasepaint"

"'These also" "exist in you?' I asked" "'There have always been"
"such men,' he said" "'They must be natural…'" "inevitable" "But come see"
"some other masks" "He took me" "to one more display:" "Masks of Jesus,"
"of Buddha" "Jehovah-like" "faces" "Masks of nameless" "tribal deities"

"Masks of gods" "from everywhere" "He placed a golden" "Buddha-mask"
"on his face" "'Why would you want to" "kill such as this?'" "he said
playfully" "'Such a mildness" "as this?" "Am I not this too?" "Or,"
"for that matter," "am I not you too?" "What would be" "left of you?"

"If you killed me?'"

188   THE SCARLET CABINET

"'Now step behind" "this display case,' he said" "The case itself—"
"it sat some feet from" "the wall—" "was full of" "feather fetishes…"
"bark placards…" "sticky-looking" "lumpy spheres" "of whatever"
"dark secretions" "'You own their magic too…?' I began" "And then saw"

"on that wall" "a large" "lone mask" "of the woman" "who had been
headless," "our first mother" "The mask of her" "was lifelike;"
"flesh of painted wood" "well-colored" "Its warm brown," "smooth brown,"
"picked up green &" "violet highlights," "skimming," "elusive"

"The hair was spread out around her head—" "tangled" "coarse real hair—"
"as if she were" "a pinned sun" "And there were no eyes—" "black
holes," "empty sockets" "Though her wide nose," "her flat pretty nose,"
"was well-rendered" "Her lips were parted" "revealing blackness"

"But were parted" "in ambiguity" "of expression—" "about to speak?"
"At the threshold" "of some unpleasantness?" "'Yes, it's she,'"
"the tyrant said" "'It is her mask" "her head'"

"'She left us long ago" "Found it intolerable" "to have become"
"a symbol," "empty symbol'" "'You destroyed her,' I said" "'Enslaved
her" "& destroyed her'" "She expected—" "at least at first—"
"power & influence" "equal to" "any man's'" "His eyes tried"

"to hold me still," "hold me" "& impress me" "'Soulfulness,'" "he
continued," "'cannot hold power" "or hold its own" "What she had could not"
"hold its own—" "wit & warmth" "& beauty" "are weak &" "exploitable,"
"vulnerable" "to our enemies—" "'Our enemies?' I asked" "'Don't you"

"contain them too?'" "He ignored me" "& said," "'Such qualities"
"are contrary to" "Nature's scheme for" "who holds sovereignty'"
"'You are, I take it,'" "Nature," "contain Nature?'" "I said mockingly"
"He modestly inclined his head" "'As the scientist I am—'" "witness my

house—" "I do,' he said" "'From the outside, I admit, but" "I do"
"rule Nature" "Understand" "& rule it" "& have increasingly" "since she
left us" "for the darkness...'" "He regarded" "her mask now" "'After"
"she left," "we began" "to forget" "exactly who she was" "Though we

remembered" "the feeling of her" "We invented" "songs about her...'"
"The tyrant quietly" "began to sing:" "'When the snake," "was our mother,"
"when the snake" "was the train...'" "Sang several" "of the old verses"
"but added ones" "new to me:" "'We serve her memory now" "in pain"

"We serve her memory now" "in pain" "When" "we ride the subway,"
"we ride inside" "her memory;" "when" "we ride the subway," "her metal
ghost," "her worthless ghost" "For she was generous," "she was sinuous"
"And when we ride it," "when we ride it," "aren't we lifeless?" "Aren't we

worthless?" "Aren't we metal" "but for our pain?" "Except for" "our pain?'"

"The tyrant's" "song was over" "He stood staring" "marble-eyed"
"at her brown" "distressed mask-face," "brown" "sunburst head"
"I myself" "felt my own face" "harden further" "into its sorrow mask"
"'Let's move on,' he said" "He took me" "through a back door" "to a

stairwell—" "where there was" "a small window" "with half-"
"open slats:" "the light that fell through" "the slats" "was muted,
greyed," "almost twilit" "I paused" "at the window" "Why is your house"
"so shadowy?" "And why is" "the light so dim?' I asked" "'Because,'

he said," "'we're in my body...'" "It's all inside me" "quite literally"
"And outside" "this building" "is inside me too..." "My thoughts are"
"half-material" "& make a screen in" "the sky" "above the world'"
"I looked out between" "the slats" "I saw clean white" "apartment buildings;"

"& trim avenues" "adorned with" "beds of red but" "pale tulips—"
"a tomato-cream" "color—" "interspersed" "with grape hyacinths"
"whose purple was" "mostly grey" "There were trees," "young trees,"
"groomed &" "unfertile" "Well-to-do-" "looking people" "walked briskly,"

"hailed pale cabs" "They looked very like—" "from where we stood—"
"the people" "in the small" "dioramas," "as if their features"
"had been painted on" "by a tiny" "fine-haired brush:" "explicit eyebrows,"
"nostrils, mouth-line" "All & only" "in place"

"The sky, the far air" "had a grainy," "a patterned" "grey look,"
"as if there were a" "thin lace curtain" "hung in front of it"

"'There are other wings" "to my house,'" "the tyrant then said" "'I can show you" "libraries," "art galleries," "& gardens—" "gardens full of" "statuary" "I can show you" "old manuscripts…" "ikons…" "codices…" "Scrolls & tablets…" "Or greenhouses," "if you like:"

"I have orchids" "& begonias…" "Also herb gardens," "wild flowers'" "Suddenly" "I heard a rumbling," "a rumbling noise" "The subway," "is it the subway?' I asked" "'Of course,' the tyrant answered" "'Can you take me there?' I said" "'Is that really" "where you'd like to go?'"

"'I haven't been home" "in a long while,'" "I said carefully," "wondering" "where my home was," "where my home now was" ("Where my true home" "Where my true home…") "In that great" "unhappy subway world" "some calling" "homelike element—" "something" "black &

ragged" "like a lost piece" "of soul—" "seemed to" "reside" "Something" "that needed tending to" "'I haven't been there" "in awhile" "myself,'" "he said," "'…remiss in" "my duty'" "We began to" "descend the stairs" "Then at one landing" "he said, 'Wait here'"

"He slipped through" "the door there" "Soon came back in" "an old suit," "navy-blue" "with shiny" "& slightly" "frayed edges" "'I'm in disguise,' he grinned" "He was now" "brisk & light" "At the bottom of" "the stairwell" "he took a key from" "his pocket" "& unlocked" "the steel door"

"When the lock turned" "he winced slightly," "his hand flew" "to his chest—" "some passing pain" "Then we entered" "a darkness full of" "a familiar" "roaring sound" "Engulfed again," "engulfed again in" "that sound"

"As" "my eyes adjusted" "I found that" "the darkness" "was actually
dimly lit by" "naked low-wattage bulbs" "We stood" "on a ramp,"
"the other side of" "the door," "that was meant to" "bridge a stretch"
"of abandoned" "subway track" "The ramp was broken" "in the middle;"

"could not be used" "The tracks were covered" "with rats—" "open-"
"mouthed rats" "Their heads & mouths" "turned up towards us" "Everywhere I
looked" "below us" "were only" "open rats' mouths," "mouths with
bared teeth" "'The subway" "has become" "more extreme" "since you left it"

"More strange &" "dangerous," "more violent,'" "the tyrant said to me"
"'How can we enter here?' I asked" "The tyrant, who was" "excessively
long-legged," "like a dancer," "a ballet dancer," "leaped across"
"above the rats' mouths," "his legs split straight out" "Then stood on"

"the other side" "'Leap across,' he said" "I stood frozen" "I was no
athlete" "'Isn't," "isn't this" "your *home?*'" "he taunted" "Enraged I
leaped out" "& fell downward," "towards the rats" "Then time slowed"
"Slowed" "For in" "the split-second" "in which I was" "in air"

"I heard" "the word 'SAVED'" "spoken three times" "by an unknown voice"
"Then I hovered" "above" "the open rats' mouths—" "perhaps I"
"lost consciousness?" "lost consciousness" "just a second" "Then"
"I was beside him," "stood beside him on concrete" "with no sense"

"of having actively" "crossed the space" "'I don't know how" "I came across,'
I said" "'It felt as if" "I were dreamed across," "another self in me
spoke" "& then dreamed me" "across...'" "'You became an owl,'"
"the tyrant said" "'For an instant," "a brief instant," "you looked like"

"an owl's shadow" "& you flew" "You flew across'"

"Then we passed through" "another door" "& onto" "an ashen platform"
"I was back now," "the air unmoving," "the stained walls sallow"
"Bodies of sleeping men" "in colorless" "dirty blankets like" "grimy
pale flesh" "lay" "at my feet" "A woman" "was begging," "was begging"

"with a cup" "She wore a ragged blouse" "that was a map," "that was
printed as" "a red-lined map" "'What map is" "on your blouse?' I asked"
"'Map of" "Map of" "Map of the subway,' she said" "'But it looks,' I said,"
"'so arterial—" "the lines so red & thick'" "They seemed to thicken"

"as I looked at them" "One line upon her chest" "swelled especially,"
"as she" "began to speak:" "'He said we were" "his lifesblood" "He
said we were" "his heart" "Am I inside" "someone else's," "someone"
"else's self?" "How can I live?" "How can I live my life?" "It's all"

"too close in here..." "Living" "someone else's..." "Dying close..."
"You're all too close...'" "She wandered off" "babbling lowly" "to
herself" "I looked at" "the tyrant's face," "shadowed," "unsmiling"
"'You look frightened,' I said" "'May I confide" "in my would-be"

"assassin?' he asked" "'The darkness—" "this darkness—" "scares me,"
"always scares me" "Rises up" "inside me" "like a disorienting"
"substance," "something" "close to deadly...'" "'Why have you not"
"tried to change it?" "Tried to change this dark place?'" "'Because"

"it *is* inside me" "It *is*" "my heart" "My lifesblood, my heart" "It is
my real heart:" "how could I change that?" "This being has this heart"
"Of course, my dear," "it is not flesh—" "I am not vulnerable—"
"But being this way" "for thousands" "of years," "I cannot change"

"It cannot change'" "As he spoke, I" "became more certain" "he was
vulnerable somewhere" "Perhaps somewhere not far" "I did not speak this
thought" "Instead I said," "'You consider" "your heart" "to be dis-
ordered?" "In a state of" "disorder?'" "'It is chaotic,'" "desperate'

"So full of feeling," "it is intolerable..." "It is also" "my courage'"
"He gave me a" "fierce look," "a sudden hard" "all-alive look"
"'And that is why" "you won't kill me" "All these feelings" "are
empowering" "Their intensity" "gives me power" "Look" "a train is coming"

"Let's get on it,' he said"

"The car we entered" "contained a crowd" "of people" "around one bench,"
"around one bench only" "We pressed through them" "to the front"
"'He is dying,' a woman said" "The man lay outstretched on the bench,"
"his space" "demarcated" "by a rectangle of" "small red lightbulbs—"

"lay" "on his back—" "a dark man" "with a dusty face," "emaciated,"
"in torn clothes—" "cheeks sunken, lips drawn" "Eyes protruding,"
"eyes huge" "'He is going now,' a voice said" "And he had died—" "he had
died, though" "his eyes" "did not close," "but his face" "became still,"

"its color fell" "a shade greyer" "& all" "electric force," "all
spirit was gone" "A brown" "rough blanket" "was drawn up over him"
"The tyrant" "began to weep" "'Are your tears" "precious jewels"
"as they say?' I said angrily" "For a woman knelt" "near the dead man"

"weeping red tears," "weeping blood" "'I cannot,'" "said the tyrant,"
"'be held" "responsible...'" "His sentence" "was interrupted"
"A man had shoved through," "pushed us aside" "& stood near" "the victim"
"He was trying" "to speak," "but his lips seemed sealed shut;" "protruding"

"were sealed shut" "Then" "the words finally" "forced" "themselves out"
"His lips shot open" "with a loud smack—" "we almost" "laughed aloud but"
"he spoke with a" "rich deep voice:" "'The radiance" "of a death"
"cannot now" "justify the" "travail," "the travail of" "this" "hard life..."

"The tyrant robs us" "of transcendence" "by making it" "all we can have..."
"our ordinary" "coinage..." "coinage..." "Who wants it?" "Can we
not have something small," "a bit of daily" "air to breathe?'" "The man
went silent" "The red lights" "around the victim" "went out" "Everyone

turned away" "& filed silently" "into connecting cars" "We followed,"
"we followed"

THE DESCENT OF ALETTE

"'All inspiration" "comes from here,'" "the tyrant whispered" "as we changed cars" "'All stories," "all drama," "all poetry" "come from here now" "My heart" "is theirs" "I feel all" "I feel as they feel" "What else can" "a heart be like," "tell me that?'" "'Your heart"

"is not your own," "is composed of" "the hearts of others," "lives of others" "Blue stone" "is your true heart," "your only true heart'" "'They cannot exist" "without me" "Was the woman" "crying blood" "not crying my blood?'" "'She should not be weeping blood" "She should be

crying" "free water," "free water," "transparent water" "We must see the world" "through our tears" "Not weep" "the thick substance" "of another's" "reality," "another's" "reality...'"

"'Let's get off at" "River Street,'" "the tyrant said" "We
soon arrived there," "exited" "'Have you ever" "seen the river"
"the stop is named for?' he asked" "I shook my head" "'Behind the
wall" "Behind this wall,' he said" "He opened" "a ramshackle" "door"

"of boards collapsing," "in a dirty" "bare wall—" "line of black dirt"
"where wall met floor—" "& we were then in" "a damp darkness"
"that smelled of" "something else," "something else than" "only water"
"The tyrant pulled" "a long flashlight" "from the inside" "of his jacket"

"& shone it on" "a river" "running between two" "subway platforms"
"which were quite" "wide apart," "wide apart as" "riverbanks"
"The water—" "but the water" "was red," "red-black" "'Your blood?'"
"I whispered" "'Yes,'" "he said" "The current" "of this river" "was

slow," "quite slow" "Into" "the lit area—" "of bloody liquid"
"lit by the flashlight—" "flowed something" "on the surface," "a dark
cloth, a" "black tatter," "a small" "black-handkerchief-like" "fragment
with tattered edge" "'It is mine" "It is something" "of mine,' I

said to him," "'How can I get it?'" "Alarmed," "alarmed-seeming,"
"he snapped the" "flashlight off" "I had sensation then" "of enlargement of,"
"enlargement of" "my eyes" "And could see" "the black cloth" "Could
see it" "in the dark" "Time slowed" "as it had" "at the entrance"

"to the subway" "when I had had to" "cross over" "the abandoned track"
"full of rats—" "But I was conscious" "in this dream, this" "dream-like"
"real happening" "For I was winged" "Slow & fast," "wide-winged
quiet-winged," "I hovered" "next instant," "mid-instant" "above the

black thing" "Then plucked it up" "in my beak—" "which felt like having"
"stiff-fingered teeth—" "I was soon back" "on the platform," "stood"
"as a woman," "holding" "the black fabric" "in my hand" "The tyrant
now switched" "the flashlight back on"

"I held the cloth up" "before the beam of" "the flashlight"
"It was diaphanous," "black-airy" "'May I see it...'" "the tyrant said"
"& began stretching" "his hand towards it" "I popped it into" "my mouth,"
"into my mouth &" "swallowed it" "Swallowed" "it down" "There was

within me" "at once" "a bleak dawning," "a sky turning" "from ob-
sidian" "to sickly" "bluish light" "'Why was my memory," "my memory,"
"floating in your" "heartsblood?' I cried" "'I must have" "let go of it"
"It was too painful" "I loosed it from me" "& gave it back to you"

"back to your body," "from where its pain came" "My name is" "Alette"
"My brother" "died in battle'" "I sank" "to the ground &" "sat,"
"sat & thought of him—" "his pure profile," "his head's shape" "un-
changed since babyhood—" "well modeled," "rounded well-made above

delicate" "neck's nape" "neck's nape" "The tyrant stood stiffly near"
"holding out" "the flashlight" "with an almost military" "cast to"
"his demeanor" "He was again" "deeply moved" "& thus I found" "my anger,"
"my life-" "giving anger" "'He died,' I began again," "'when you last

fought...'" "yourself" "When two of your..." "warrior masks," "two of
your leaders" "last fought," "when two armies" "were amassed from"
"the subway populace'" "'Men fight,' he said" "'Men fight'" "Don't you
think they must sometimes?" "And there's a shape to—" "an intensity"

"to battle—" "to war—" "a proximity to life & death—" "that captures
many men's" "imaginations...'" "'That's exactly what women" "are enslaved to,'
I said dully" "'But this is all a cliche" "All a cliche, anyway"
"I don't" "want to live" "in a cliche,' I said" "'Your" "house of insults"

"of science," "of art," "your trivial politics," "your inspiration"
"drawn from the hardships" "of others..." "my grief for" "my brother"
"so moving" "to you..." "I must" "have been searching" "for him"
"as well" "Or I was searching" "for her voice—" "the headless"

"woman's voice—" "so that I could" "speak to you'" "'Beautiful,'"
"he murmured" "'It is not *beautiful*" "It is what was!'" "I was nearly"
"screaming now" "'He is in" "the black lake" "I have been there too"
"It is all" "that there is" "that isn't you," "that isn't you"

"Infinity" "isn't you!'" "But it's all" "so beautiful," "so moving,'"
"he kept murmuring" "with tears" "in his eyes"

"'You are vulnerable" "somewhere near here,'" "I said to him"
"'If there is blood," "all this blood," "if in this river" "flows your blood,"
"there must be flesh" "somewhere...'" "'It has long since" "turned to
concrete," "to brick & steel,' he said" *"'I am not vulnerable"*

"anywhere'" "His eyes" "tore into mine, but" "there was a glint there,"
"I thought," "of hesi-tancy" "'I will find" "that place,' I said &"
"became an" "owl again" "contracting lengthwise," "spreading widthwise,"
"becoming" "wings & eyes—" "such a lightness—" "I felt hardly formed"

"I began to fly" "along the" "bloody river," "corridored river,"
"looking into" "the darkness" "for any trace of" "fleshy softness,"
"fleshy softness"

"The tyrant" "pursued me, running," "at first" "as I flew" "I began
slowly," "searching, looking" "Stopped & hovered sometimes" "He lunged
at me" "once or twice" "as I flew low" "But I was quickness," "speed
of thought," "unhinderable reflex" "As I became" "used to my search"

"& speeded up, he" "fell behind" "Then he disappeared" "entirely"
"I had no mind now" "but flew & looked" "My brother's image" "had vanished"
"Had vanished" "from my thoughts" "Beneath a lightbulb" "I saw myself"
"on the surface" "of the river:" "unnuanced owl eyes" "amid feathers"

"distorted, shadowy" "in liquid thickness" "Along the river, here & there,"
"people slept" "huddled upright" "or spread out" "on the concrete"
"I saw" "a strangely shaped," "almost potato-" "shaped man," "bald,"
"thick-necked—" "his head was like" "a rounded neck—" "pale, coarsely

fleshed," "peeled-looking," "his facial features" "sketchy-seeming"
"He stood chanting" "to himself," "'Am I" "the man the father?" "Am I"
"the man the father?'" "And someone else" "in bandages," "someone
wound with" "strips of white gauze—" "like a mummy—" "wandered up & down,"

"up & down this" "heart river—" "a man," "a tall man," "who would
scream or weep" "or cry out" "these words or" "a variant:" "'Where is"
"my body," "my sacred" "body?" "Where is my corpus" "sagrada?...'"
"Cardboard," "bottles, faeces," "unnamed dirt blacknesses" "were strewn"

"upon the platform—" "the river" "itself" "was plain," "unlittered,"
"glittered redly," "red, black & silver" "beneath the" "occasional
lightbulb"

"Thus I followed" "the river" "as it curved," "curved & straightened,"
"unhindered," "unpartitioned" "Finally" "I heard a motor—"
"the tyrant" "was now driving" "a small" "open vehicle" "Had caught
up with me" "in this cart" "He rode beneath me" "a short distance;"

"then I saw that," "ahead of us," "the river branched into" "several
small streams" "But their paths thence" "were cloaked in blackness:"
"all" "illumination" "ceased where" "these rivulets began" "I paused"
"& hovered" "at the edge of" "the darkness" "The tyrant stopped too"

"& shouted up at me," "'You act wrongly," "act wrongly" "The order"
"of things" "has" "its own wisdom" "formed by everyone's" "will'"
"I opened" "my mouth" "to reply, but" "my mouth" "was a beak"
"The hoo hoo hoo hoo" "that issued from me" "echoed" "off the walls,"

"filled the corridor," "filled my owl self" "I faced him downwards,"
"circled looking down" "Loosed a slow stream" "of owl sound,"
"a stream of crying" "mournful notes," "mixed with screams &" "low
growls," "with scornful" "laughing sounds" "His eyes were frozen wide,"

"his face tense," "bone-naked," "pure in crisis" "He stared &"
"stared at me" "Searched me out, but" "I wasn't there" "I wasn't"
"there at all" "I continued" "to sound at him" "in purity," "in purity,"
"in purity" "of owl's own" "Then I flew into" "the dark"

"The pupils" "of my owl eyes" "grew even larger" "I could see, faintly outlined," "the rivulets" "& their nearby" "destinations" "Beyond the threshold" "of the darkness" "the river's corridor" "widened" "into an immense chamber" "The streams flowed there into"

"a semicircle" "of grottos," "room-sized" "smooth cupolaed caves—" "each stream had" "its own grotto" "There were five of each" "Four of the grottos" "were constructed" "of grey cement," "made by techno-" "logical process" "But one grotto" "was pink" "soft &

undulant," "uneven," "soft & fleshy," "soft & fleshy—" "though firm too," "rather palate-like" "It was surrounded by" "a high" "spiked mesh fence" "with a padlocked door" "A sign hung" "on the door:" *"This fence is"* *"electrified"* "I easily" "flew over it"

"I flew" "beneath the round" "flesh roof" "of the grotto"
"There was a light switch on the wall" "which I pushed up" "with my
beak" "A pearl-" "like fixture" "now illuminated" "the cave"
"The bloody rivulet" "flowed" "into a small well" "in the floor,"

"sunk beneath" "the flesh floor" "near the entrance" "to the grotto"
"But also in the floor—" "in its center—" "something grew,"
"a small plant" "that was rooted" "in that flesh," "a bush of"
"different textures," "though symmetrical" "in form:" "It was

composed of" "long-fingered" "stiff branches" "But it was leafless"
"& each branch had" "a different surface" "One branch was furry"
"with brown" "short thick bear's fur" "One branch" "was a length"
"of reptilian skin," "thin & dry" "like a shed snakeskin," "though

stiff" "& erect here:" "it was palely" "brown-striped" "One branch"
"was vegetative " "but spiky," "dull green" "And one branch"
"was feathered" "with pale small downy feathers" "But one branch
seemed to be" "a very thin long human arm" "less than" "two inches

wide—" "a hand small" "as a baby's," "which held" "a dead rose,"
"a dried black dead rose"

"The tyrant" "was near the fence now," "working" "the switch" "which de-" "electrified it" "Then he unlocked the door" "& entered" "I panicked" "for the grotto" "was not" "very high" "I flew at its rear wall" "& extended" "my talon—" "Sliced into" "the flesh wall,"

"clawed it repeatedly" "It began to ooze" "drops of blood, but" "the wall" "was not vital" "to the tyrant" "I heard him laugh," "laugh behind me" "I turned & faced him" "A white liquid" "now seeped" "through the arm" "of his jacket" "'You can't kill me!'" "he shouted,"

"exultantly," "then rushed at me" "I flew out" "of the grotto" "He sat down" "& laughed again," "Then reclined next to the bush" "'Come & keep me" "company" "Keep me company!' he called" "'We're both weary now" "Let's rest awhile" "together'" "I could in fact"

"barely fly" "'Why not?' I thought—" "& was beside him" "a woman," "a tired woman" "'Even if,' he said," "'you pierced through,'" "all the way through" "these walls with" "your talon," "I would not die:" "it is such" "a small part of me," "this grotto..." "Flesh is not my"

"nature now...'" "But I thought that" "the wound" "I had made in" "his arm" "was tiring him," "as well as" "the physical" "exertion" "But what use was" "his fatigue to me," "if he was" "immortal?" "'What is this bush?'" "I asked him" "But he had fallen" "asleep"

204   THE SCARLET CABINET

"I sat & stared at" "the bush" "Gradually" "I discovered" "that the
attenuated" "arm-like branch" "was making small" "twisting movements,"
"slight motions" "periodically" "And the flower," "the dead rose that"
"it held," "began to change" "Its petals" "became moist & full,"

"became dewy red…" "The tyrant muttered" "in his sleep" "Then his
face" "composed itself," "became youthful-looking, tranquil"
"The whole bush now came alive" "The branches rustled" "& touched
each other:" "The scaled branch lost" "its dryness," "its thinness

of molt" "& gleamed sinuously" "Likewise the" "other branches"
"became more vital" "& lustrous" "The green of" "the green branch"
"deepened" "The feathers broadened" "& took on color" "The brown fur"
"grew longer…" "I understood" "what to do now" "& searched myself"

"for a cruelty" "& temporary" "heartlessness" "I didn't know of"
"in myself:" "my owl self" "had to do this" "But I thought" "my
woman's body" "had factually" "to do this" "I closed my eyes,"
"saw the winged" "shadow shape of" "my owl" "I seemed to empty" "I

extended" "my arms in front of me" "Grasped the bush" "in my hands"
"& yanked it out of" "the ground" "Pulled it up by" "the roots"
"which were long thread-like red," "glistening" "with blood" "But
one root," "one slender strand," "would not dislodge" "from the ground"

"I pulled as hard as" "I could—" "heard the tyrant" "stir & moan,"
"make, still in his sleep," "low pained moans" "I dropped" "the bush
suddenly" "Rose, rushed up" "in weightless smallness" "Hovered wide-
winged," "an owl again" "Then settled on the floor" "& with my talon"

"dug into it," "the fleshy floor" "I gauged out the" "stubborn
last root" "Blood spurted up" "in a small jet" "Then I changed back"
"into a woman," "sat breathless" "& blood-spattered" "near the
tyrant" "still tossing, moaning," "not yet" "fully conscious"

"There was" "a full moment" "of silence" "& stillness"
"which spread out" "around my action" "I felt encircled by" "time-
lessness" "As if in" "another realm" "I had not acted," "had never
acted" "Then the tyrant jerked awake," "convulsed & clutched at"

"his chest" "Eyes enormous," "amazed" "He spoke with difficulty,"
"in fits:" "'I think...'" "you have killed me..." "I am..." "really
dying'" "He seemed so" "bewildered" "'How could you be" "this cruel?"
"And do you not" "kill yourself?" "your own culture..." "soul's breath?'"

"'I'm killing no one" "You are not real" "You said so" "yourself,' I
said" "'Forms in dreams...'" "forms in dreams...'" "I searched within"
"for right words" "'I will change the" "forms in dreams'" "I lifted"
"the dead plant" "& flung it" "across the grotto" "'Starting'

"from dreams," "from dreams we" "can change," "will change" "In
dreams," "in dreams, now," "you will die" "You will die'"
"He turned" "away from me" "Lay looking upward," "wide-eyed, panting"
"His body seemed" "to become" "more & more" "transparent," "lose

substance" "From within it," "within him," "a ghostly tableau
emerged," "hovered," "above his body," "was performed in" "air above him:"
"There was a thicket" "in which a knight" "lay dying" "on the ground"
"A woman tended him," "bent over him" "in ancient" "Greek costume"

"But she" "was a skeleton" "with long hair" "She spoke & told him:"
"'What you have made me—" "what you now see—" "is your consort"
"in eternity...'" "The knight took" "her bone hand" "They clasped
hands," "the scene dissolving"

206   THE SCARLET CABINET

"'Have you" "no forgiveness?'" "the tyrant turned his face" "to me"
"'The question" "has no meaning," "has no meaning,'" "I said"
"'For when you ask" "me that" "I am an owl...'"
"'Your wings are covering me,'" "he said" "Then he died"

"The red river" "stopped flowing—" "the small streams" "became still" "And the light" "went out" "The light went out," "a door swung open" "Near the grotto," "atop a staircase—" "an iron ladder-" "like staircase—" "a door" "opened out:" "a shaft of" "bright

sunlight" "fell hard against" "the stairs," "against the" "floor below" "But I didn't leave quite yet" "I knelt down" "beside the tyrant" "I supposed" "all lights had gone out," "all doors had opened," "the trains had stopped" "Outside, the veil of" "his thought" "that had

obscured the sky," "would be gone" "I touched his" "so-called body," "then lifted" "his hand:" "it was light as" "a rag" "He had no substance now at all" "So I picked up" "the body" "in my arms—it" "hung down like cloth—" "& proceeded" "to carry him" "up the stairs &"

"outside"

"As I emerged from" "the subway" "a brown darkness" "gathered"
"before my eyes," "took on a shape" "Became a swirl of" "blurred wings,"
"which then steadied," "held still in air" "It was my owl self"
"confronting me" "but spectrally—" "unreal & real," "transparent,

present" "It looked at me" "dispassionately," "with yellow" "ungiving
eyes," "as if" "I were of no" "real consequence" "to its exigencies"
"Then re-merged with me," "disappeared back" "into myself—" "I
accepted it," "I accepted it" "Carried the tyrant out" "beneath the

new sky" "The street was" "already" "filling up" "with people"
"They knew he must be dead" "Stood staring into" "the clear air:"
"it was early" "in the morning" "The sky was jewelled blue, rich blue"
"'What we can have now,'" "a woman said," "'is infinity" "in our lives"

"moment by moment," "any moment" "He no longer lies" "between us & it"
"The light is new now," "isn't it?" "The light has been made new'"

"The city" "looked ancient," "still & ancient" "that morning—"
"all traffic" "had stopped;" "all commerce" "had stopped—"
"bricks were artifacts;" "windows, holes" "in the stillness" "in the
light" "I laid the tyrant down" "on the street," "before the crowd"

"'This is not really" "his body,'" "I said to them," "'The structure
we've just left—" "those around us—" "this city—" "how we've lived,"
"is his body'" "A woman" "then picked him up" "& folded him," "his
cloth-like body," "till he was" "a small square shape" "Then she

laid him" "aside" "'Must we continue" "to live in" "this corpse of him?'"
"a man asked" "'We can change it," "of course," "someone said,"
"'but the earth, all life here" "is structured on," "conducted through,"
"the medium" "of corpses," "remains of corpses" "Very little"

"that is real" "just vanishes" "when it dies...'" "'But can't we make"
"something new now...'" "another" "began" "I left them" "& sat down"
"on a curb" "beneath a tree" "to rest & watch awhile," "rest & watch"
"I saw those from" "above the ground" "Their clothes had" "become

unwoven" "They stood half-naked" "here & there," "forms to which"
"thread clung" "like hanks of corn silk" "But they had also"
"lost their voices," "most of their" "vocal powers—" "they whispered"
"to each other" "& retreated" "to the periphery" "of" "the growing

throng" "of those who came from below the ground" "And many" "who
emerged" "into the daylight" "then took shovels," "picks & shovels"
"& began to dig" "holes in the ground" "In places" "the surface"
"of the earth broke" "spontaneously" "Cracked & parted:" "all the

lost creatures" "began to" "emerge" "Come up from" "below the subway"
"From the caves &" "from the dark woods" "I had visited" "they emerged"
"I watched through" "tears of clarity" "many" "forms of being"
"I had never" "seen before" "come to join us" "or come to join us

once more" "Whatever," "whoever," "could be," "was possible," "or
had been" "forgotten" "for long ages" "now joined us," "now
joined us once more" "Came to light" "that morning"

Sophia Scarlett

A Historical Romance

by

Douglas Oliver

**Dedicated in the hope of amendment to any
prig-rats, of whatever religion or sect and
wherever they may be, who make of
their metaphysical beliefs
a cause for enmity**

Note: Sir John Cochrane is only half out of history, the rest of his character being coloured in from 'fancy's paintbox'; so may his shade forgive any distortion by a novelist who doesn't like the aristocracy all that much as an institution. Isabel Harvey's name combines those of two Covenanter martyrs, Isabel Allison and Marion Harvey, who faced execution with a bravery that matches hers.

Editorial Note

(Dr. Agnes Christmas (1947-1992) was born in Edinburgh and educated at Stirling University. She later became an itinerant university lecturer in Europe and the United States, latterly in New Orleans. After some early poetic collections, her books included: Outlaws: A Study of Physically Unusual Women in Literature, London: Macmillan, 1976 *(feminist critical theory);* RLS: The Years in Samoa, London: Macmillan, 1980 *(biography);* Derrida as Male Charlatan, New York: Privately printed, 1981 *(feminist critical theory); and* The S/he Cook: The Parrot Heroines of RLS, Tunbridge Wells, England: Academic Monograph Press, 1985. *Increasingly isolated academically, and awesome physically (six feet four inches tall), Dr. Christmas became clinically depressed in mid-life and hanged herself in the stair well of a Bournemouth, England, guest house. During this Bournemouth visit she was researching R.L. Stevenson's years in that town and paid several visits to Shelley Manor, now a municipal technical college, but owned in Stevenson's day by his friend, Sir Percy Shelley, son of the poet. The following manuscript, not entirely complete, was discovered by a custodian, Mr. Robert Keneally, in Shelley Manor in 1991, along with its Preface.)*

Preface

WHEN I am but sorry dust they may ask why I have created such an old-fashioned romance in the manner of Robert Louis Stevenson. Was I not, throughout my undistinguished career, a devoted follower of the avant-garde? Had I not begun with poems which deserved the accolade W.H. Auden gave to that founder of the modern French school, Mallarmé, who, like me, had too much to say, for:

> ... he could never quite
> Leave the paper white.

Then did I not strive to become a specialist in that Continental theory, according to which our consciousness is so language-like in its every move that we never know whether we make a book of the world or whether the world makes us its readers? And here am I now labouring in a neglected style, in a forgotten corner of history, aware that this novelette, devoid of interest for the smart modern public, will see light only in another small press edition.

For who cares nowadays about Scottish 17th century Christian history? Who, much, cares about Stevenson, half-outlawed by influential critics as a sexist and High Tory? Who cares for his famous artificialities of style, when we have such plain talk, such sophistication of narrative philosophy, of non-closure, of fragmentation, of parody, in our contemporary knapsacks?

Well, I have been an outlaw all my life because of my great size. Christianity? In Britain and America some 80% of people profess themselves Christian and seem prepared to cite those beliefs among their reasons for supporting wars. Scotland? Tell me of England or Ireland or America! But poor wee Scotland, so often torn by prig-rat quarrels, has seen its own history almost outlawed from modern consciousness. Yet, the miserable stories of Northern Ireland, of the U.S. white "backlash", and of the plummy securities of the English religious class system show that religion has still to be confronted — not in the sacredness of individuals' beliefs — but in the domination of churches and priests. Of all possible examples, the Scottish of the 17th century shows the issue at its most pointed: purity of the church or corruption of the state? Or some third attitude of mind, non-religious probably, free of all dogma, of all sacred books, of all religion as such, and truly liberal in its spirituality?

I have spun this tale out of two hints. The first is the evidence that at the time of his death in Samoa, in the South Pacific, Robert Louis Stevenson was planning a novel, *Sophia Scarlett*, of which nothing more than the briefest outline survives. It was to have had three central female characters and a hero who died mid-way through the story.

So we shall now have a pastiche? No. I have utter contempt for the modern Victorian pastiche — that nostalgia for genteel, class-ridden, patriarchal, religio-ohso!, patriotic pomposity. Instead, this will be a travesty, a calumny: I shall make RLS speak with the voice of a woman! My voice! And my characters shall speak, like his own characters, a hybrid Lallans that probably no-one ever spake.

The second hint is the only holograph I possess from Stevenson's hand, a letter whose authenticity some of my male academic colleagues have doubted. It's a letter to *The Times* newspaper but was evidently never sent:

                                      Skerryvore,
                                      Bournemouth

                                      18th November, 1886

Sir,

"Right" is a sacred term notorious for its misuse; and yet surely we may talk pleasantly of a right to create one's own legend, providing the life lived be sufficiently prodigious? The lady known among her own river and dockyard people of Lothian as Miss Christmas Bessie Queensferry has certainly earned her legend, as I may put to your readers' judgment.

What man, six feet eight inches tall in stockinged feet; what man, tougher, more foul-mouthed than the foulest stevedore, able to carry a cask of flour under each arm while balancing another on the head, holder of the record for unloading sugar bags from ships docked at the Port of Leith, capable of towing heavy barges effortlessly upstream along 17th century river banks, cock of the walk among the roughest class of person and able to thrash any plaid-cloathed bully, male or female, throughout south-eastern Scotland, renowned for an awesome necklace which bore one bead for every ear or nose chawed off, with two beads, and I almost fear to write this, for every eye gouged out — and that includes but those ears, noses and eyes of the male sex —; what man, I say, would be denied his legend?

Evidently, Miss Queensferry's history comes to us coloured by myth. But I am an old trafficker in stories; I know how important are the brighter pigments in fancy's paintbox; and I would hold my pen like a lurid brush could I serve her memory the better.

Three months ago a "delegation" of two Leith stevedores and their wives, touchingly dressed as for Sunday service, journeyed long from their native haunts to seek out "the author" at his residence in Bournemouth Bay; and most modestly they requested that I compose an inscription for a stone obelisk in memory of Miss Queensferry. My new friends, staunch in the old Covenanting traditions, knew of a history of the Pentland Rising that was one of my earliest sorties into the Scottish history; and so, unjustly as may be, thought me fit to write the paean to a heroine of their faith.

Now Miss Queensferry was no Covenanter herself, but, as I have related, a fighting-rough ferry woman in the Firth of Forth during those religious wars in Scotland brought so cruelly on by the policies of Charles II, his bishops and ministers. This female bargee, because she hated King Charles and admired courage and patriotism, would give clandestine convoy to Holland for Covenanters, who were defined as traitors purely for believing that Christ alone, and not King Charles, bore the True Kirk's crown.

I promised to look into the matter. Their fund-raising committee informed a London journalist; he inquired an opinion of a retired Minister of the Church of Scotland; who thereupon wrote to you, Sir; certain Edinburgh authorities took ware; and I found myself at the centre of a public row in which churchman and official alike impeached Miss Queensferry's morality and that of her faithful commemorators. It seems that the boat on which she lived — of which one spar resides in a Glasgow museum — was in its own time a resort for sailors of loose life. Permission for the monument was refused.

No more doughty a defender of the public good arose than that retired minister of my own sect, the Reverend Angus Abercrombie, late of St. Andrew's-in-Mussleton, by Tarbolton, Ayrshire, now of Bournemouth, a clergyman who, I understand from diligent inquiries, is five

feet seven inches tall. He must stand on tiptoe to reach the height of moral indignation shown in his letter of August 4th to your journal, from which I draw the following citation:
> To erect a tablet, even a pagan obelisk, to a reprehensible and violent whore, who ever lived outside the civilised pale and who traitorously offended all moral, religious and political scruple, etc.

Leaving aside the considerable hint of religious bigotry, has Mr. Abercrombie adequately considered from his safe place in the bosom of conformity what it means to be a rude, uncultured, unlettered woman six feet eight inches tall? Cannot he understand that her size alone placed Miss Queensferry "outside the civilised pale"? To be a social pariah, the butt of jokes, the target of lawless desperadoes -- can any of us know what that means?

No-one can condone violence or the bawdy house, but my researches show me a woman of crude understanding, bereft of guidance from infancy, but one prepared to risk life on behalf of the persecuted. She was a Penthesilia, Queen of Amazons: another fiction. Can the obdurately self-righteous Edinburgh authorities not learn that a story is but a story, that an old religious quarrel may be laid to rest, that an illiterate giantess has the right to her legend; and that courage deserves its obelisk?

I bought this document when it appeared at Sotheby's quite simply because it made me cry to see a name similar to my own in such a context. Here was my archest of arch enemies — the gallant, the false-heroic, the pompous-moral, the patriotic exiled Scotsman Robert Louis, the novelist who died before he ever quite learnt to draw a woman true, RLS the agnostic, the quasi-religious prig-rat, the sitter-on-both-sides of Scottish politics — appearing at his most noble. Had he not possessed nobility he would not be a worthy enemy. This is the Stevenson, bourgeois to his very shoe soles, who could yet share an infected man's cigarette in a forgotten South Seas leper colony because he hadn't the heart to refuse; this the man who loved "all classes" but could never make a *heroine* out of the lower ones. And now he had given me my opening. Here he stood in defence of a working-class, sexually impure, politically active, *grotesque woman* (I myself have been called *grotesque* by my enemies). Could I not borrow a little the Stevensonian voice (not too much) and make it my own; that is, force RLS, that genteel Edin-burgher to rub his nose in the female sex organ, in shit, in witchcraft, in lower class, female honour? Call my story, *Sophia Scarlett*, or call it by another Stevenson title, *The Story of a Lie*. If he wants three women, let me give him them; if he wants a moribund hero, let me model that hero after himself, RLS — let him play the flageolet, make up poems, wear a blanket with a hole for his head. Call this hero Percy after Stevenson's aristocratic Bournemouth friend, Sir Percy, son of all those socialists and women's righters and of the great poet, and make this RLS-hero die off halfway through. Let him leave the battlefield, and then I'll change the narrative and give the martyrdom to my three glorious women, one of them a giantess!

When RLS was a young smout and writing to his "mother", his "friend", Mrs. Sitwell, he would dream of coupling with a mountainous woman like the monstrous females on the Parthenon frieze in the British Museum.

And that part of me which is not scholar adds: "Well, I love thee a little too, Louis, though I think ye wud have had a little PE (premature ejaculation) had *we* lain thegither ane time, so awed ye wud have been by Agnes Christmas!"

When I was young, I was *seduced* by Frenchified feminism and would write my criticism with those awful punning titles, *The S/he Cook* and so on. And I used to think that massive as my own body is, there could be nothing but a phantom "self" residing within — the thought used to comfort me. Now I *know* that self because I have *seen* it, just as surely as Stevenson saw his:

> So, to the man, his own central self fades and grows clear again amid the tumult of his senses, like a revolving Pharos in the night. It is forgotten; it is hid, it seems, for ever; and yet in the next calm hour he shall behold himself once more, shining and unmoved among changes and storm.

Big as I am, misfortunate as I am, my central self is yet more huge and, though I canna see it, I must believe that it is happy, will be happy. Robert Louis, I ask thee, I ask thee beyond the grave:

"D'you think Heaven sends back women who are too tall?"

He answers me: "Surely they want their angels as big as possible."

"That's very kindly meant, RLS. One day I might just go and ask for my wings, as there seem no kindly friends on earth but your books. And they are my enemy. Here is my final message to the world:

"From a woman too tall to be an angel."

CHAPTER I

Orphan in the Stooks

AT the criminal court, one Bessie, quondam sirnamed Queensferry, is sentenced to be hanged, for strangling a child born by another, in adultery, and for other notorieties. Item, three other women are condemned for the same crime commited by them on their bastards; which sentences were accordingly put to execution on the 25 of January, thereafter, on them. As also two other women were hanged for their opinions and principles, disowning the king and the government, and adhering to Cameron's treasonable Declaration. They called the one of them Isabel Harvey, from Lanark, and the other Sophia a-Sop, so-sirnamed Scarlett, foundling, from Tarbolton.

So reads Fountainhall's *Historical Notices*, vol. 1., p. 288. And a few lines are found in the private papers of Sir George Mackenzie (the "Bluidy Mackenzie"), Lord Advocate:

It was said by one James Robinson, of North Queensferry, that Sophia Scarlett, prisoner, was discovered, a bratty bairn, lying by the oat stooks in her native township of Tarbolton; and, further, that Andrew Hood, farmer in the vicinity of Ba'al's Hill in that parish, did take her in and nurture her until those evil days when, woefully instructed by Phanatic pastors, she evaded the circle of those who loved her in conformity and holiness, and began her dissolute and wandering life, tainted by unfounded suspicion of Witchcraft.

Were your historian Mr. Henry Fielding, who indeed loved another Sophia, you should be served up piping hot with this orphan mid the stooks and with a late-minute revelation that she was of genteel origin; but we shall not exceed our documents; what we have mostly on record of Sophia is her prison "testimony", which was not written in fully sound mind; other Scottish family papers supplement what mental distress leaves out. Her name, we are told in Hood family lore, derived from "a-Sop": that is, "in the straw". As for "Scarlett", it will become a question whether such an appellation was well deserved. Low-laid in the stubble at birth, Sophia never rose much higher in a narrow-minded society's estimation; and yet, though the story is set mainly among the lowly — for such the majority of the Covenanters were —, and *though I must consider matters of greater salacity than have before sullied my pen-tip*, I wager that by the end we shall admit to the high moral tone of her adventures.

In those 17th century times, before the death of that oversubtle Stuart, Charles the Second, the Hoods of Tarbolton were a minor branch of a greater family; they were but yeomen and farmers, and yet of long standing in their clachan. "There were Hoods in Tarbolton long before there were Boswells in Auchinleck," went the family saw. We find in the Ayrshire county records a farm in the parish of Stair called Hoodston and a group of houses on a Hoodshill in the parish of Tarbolton. This is the pagan mount mentioned by "Bluidy Mackenzie" as Ba'als Hill; it was legendary for Druidic rites and, in Sophia's time, surrounded by bogs. The name changed from the pagan poetry to the prose of Hoodshill when an 18th century schoolmaster, John Hood, rented it as a playground for children.

Farmer Hood, Sophia's foster father, would boast that his family derived from a brother of the famous outlaw, Robin, a brother who fled to Scotland. Lately, Mr. Hunter has shown Robin Hood's king to have been Edward the Second, not Richard the First of the later ballads. As Robin's feudal lord was the Earl of Lancaster, so not inconceivably when that restless noble unsuccessfully challenged Edward at Boroughbridge in 1322, Robin and his supposed brother, like others in the defeated Lancastrian army, would have been declared outlaws and would have forfeited their property to the Crown. Motive is complete: the egregious Robin forced to lurk in the forest, the mysterious brother flying north, probably to join the Bruce strongholds in Ayrshire. Well, these historical threads are slender; nevertheless, more than one armorial crest of Hood family collaterals bears a bow and arrow, a typical one from Honridge being superscribed with the motto *Olim sic erat* and subscribed with the legend, "Sherwoode".

Excursus over, we return to our 17th century. Andrew Hood's clachan, his county, in verity the whole of the South West, were fervid Covenanters in the time of Charles the Second; and during much of Sophia's childhood rapacious government troops invaded and quartered themselves on a populace judged by a Royalist Edinburgh Parliament to be no longer Scottish and patriot but mere weasely traitors. By "traitor" was meant one who denied the Royal Stuart authority over the True Church or Kirk.

Sympathiser Andrew Hood must have been, one who believed that truth lay in the Bible read by his unerring conscience over which Christ alone held sway. All round him in villages to the west, elected church ministers, dwelling in pristine New Testament equality, had bowed down in spiritual matters only to the divine Chieftain. Hood's forefathers had joined the great Edinburgh gatherings to resist the prayer book of that fierce primate, Laud. First, they had signed one Covenant; and later they signed another, as though God Himself could twice subscribe His name. Now, in the Stuart Restoration, Tarbolton villagers would have allowed the king all the *civil* power he wanted, yea and some would declare it divinely ordained if he must have it so; provided that he meddle not one whit in church affairs, nor seek to pack its administration with his time-serving bishops; all of which consorted ill with Charles's Hobbesian wish to control both his kingdom and his church.

That wish set poor Andrew into the toils of a civil war all the more dangerous because undeclared: Royalist Edinburgh authorities had judged him and his friends guilty just for their beliefs. In his South-West, Covenant ministers were ousted from their churches and illiterate opportunists pasted like cardboard figures into their pulpits. The Tarbolton minister, old John Guthrie, "left his parish in 1660 never to return"; ancient as he was, he became a religious outlaw, a religious Robin Hood if you will, flitting in secretly to serve the poor with spiritual comfort, preaching at conventicles held in field, byre, or darkened cottage. We learn of him again at Lanark in 1666, working upon the souls of the Covenanting party who suffered so calamitous a defeat in the Pentland Rising of that year.

See this little fostered girl, growing up a servant in the rough-hewn farmhouse on the Bogside, under the witchcraft hill of Ba'al, the cluster of clachan roofs below marking the edge of her world, and the kitchen and living room alike resounding with Bible citations. Further details of Sophia's infancy are lost, for the first pages of her own account are wasted away, from which raggy edges emerge the words, "... and so my troubles began that sad day my benefactor was roastid." An unaffected phrase; behind it perhaps horror lies; for the soldiers, given peremptory authority by the Edinburgh Council, had been extorting by threat or torture unconscionable fines from Tarbolton villagers who absented themselves from the Royalist churches or who harboured conventiclers; if, alas, Andrew was held over his own griddle until he squawked, it would but have added one nightmare more to history.

Let us suppose that a field preacher had held his forbidden conventicle on Andrew Hood's marshy farmland too little distance from the village to remain unobserved by ignominious local spies. There'd be the fracas on the hill as the troops invaded, Covenanters leaping over the heather, the soldier-rabble chasing them down into thick mud, the minister — perhaps Guthrie himself, certainly his old assistant Peden — escaping yet again from a raided prayer meeting, quick fumbles as besotted troopers grab a fleeing worshipper, a horse stuck knee-deep in the bog, the clamour gradually quietening, the sun going down on the bronzed hill, hollow blues and greys along the heather tops, a few prisoners hustled down the rough track to Ayr — all this lies outside the fencework of our story. We hear briefly the hoarse shouting of the farmer tortured over his kitchen fire, then that too dies out. The hill finally black; and, after an hour or two, along a shadowy footpath comes a rill of white petticoat flouncing under heavy plaids, as a dawdling maid emerges from the safety of the swamps, re-enters her village past the Hood farm cottage blazing with light where a rear-guard of soldiers swigs the carefully stored malt, fogging out of mind their worst deeds. There we have the Hoods ruined financially, or imprisoned, or executed — and, the heart fails, this 15-year-old Sophia cast out a second time on the mercy of the parish!

At first she sat by the market cross and looked gloomily at the manse on Burn Street, where the despised toady minister, Murdoch, had usurped Mr. Guthrie's honoured place. Having let the pump water trickle mud from her calves, she felt colder yet; so she sank down in the Cross Keys archway, sore wearied, her bare feet in cart ruts as she inspected some herbs she had gathered; yet be sure she wept her heart out for what she'd seen and for her maister and his family. She heard distant lowing of cows long called to the bye; the dark Sandgate was deserted, not a villager daring to stir between the crooked shambles of cottages: oh, her nation's religious quarrel seemed a grievesome weight around the neck of a 15-year-old servant lassie fast bogged in her ane trochle.

Dozing, she only half-heard the burst of chatter that signalled one leaving the inn, but a polished boot nudged her gently awake, and a captain of troopers — his footgear evidently burnished after the day's work — stared down at her; she gazed back into the enemy face above his own plaid, framed by the black wig of an Edinburgh Parliament man, a king's man, a Malignant as her unfortunate protector had still called them. The face was wise with soldier experience, sly, almost whimsical with cruelties committed.

"Hoot! We've been hearing your greetin' these two hours — fair spoilt ma punch. Now I'd hope ye'd be one who attends her church like a good lassie?"

Though this was neutral in intention, Sophia imagined it to be fraught with traps; here was, if not the instigator, at least the tolerator of farmer Hood's tortures.

"I suppose I'd be the foolest girl to tell't tae ye."

"Ha! Mettled like ma Black Robbie! And ye'll know of penalties for your maister if his servant lassie's no too guid behaved?"

"I wouldna ken where ma maister may be," she replied hotly.

"An' which is he?"

"'Twas Mr. Hood, an honest proprietor, always at praising the Maker."

"Sorrow to his thank, then. Now, don't open your mouth or a troot may jump oot. A bonny lass like you must have a care — Humph!"

With a quick movement, the captain lifted from Sophia's hair a scarf in bright yellow tartan and examined her face. Who can presume to know whether masculine taste for feminine beauty has changed after two centuries: whether a saucy expression and a sturdy ankle fringed with ginger down and stuck out nakedly from muddy woollen plaid would attract the eye *then* any less than a silk-clad ankle immodestly glimpsed under a brocaded ballgown might *now*? Even at her age, Sophia sensed the man grow lustful and the interview become dangerous.

Something caught in the captain's voice and he said gruffly, "Now get you on your solid legs. We have a pony you mun ride, for you're coming wi' us this nicht."

Sophia, thinking herself arrested when in reality she had been appropriated, dropped her herbs, shut her mouth like a salmon and stumbled beside the captain's broad bulk as he re-entered the inn yard; she could discern over the low stone wall a few troopers, still carousing as they saddled up in the back field.

CHAPTER II

The Scarlet Apple

"CAPTAIN Glenmuir." Not a loud voice but a confident one; not an order, but a cultured remark, which caused the soldier to mutter, "Deil a fear", yet turn as if to a command.

Dimly outlined in the archway, a broad-shouldered but ill-shaped Scots gentleman stood looking after them.

"Why, Sir John, what is a member of the noble House of Cochrane doing abroad on such a woefully misbegotten day?" said the captain, a grimace making noticeable a scar which dragged at his nether lip.

Like a boy caught at the parlour jam, he relinquished a hold that he had taken of young Sophia's person.

"I have been visiting my good neighbour, Blacklock of Enterkin, who as you'll recall, Captain, is chief proprietor here in Tarbolton and has his away house over yonder behind the kirk."

Never a step could that captain take but he must deal with Ayrshire's feudal loyalties. Old William Cochrane had been fined by Cromwell himself for loyalty to the Stuarts; after 1660, a grateful Charles appointed William Privy Councillor, a Treasury commissioner, and Earl of Dundonald. This present Cochrane was Sir John, his second son, who lived at Ochiltree close by Tarbolton, and was friendly with Mr. Matthew — the chief Blacklock — who owned half of Sophia's village and was suspected at Court, like most of the Ayrshire gentry, for Covenanting sympathies; and on this knowledge the captain drew for small shot.

"Then Mr. Blacklock has, unwittingly I am convinced, harboured a neist of traitors, couching like partridges in the bogs beyond."

"You have your duty, Captain; but you may concede that it need not extend so far as to snatch up the meek chicks scarce out of the eggshell."

In the dark, the captain squeezed Sophia a horrid instant, then nudged her aside and chuckled sarcastically:

"It's a mercy, divine-like as ye will Sir, that we chance upon sae Godfearing a laird as yrsel', when here's me wondering what to do with yon backsitter in the neist."

The laird came forward then and his hand took that of Sophia's strongly, so that she felt a child again rather than a woman lustfully desired.

"The Lord will find a berth for this one right enough, Captain Glenmuir. Now you have a troop to look to; and, since the word 'mercy' rolls in your mouth like a marble, may you ride with ilka virtues."

"God save His Majesty," retorted the disgruntled Captain, turning to join his troopers.

"May the Divine Maker take His good care of that indeed," came behind his back.

So it fell out that Sir John Cochrane made an enemy in the King's camp and Sophia stepped into the austere protection of the gran' folk who, though out of power at Court, in their own world still exercised a baronial importance. While she walks hand in hand with the laird as if they had been young lovers after all, and before she starts her adventures, we have a moment to take a closer geek at this young heroine.

She was the green bud which, kept in its pot amid the granite corners of Farmer Hood's high-principled kindness, waited to blossom in the sunlight of warmer affections; and nevertheless that bud had felt strained to bursting at the ripening to come; but now, uprooted by the hand of civil discord, she knew not whether she would be discarded carelessly by her temporary protector or taken as a servant into a noble family with many estates. The one moment she felt the ambition of that latter prospect like a hard knot in her mind; and with the next moment came a bleaker fear of being adopted by the king's more prominent enemies. Then she recalled to herself the red flames of her hair, the freckles on her cheek and the scornful blue eyes; she knew herself to have a power. So came a harsher thought: she would bloom whatever they tried to do to her.

"To my binifactors, Mr. Hode and Mr. M'Fail, I ow all rivirince and loyaltie, but to Cockranes and Blacklockes in this earth I ow loyaltie only. They niver did naught with me except for thyr pride and skemes."

Her spirit lies well disclosed in her wretched prison testimony.

Sir John's ugliness was a little proverbial among the villagers, but he inclined his dark and damaged features in a considerate way and regarded her feet stumbling in sodden ruts.

"Are ye the one they call a-Sop?"

"Some folks do and some folks have nae sense," she retorted, looking keenly into the murk where low buildings of the Blacklock residence gathered behind the kirk.

"And do ye always lack your shoon?"

"Ma feet walk nakedly aboot wi' me on their ane business."

"Then you have mettle, as the captain observes, for I overheard you both from the beginning. As yet, you require the bridle of good manners and the bit of devotion. He who rides the cross may yet choose to ride thee."

Unsure whether this was Biblical, she withdrew her hand from the laird's grasp but let him lead her, tired enough for slaughter, into the low-ceilinged Laiche Hall of Blacklock's place.

By midnight, still unfed, she was lying on a straw pallet in an outhouse amid the musty rashes-o, while all around breathed other female servants. At three o'clock she waked when a cow mooed close by; and she lay listening to the sea wind blowing inland long miles to crack and swash through the elms and yews around the church; a little owl skeeted; her mind was full of frightful phantoms, recently real: the benefactor tortured; a man's whole arm slashed bloody from his shoulder; heads thwacked half open with gun butts; and, somehow the most fixed image, a soldier's horse urged on, foaming red at the mouth as the bog sucked at its hocks; it had been stuck through the lugs with a hoe. In her anguish and hunger, she rose and brushed her hand along the great Cromwellian sideboard that lined the wall, finding there an apple which she carried back to bed; she realised only the following morning that she had swallowed a worm beside.

By 5 a.m. the martial tuck of the village drum prompted the groans of reveille in the outhouse: in autumnal darkness, the women rose on all sides as if from graves, chatting solemnly and shivering as they put outer garments on over their shifts. A stout wifey with hair flat as lampblack under her lace cap hoisted her hips like moving a table and crossed to the great sideboard to light a candle in its stick, muttering over the flint while Sophia hid behind her elders and wondered at the extravagance. The woman bent and, below the long shelf, unhinged both ground-level cupboard doors by a quick movement that indicated they had been specially designed; a fair-haired man dressed in sleeveless leather jerkin was discovered lying inside the lower space from which interior walls and shelves had been removed. He snaked his way round the central door post, dusted himself down, and with a fierce look acknowledged the gasps of some uninitiated servants as he stood upright. It was their minister of the day before at the conventicle, the celebrated Alexander Peden.

"The Lord has aye a place for dishes and aye a place for auld Sandy," he chuckled, gazing round as if to receive applause.

"Ye look a bonny labourer, Sir," said the stout woman.

And truth the man was in his prime, lean and muscular: with an alert expression, a mouth permanently pursed into smiles, a bitterly-weathered face garish in candlelight, dominated by eyebrows darker than his hair. He, who had just arisen from being the bruised worm to being their shepherd, replied sententiously, "Ah weel, Jessie, is the shepherd not just the labourer?"

As if sensing he could outstage himself, he raised his arms dramatically.

"There be those who have got up a fashion of professing Christ, and they sit closely in favor with the corrupted; and there be those whose houses be bare and ill-provided; and yet Christ visiteth them with His riches. Let us pray, sistern."

The hoarse voice of the hunted preacher rang out fearless as the candlelight flickered over his face: "Oh dearest and Divine Master, hear the voice of auld Sandy whom again Thou hast delivered from Thine enemies as he prays for the servants of this devout household who also are Thy servants. Though we may think our cupboards and hidey-holes be barer and harder than we looked for, assure us daily that Christ minds only to diet us for the good of our souls while yet He feeds our hungers.

"We have loved ones whom Thou has suffered to lie down in the heather, their tongues now gone cold in their mouths; and Thou knowest that Thou has drawn their souls to Thy bosom and warmeth them even this moment; so that those tongues speak miracles to us, prophesying the sufferings we must yet endure until this our homeland shall be a beacon of blessed religion to the world. Others of Thy servants huddle close together in the prisons of the ungodly and no-one save Thou yet knows their fate. Give us all courage to succour the afflicted in this unceasing fight and to bear Thy banner onwards. Amen."

As he drew out the Amen, Jessica, the stout woman, sighed deeply as if the sounds came from between the ribs of her tight bodice, for the soldiers had taken her own cousin the previous day.

The preacher snapped out. "But whaur's ma apple?"

Sophia, who until then had stared fascinated at the fabled hill preacher standing alive, so to speak, in this servants' bedroom, now sidled closer to the wall: Mr. Peden's pious theatricality threatened to involve her, a newcomer anxious to make the best impression, in a public process all the worse for being so trivial. But the preacher's professional eye for guilt picked her up immediately.

"Come forward, lassie," he said.

While Sir John Cochrane, a noble close to the Scottish Privy Council, had failed to dash her, that morning she had to brave the eye of God peeking out under the bushy eyebrows of Peden — Tarbolton's most famous fugitive. And she blurted out her confession as hastily as could be.

"I hadnae tae eat yesterday: I found it in the night, so much I was hungered. I didnae thunk onywan wud fash themsel's ower a wee pipkin that I found in the dark."

Her shoulder was gripped eagle-hard as the minister, who smelt rank and heathery beside her, steadied her before him.

"Ye'll no be makin' licht o' a theft, I imagine, lass? Was it not Eve herself wha made licht o' sich hasty pilferin?"

To Sophia's hot honesty there seemed such disparity between the suffering she had witnessed the day before and this peevish fussing that she spoke without thinking:

"Eve wasnae hungered. I'd gi ye *ma* apple if ye were hungered."

Audibly, the other servants drew breath at this insolence to the man of God and a pretty housemaid, Mary, called out in a shocked voice: "'An' she took of the fruit thereof, and did eat' — and wasnae Eve an hungered to be sinnin', Mr. Peden?"

Mr. Peden quelled the maid with a frown and a gesture, though Sophia observed his eye winking with gratitude.

"Ach! Let no-one say auld Sandy will grudge an apple," he said with oily kindness.

She relaxed a little under his grip but was deceived because he suddenly went rigid and silent, as if aghast at some inner thought. A time passed, then he raised his right hand as if for a holy oath and shut his eyes.

"Lord, my eyes are dimmed in Thy sight, and yet Thou givest glimmerings. I fear, I fear, one day this unhappy lass must be put from this house lest she be a stain to the family, though I see not the cause and must hope it will be a mickle sin, e'en as this apple, being but an earthly fruiting and not that which burgeoned in Paradise, stood not in thy direst prohibition."

Half of these words flowed over Sophia's untutored understanding, yet it seemed a great deal to pay for an apple; she flared round at her fellow-servants to see who could be taking the minister's prophecy seriously. Her overture was refused with prayerful nods. Peden opened his eyes, turned her again towards him, and looked benevolently upon her as if he had just rescued her soul instead of wrecked her reception in that house.

"How do they call thee, child?"

"Sophia. Sophia a-Sop," she said angrily.

At the anger, his canny eye glistened and his lips pressed into smiles. "A-Sop? An' baby Moses was found in the rashes. Weel, I shall call thee Sophia Scarlett, on account of ma scarlet apple that ye have so unjustly swallowed, an' we'll spell ye wi' a double 't' just to *tease* ye. Now go and take no more the fruit from the mouth of the godly who are hunted aye in their caves and by *you*, Sophia Scarlett, in their cupboards."

He gave her a little push to join the others, swept his smiles all around to answering laughter, and left. ("I cannae doot," thought Sophia, "he's off to report to the Blacklocks and ruin ma reputation some mair.")

Saving stout Jessie, the others went directly to their tasks in kitchen, barn, and byre; no time was wasted on mere washing of the person, or on greeting Sophia except with those nods; and to say truth it did not seem a merry household. Under the smear of black hair, Jessie's expression held a resigned pity.

"I doan't noo what the gran' folks will say to this," she said with the ponderous sigh.

"But what he says cannae be true," retorted Sophia, herself fearful, for that age's superstition made her wonder if she had not just faced the foreknowledge of God.

"Now just sit ye doon on your bed, lass, and I'll tell ye about Mr. Peden and his divine gift of prophecy and ye'll ken better why folks may take this so truth-like an' why it's skaith tae yoursel'."

CHAPTER III

Jessie's Tale of the Prophet

LEANING back against the sideboard, the housekeeper found a *point d'appui* and her body subsided around that point. Twenty years previously, she said — in terms which we shall adapt to our narrative — Alexander Peden had been a young callant from college, arrived in Tarbolton to be schoolmaster, precenter, and session-clerk to Mr. John Guthrie, the same minister who was eventually outed. Now, a village girl lay adulterously with a servant in the house where the young cleric was staying; when pregnancy followed, said some of the gossips, the serving-man fled to Ireland with this parting shot: "Father it on young Mr. Peden: he'll better provide."

On the very day Peden went to the Presbytery to get his minister's licence, the woman slipped ahead and accused him to the Moderator. Peden replied: "I am well surprised, I cannae speak; but let nane entertain ilka ill thocht of me, for I am utterly free of it, and God will vindicate me in His own time and way." ("It was something that way of it — I didnae come to Tarbolton until some years later," added Jessie.) Peden walked beside the Water of Fail upwards of twenty-four hours and would neither eat nor drink, but when the Holy Spirit finally answered, said: "I hae got what I was seeking, and I *wull* be vindicated, and that poor unhappy lass will pay dear for it while yet she lives, and will make a dismal, dismal end; and for this surfeit of grief that she hath given me, there shall never a wan of her ane sex come into my bosom." And thus he never married.

Sophia, for whom such a man's word should be crystal truth, cried out: "And what for consequence?"

"Some say, some say, and some say," said Jessie judiciously. "Some say, Mr. Guthrie speired the wicked whore on the stool of repentance tae announce who had fathered the bairn, and discharged her from his employ for tae be helpfu' to her. Others say she dwelt faithless in her obstinacy. Some say, Mr. Peden was excommunicated. Oor shepherd, Dickie, who blethers to hisself as he goes aboot his sheep, tell't me that Mr. Guthrie stood up wan day to give the congregation account of the sorry sin, and the father had returned repuntant frae Ireland, and confessed in church crying like the bairn to be born: though that seems too guid t' be true. Howsomeeever, certain it is that after she was married tae that servant — I dinnae ken where — everything went cross to them; and they journeyed from place to place like tinkers withouten wares, and were reduced to great paverty. I was here myself that day when she came to the Water where Mr. Peden had prayed so lang; an' there she made awa' wi' hersel'."

Her own telling made Jessie a little tearful. Had Sophia not been so barbarously prophesied against by Mr. Peden, perhaps she would also have swallowed down the story sentimental-whole and not wondered whether, in that lassie's worst of despairs, there were not at least two explanations why she had flung herself to drown just where the saintly man had prayed so long.

The feared summons to the sprawling Blacklock halls never came: Mr. Peden vanished as suddenly as he had appeared, leaving his prophecy behind like a miasma to infect Sophia's growth to womanhood. Owing to her bodily vigour, she was appointed dairymaid. The Blacklocks spent only the summer in their Tarbolton residence, and that first summer Mrs. Blacklock was away tending her ailing mother-in-law at Enterkinfoot, and her husband, a lawyer, had much business in Ayr and Edinburgh; this left the redoubtable Mrs. Mauchline to rule indoors; the milder Jessie outdoors; and Sophia thus fell under the milder yoke. Slopping about in second-hand shifts and crude-cut shoes, she bowed under many an admonition to mind her ps and qs "Miss *Scarlett*"; and sedulously did she cultivate a demure step and righteous comportment — when her very being sprang with energy and her blue eyes flamed at every unearned reproof: should she just peer into a water bucket to straighten a lock of hair, some fellow domestic would hiss disapproval, all on account of the prophecy. In loneliness, she carried herself so reverent-solemn that sometimes within she felt fit to bust at the thought of herself; and other times she felt herself slipping body and soul into this other solemn person she had made of herself; and would draw back well-nigh panting with fear.

Jessie gave her that minimum needed for a warm heart's affection: a complacent, fatty grin, a kindly shoulder-clap when she had tended a calf shining fresh from the womb. Darker in mind was the whipping administered by Mrs. Mauchline when, from an upper window, the toady housemaid, Mary, spotted Sophia dancing on her leelane behind an oat-field hedge: Sabbath, but the reveller had thought herself hidden. Mrs. Mauchline, her crinkled brow perspiring with her cruelties, muttered as she wielded the taws: "It's no for y'r ain sake; nae dootin' that's past perdition; but the reputation o' the hoose in such peerilous times!" That night, the lass lay shocked and shivering in the outhouse and fell prey to wildness in her thinking, since she could draw comfort from no coherent centre in her orphan upbringing.

Poor Sophia laboured to redeem her stolen reputation, but many a time she leant her head for warmth against the heaving flank of a milch cow and repented she knew not what.

About this time was declared an "Indulgence", when the King's government would double or treble up formerly outed ministers into vacant parishes, although the stricter Covenanters viewed such conformers as trifling with the Gospel itself. Ah well, it was but a respite, a salving of Scotland's wounds with ineffectual balm. But Tarbolton already had a despised placeman, the half-educated, half-English, blabbing lump, Reverend Murdoch, living in his manse cheek by jowl with the stern Blacklocks. He was so full of self-love he would weep publicly, sometimes, at his own *soi-disant* eloquence.

A famous Scots anecdote was also told of Murdoch, that one day, short of a sermon for his Sunday, he found a manuscript, a little eaten away, that the previous incumbent, Mr. Guthrie, had left in the attic. Murdoch rose in the pulpit, smacked his fat lips, and began, "Eh... I'm just going to begin where the rats have left off." True or not, ascription of the anecdote shows the woeful image that Murdoch left in village memory.

One problem the indulged minister had: he could never get his tithe corn ground peaceably. Stoddie, the miller, like a good Ayrshire man o' business, was willing right enough, but once the stones were churning the Murdoch grains some malicious prankster would surely drop by and there'd be "a accident": a flour bag contaminated with earth, a leaky or a spilt sack. In desperation, Stoddie would leave the water cock on after work and the unpopular cleric would sneak in at night along with his man to grind and bag; and the clopping of his mule loaded with a boll of meal would be ignored by the nightguard of soldiers.

Sophia regarded such ironies as a distraction from a severe life. As a mere dairymaid, she was barred from sunning herself among the old-fashioned bankside gardens of the Blacklock mansion but, left to herself in the poultry yard or dairy, or bouncing on the sledge of sheaves after the hay harvest, she could never quite restrain a natural vivacity; she would sing a romantic village catch, and seeing the frozen looks of her Covenanter colleagues she would sing out louder yet, clutching for luck a forbidden amulet an old village witch-woman had given her:

Ma gudeman hadnae hame nor plow
  Sae tae the wars he rode.
He met an army in a howe
  And in that howe abode.

There were pleasures to sing about too. The dour Blacklocks gave three annual entertainments, the first for their own grade, the second for their tenant farmers, and the third for villagers; at the last of these, Sophia could dance and sing. Or, when the household gathered round the spinning wheels for a "rocking', she displayed a talent for story-telling equal, some thought, to Jessie's own. Or evenings, she could stroll before milking under the willows by the water of Fail while the curlew wailed and peewits flashed black and white across the darkening marshlands; and she would search out plants the witch-woman had told her about. Or the better class of beggars, received out of Christian devotion by the laird and lady, would bring news, ballads, and cattle cures which they would relay from their night's lodgment in the barn. What with "ane thing and the ither", Sophia was warming her climate by her uncertain inner sun.

Her first friend was the farm "gyte" or brat, Donald, whose talent was for poaching the fish out of the laird's burn and snaring his hares with fiddle wire, afterwards selling his catch to the locals. Other friendships followed, but one critic she seemed unable to conquer. Suspect not that the housemaid, Mary, fell jealous at the dairymaid's robust good looks; for Mary had a pallid, vulnerable fairness that often charms men; fresh adornments and sinuous lightness of step added to her attractions; and the stablehands were mostly in love with her. With Sophia they merely had *jokes*. To the admiration she excited, Mary returned an expression of sallow devotion as if to Higher commands; thus links were added to her lovers' chains, increasing their distance but not unlocking their enslavement. A kind of jealousy there is, nonetheless, most fierce against anyone non-conforming to the group of which oneself is the cynosure. So Mary, profiting from closeness to the black-clothed, beetle-browed Mrs. Mauchline, did her best to put Sophia to the outer bounds of farm life or, on occasion, draw her under the lash of the taws, as if the housemaid's respect for Mr. Peden justified hurrying onwards Sophia's prophesied expulsion.

The throstle sang blithe in the orchard blossom one sparkling morning when a low cart hauled by two strong piebald mares creaked into the yard and drew up alongside Sir John Cochrane's glossy stallion, for Cochrane was making one of his frequent visits to his neighbour. The carter, John Brown, was known shire-wide — a stocky, quiffed, Bible-spouting humourist who this day bore a pair of fine chairs and some bales of cloth to the household from a sale of effects in Carrick. Sophia helped him with the chairs to the laiche hall and saw to her consternation that they were royalist chairs with the queen's monogram "C" on the leg struts. (During the persecution, many a Covenanting family would keep their loyal chairs downstairs in their bare halls and reserve their writing desks with hidden drawers to the backest of back rooms upstairs.) The owl-eyed, bewigged figure of Mr. Matthew Blacklock, Sir John Cochrane beside him, almost made a leg at the carter; with the same unusual courtesy, Blacklock himself sent Sophia for Brown's refreshment. The laird, not notable for generosity, began arguing expenses *sotto voce* with the carter, while Cochrane lent an amused ear. Mrs. Mauchline called for Mary to dust the chairs so that their value could be estimated and the housemaid overheard a few words of the laird's conversation: "Peden... hiding place... escape", no doubt something like that. Finally, Mr. Blacklock announced himself loudly to be satisfied and said Brown could, for good measure, take away the old Cromwellian sideboard in the outhouse in hopes of selling it at some farmhouse; and getting that piece of furniture on the sturdy cart became a minor festival.

The same night, as Sophia was wearily washing her wooden buckets in the dairy, the lad, Donald, came in crying and crouched by her side. His clothing hung out little ragged flags all round him.

"I haddae skelping." He was bald-eyed with pain and fear and marks of the switch showed through the rents in his shirt.

"Then ye'll hae deserved it. Who from?"

"The laird hisself, all ower his trouties that ah've fished."

"Ye're the gyte and gytes get skelped. But ye'll no always be the gyte. Just wait two years and we'sl have ane ither gyte and ye con be ma man."

She reached to comfort the trembling bairn, but he drew away from any touch on his smarting body.

"It was stuffy-nosed Mary that tell't. An' she's worse than ony o' us."

"Awa'. Hush now."

"Ye just ask her Soph, why she meets wi' the Reverend Murdoch at midnight in the mill."

This was so improbable that Sophia nearly slapped him herself.

"Gang y'r ways. Don't be scandalous, bairn. Just think y'rsel' lucky ye're no auld eneuch tae be hangit for y'r thieving."

Now he gripped the girl's arm with a filthy hand: "She'll be grinding the minister's or somebody's corn at the mill this nicht. I heard her whusper those self-same words tae him in the Sandgate."

"Ye know not what y'r saying," said Sophia, now whispering herself and scrubbing her pail vigorously.

Eventually, she was able to send Donald, comforted, to bed; but she had begun to think hard. Here, it is necessary to understand the secret reputation of Brown the carter, whom she had seen the laird treat with unusual respect. In later years, Covenanters would call him the "Christian Carrier": under cloak of his employment, he bore messages from one group of the faithful to another, until that day when he was shot down by the king's lieutenant, the frightening Claverhouse, for refusing to take an oath of loyalty. Sir Walter has this story, out of Patrick Walker. Of Brown's true role, Sophia had an inkling; she had observed that before the previous year's savagely-interrupted field meeting, Brown had much carrying to do in her district; and... well, revenge may have sharpened her nose for scent — we are speaking of no saint... but she smelt treachery in Mary's behaviour.

CHAPTER IV

Treachery at Stoddie's Mill

SOLDIERS were still billeted on the village and curfew had long sounded when, at 10 p.m., Sophia stole from a room of sleeping servants, hissed at Cadger barking at the gate, and footed it stealthily down the path. She journeyed alongside the kirk's yews, round the village cross, towards the Ba'al Hill. And as she flitted along the underskirts of the mount, her mind relived the cries of her old benefactor from the slopes, cries become the more eerie in dark imaginings, and she skipped past the abandoned farm house rapidly. Two miles beyond the mount she found Stoddie's Mill — for Robert Burns later, the miller would be the celebrated "Willy"; at Miller Stoddie's epoch, its crude heather-thatched buildings of clay-mortared whit-stone lay hidden in a deciduous wood that encircled a river-bend.

Leaving the beeches behind her, she ducked under a stone wall by a dunghill; there she intended to await Mary or the minister. Discommoded by the reek, she looked round for alternative hiding-places; and her eye fell on the mill itself, an appendage to the house where Stoddie slept. Behind, on the damp river bank, she crouched by the horizontal water wheel as it churned round in the rush: Stoddie had left open the water gate for the Minister Murdoch's nocturnal usage: he would grind only small amounts at need. Old Hood had often taken Sophia to the mill as a second pair of eyes to make sure that the canny miller while sacking up filched no extra flour than his allowed thirlage. This memory set her to thinking that a placed minister such as Mr. Murdoch, profiting from enforced tithes, was in effect stealing his corn from her begrudging community: and a spark of mischief caught light in her.

The wheel, a venerable mechanism, was geared upwards to quern stones on a second floor just sufficiently raised for bagging operations below; and the bankside grass swelled against the wall outside, making it easy for the tallish girl to stand on tiptoe and pull herself through the open arch of the upper window. Sneezing in the shadowy quern room, she blew her nose on her yellow plaid head scarf, set it aside, looked around, and spotted the metal flour chute leading out from a boss under the two great round grinding stones. The chute, which delivered ground meal to the sacks underneath, proved to be on a swivel and she heaved it around until it poked out the back window which overlooked the river. She tightened it with all her strength. When the minister in the pitch-black room poured his barley into the quern-stones the chute, instead of filling his bag below with the flour, would embrown the river outside. But then he might notice.

On this second thought, she jumped down to the bagging room and found the water lever; by unscrewing its grip on its spindle and by pushing the spindle nearly through the wall, she made it probable that, when the minister tried to close the water-gate to save his flour, the spindle would, like that of a loose doorhandle, slip backwards into the mill-race. Chuckling, she climbed back out, and crouched, now more securely hidden, under the thickest bankside bush; there, she shivered and waited.

She heard a rider dismount at the front of the main house and tether his steed; from the jangling, he sounded to be a soldier; and that betokened considerable danger for Sophia, not just as a curfew-breaker but, from her situation, as suspected burglar or immoral woman. The soldier entered the bagging room on the other side of her sheltering wall. After an interval, came the softer pad of what turned out to be Mr. Murdoch's mule, and the minister entered the room to greet Sophia's old aggressor in whispers: "Glenmuir!"

"I am not inclined to condone the means," he continued, "but this is a business which may expose the king's enemies to you, Captain Glenmuir, thus redounding to your profit, while aye ridding me of some of the discomforts that have assailed my holy office."

The captain pierced this long-winded hypocrisy with a gruff: "Aye, and ye'll mean that ye'll get rid of y'r field rival, the traitorous Peden, while I'll gain a nifty sum of forfeitures and fines and may hae a moment or two of pleasure intae the bargain."

"Now what passes 'twixt you and Mary comes not within my ken. We have agreements, captain."

"Haith, man! An' there's just the twa of us here. I'm dazzling the lass wi' marriage or what seems like it, a loyal sort of breach of promise wouldn't ye think, for just an oat of truth an' a scamper in the barley sacks?"

"All dignities attach to the cloth, Captain: I'll not have it sullied by scandal. My only purpose is to win the villagers' hearts to my placement here, for the public peace depends on it."

"An' a holy deal of stipend."

"There's enough. I hear a low cooing and I mun hide to await my time of milling."

"Aye, while I hae mine the noo," the captain replied coarsely.

With surprising agility, the stout minister climbed out the window and crouched by the wall just up the bank from the bush behind which Sophia herself was installed; both of them heard the ensuing dialogue; but one of them in fear and chill had to stop her teeth from chattering; but one of them, *voyeur*, in his thick-throated lasciviousness, licked his lips.

Of what followed, Sophia's prison testimonial shows such abhorrence that only the words, "I sd nither hopid nor antisipatid that Marie sd fall so far fram grace", are set down. The gist of the conversation between housemaid and captain may be reconstructed. Mary's voice would have shaken, so different from her haughty tones to stable lads, and her body would have trembled like a hare entranced in its captivity. The captain would have promised her finery, a position in his camp, an end to drudgery, and apparent status as his wife; and Sophia would instantly have seen how much of policy had lain behind Mary's pious demeanour in the Blacklock mansion, since she now stood revealed as the informer who had brought the soldiers to the previous year's invaded field meeting and now again threatened her employers with treachery.

An interview with an unnamed farm labourer conducted later by Mr. Blacklock and stored in his family papers enables us to add a touch or two of salt but not of spice to this tale. As the captain tried to seduce the maid, she refused his offer for her to become a favoured military camp follower. Next, he proposed marriage; and this was accepted even at the cost of the present prologue to wedlock.

At that, the spy told what she knew.

"Everyone thocht the Reverend Peden had fled the Blacklocks the day after the field preaching. But he's been mostly hiding there, on an' off, ye ken; they have a secret panel I'll draw for ye."

A flint struck and eventually a light glimmered.

"Here the hall, and here the outback, and here the mantle, and here the lever," muttered the trembling voice of the maid.

"Well, and can we catch him?"

"Oh noo, nat here. The carter, John Brown, came this day — he kens naething perhaps — bot they laded him up wi' a gran' sideboard and the Reverend is surely hiding inside."

"In which direction do they go?"

"That I ken nat, but I think somewheres to Carrick, not 30 miles distant. They'll be travelling slow, surely, for the carter will have ither calls tae make."

"And is the carter a fanatic?"

"It is thocht nat," said Mary, perhaps in the vestige of her conscience willing to protect a less prominent Covenanter where no need presented itself. "It'll just be a job of carting but he may be surprised to discover his true load."

The attempt upon her honour then began, against Mary's initial acquiescence and then standing out for the promise of marriage. Some violence succeeded this refusal, rather to the whetting of the captain's appetite, and he even uttered a *mot*: "Marriage, hoot! Your corn's already brought to harvest for the milling."

By then, an outraged Sophia, making about as little noise as an otter, had crept over the river bank and crawled under its shelter to a safe exit. Muddied and wetted down one side, she ran and walked stage by stage to regain body heat, wondering the while that she was hurrying to save Minister Peden, the man who had blighted her. Halfway along the road she missed her yellow headscarf.

The Blacklock mansion was still abed. Her station was too humble to permit her to wake anyone; so she slept for a warm two hours before that solemn rising of servants. She went immediately to seek Mrs. Mauchline, who came to the door of her room in deshabille, in hair papers — and in a foul mood, worsened by seeing Sophia's muddy condition.

"Michtie me! Look at ye! Yer dinnae come tae the gran' hoose like that, niver, niver, niver!"

First she shook the girl; next her expression became highly suspicious as the tale began, since she knew Sophia and Mary to be enemies; but finally she grew grave and responsible, for the truth shone naked.

"Now we'll leave the wee harlot to hersel'. No a word tae her. We dursnae let the captain know by her traitorous offices that we're close wi' their schemes to arrest Mr. Peden. I'll awa' tae Mr. Matthew and ye're tae gang aboot y'r business as if naething has chanced."

Her eyes smiled about as brilliantly as a claypool in weak winter sun. In this emergency, the fearsome housekeeper showed her other, more admirable side, full of courage and resource and, even, a bleak kindliness.

At eight o'clock that morning, Sophia was called to the big hall. Waiting there were: Mr. Blacklock; Sir John Cochrane; Mrs. Mauchline; and — terrors! — Captain Glenmuir and the Reverend Murdoch, the clergyman clutching her yellow tartan which he shook threateningly as she entered. Mr. Blacklock's studious eyes looked stern and he told Sophia that he'd let the minister make his own complaint.

Setting one plump hand on his velvet-covered belly and leaving the other free to shake the scarf, Murdoch began with a sanctimonious wobble of his jowls: "You have stepped in. Stepped in. Sophia don't they call you?" (Shakes scarf.) "You have jetted e'en a wee stane between the annointed vicar and his flock's sacred duty of tithe. Did you think to listen to the japes of fools and e'en copy them? *Habetne animus tuus satis sapientiae?*" (Shakes scarf.) "Which I will construe for you, silly lass: 'Has your soul e'en the wherewithal to meddle in matters that you dinnae understand?' Did you think to cast *my* bread upon the waters and the heavenly maker of all harvests who marks a sparrow's fall would not notice? Can you e'en understand me when I translate the Latin for you?"

There was much "e'en" here, but the girl was thinking too hard to listen. Since her employers had no sympathy of religion with the huff-puff Murdoch, he posed no threat, but Captain Glenmuir, she saw by this morning light, filled his muddied uniform with well-muscled middle age; his lascivious lips lay together like uncooked dough within his touseled grey-ginger moustache and beard; his eyes were hooded and cynical, fully of policy. He would have come to see if she had overheard Mary's confession and her own game in this conference was to remove his suspicion. By admitting her practical joke, she might twist the evidence to her purposes: but that was to rely heavily on her employers' protection because she stood within sight of a whipping and perhaps a prison sentence.

She put on a sob or two. "I was just playing."

"We shall take that for full confession, by your leave Mr. Blacklock," said the rasping voice of Glenmuir. "I mind pulling that yellow plaid from the girl's hair a time."

"You have my leave," Blacklock replied quietly, while the girl started with alarm to find herself so quickly handed over.

The captain's eye was not to be avoided. "When did ye y'r prank, Sophia?"

"After the coos waur a' doon, an' I had an hour, I went walking down by the cottage whaur I used to live, for the memory's sake, and carried on a bit ower the bog, and came to the mill. And I minded what one of the beggars who came here to bide a night told me about a miller playing sich a game on a greedy man."

"Would that be an aspersion?" asked Murdoch.

"I dinnae think there waur ony aspersions in the man's tale."

Glenmuir pursued his point: "And after ye had caused such lamentable mischief, which surely must be punished — I should be glad to see to this, Mr. Blacklock, again by your leave — what time did ye return home? Were ye no missed?"

"Och! Wha cares aboot a dairymaid wham naebody likes?" cried Sophia bursting into tears that were genuine. "I went tae ma bed just after the ithers: naebody missed me."

As the more recondite pages of later Scottish history show, Mr. Blacklock was a learned lawyer but no man of action, whereas Sir John Cochrane was to carry his appetite for conspiracy some ten years later even so far as the Carolina scheme and the Rye House Plot upon the life of Charles the Second. He it was who now came to his friend's rescue.

"A word, Matt, if you will permit, for I see the grounds of your hesitation. The dignity of Mr. Blacklock's house, captain, forbids that he resign unto the military his own rights of discipline in this orphan child and of bringing her to penitence. Have not all recent proclamations of His Majesty's government so emphasised the master's duty to control his servants in all matters pertaining to religious conflict? You read me, do you not, Matt?"

"Ye sit nearer than I to such affairs, Sir John," muttered Blacklock warily.

"Then I counsel you, Matt, to satisfy both law and dignity by casting this sinner forth from your house, there to take her chances on the public road. And may she serve some new master more faithfully than she hath served you."

Sophia was astonished at this betrayal, to which Mr. Blacklock after a pause gave his assent, silencing Mrs. Mauchline with a hand. The accused saw no way to protest without re-opening the process and by her answers endangering Mr. Peden's life; yet she realised instantly how well the judgment would suit the captain since, once outside these gates and a beggar herself, she would lie at his mercy in all ways.

Murdoch complained: "Punish the girl as you will, but where's my bread coming from? The labourer is worthy of his hire."

"Mr. Murdoch, we'll pay you your baubies; don't get too fashed over a few bannocks."

"I'll not be disgraced by this, mind," Murdoch was saying as he was ushered out. On mule and on horse they left.

As the two lairds returned to the hall Sophia turned fiercely.

"How *could* ye?" she wailed at these nobles who had just dismissed her to all the perils of Scottish wayfaring life.

But Sir John replied with a gentle smile, "Ignoring your disrespect, we'll immediately explain. Once before, Sophia, I took you under my protection and remain in it you will. Mr. Blacklock has told me that our good friend the Reverend Peden has uttered a prophecy in your regard, that you will be dismissed from this household for wrongdoing. Now I have seen a way to make that prophecy come true in a way that will redound to your eventual credit, though not, I am sorely afraid, to your present renown."

Had Sophia's cradle been festooned with embroidered linen instead of spiky with stubble, Sir John would not have spoken as he now did: in truth, all in his plan exposed Sophia to danger and cloaked himself and his friends in safety. she was to take on herself the shame of banishment, while an unsuspecting Mary was to stay in favour — although doubt not that discipline would be severe for the housemaid in due course. Sophia was to leave on foot, but accompanied by Mrs. Mauchline as if to make sure she did not return (in reality to deter any move by Glenmuir); in a hollow she would find Mr. Blacklock's best mare and would ride the 30 miles to Maybole crossroads, there to await the labyrinthine progress of Brown the carrier with his stowaway in the sideboard, Peden; and she was to warn Brown not to proceed to the house of Hugh Ferguson down in Carrick because soldiers would be awaiting the fugitive minister.

Thus, by making his prophecy come true, she would save the man who had cursed her.

CHAPTER V

Brown the Carrier

ONCE again cast out, Sophia left the Blacklock gates that same morning, with the housekeeper for sober company, her few belongings tied into a draw-string gunny sack, and a shoulder bag for more personal things including her precious herbs. It was a saft day of drenching mists. After a mile or so along a rough path that led round the back of the village, Mrs. Mauchline looked behind and before and dove into a subsided wood to find there Mackie, the head groom, holding the laird's chestnut mare. He addressed Sophia almost with respect, being privy to her errand and awed that she should have been deemed worthy the mare.

"Ye know the paths to Maybole? Good. Just gi' Maeve a wee glimpse and she'll tak ye there out of her own fine intelligence onyways. The laird is no a man for the hunting and, like the scholar he is, prefers breeding above temperament in this one."

Sophia knew not how to ride side-saddle, more used as she was to the barrel backs of farmyard dobbins; so Mackie helped her to mount astride, her plaids damp above her knees. He slapped the mare's rump and the ride began without even an adieu from the two grave servitors. "I dinnae ken whaur I'm gangin' — but at least it may be more fun than that household," she was thinking, as the thoroughbred suddenly galloped up a bushy bank and took her, gripping on hard, over the crest and on to moorland heather interspersed with gorse clumps, where progress modified to a deceptively fast trot. Blacklock had made sure of his maid by being sure of his horse.

Ayrshire is sliced in three, north to south: Cunningham, Kyle, and Carrick; Sophia's ride, beginning in mid-shire, headed south. By lifting the mare's head to the southern horizon, Sophia gave the required "glimpse" of destination; but the animal's notion of direction had this limitation: it was little more complicated than a crow's: turn the mare's head towards environing woods though Sophia might, Maeve knew the difference between her master's curb and that of a novice, and continued without strategy across wide-open, though misty, moorland. At one point she heard a crack!, perhaps a gun, from the trees but saw no smoke.

Two miles later, the Reverend Murdoch on his grey mule emerged from behind a large clump of gorse fringing a shallow vale; he levelled a long barreled pistol.

"Halt! You little runaway," called the placed minister.

She tried kicking the mare into a gallop but, infuriatingly, the animal came to a docile stand just by her assailant.

"Why, Reverend Murdoch," she said as sweetly as a choked throat would let her. "I was just following the instructions of my betters and leaving my hame behind."

"Have you lost y'r little yellow cockernonie a-filching ma scones," he sneered, nodding his gun for emphasis as he added: "And have you now turned horse reiver — a hanging matter to steal a mare from the heritor."

"Ye seem tae have a fine mear for y'r ainsel'," she replied, indicating his droopy mule.

"You loopy quean, unless you prove co-operation an' loyalty there's a day coming when they'll set up the gallows for you, an' you'll no cheat that piece o' woodie. We have a little twa businesses to discuss, you loose limmer. Now come you down from that mare an' answer my questions. Captain Glenmuir mun know where the renegade Peden is heading and it strikes me that on y'r fine horsie you might just know. You might just be taking messages somewheres."

She maintained her seat, waiting, tight-lipped, clutching her shoulder bag.

"Come down I say. We have no instruments to put the question out here on our lee lane, Sophia Scarlett. But man must invent where God neglects his situation. I have a good stout belt round me, or a thorn from the broom under the fingernails wud speed our business. *Quis est qui tantum dolorem ferre possit?* I must construe again for you: 'Who is there who can bear such pain?' I transact but the king's affairs: my heart will be clear."

"Ye'd do better drifting your black gown i' the water to dredge up y're lost corn meal," she replied, sick at heart and desperately painting her bravery.

His hairless brows hung over his eyes like sashed window curtains of flesh, and the pinkish eyes which could raise to heaven so saintly-like, now looked glutted on cruel visions. He levelled the pistol meaningfully, and unable to control Maeve, she saw no option but to dismount.

As her leg began to lift, the mare, whose academic attainment so touted by the head groom, was mostly in the subject, *destination*, sensed the journey was ending before its term was out; so it reared mightily, while Sophia clung to its neck. As if its soaking hindquarters had become a broad-hipped woman, it staggered round and barged the portly minister into the showering thorns, his gun discharged harmlessly in air. Then the mare's front legs juddered down and it set off at a furious gallop across the heather, leaving Murdoch and his ashen-faced mule no chance of successful pursuit.

After holding on for dear life, Sophia became accustomed to the new pace and had leisure to reflect that, if pistol shots were signals, Glenmuir must have posted guards to observe her route from the village that morning. Her mount seemed as convinced as she that it was imperative to reach Maybole without delay.

The drizzle stopped; the gallop declined to the speedy trot; and they crossed barley rigs into unending moorland stretches or sheep pastures climbing above farmsteads. The sun was declining when she turned right on the main track towards Maybole. Passers-by stared at so young a peasant girl on a fine, steaming thoroughbred and she was glad to spot eventually the laden cart of Brown the Carrier waddling down the road, the great sideboard now bedded down among mattresses and rolls of cloth. From alongside, she called on Brown to halt.

What happened next took just seconds. She had time to gasp. "They're after the Reverend Peden!" and, as Brown woa'd his double team of horses, she began to dismount, forgetting what a signal that was for the mare. Maeve bucked high once more and dashed off down the road while she pulled at the reins and Brown ran after. This time she succeeded in diverting the animal into a clump of pines where, too tired for further games, it stood heaving its sides and letting Brown take it by the bridle. She slithered to the ground and a man suddenly gripped her shoulder behind. She turned to meet a stern, sandy face: it was the Reverend Peden and she scabbled out that soldiers were looking for him.

"Why, I mind the bonny Sophia Scarlett, who took ma apple," said the minister in warm, friendly terms, very calm.

"And little thank I'll have for saving y'r neck, your reverence, but--"

"Och aye, Sophia: ye'll have thank enough for there's another thanker, ye ken. But we mun hurry. I have seen dragoons coming over yonder hills towards the road."

"What mun we do?"

"Lass," said Brown, "we mun surely lend the minister the mare so that the divine work in this bluidy kingdom drives onwards."

"An' ma anesel'?"

"Ye can just ride wi' me, because there's no law against a girl travelling with an innocent carter."

Peden took Sophia by both shoulders now and looked sincerely at her: "Ye also are called most mysteriously to the work," he said. "And we give thee thank indeed, earthly-wise. Abide in the Lord and thou shalt not fall into the hands of men."

And he and the mare were gone in a thumping of turfs.

Back at the cart, Brown said hurriedly: "Ye must gang inside yon sideboard y'rsel': I canna think o' better, for if ye run they will surely pick ye up. Neither can there be law against travelling within furniture," he chuckled, "and the soldiers may not be fully informed."

They had gone a hundred yards before the dragoons came over the bank that bordered the road and they reined up to stop the cart. Sophia was now lying down in darkness on comfortable bedding that had been laid inside the sideboard for Peden's journey. She heard the voice of Captain Glenmuir, sleekit with false friendliness:

"Hey, carter! Whaur ye heading?"

It was evident the captain had not seen Peden's escape; so to understand the next sequence of events we have to peer into the minds of the actors in the little drama:

GLENMUIR: I don't know where they're going but obviously the girl had not yet reached this carter fellow; so he will not realise that I know he has Peden inside his furniture. He may think he can deliver him in safety right under my nose. This means I can catch him, Peden, and whoever is ready to receive that malefactoring clergyman. *Ergo*, I ride with this carter.

He *said*: "I'll be going your way but my dragoons will not. I hope ye won't mind a bit company." (And, privately, while dismissing the soldiers: "Keep out of sight but follow along.")

BROWN (Owing to her skittish mare, Sophia had not had time to tell Brown the extent of Glenmuir's information): Mr. Peden has escaped and the captain may not know he would be in the sideboard. This means I can deliver the furniture to Hugh Ferguson with the lass inside and, as Hugh is friendly with the Blacklocks, he will take her into service on a mere nod from me. Even supposing the captain became suspicious he could not trouble me for giving a ride to a dismissed serving lassie; so, at worst, I should fall under suspicion.

He *said*; "The road is long and I shall greatly enjoy your company, captain."

SOPHIA: I cannae cry out, for that will put me in the captain's power and prevent Mr. Peden's escape. I wish I had told him his hiding place was known of -- an' here am I in it. *But whuur we going?*

She *said*: nothing.

Thus three people continued as travelling companions who were ignorant of each other's intentions: and the journey should have concluded difficultly for Sophia unless the Ferguson of Carrick could protect her -- and for Brown too, insofar as he would fall under suspicion. However, we have not yet added the thoughts of the fourth actor:

THE REVEREND PEDEN (turning his mare on the widest of circles across moorland): The girl's appearance was strangely fortuitous and I thank thee Lord for it. Is she destined to keep crossing my path so luckily? I would that she had spoken more, but the soldiers will have been making their usual hunt for me and will not have guessed I was to be in the sideboard or that I have now escaped. I therefore judge it safe to proceed to Ferguson's house: it's either that or a cold, saft night in the heather.

He *said*: a prayer. Naturally.

Back on the Maybole road, Sophia lay in a desperate semi-darkness, for the bedding piled about the sideboard had, in the carter's hurry to hide her, prevented the doors from properly closing. Should the captain once ride to the wrong side, he would remark her. She stared from night into day, the loose doors and the cart springs jiggling and jangling all round her. Knowing her danger, Brown the Carrier kept his nerve by losing it, so to speak: he began an extraordinary outburst designed to engage the captain's attention fully.

"How think ye of the troubles on which ye are engaged, Captain?" he asked.

The topic could not have been better chosen for a military man who designed to interrogate this suspect, and Glenmuir made the mistake of trying to draw Brown out with a devout text:

"'Sion is wounded and I will heal her, saith the Lord.'"

"Ach certainly!" Brown cried like one suddenly gone mad. "Homping pomping gaeth the Word in their mouths. The mortals hae gone sand blind. 'Yea, yea, is the whiteness of desolation tae lie still on the mountains o' oor land forever?' asketh the holy ones in their forbidden conventicles as they beat thin the gold of the Lord's word into mere wind across moorlands. And the law is held for a minion. Oh disgrace! The flocks o' a thousand hills are thine, and their lives or deaths wud be naething tae Thee — Thou wud be neither richer nor poorer, but it is a great matter tae us. Homping pomping, gaeth their proud words."

"Eh? What's that ye say?" muttered Glenmuir coming closer and unable to decide whether Brown was for one side or the other. "Talk ye o' the fanatics killed about their sorry business? Talk ye disloyally?"

"Never mind, they're deed an' they'll stay deed. Homping pomping," said Brown as if he scarcely heeded. "Sion is wounded, as ye say, well wounded with a sword struck through her ear to make that organ deef."

("Ah, then, he sides with the outlawed ministers," thought Glenmuir.) Affecting disinterest, he inquired: "Hae ye by chance come against the Minister Peden a whiles?"

"I cannae condescend on ony particular time I hae seen him lately." The carrier dropped his voice to a crazed whisper: "Though *they say* he was once in Tarbolton."

"Aye. When?"

"Why when he was a young man homping and pomping out God's word, though he was but a session clerk. Then I saw him a time."

"I cannae the deil reach your meanings, friend."

"Aye, ye signify the master, I'm thinking."

"Who the master, the deil or the outlaw Peden?"

"Och but there's another master whose fields will whiten unto corn. Therefore shalt thou plant pleasant plants, and shall set it with strange slips. In that day shall his strong cities be as a forsaken bough, and an uppermost branch."

And Brown hooted with laughter.

"Ye cant like a conventicler, yet ye make them into clowns. Ye have oddly-sounding drifts, friend."

"Aye, the truest friend am I of all that is military."

("Then he may be for the soldiery," thought Glenmuir, but Brown was calling out.)

"Halloo there, young Graham! Come oot and pay your respects tae the militant."

Brown had stopped so abruptly at a large cottage in abysmal state of repair that the captain had ridden half down the road before he realised; so he reined back and waited, watching for any move to shift the sideboard. But this was a preliminary delivery, evidently, for the carter climbed down and went round to the bedding.

"Come oot, I say, ye with the fierce pike of matrimony about tae stick ye in y'r puddings, come oot, young Percy Graham."

A limp young man with straggling black moustaches emerged from under the mangy thatch and grinned broadly at Brown, flashing bright glances at the soldier some 20 yards off.

"Gi' me a hond wi' the bedding for y'r new bride. When ye carry off a lass intae y'r bedding," and Brown winked lewdly at a mattress, "then remember there's Exodus 6, verse 5, an' Galatians 6, verse 2."

Nodding to the captain, Brown and Percy Graham staggered into the house with heavy rolls of mattresses and cloths. Brown went back to his cart and firmly closed the doors of the sideboard, now the only item of carriage. Percy Graham, who had never spoken, shook his head with a smile as he listened to Brown set off again, his rich voice resuming:

"I see the fair one enter the castle on the hill, there where princes ride, and in the distance stands the dark presence of gallows, reminding us that richness shall emerge from sinners."

"Sinners?" exclaimed the now utterly bewildered captain. "D'ye mean those whom the outlaws misguidedly call the saints?"

"Whisht! I cannae mind y're interrogatories. D'ye not see, man, I talk of that young man's bride, whaur she stays in Edinburgh and waits for him to make ready their betrothals here in Carrick — an' she waits wi'in a mile o' the Grassmarket whaur so mony have been hangit?"

"P'shaw! I cannae make nor head nor tail of ye and y'r homping pomping."

CHAPTER VI

Escape on the Mules

AFTER a further mile of this dislocated communication, a major of dragoons cantered up on to the road from its declining side and called on them to halt.

"Major Cockburn!" exclaimed the captain, saluting.

"Glenmuir, I must ask you not to proceed for a while," whispered the major.

The two of them rode aside and Major Cockburn kept his voice low.

"We have the traitor Alexander Peden holed up in the house of one Ferguson of Knockdow yonder in the howe."

"But major, that's nigh impassible!" said Glenmuir, controlling his voice with difficulty. "My advice is that the same traitor is hiding right here, in that great piece of furniture on the cart."

The major gave a cold grin. "Then ye have been well fooled, Captain Glenmuir. For Peden was seen by our informer, Mackintosh, to ride up to Ferguson's house just this very afternoon on a brown mare."

"Then I'll know who is hiding in that sideboard," grunted the captain. "For someone I've heard moving about in there."

He spurred his horse towards the cart and jumped from the saddle on to its boards. The carter did not trouble to turn around. Glenmuir threw open the sideboard doors: no-one was inside: empty — even down to the palias on which Sophia had been resting.

Much later that evening, on a hard ride east towards Edinburgh, the captain made one correct deduction but failed to make a second. Correctly, he deduced that Sophia had ridden on to some meeting place with Peden and had handed over the mare. Incorrectly, he deduced that the frightened housemaid, Mary, had overheard some plans for Peden but too imaginatively assumed that the minister was inside the sideboard Brown had loaded on to his cart. By then, Glenmuir had returned to Percy Graham's cottage and found that the young man had left, so that his suspicions were renewed.

The arrest of Peden at the house of Ferguson is matter of published history too celebrated for our obscure narrative — the minister uttering divine curses upon those involved in his capture as he strode from the house raising his arms to heaven as if to escape upwards. We should return to the humbler abode of Percy Graham where, as the reader will have surmised, Sophia, clutching her gunny sack and shoulder bag, had been delivered safely wrapped up in a mattress. During the journey, she had crawled out of the sideboard, down its lee hidden from view, into this safer refuge of bedding, thinking she might have an opportunity to run off. Brown, catching sight of her feet as he went round to unload the mattress, had managed with Biblical quotations to alert Graham not to betray Sophia's presence. Thus:

Exodus 6, verse 5, a text all Covenanters had by heart, warned the young man that some Covenanting business was afoot: "And I have also heard the groaning of the children of Israel, whom the Egyptians keep in bondage; and I have remembered my covenant."

The equally well-known Galatians 6, verse 2, along with the lewd wink and reference to carrying off a lass, had warned that the mattress might be unusually heavy: "Bear ye one another's burdens, and so fulfil the law of Christ."

We return — but Percy Graham and Sophia Scarlett have already fled; the cottage is deserted save for neat piles of bedlinen; in the dusk two white mules climb shadowed hillsides towards the newly-risen Eastern stars.

The moment that Sophia had unrolled from the mattress, Mr. Graham had seen that escape was imperative. He seemed to take a glee in it: "We are in for adventures, Miss Scarlett," he blurted, once he had discovered her name. "I see no way of it but to accompany you across the hills to Edinburgh."

"I barely know ye!"

"Well," he replied cheerfully. "Look around you at this bare, bachelor farmhouse. These are the works of Monsieur Montaigne. These are my study papers. Now you know well enough for me to act as chaperon."

"These books are foreign."

"You see how you know me already. Miss Scarlett, we cannot bide more courtesy. Mr. Brown will not hide those whom soldiers will easily forgive: that captain will return."

His smile displayed a mouth of over-crowded teeth; he snatched up his Montaigne, and began bundling up a pannier sack for the journey. She, too, flitted about his house packing flints, salted meat, other usables, and the bag with her only worldly treasure, her herbs. Mr. Graham had fallen into a shy silence; he had the slender form of a gnat — only you have to imagine that translated into human form and graced with that lank black moustache.

"I call these two mules Ingram and Umfraville out of the Bruce poem. You may have Umfraville."

Once he was mounted, his shyness returned, added to by something pensive, even troubled; he slouched, the sickliest of horsemen though young-faced and his thin cheeks drew away from those teeth. He laconically described himself as descendant of a minor family of merchants and factotums, not of landed stock, and his dialect was the Southren one of Edinburgh, educated into the latinate at St. Andrews.

"But ye are leaving everything for tae aid me!" she protested as they rode uphill.

He became suddenly voluble again: "Here is the difficulty compounded. I have been away from Carrick many years: you are a suspected person. I know none in the locality save Mr. Ferguson who could have helped us in our predicament, and I greatly fear that the soldiers have descended upon him. My father was his factor and lies in prison for strong suspicion of recusancy."

Sophia digested this before saying she was sorry.

He resumed: "And here is your personal difficulty removed. You do not discommode me because I was to return at all events to Edinburgh, there to find my bride, Isabel Harvey, and to return with her here to my father's old house. This may now have to wait, but Isabel, as a member of the True Kirk, will never mind for she dwells in the city among fellow believers; and I shall not mind if I am with her."

"An' ye say ye're affianced?"

He snatched at the unspoken and cried out unaffectedly, "Oh, but will ye trust me?"

"An' if I shall?"

"Then we ride indeed together, to Edinburgh, where I shall endeavour to find you a place. But our days and nights will go hard with us and our reputations stand sorely at risk, for we dare not use the public ordinaries awhile and must lodge under the hedges in bitter cold, shielding small fires from over-curious soldiers."

"What of your ane reputation wi' y'r intended? I'll no cause honest folk trouble o' the heart."

"That is valiantly spoken," he exclaimed with his alarming enthusiasm. "If you but knew Isabel's purity of soul — oh, but you will meet her — you would not be afeared. Now let us head towards yon cliff, whose stone admixes the colour of lime, and likely holds caves."

They led their mules among the moorland tors; and above a lake found a convenient cavern. Tethering the animals nearby, they cautiously lit a fire, and nibbled oatcakes that Sophia had taken up in the pantry while fleeing the cottage. He pulled two blankets from their packs, quaintly cut jagged holes for their heads, and thus attired they crouched in the smoky cave entrance and looked beyond the firelight at dull wreaths of mist that dressed the dark valley.

That first night, she told him of Peden and his prophecy, so unlucky for her.

"It's for this I am turned out as if I were tae be as feared as some witch-woman and so I wear the name in pride."

He shocked her country superstitions by replying: "Oh, we are not to believe in witchcrafts. But prophecies may be of our very nature! Have you heard of the advocate, George Mackenzie? I suppose not. He has written that prophecy is no miracle but is natural to the soul, since the soul is God's placement in us and God has foresight. Dying men may have foresight because the soul then begins to act like itself just before it is assumed into glory. I find this in his *Religious Stoic*. But you should read, lass, read our best Scotch authors, Buchanan, Rutherford, Dunbar, Ferguson, Mackenzie."

Sophia, who had never heard a companion talk of intellectual matters, conquered her incomprehension sufficiently to answer indignantly, "But ye're no listening, man! I myself made Mr. Peden's prophecy come true. I'd fain that Mackenzie person shud try his wits agin mysel'."

"As the poet Spenser says, our self is our true genius, our ancestry of spirit, and our life to come. We live as if we stand always at a cave mouth, like this cave mouth, speaking our words into the wind, and we know not that in the darkness within us our true self is eternally shining. We peer across these moors seeking our worldly future — you and I do this now, out of anxiety for your danger. In these misfortunes, we neglect to look inwards; but we are each caves, you and I: our eternal futures are stored up already in our souls lying deep inside our own mystery."

"Och, Mr. Graham, Mr. Graham, who I thocht so silent, what manner man are ye, tae speak sae?"

"I have told you that I come from border people, wine merchants and factors, we Grahams, most of us exiled to Ireland longtimes since, a minor True Kirk branch of a mostly Cavalier family. My father, lying now imprisoned, follows the divine faith of the family, although I am but his weak successor assailed by doubts. Wait! Let me tell you a Graham story anent the spirit of prophecy; it goes with a wee song I made up for it."

He plunged into his bundle of belongings, retrieved a crudely-made flageolet, and whistled a plaintive air upon it before singing in a cracked but melodious voice:

Graham lang and Crawford small
They brought twa ladders to the wall
In Lennox' cause, for good or ill
For to scale that castle hill
The Castle of Dunbarton.

Dunbarton, Mary's fortress sheer,
Where absent queen was held so dear
That every man his life would spend
The royal castle to defend,
The Castle of Dunbarton.

Alas poor Mary where you lay
While foul usurpers held the sway
And troopers came to take the men
Who held that stronghold for you then,
Your Castle of Dunbarton.

> Dunbarton's pride came tumbling down
> Crawford small gained great renown
> Of hundred men not one that died
> Yet captives made of all inside
> The Castle of Dunbarton.
>
> O Graham bring your wine to me
> That we may drink to Regency
> All our merry men amang
> Said Crawford small to Graham lang
> In the Castle of Dunbarton.
>
> As Graham drank, a vision he saw
> Of good Queen Mary greetin' sore
> From a blue place in the sky
> And knew he for his queen must die
> In the Castle of Dunbarton.

"To interpret: our family has been always thus, caught 'twixt and 'tween," he said. "It concerns the siege of Dunbarton Castle, a seemingly impregnable fortress which at the time held out for Mary Queen of Scots against the Lennox regency which held her throne usurped. With two ladders, Captain Crawford scaled the unscalable castle cliffs at dead of night, and you may have heard — no? — that one of the invaders, who was subject to fits, had convulsions because of his fears there upon the second-most ladder. Crawford in his charity would not kill his own man but strapped him to the ladder and turned it round so that the other invaders could mount over him. What is private to our own family legend is that my ancestor, Hugh Graham, border merchant, would make two trips each year, one to supply the Irish coast of Scotland with wines and one to supply the Dutch coast. As he landed his ship upon the northern banks of the Clyde, it had grown late and he found himself seized by Crawford's troop and forced to join in their famous climb up the ladders. When Archbishop Hamilton had been captured and the defenders secured, the soldiers sat down amid the ruins of the hall and, while they feasted upon plundered venison, they quaffed the wines so fortuitously brought there by my ancestor, who was made the butt of all jokes. All at once, he rose, with eyes become glassy, and gasped: "I see the bonny queen in her end, captive in a foreign land." And he dropped down dead on the spot. Now what think you of that for prophecy, Sophia?"

"Your ballad seems to need its explanation and I was fair bewildered by the 'And knew he for' line. But it's no bad for a beginner."

Mr. Graham was at the cave mouth again, darkly outlined against the night, and had been using it rather as modern actor uses a stage, only with his darting insect-like movements. He chuckled with delight at her criticism, then coughed harshly, the sound echoing. He dropped down dead and got up laughing.

"An' where d'ye fix y'r ane thocht, Mr. Graham?"

"Through my father, I owe my loyalties to the True Kirk of the Covenant, although I may be a sorry backslider and do not always know the difference 'twixt loyalty and faith."

"Now ye sound on the borders, like a Graham."

This time in her dialect, he added softly: "D'ye think we could look from ourselves truly, shining by firelight within this cave, and see our future gathering across these darkened moors?"

"I dinnae care to even *thank* aboot it," she cried, trembling, for she felt a strange constriction at her throat and a thumping at her heart, as if those bodily sensations themselves were her future.

CHAPTER VII

A Herbal Remedy For Sorry Behaviour

AT fall of the next day they stopped their ambling steeds beside a burn running golden through the heather, the landscape purpling into distant folds, gnats darkly busying at their heads or becoming sparks in the declining sunbeams.

We may considerably abridge the conversation that followed. Percy Graham told her how in the Classical story our lives are spun by the Fates; and he described a dream of a giant, mythical woman who summed up those Fates in her one body, and of his yearning to love such a giantess a single time and then die: to have his whole life at once in an ecstasy. She barely comprehended him, for it was her introduction to all philosophy; the discussion was accordingly prolix.

But then he added: "Such a woman assayed to come to my father's aid when he was arrested."

"What like of woman could that be?"

"A woman considered wrongly to be almost entirely without wits. My father, pursued by dragoons part of the way, had taken such a journey as ours to Edinburgh, hoping to find in the anonymity of the city either refuge or, in its Dutch-facing ports, escape. Not a strong man, he was seized by a soldier, down by the Shore of Leith, as one who had been asking about shipping — when suddenly this giant of a woman burst upon them and killed the soldier with two blows of an oar. This was the woman they call Miss Christmas Bessie Queensferry, but she plies a ferry across the Firth of Forth. Despite her aid, my father was taken and lies now in the Edinburgh gaol. The bargee escaped to Holland, though it is said she will convey dangerous cargoes across the German Sea.

Musing, he added: "Mark you, this is a woman of unsavoury reputation. 'Tis said...," he barked a laugh. "Well, maybe some young smout might be tempted by so tall a woman."

"Ye are not tae come in on me in that gait," she reprimanded, understanding both finished and unfinished phrase.

He was instantly confused and apologised. She found herself studying his pallid cheek, how the frosty evening air had flushed it, and, relenting, began to tell him things she knew:

"These are the vetches and those the false parsleys. Here is old man's beard growing beside the kingcups: does that not make ye think o' the old men in Edinburgh sitting down for tae toast their tyrant king? And that wee bird flitting there ye'll know as the titlark, and that wi' the flash of white's the chat." They came across two sundews and she lifted a little pad to show the sticky hairs of the fly trap and the insect caught inside.

"Naething should be done in haste but gripping fleas," he remarked, watching the hairs slowly curl in upon her fingernail.

To her amazement, he solemnly wrote down these common things in a little notebook, for he had a contained ink-and-pen device which he had made out of a bottle, a cork, and a clipped-off quill. Meanwhile, she put some of her finds into her shoulder bag.

"And what is that around your neck?"

"That is my amulet, given tae me wance by a wise woman. It has the peony seeds within it."

"Is that so you may pine with love?"

"That is a little mocking. Nae, they protect me agin lunacy."

"Faith, do you think you shall become lunatic?"

"I might. Straunge thochts afflict us a'."

"You may be wise yourself beyond your years. And what else do you have within your bag?"

"They are herbs the wise woman gave me, and some I have collected. Ye wud spy the deadly aconite, fram some peaks in France — she said 'pair o' knees' but it cannae be that."

"Pyrenees."

"Aye. An' oil o' rue, that women use, for things ye shud nat ken — an' some for tae end their unborn bairns. An' some medicines an' some poisons that are medicines."

"But this is terrible!"

"Oh, I'm a kindly soul, Percy Graham, and there are jauncier things: myrtle for love, Piss-a-Beds for warts, and elder for skin and for the headache. I have mony a time conducted my little cures amang the ailing, but a body has for tae be careful with sich like as yon Blacklocks."

"How so?"

"The Black Arts," she whispered.

"I should be serious with you. Not just the Blacklocks. Every village has its wise woman, but beware letting the superstitious know of your wisdom lest they turn enemy one day and persuade other credulous people to suspect you for a witch."

That night, as they lay separated by the stooks in a kindly farmer's barn, she heard him coughing sorely.

"What ails thee, man?" she called.

"It's but a weakness in the chest traditional in my family. Not of consequence."

"An' is there blood in it?"

"Oh, you know... maybe. Now talking has got it over; so goodnight."

Yet she dreamed of darkness from which came harsh sounds, and when she looked for their origin, lo!, there was a weak light as if a candle glimmered in an echoing cave.

The following night they slept in a ditch like vagrants and she feared for his health and gave him a balmy tincture.

"Wud no' your intended be fearful too if she knew how ye were lying abroad?"

Ignoring that, he said: "Have I told you of the sublime manner in which we became betrothed? While my father secreted himself in Edinburgh, he fell naturally into the care of the True Kirk and, being much struck both with the beauty and the purity of a young woman at a house conventicle there, gave it as his wish before he escaped that she and I should become acquainted."

"Were ye no there y'rsel?"

"An Elder proposed that I approach this young lady, Isabel Harvey, for her hand, her father, a gentleman of the most modest means, having suffered execution after the Pentland Rising. I could not track the Lord's purpose in it, however, but rode from university to Edinburgh in a state of great timidity. As the match had really been proposed by my own father, I courted Isabel first through a chaperone and was indeed struck by an air of great freshness and decision that she has; and yet neither of us could be sure what was purposed for us. For six months I durst not approach her again, but one Sabbath a meeting had to break up hastily upon false report of soldiers and she and I found ourselves hiding together in the larder. The alarm over, we dropped to our knees and prayed what this chance could mean. And thus after a further two months of mutual devotions matrimony was decided."

"It was a very prayerful courtship," Sophia remarked.

"And now I hope to get well and repay my debts to the world. Money is the sign of civilized transactions between people," he said as pompously as he had described his engagement.

"If we're spared for tae gain it," said she, so freshly escaped.

He thought a minute. "I should not tell Isabel of your herbs. Another thing. She dwells in Edinburgh under incognito, for she is so near the inner compass fulcrum of True Kirk circles that the authorities would love to pluck her up."

"The compass I do not understand but the incognito I do."

Their worst night came in the Pentland braes, just where Isabel Harvey's father had ventured, and finally lost, his life. For shelter they had only a declivity beside a mountain burn, and rain set in at 3 a.m. After three hours, dawn rose as feebly as a fasting penitent; under its watery sunlight they cantered, soaked and weatherbeaten, down the hill-slopes towards the yellowing blocks of Edinburgh Castle high above the roofs.

They rode under the great castle rock towards the old city defences, heading for West Port which opened on to the wide Grassmarket, hub of commerce, and notorious theatre for public hangings. Outskirt housing now lined their road, and a dumpy fellow squatting cock-legged on his own dry-stone wall chuckled as the drab couple clopped towards him. He called out:

"I wud gi' some drowned rats some cheese for nibbling an' they cared for it."

Thinking to tidy their appearance before visiting Mr. Graham's betrothed in the city, they steered their mules across to him.

"We accept a kindly offer," said Percy.

They followed him through a narrow door, and once within, they were set upon by waiting soldiers who had commandeered this cottage strategically sited on the main approach road to the western city. It was a trap; and the man who had sprung it was easy to be guessed.

In the dirty front room, Captain Glenmuir sneered aloud at their easily-accomplished captivity, as he hung a foot over the arm of the one wood chair. His men stood at angles in the narrow space. Through the window hole their horses could be seen hidden in a barn.

"Why, we have the lass who sneaked intill her lover's hoose while ma back was turned," said their enemy, the light of morning sculpting his face into white lard under his ginger-grey hair. Loose tartan trews could not disguise the bulge of his well-fed stomach, but there was no mistaking the muscle of his torso.

"Or could it be," continued Glenmuir, as Percy made no reply, "that a certain Isabel Harvey, whose acquaintance I should much enjoy, waits for her betrothed?"

To Sophia's surprise, Percy replied: "I-I have heard of that lady but, as you see it is Miss Sophia to whom I am betrothed."

"Oh hah?" said Glenmuir.

"I believe you the captain who stood by while Mr. Brown brought our wedding things within. Miss Sophia, you understand, was already within. I-I have been acquainted for some time with Mr. Blacklock of Enterkin, and thus came to know Miss Sophia. Although my father would hardly approve the match did he but know of it, we have decided in his incapacity to proceed to marriage."

Glenmuir hooted. "I like this young man," he told his troops, "for he spins yarns tightly. His father, ye ken," — he spoke at random to a dragoon — "his father lies e'en now in the Tolbooth for recusancy an' here's his son rejecting his true betrothed and scooting hither and thither o'er the Pentlands wi' a pretty farmyard lass."

He straightened in his chair and became a different man. "Now see ye here: farm lass, you go intill the back room and finish making oor oats — Bell, you go with her — and meanwhile we shall see if we can tease oot o' this man Graham just wheres Miss Isabel Harvey might be staying."

"I cannot tell you of an old love, now past recounting."

The soldier Bell drew his sword and held it low as he pushed Sophia into the small back room, where a hearth fire glowed under pan water which had already come to the boil. She heard next door a long cross-examination in which she apparently maintained her false status as Mr. Graham's betrothed. Glenmuir told one of them to bind their prisoner's fingers with twine — at which her guard became more interested in the next room's proceedings — and then bind his wrist to the chair arm. There followed a terrifying fifteen minutes in which she heard, for the second time in her young life, a grown man screaming, for they had lit splints of wood between Percy Graham's fingers.

"Stappit! Stappit!!!!" she kept shouting, but her guard struck her full on the mouth and thrust her into the hearth, scalding her with porridge water.

"An' ye need nat think tae knock me wi' y're ladle or ye'll find a sword point in y'r dainty bosom. As ye wull if oor parridge doesn't ready."

She blocked her ears and thus felt the drag of her shoulder bag. In intolerable anguish, she dropped her hands and took a bag of oats, watching Bell sidelong. When young Graham hollered very loud, her guard edged to the door to look. Sophia was flicking the leather stopper from a stone bottle in her bag and under cover of stirring the porridge managed to pour in a weedy liquid. She felt herself, as a healer, to be doing a terrible wrong, like stepping into inevitable darkness, but Mr. Graham's screaming was all about her. "I am but a weak woman; I have no other weapon against these dastards." The inner voice sounded somehow off to the side of the events and it had a melody.

"Stappit! Stappit!" The torture was ending: Percy Graham had given what would turn out to be a false address for his Isabel; and his acting talents had persuaded Captain Glenmuir to believe him.

"Ye may be a guid man an' a foolish, Graham, but we shall send a man of ours to see."

When they had untied him, the captain called out impertinently: "Now we're all friends again, let's have oor oats!"

Tears streaked Sophia's cheeks and she shivered and trembled as she carried the pot of porridge out to the table. Mr. Graham had been freed and the householder, horrified to have invited the couple in to such an ordeal, was applying butter to the scorched skin of the shocked, nearly fainting young man.

"Fall to," cried the captain jovially, himself now reoccupying the sole chair. "Tonight ye shall have prison fare."

"We choose nat for tae eat with ye," Sophia said firmly. "Neither me nor Percy."

The soldierly appetite had been rather increased than diminished by the brutality, and they dug lustily into the pot using pieces of bark from the yard for plates. When all were replete, they sat there gossiping and calling for more ale, until Glenmuir looked again at his prisoners.

"It seems unfair, don't ye consider it, Mr. Graham?"

"How do you mean, captain?" The shivering youth had to be held to stand semi-upright, yet he had not lost his resolution.

"It seems unfair that ye shud have a' the pain and torment when it's your betrothed — I mean, this wan — that ye have rescued from horse-thievery and perhaps from re-setting."

"She is no horse-thief."

"There we shall see. But I hate the unfair and love the fair, such as she is. Will ye bide a while, for I must accompany her tae the pains o' a sweet bed."

Mr. Graham tried to thrust the householder aside and leap forward but the dragoons, knowing their captain well, had already anticipated this moment and held him without difficulty.

There was one bedroom with sloping roof under the eaves, and the odious soldier half-carried Sophia up the ladder to it. Once inside, he faced away from her and fumbled at his trews, calling behind his back that she should prepare herself for happiness. She did not move. And there seemed some delay. For now it was the captain's turn to shiver, and he turned with an odd look on his face, his hands now making meaningless gestures at his belt.

"I am unwell," he said. And sat heavily upon the low bed. Then: "There are large spiders." He held his plump stomach and groaned. After a short while he vomited into the corner of the room. From downstairs came similar groans and angry voices. Glenmuir tried to speak but his words cracked in his throat and he let himself fall again on to the bed. "Bring water, ye hussy!" he managed to say, but spasms caught his limbs, he heaved great sighs, his hand sought his sword still dangling by his side, but clutched it uselessly, his chest heaving, the facial skin pasty. He shut his eyes. "I am verily dying," he said.

"I will get help," she replied, making her escape down the ladder.

Downstairs, all the soldiers seemed similarly stricken, and she instructed two of them, "Your captain has asked for ye. He lies ill, just as do yoursel's."

They tried to climb to the bedroom but sank down at the foot of the ladder. That left four men whose only desire was to seek the yard to rid their bellies of wretchedness. One remaining soldier, Percy found to be as weak as he himself and thrust aside; the couple stumbled out of the front door and round the wall to the barn. They took two of the military horses, scattering the rest, and resumed their ride towards Edinburgh at a gallop, slowing as they approached the West Port so as not to arouse suspicion.

"What did you manage for those poor soldiers?" asked Percy, suddenly bursting into laughter, though he could hardly hold his reins for his agonies and shivered and winced at each vagary of his horse.

"I have used up all my aconite from the Pyrenees," she replied solemnly.

"Will they die?"

"Nae chance."

"Well, why do you seem troubled?"

"It wasn't witchcraft, would ye say?"

"It was sheer poisoning, you fool!" he bellowed. "I apologise for calling you 'fool' — it was just by way of expression. And will you forgive me, too for calling you my betrothed?"

"It's just as might be," she replied cryptically. And they rode on; and she was humming a tune to herself despite her care for Percy's torments at each falter.

CHAPTER VIII

Branded A Thief

THEY tethered the horses beside an inn's trough, and shortly the two friends have entered a lane behind the High Street and Sophia is taken into the front entrance of a *land* -- a tall tenement in harled stone — then down innumerable stairs into a bottomless pit before being brought out still at ground level — Percy chuckling at her surprise — on the far slope; whereat, he turned about face, entered a yard, and mounted arcaded wooden stairs up an external wall, before knocking at a poky door just below the bellying of a turret. They were greeted by a bonny young woman, with raven hair falling from under a lace bonnet on to narrow shoulders. Her small, starry eyes tried to widen yet more but had no capacity; so she chastely embraced Percy Graham and presented a cheek to be kissed.

"Then you've come. The Lord be praised. And Percy, what have you done? You look all in!"

"We've had adventures," he cried. "May I introduce—"

She forestalled him. "And you'll be Sophia Scarlett. Sir John Cochrane has told me of you."

"Merciful heavens!" breathed Percy, bringing the slightest of wrinkles to Isabel's brow, although she kept holding his arm and inspecting his condition rather anxiously.

"I'd be heartily surprised he would much remind my name even, were it not that I lost his friend's horse," Sophia said.

"Oh but you do him wrong. Sir John, being also a friend of Mr. Ferguson, heard immediately of Mr. Peden's disgraceful arrest and has sent messages to Edinburgh for you. How old are you?"

The question was strangely placed, but Sophia answered that she was eighteen, although just turning into seventeen.

"Then you are five years my junior. I shall always have that over you."

Isabel laughed throatily, even though her brow had something set about it.

"What messages?"

Isabel inspected the courtyard.

"Sir John said I am to get to know you first. What a *time* you two must have had over the moors. Just look at you, a couple of tinkers coming to my door begging for a bit parridge. Well, it shall be provided; so come away in."

Once in, she exclaimed, "Percy! What's happened to your fingers?"

She took him through an inner door to treat them and to hear the whole story in privacy before sending Percy to bed to recover. But he was up in two hours — an unpoisoned pot of kyle porridge bubbling ready for him — and he making a spoon-hold of his bandaged fist on the table and saying breezily, "Now this I'm ready for."

But Isabel would first search a chest for a warm grey dress of wool, inspect it for moths, and hand it to Sophia with a brilliant smile. Outside, the cries of street hawkers cast their echo into the courtyard and provision carts rattled at a distance. City life was already dazzling for a Tarbolton lass.

Over the porridge, Percy again related their travels with so many compliments to Sophia that Isabel grimaced at the other girl, who then wanted with all her heart to become friends.

"I have grave news, Sophia — let us stop these Mr. Grahams and Miss Harveys. I think I may now give you Sir John's commission. He sends first to tender apologies, but he has declared you publicly a horse-thief." She continued hastily, "And yet he has rescue to offer. His messenger waits at the law offices of Mr. Blacklock for your answer to his proposals."

Sophia pushed away her porridge and sat stunned.

"By what manner right, cud he do a thing like that? They can put me tae the gallows ony time."

"To have done otherwise would have set the whole south-western communion in danger — Mr. Ferguson is already in difficulties, Brown the carrier, our informers... but everything stands at risk."

Sophia retorted, "Ye neglect Sir John and Mr. Blacklock."

"I also left out myself, for I am embroiled in my Saviour's work. But you are to remember, if you want Sir John's continued help, that the great ones must preserve themselves to be promoters of their faithful tenants."

Percy had been as shocked as Sophia and now he interrupted, quite furious:

"No, no, no! This is not honourable. I mean in Sir John, Isabel: it's danged treacherous even. We cannot in conscience set our hands to it."

At a stroke, Isabel lost her willed brightness, as if another more doubtful self lived within her fervour.

"My truest friend," she said, "be not so moved as to profanity. You stab me where my heart is already divided. Sir John has acted, and a cloth cut in such haste cannot be sewn back together."

"Yet it is most serious, Isabel, to place Miss Scarlett — Sophia — in such peril," Percy Graham said.

And Isabel nodded anxiously many times at the seriousness of it.

"I must ask you whether you are a true believer, Sophia," she said at last.

"I havenae rightly decided what I think. I see the killing and I hate it all."

"Oh! Oh! That is misfortunate because it makes it the more difficult to help you."

"Isabel!" Percy exclaimed, his anger not appeased; but the women's eyes were engaged with each other.

"I cannae say what I dinnae believe properly."

Percy stood up and walked aside a pace.

"In such a way, our martyrs charged before the Royal Council refuse to renounce their proper beliefs, even for their own safety."

"Aye, but this is failure to renounce *lack* of belief. Oh we must hope and pray Sophia comes to her election right soon! But now, for none of her own fault, we find her vagabond and uncertainly chosen, perhaps with blame in her heart against Sir John for his necessities of policy."

Sophia felt trapped: unbelief gave her no strength to contradict such certainty as Isabel's.

"Yet I would vouch with my life for Sophia's loyalty," countered Percy.

"I too would lay down my life for one who has well served, yea even in her unbelief. I decide, therefore, to risk the cause by resetting her into the networks of safety."

Isabel renewed a smile, but Sophia remained in awe of this devout austerity to which even Percy seemed thrall.

"We are to wait here three months; then we are to convey Sophia on board a barge at the Queensferry, Percy, for she is to sail as Sir John's messenger to the Estates of Holland."

"Holland!"

"But you see, Sophia, there's *such* warm welcome awaiting you from the exiled Scots in Rotterdam. You will find a home and great kindness there when you deliver certain letters."

Here am I, Sophia thinks, orphaned, lusted after by a soldier, cursed by a minister, outlawed, and now thrust forth into exile if I grasp the hand extended to me!

"I see Sir John pushing me tae the wall, so tae mak me his spy. And what wud be in the letters?"

"How strange and admirable that you ask that first before inquiring further about yourself," said Isabel, staring at her. "It is purposed to protect people who would otherwise die for their faith: more you cannot know.[1] Sir John has been so struck by your faculties, that you will be tutored in Rotterdam as befits a superior housekeeper, and he will thereafter take you into his protection."

"I may think first of my country, but d'ye just see Sir John has practically murdered me, what he wouldnae hae done tae a person of quality?"

"He had to choose who to place under suspicion, you on your own or all

---

[1] (This letter being not germane, we may add that it warned the Dutch of coming British pressure to expel prominent Covenanters. Two years later, the Dutch complied with such a request but promptly re-opened their borders to the fugitives, frustrating British hopes of kidnapping them and putting them to trial.)

these other people who have more power to serve the Kirk."

"But I've never *done nae thing*! These others are all constantly in rebellion."

Isabel came round to hug the girl's shoulder.

"You took the first step when you warned Sir John that Mr. Peden's life was in danger. For that, our communion will protect you."

"And I shall lay my sword alongside Isabel's promise," declared Percy, coughing in his frail fervour.

That said, Sophia rendered Isabel a better justice:

"We'll have put ye in danger by arriving directly from the troopers and their tortures."

"Toot! Below me two floors is a Lord of Session to whom I have been muckle obliging and who will vouch me to be no Isabel Harvey but one Marion Allison."

More thoughtfully, she added, "We must live like mice behind walls until you depart. A further aspect will intrigue *you*, Percy, for you will guess her conveyance to Holland — or should I say her conveyor."

"It will be the giantess, Bessie Queensferry."

"Yes, the dreadful woman who rescued your father a time and for whom our cause still has uses."

All this hardly settled Sophia's outrage; but in deciding for Rotterdam she found within herself an obscure ambition which she did not yet know was intellectual. During the coming months, she would lie awake at night, downed into humility by Isabel's kindness and fanaticism. Then, outside, a sword would jingle and her heart go panting: a soldier would emerge from a courtyard doorway, and she would watch him idle off, heading up towards the Castle. And she would think of spies and know her own original loneliness and lack of centering.

The older girl bathed in intrigue as if in ass's milk: when on church business she left her own dwelling in the wee hours like a thief and returned at nine, her complexion shining with faith. Merely to assemble a Sabbath gathering, now here, now there, incurred threat of execution; and not a prayer was uttered by the faithful but with an armed worshipper at door and window. Percy added his own brand of fun, for he contrived small woven baskets on wheels to ride down washing lines between the facing windows of the tall *lands* as missive bearers, while those who preferred the washing pole developed a crude semaphore of laundry under his instructions: blue... blue... red... yellow... yellow: so passed the arrangements for one house conventicle. Alas for fun, he concluded that the very romance of the system would make it talked of, and he burnt his baskets under Isabel's amused eye.

After a month of skulking indoors, Sophia learnt that a cousin of Jessie the under-housekeeper -- that cousin captured at the Tarbolton field meeting — was now in Edinburgh Castle for execution. Long held in Ayr garrison, he had got news out to a Covenanter cell that a fellow prisoner was being taken to Glasgow: an ambuscade failed and his role stood revealed. At 6 a.m. on the following Saturday, half the city would witness the hanging in Edinburgh's Grassmarket, and the man's head would be spiked at the West Port gate. With this as unhappy diversion, Isabel seized the moment to pay dawn calls to unnamed church Elders. By six of the evening, she had not returned and Percy and Sophia grew alarmed.

The young man slung his sword and Sophia put on one of Isabel's best dresses for disguise. So, like gallant and lass, they made a forbidden sortie into the streets.

"It's a *huge* city, but it all grows upwards," murmured the village girl whose fugitive status made rare any chance to inspect the metropolis.

True, the circumambiating walls of Edinburgh squeezed the *lands* higher and higher; commoners' rooms piled rickety-tickety ten or twelve flights high upon those of nobles: she saw m'lord's rippling black wig and port-wine face framed in a window below, while far above against the jig-jagged sky a slack-mouthed tavern maid hung out her sheets on a reclaimed ship's bowsprit. Black alleys arched through these collapsing precipices and led to cobbled yards where yawling urchins were cursed by jail-birds temporarily freed from their lockfast cages, and footmen jolted m'lady's sedan supperwards past ladies whose station was more *dégringolade*.

At a known address, a man hiding behind his window sash, told Percy that application of the thumbikins might have torn from Jessie's cousin secrets of the Edinburgh communion. In this uncertainty, Isabel was to remain overnight at an Elder's house. They began to retrace their steps relieved that at least their mutual friend was safe.

The night following a hanging in old Edinburgh was dangerous because vainglorious minds discharged their own fears in tavern brawls. Percy had to steer Sophia across the street from more than one loud argument.

"Now I have emerged like the mole, I feel like the tiger," he was saying. "I'm minded to have down that poor cousin's head from its spike once I have returned you home."

"You'll have gone saft in y'r ane head, man," retorted Sophia. 'It'll be fair surrounded wi' the sodgers."

But beside her borrowed, gentlemanly beau, she was thinking, "He has such a bonny air."

A quarrel across the street grew louder, and hated, pompous tones suddenly declaimed, "Ye may not disrespect God's minister with names. *Nihil metuenda est quod animo nocere non possit*, which I shall construe: 'Nothing is to be feared which cannot injure the soul.'"

"But that is lamentable bad Latin," Percy chuckled, seeing a band of louts descending upon someone in their midst. "So poor a scholar must be rescued."

Before she could stop him, he strode across to the knot of people under a tavern sign, thrust firmly but cheerfully aside four or five ruffians, and dragged out fat Murdoch, the placed minister from Tarbolton, bleary drunk and abusive.

"Sir, you must say *metuendum!*" he advised gleefully, brushing the man down with his hand.

"I, Sir, am too drunk for exact quotation," said Murdoch deliberately as he might. "And I was beset."

"Then we shall excuse it as neck verse. Here is another, *Nostris temporibus omnes plus metus et minus spei habemus*," Percy rattled off.

"There is no need to construe such school Latin."

Murdoch spat irritably to hide his confusion. He leant against the wall, his eye narrowing.

"But I am not so drunk as to mistake Mistress Scarlett of bad repute, she who stole my flour and became a loopy horse reiver."

"This is our placed minister," Sophia burst out.

Only then did Percy realise he had rescued an enemy. He beckoned to the ruffians and dragged Murdoch along towards them.

"I give you back your lard-bag, for I find he deserves all your injuries."

Seizing Sophia's arm, he started them both running as the hooting louts grasped their victim.

"That will buy us time," he muttered, sprinting in a direction away from Isabel's house.

In a moment he was puffing: "How does it arrive that so inactive a man should be following you?"

"They say of Murdoch he comes aye tae Edinburgh for tae see his parishioners hangit, sich as this misfortunate cousin, but I think there was verily ony wan ither time."

She was breathing easier than he; running was not his *forte*.

"Then I hope those blackguards dust him well. But we must take refuge: while we are exposed on these few principal streets an enemy can find us as easy as bowling down ninepins."

On the west of town, they hid in an entry to make sure they were not followed. Percy clutched at his chest.

"We neednae fear," she said, distressed for his physical weakness. "Murdoch has the spirit of a corncrake and the beak of a loon."

They stood too close together in that darkening alley; his thin limbs would brush her satin dress; she could hear the harshness of his breathing, catch the merry glint in his eyes; and they were truly in no danger; and they didn't want to leave that hiding-place for they knew it was a trysting-place too. The merry eyes were growing lustrous and sad; his hand wandered from his chest to grip her firm bicep.

"This cannae be," she whispered. "But gi' us, just this wance, half of the plenishing."

She rose on her toes and kissed his lips; his thin body shivered; his eyes slid to the side desperately.

"This is great sweetness, perhaps the greatest I shall know," he whispered back. "Help me now, Sophia, lest we be punished above for our dreadful miscarriages. And yet I must return kiss for thy kiss only for this one time."

Hardest for Sophia was that journey home, the night alone in Isabel's lodgings, and the return of the heroine herself, welcomed by Percy with extra fuss.

And so, to her alarm, she was full in love with Isabel's betrothed.

Percy spent his nights at a neighbour's. Sophia hated most that moment at bedtime when she would hear her hostess's voice wailing in prayer like a good Covenanter's, and the prayer turn severely upon her impending nuptials:

Lord, the voice of Thy mercy never tires. Notwithstanding the encouragement of my call, I feel Satan close-writhing around my soul, for, though I perceive with much solidness the weight of a married life, avoiding the tongues of licentiousness and scandal, I fall nightly into these strong enticings from the flesh. Be Thou undertaker for me in this betrothal and unwrap me from these coils of death, that in earthly love we, Thy servants, may foretaste eventual sanctification, not for our sake but for Thine own.

Sophia, turning in bed, felt overmatched by repellent asceticism: no wonder such a saint was loved better! She saw no escape from Isabel, to whom she was beholden for clothing, food, friendship, and her very safety. Yet the older woman constantly tried to lighten her burden, promising that the friendship would be for a lifetime and that this sheltering was but a small reckoning. Still more considerately, though Isabel observed Sophia's love for Percy, she essayed to lessen even that burden, contriving that contact with her betrothed should concern the girl's education only; and thus, the forthcoming absence in Rotterdam. Meantime, she curbed Percy from intimate enthusiasm for herself and arranged their marriage to post-date Sophia's departure.

In all this, lay some policy, since while Sophia was unobtainable for Percy, Isabel would not suffer herself to be more obtainable.

Percy's unconscious defence against romantic involvement was to talk constantly about Isabel.

"You may find it difficult to believe, but she was once a sinner herself," he would say.

It was his only dead story: Isabel was the daughter of an Abel Drugger of a Perth apothecary, a signatory to the Covenants. At first, she "rebelled" against her strict parent, but was saved from "blasphemy and Sabbath-breaking" when she wandered into a field conventicle one day.

"I hope she had done naething too dreadful," said Sophia.

Percy side-stepped the irony by pointing out how full Isabel's present life was with excitements.

"Do you suppose that if the Reverend Mr. Welsh preaches to a thousand people amid the moors of Carrick the congregation simply leaps fully-clothed out of the heather?"

No, he continued, there needed this network to perform the magic before the authorities took warning and sent out the soldiers: an inter-shire system of setters, spies, messengers, and secret cells. In Edinburgh, her ear close to Parliamentary gossip, some of it whispered to her by Sir John Cochrane, Isabel was indispensable.

Since her own risk as horse-thief was less than all this, Sophia's debt to the older girl appeared all the greater after that conversation.

One morning Isabel went into the street and heard talk that Prophet Peden had been sent to the Bass Rock, that massive lump stuck sheer-sided into the East Coast seas and now become Scotland's newest State prison. Isabel hurried home: during her absence, a messenger from Mr. Blacklock's Edinburgh law chambers had delivered two letters bearing Sir John Cochrane's seal, one to the Prince of Orange, the other to the Scots kirk in Rotterdam; and Sophia was to be their carrier. The danger they all courted seemed to draw nearer.

CHAPTER IX

The Queensferry Fracas

THE sweet agony ended. Another morning, a certain James Robinson, who announced himself as from North Queensferry, climbed the wooden stairs. He wore a black smock that emitted swart pollen dust when he brushed at it. "I'm a coal-hauler, ma'am," he said, as if that was an explanation constantly necessary. An obliging, bald-headed man to whom wings of black hair and dirt-streaked cheeks gave a badgerish look, he reported that the previous night the Queensferry bargee, Bessie, had told him she stood ready to carry Sophia to Holland. Robinson backed out conspiratorially, leaving a smudgy spoor across the rushes.

One afternoon, the three of them — not daring to hire horses since any Edinburgh ostler was, odds-on, a king's man — were walking briskly down the eight-mile road to the Queensferry, where the female bargee would await them at dusk. The girls were warmly cloaked and bonneted and Percy prudently tucked a brace of pistols beneath his jerkin.

The thrill of danger, the incipience of unrequited love, and the whitened May sunlight across ploughed fields hairy-green with new corn, made Sophia yearn for poetic expression. A tightly-budded ash bough overhanging the path trembled in the firth breeze, becoming emblem of her own prospect. She inwardly exclaimed, "This is ma native land an' it has such a canty, such a canty..." and the vocabulary of the mind would falter. Or to see burn water rushing out of woodlands as if in haste to transmute its own brown incontinently into whisky made her cast her thoughts outwards and whip them across the water like a fisherman's fly, though no metaphors rose to her as-yet empty hook. "I cannae e'en hold his hond."

An odd encounter made them uneasy. A muscular man came up from shorewards, turned, and fell into step with them. He had a massive black beard, a fly-away tartan bonnet, a loose blouse of white calico, and baggy tartan breeks caught up between his legs into the belt in front. With a broad sword dangling from a leather shoulder strap, he was a regular-looking villain.

"It's a fine day for walking with twa sae bonny lasses," he remarked with gruff impertinence.

"I'm sure we thank you kindly, though we much prize our privacy," said Percy, not liking company which had a semblance of the military about it.

"Are ye not Hugh Miller, that owes me 50 merks?" the man said, peering suspiciously at him.

Percy replied that the stranger must be mistaken.

"I'm sure that if ye were tae pay me ma debt we wad be left in a peaceful way, for I have the law of it."

"We have no part in such a discussion," Percy retorted. "You have mistook your man and must press your point no further."

"Aye," growled the ruffian, giving a savage grin, and then turning back into his own direction.

They watched him go far down the road and walk into a by-lane, before Isabel inquired of Percy, "Do you think it safe to proceed?"

"I'm asking myself, or did he think to rob us? Did he look for a bribe to warn us of coming dangers? Or did he indeed mistake me for a partner in some rough card game and then see I was a gentleman?"

"Belike the last," said Isabel. "What say you, Sophia?"

"If we return, I cannae see there's mair safety than ganging forwards, for if he was a sodger-man they'd have been watching the hoose, as I've sometimes suspected. So the quicker I'm awa' the better."

"Then we must be circumspect," said Isabel. "We are not to meet with your boat until evening; so let us turn aside into a hollow and pass the time until then."

They found a woodland stream where they squatted on boulders, and talked quietly but with hectic gaiety, although Isabel always looked about to turn things into a prayer meeting. When dusk began smoking through the hollow, they regained the main road. From a rise they could look one way to the taller ships standing in to the port of Leith and look the other way to the fisher-boats ploughing white scalloped waves off the Queensferry station. A great sea was breeding the darkened heavens' copper coinage with silver glints decreasing eastwards towards the night rim of the Scottish horizon. "An' I am tae gae there, yonder past the final rocks."

Isabel knowing the way, they turned from the road, crossed the pine-covered links bordering the cliffs, and entered a gully of fallen boulders and grim grey sand flecked with granite. Presently a tiny creek began to weep from a wrinkle in the sand; and presently it broadened; and presently the gully opened outwards on to the firth where divided cliffs bore low shelves tabled with dark green grass; and as they neared shore their creek was fulling as the tide purled inwards with grey rills of froth. A collapsing boat shed was there, worn by one bank like a lopsided bonnet; two craft and a dinghy held offshore on looping ropes and rocked in the stiffening breeze. One, an antique fisher-boat, groaned in its teeth and sank tarred planking deeper into the waves. Its companion, a ketch-rigged barge with wing-shaped side keels, had its sails loosely bunched under the collapsed gaff ready for a voyage, the mast a dark spike against the last light, the forrard loaded with timber and, probably, bundles of hides, while from the stern a dingy-tender swayed on its painter. A guttering oil lamp at the main-mast cast a Rembrandtesque chiaroscuro upon the skipper, who, straight-legged, squatted against the mast. Her identity could hardly be doubted: she was the giantess, Christmas Bessie Queensferry. Mouse-coloured hair hung in swags on either side of a great heavy-browed face dark with sulkiness, almost negroid in the pouting lips. "Merciful heavens!" said Percy, and Isabel did not stop him, for the shirt of the giantess flapped carelessly round her naked, almost flat chest; and you would have called the body a huge man's so prodigiously did the biceps bulge against her side and the calves swell under linsey-wolsey leggings.

"Hail! Hail the *Mary Cutler!*" — for he had seen crude white lettering on the tarred stern. "Your leave to step aboard?" Percy called softly across the intervening 10 yards of water.

The woman appeared to deepen her sulk; she sat utterly listless. He hailed again, and now she shook her head furiously. And again, till she replied like a grumpy child:

"Is that Scarlett?"

"Sophia Scarlett," the girl agreed.

"I'm not sailing, Scarlett."

And she folded her arms into renewed silence.

Attempting an absurd bankside conference, they began a pleading and a negotiation but she just kept frowning. Eventually, from behind the cabin arose two identical black-bearded men, either one of whom might have been the rascal who had earlier accosted the party on their journey.

"Now ye may come aboard and pay y'r debts or stay there and be murdered as ye stand," called one of them while his twin brother — if that were the case — laughed sarcastically.

Bessie Queensferry chewed her jaw as if it were a muffin.

Percy muttered: "Look behind us."

In the gathering darkness, an incertain number of soldiers had invested the head of the gully; there could have been 10, there could have been 20 hiding behind boulders. As yet, their aggressors were cautious but would move confidently forward once it was clear the little party had few weapons.

"This barge woman tells us she is a loyal subject of the King's Council; so whaur's now y'r fine winds and fair passage?" taunted the soldier twins on board.

On shore, the three friends drew closer as Bessie Queensferry now rose slowly to her magnificent stature and regarded them mutely. "Maybe if we reached the boatshed..." said Isabel. They ran and climbed to it. "No, that would merely entrap us," said Percy, peering at its internal collapse. Sophia darted in and emerged with two carbines which rust had made unusable, but she handed one to Isabel, saying, "Let's gi' 'em a fright, onyways." Percy was drawing the more serviceable pistols from his breast. They ran round the boathouse, jumped down the bank and took shelter behind a rowboat upturned on the creek edge.

A shout now came from far up the gully: "Will ye turn yoursels in wi'out bloodshed?"

Glenmuir's voice.

Percy called out an imitation of the man's tones: "Never! Ye shall answer for my burnt fingers."

Glenmuir back: "Did ye not suppose our surveillance of ye frae the minute ye left the king's horses by a water trough? And think ye we sall let free a horsethief, a resetter wi stumpy finger-ends, and Miss Isabel Harvey wha has bin known tae us these past many months as a fanatic?"

The captain was evidently shouting into night air for sheer enjoyment.

"Our best chance lies across this inlet, though we may now need to swim it," Percy was meanwhile whispering. "I don't swim," replied Isabel. "We cannae shift this boat intill the water: they'd a' be on us," said Sophia. "A better chance lies in grasping that wee dinghy out at sea behind the barge," said Percy with an excited edge; but here again lay the problem of Isabel's inability to swim.

They looked over the boat keel up the gully and, to their astonishment, a man suddenly poked up behind a boulder not yards away. Percy levelled a pistol at him. "Kill him!" screamed Isabel. A shot rang out and blood sprouted from the man's blouse breast as he lurched, half stood, span round, and fell. Percy had not fired. In the gloom, no doubt seeing the silhouette of Percy and his pistol against the water, another soldier behind his fellow had taken that unchancy pot-shot. Then a great roar resounded from higher up and white blouses began leaping towards them in the gloom. Everything next happened at once.

On board, Bessie Queensferry seized an oar and broke it on twin number one, who dropped like a stone. As the second twin struggled to draw his broad sword, she gripped his neck under her mighty forearm and — the air rent with the man's screaming — she... the narrator hesitates. She gouged her fingers into his eye. Her half-sightless victim continued to wrestle and writhe, powerlessly gargling, until his body, now strangled to death, stilled, and was heaved overboard. Percy meanwhile had fired one of his pistols over the heads of the nearest shore attackers, and, alarmed, they held off in a half-circle which blocked escape by the creek, while Percy and the two women swung their guns warily side to side. At their backs, the great sail of the barge creaked upwards and became a brown wall against the sky; the craft took a lean against the freshers as Bessie hurled ropes into the sea and the boat slowly got under weigh; the semi-circle of soldiers jeered to see their prey abandoned for them on shore. Trailing its precious dinghy, the barge broke further from the bank to slide majestically on a preliminary tack across the creek.

"It's our only chance," cried Percy, and, grasping Isabel by the hand, he chased to the steep sea bank where the two of them plunged into the tide, Sophia following behind. Water immediately dragged at Sophia's heavy clothing and others of her cloths ballooned around her. Choking on gritty salt water that swamped her head, she felt air panicking in her chest, and during a slow passage of time a bullet zipped the water. But the barge, reappearing from its tack, suddenly blacked out the sky and its tall sides nearly engulfed her as its planks sped past on the turn. Wallowing, her eyesight darkening, she grabbed a rope that rasped along her arm and was incontinently dragged horizontal, bursting through the water as the vessel turned again, gathering speed. She held the trailer rope for the dinghy; so, paying it out hand over hand, she let the gulping wake carry her backwards until she could first grasp and then scramble into the little boat, where she lay gasping. In the obscurity, she thought a body floated past and she put out a hand to haul at it, recoiling at its bushy black beard. Crackling gunfire sounded from shore. With another start, she realised that a hand had been gripping the dinghy gunwale all along; and she bent over to face an exhausted Percy still supporting Isabel with his other arm. Providentially — or because its skipper had been watching them — the barge went about so that a half-drowned Isabel and her rescuer could clamber aboard on the dinghy's lee side as it swirled easily round.

Inside their seat-less boat shell, the refugees wallowed in a flooded pile of ropes and oars while Isabel revived, coughing, gasping, and shivering only one whit worse than the other two.

When she could, she said, "We are being towed out to broad sea. There is no time to lose. We must hail that fearsome woman and separate from Sophia immediately."

But even as she spoke, the barge came off a fast reach and turned at right angles to them, head-to-wind, caught noisily in stays; meanwhile, their dinghy was tugging rhythmically forwards like a hooked sea trout. The stiff breeze backed the barge across channel, so the craft, like an intelligent being, leant over on its reach to regain sea room. The manoeuvre was repeated until they drew near enough to see the giantess in the stern, her naked foot holding the tiller, hauling them steadily alongside.

"Can we trust Sophia to this monster?" wheezed Percy, for he was coughing, and coughing blood. But they had arrived.

"We cannot accompany her on this voyage," said Isabel. "You must seek medical help immediately."

"Forwards or backwards lies danger for us all."

Miss Christmas Bessie Queensferry, a pale bewigged fury in the gloom, pointed a finger down over the side of her barge.

"You, Scarlett, come," she said, her voice like scratched amber.

The girl hesitated, but two forearms — or two legs of beef — flashed downwards; she was grabbed at the collar and seat of her dress and carried up like a baby before being stood in the well of the barge. The girl stared in astonishment to be so abruptly restationed in a boat alongside the mountain mass of its skipper.

A cry from below: "The letters!"

Bessie leant over, snatched the document from Percy's outstretched hand, and thrust it at Sophia behind her. A tarred paper wrapping had protected Sophia's passport to Holland from substantial water damage.

"Now go!" Bessie called down. She let the painter fall and kicked her own tiller so that the barge swayed sideways and the dividing water widened. Without time for more than yells of farewell, her friends were lost astern as the giantess swung her craft on to a broad tack. "She must be six feet *suvven*." The thought cast Sophia into terrible loneliness, to lose her new friends so quickly; and she kept trying to re-decipher the last shouts as the wind spread them wide. Isabel had screamed: "Robinson - Queensferry - for - messages"; and Percy: "We'll .... again": the missing word could not have been "meet".

CHAPTER X

By Barge to Holland

THE farm lass had never sailed at all, let alone sailed at night alongside a monstrous woman. She wondered at the silent navigation, beating across the firth in turns as tight as the lacing on a jerkin; they would come so racily shorewards, the surf frightening-white under cliffs fuzzy in darkness; the brown sail towered above its fat wooden boom, trembled in the agonising slowness; a clap like a moment of absolute danger, a flapping, clattering, a "dong!" as one side keel went up, another "dong!" as the opposite keel went down; and the *Mary Cutler* came round at last, stiffing on her new course: all this performed alone by the half-naked female savage at the large, curving tiller. Bessie had spoken once, and that in an English accent, when Sophia had said, "Ma claes is sorely wet."

"Dry clothes is below."

In the *Mary Cutler,* cabin and hold were combined: just a tunnel below deck. Sophia stumbled across four caufs of chaff-filled sacking laid out for beds on the planks, as if Bessie were running an inn for beggars; she smelt the sickly-sweetness of grain but some sacks under the bows were full of wool yarn. Then she nearly broke a plaster statue, apparently of the Virgin Mary with Jesus, that leant against the hull; it bore a votive necklace of six beads. Further fumbling discovered two lockers and, in one, some long dresses and flannel vests. She shed her freezing things and donned two vests and a full-skirted dress which blind fingers guessed had a silk bodice and muslin sleeves holed under the armpits. Still shivering and attired in no manner fit for a sailor, she climbed back out to tie her own clothing to the rigging. Her daunting companion beckoned for Sophia to manage the side keels on each turn.

Scotland's shore's seemed to tumble rocks into the water each time they were neared, but they were gaining more and more searoom until the *Mary Cutler* picked up a northerly on a long tack towards the Isle of May and the German Ocean. The moon came out, dangerously for them, and by 6 a.m. they stole by jib-sail alone into one of the isle's inlets, where Bessie cast anchor behind a seacrop of rocks, and stepped her long mast. They were crouching together by the cabin doors and Sophia whispered: "This isle is where St. Adrian had his chapel: his stone coffin floated clear across to Anstruther Wester". The giantess put swollen finger to swollen lips. Sure enough, after a while a fast naval sloop with cannon on its bows surged past their hiding place; their moonlit progress had been followed. They hid out for a further hour on the sheltered waters before Bessie reset the mast and, since they were caught on a lee shore, bunched the mains'l ready for hoisting, edged the barge out with hands grasping at rocks, and, round the point, furiously hoisted sail as the northerly took hold. She cut out towards Denmark, before rounding through choppy moonlit waters into what proved a four-day run almost clean down to Holland. Bluffed by wind, thrilled with danger, they might have navigated the North Sea's length in silence — Sophia worrying both for self and friends — had not Bessie seen that she shivered so desperately.

The sail had squared and that versatile bare foot maintained the tiller. All at once, the giantess again lifted Sophia like a toy, sat her on her knee, and began chafing her limbs, murmuring incoherently. Dwarfed against a mighty chest, Sophia realised that Bessie was not cleanly but smelt acridly of sweat, the sea, and her cargoes: even then, the blood tang from the bundles of hides tied on deck came back mustily on the wind, and she almost retched at the thought of what those butcher hands had recently performed. Acute embarrassment perhaps more than the chafing made her quickly warm and soon she politely disengaged herself. Thereat, Bessie handed her the tiller, and made to cover her hand with a wide and murderous hand, so that she drew back instinctively.

"I'm not a witch," snapped the big woman, and, insisting, guided Sophia until she had the steering right. Then Bessie plunged into the cabin.

She reappeared with the bead necklace that had hung round the statue and, squatting on the deck opposite to supervise the steering, began untying the string. With difficulty in the moonlight, she threaded on a seventh and eighth bead, the panels of her hair swinging and her eyebrows heavily concentrating.

"Is that for the idol?" Sophia asked.

The woman grunted like an animal, "Hnnh?"

"A mother of Jesus, I think it is."

Bessie lifted her head and suddenly smiled a brilliant smile of moonlit, gappy teeth under brows thick as caterpillars.

"We don't count the ones who die. Just count eyes," she said. "Two new beads for the eye." And she grunted again over her work.

Horrified at this murderous abacus, Sophia concentrated on her steering, and then blurted out:

"But are ye a Papist, woman?"

"Could say. An' you're a harlot."

She began squeaky giggles that became a cackling caterwaul.

Sophia, looking down, realised what kind of dress she had donned.

"Oh dear," said Bessie. "Don't cry."

"But how can ye aid us, when it's aye the Papists we're fightin'?"

"That's just what you call those devils. Each eye a soldier man's. I see them killing. Eye for eye. Papists are in France. These just English piddlydoos. Scotch piddlydoos."

Rashly, Sophia exclaimed: "But ye're helping me escape, woman."

Bessie set the necklace aside, balanced her hands on the deck, and stared at her passenger.

"Might not," she said, thoughtfully. That being enough thought, she added: "Oh dear. But will. Religion is —." (She used an indecent expression.)

"I thocht ye just said ye were a Papist."

"That I am. Religion is —." (She used it again.) "Right, wrong, anything's possible. How is anyone to know? You just don't let them down peaceful people You just don't let them down — women. Eye for eye. Those —."

Sophia had never heard this second indecency before. She stared round at the beauties of the night sea, unstably smeared with green milk, flickering, draining, yawning black, stretching out and gathering into heaps, collapsing, and sloshing as it creamed past the *Mary Cutler*. The sky was now full of stars chilled into cold fires by the moon or fading under smoky cloud. The barge mast pointed towards the heaven's great pattern, as if the great finger of possibility were wavering in its choice among fixed fates. The boat yawed on a cross-swell, and the deck lifted, making of Bessie a colossus rising against the night; the vessel heaved forwards on its run once more.

"Whaur's y'r sailor boys?" Sophia asked.

"Hnnh?"

"There's four beds, ye ken?":

"Not a good question. Just me."

Sophia then realised that all the sheets cleated back across deck to the well for single-handed sailing.

Bessie added: "Oh dear. In Rotterdam there's my ladies. In Scotland eye for eye."

"What manner of woman are ye?" whispered Sophia.

"I'm not a witch," Bessie suddenly bellowed with all her force. She looked wild-eyed and the girl was scared before her.

"Well, wha says ye are?"

"Good question, Scarlett. Like it. But there's many, oh so many, have called me that."

The woman still looked fit to go a-slaughtering. To calm her, Sophia thought of her story-telling talent which had charmed the Blacklock servants round the spinning wheel.

"I'll tell ye a tale of a true witch, what I kent a time... if ye want it."

Bessie grinned the alarming smile and said, "Tale. I want my pipe."

She returned to the cabin and when she came back to the well her lips were pursed on a glowing clay pipe.

"I kent this woman. She was the niece of the Warlock Laird of Fail, hard by Tarbolton whaur I was reared. Aye, the Warlock Laird, a wrinkled auld laird he was in King Jamie's time. Walter Whiteford. Och, naebody kent that he was a wizard for sure but he looked like wan, daft-like wi' his slee twa eyen an' his kenning. Jessie tellt me he was like a school bairn, sae muckle his japes and pranks: he could aye prevent the butter thickening in the churn, halt the plough in the furrow — unless there was a rowan branch on the plough hondle. He wad make his whole hoose o' people dance till they could niver stap. But he fell deed natural-like and on the very bed promised his servants nane should come tae harm if they wad only bury him decent, which they did as ye can see by his stane at Coilsfield. Now this was before Mr. Guthrie and Mr. Peden came tae bring sanctification tae our village. What, woman? Ye niver heard tell of Mr. Guthrie and Mr. Peden? They are just the most famous men I iver heard of and Mr. Peden himself cursed me wance — but tha's anither story, an' one that sorely wrongs me.

"Weel, naebody kent whether the laird was a wizard, as I tellt ye, an' if onywan wad have kent it surely King Jamie himself wad have bin that person, for sniff out a witch that king could certain. Now the laird had a sister, Elsie, whose pride was her dochter Maggie Osborne wha they called Mother Fail later. Wan day a gaberlunzie — "

"What?" The giantess gripped the deck. Her teeth grinned round her clay pipe as to snap it clean.

"Eh? — why, a beggar-man! wha cam tae her door and he looked sae woeful-like, thin as a ghaist, that they aye lodged him that nicht an' he sat him doon in the ingle besides young Maggie. An' how he sang and ranted tae them that even, an' the tales he tellt! Maggie was fair bumbazed t' hear him. No word of what he said tae her was heard by her mam save wan: "How blythe I wud be!" which on remembrance later her mam laid up tae her heart.

"Next morning early, they went tae speir for the poor man an' the straw was cauld: he was gone. They searched through tae see if they waur robbit of their gear. Waladay! Waladay! As the song I've e'en heard sung tells us. Ye'll be half guessing what happened. Their gear was safe right eneuch: it was their own darlin' dochter that had bin taen.

"Now the Laird of Fail waxed wroth indeed tae see his sister's dochter stole by a beggar-man, and he cursed that poor gaberlunzie in the braes an' in the mountains, by his ingle and before sleep. Still, langtime, naebody heard word o' the dochter. Weel, the laird aft and died his last, and mony years after an auld auld woman came intill Tarbolton inn and said she was Maggie Osborne. They waur highly suspecting but, by the charity of Mrs. Blacklock, she was settled in a dirty hovel on her lee lane, and soon eneuch rumours cam tae be spake against her as a witch. She wud aye shudder if she shud meet ye in the byway.

"Jessie of the dairy sent me wi' a box of plums an' I found her there i' that hovel, a wee blind linnet in a cage by her which oor housemaid, Mary, said was her devil. I was that skeered and put down the plums, but she helt me by the arm and said I mun take tea wi' her."

"I hope you didn't," muttered Bessie, a great frown of worry amid her eyebrows.

"Och, she moved sae slaw, ye ken, slaw, slaw, aboot her business, wi' dust in every corner an' the walls weepin' for her loneliness. Her face had been on her for iver, an' her eyen — little fiery things that didnae see for they waur sae deep in her heed. The tea tastit weird and herbish an' she kept a-gabblin' whiles I drank it. I cleaned her hovel right eneuch and I'm a bit of a sloven they used tae say. An' she hersel' tell't me the tale o' the gaberlunzie man, saying that wance i' the woods where they repaired for the nicht he opened his shirt an' she saw a secret sign on his breest that hadnae bin there before, but she wudnae say what that sign was. I think tae mysel' she half believed what all my neighbour lasses said o' her. She gave me all her wee planties when the witch-finders took her: harmless, harmless auld biddy, but a real lady, ye ken, a real laird's niece wha cud talk your hind leggis off."

"It's just my story," said Bessie, and she was gulping with emotions like a little girl. "No-one will listen."

"It's but a story, woman," said Sophia, trying to get her companion out of that mood. "She was condamned for tae be drownded at Ayr the following year. An' when they cam tae her cell for tae mak her droon, she was disappeared intae the air. Jessie tellt me it was for the sins of her uncle that Auld Nick himself had come in the likeness of that gaberlunzie man for tae spirit the niece awa'. Sinsyne, there's a saying in Tarbolton about the Warlock o' Fail: that he wud try tae curse the divil himself."

"Jessie should not tell such things. No devil. There is no devil." Bessie had tears in her voice as she said this.

Sophia knew a Tarbolton village idiot with the same sudden mood switches; although the big woman's sailing strategies had been full of decision and sense. She felt her story tactless and then realised she had begun to treat this apparent murderess as a fellow human.

"Mother Fail wad teach me yon herbs and flowers till I kent them a', an' wance she gave me e'en this little bunchy spell wha's I carry aroun my neck in this pigskin, though I doot the water has done it nae guid."

Sophia took her amulet on its leather necklace from her bosom and showed it, but Bessie edged away in horror.

"I hae sinsynes wondered wha' it wud be tae be a witch. It's a gran' fear I have."

"Witch! Witch! All the time," Bessie wailed, her vocal cello cracking in its wood. "You're just by yourself if you're me. Witch! Witch! Scarlett! You're backing the sail! Over a bit, over."

They were lost from the shores now, alone under the moon and the wandering waters, trapped into each other's company in that boat's well. Sophia leant heavily on the great tiller and brought the *Mary Cutler* to rights.

And then it was as if they couldn't stop talking, even if one side of the conversation stuck at the very birth of grammar sometimes. As dawn rose, the solan geese were scissoring into the waves or flickering through the mist on their immensely slender white wings dipped with black. Sophia heard, "Look out!", and next she knew she was awaking the following evening where Bessie had lain her in the cabin as the breezy run continued.

Halfway to Rotterdam, Sophia thought to say, "They call you witch only for your great height. How cam ye so high."

"I was born not in love."

"Och but we're all loved when born. Even I, though abandoned in the oat stooks, was taken up by a binifactor."

"*Ma mère* lay in prison for attempting my murder."

"Who's *ma mère*?"

"My mother."

"Oh, that is a mischance."

"They gave me to her. Took her from prison and gave her me. *'Parbleu'* she would say *'Parbleu.'*"

"Is that the English?"

"Oh but this was all in France, don't you see? She was with the French king's soldiers. Here, there, she went. She was French all along, *ma mère*. Then in prison on account of nearly killing me. And she wanted to be in France no more. So she came to Portsmouth with a soldier when a French lord came to see the English king."

"Where might Portsmouth be?"

"In England, deep in England by the Southern sea. Where I grew."

In these staccato phrases, Bessie recounted her childhood, a sorry tale of beatings, of a mother desperate to earn a living in a foreign country, migrating to the dockside in Poole, and, her own looks fading, trying to prostitute her ugly daughter to the dockers from the age of 14 until she grew too tall for all except the most perverse; and that unkind woman receiving in return not hatred but a sort of animal love. Just before her death from plague, her mother sold Bessie to a bargee ("my owner") in the Poole estuary, a cruel man for whom, in the French *batellerie* fashion, she would act as draught horse along the bankside from the muddy estuary up river to Wareham. She could draw laden barges against the tide, and, performed extraordinary feats when unloading, balancing full sacks of flour on her head and carrying two others under her arm. Her hot temper made her notorious for brawls with men. The enthusiastic historians of the Fancy may not lightly be contradicted; and they record the first woman prize-fighter to have been one Elizabeth Wilkinson in 1722. Nevertheless, money changed hands when young Bessie fought and she acquired the soubriquet, Christmas Bessie, as a fighting name. On one memorable occasion Lord Rochester himself slipped away from a Royal visit to Poole to see her fight, but judged it unenlightened even for a rake to transport such a woman to the capital; and so this potential page of pugilistic history fell blank.

Her "owner", unaccustomed to prodigy, believed a combination of romance, brutality, and blackmail would control the giantess. Of "romance" it is not necessary to speak; from "brutality", we turn aside in disgust; on "blackmail" we may pause a moment. The origins of the later smuggling... "industry", let us call it... in Poole lay in privateering along the English Channel: first Spanish and French, then during the Civil War, English royalist vessels had been plundered with impunity by the puritan sailors from Poole; after the Restoration, any French vessel rash enough to hove in sight was still fair game. The patriotic pirates paid surface tribute to the Crown, but, underground, established stores of liquor and jewels on the Hampshire and Dorset coasts. Her "owner" involved Bessie in this semi-contrabanding; she did not understand what was owed to the Crown and what was not, but knew exposure would mean prison. He it was who first threatened her with denunciation as a witch.

"But ye escaped him, woman!" Sophia said, as the other had fallen silent amid her memories.

Bessie looked across the waters.

"One night, after I beat the fiercest rousterman in Wareham, my owner put my money in his bed. I wanted it and he took the whip. I was still fighting hot. I hit my owner a blow back. The only time. He died. I took his barge and his eye, the Bible says I must."

She indicated two beads on the discarded necklace. Then she pointed across the deck, to the West.

"I took his barge and I sailed it there. To Holland, where the French Huggenies went, *ma mère* said. To Rotterdam. And I am a bargee there in summer and a ladies woman, because I want to help ladies who are like *ma mère*. Your Kirk came to me there, in Rotterdam, and I sail to Scotland for them. Grain, cheese, flowers sometimes, to Scotland. Back to Dutch with yarn, ribbons, lead ore, wood, coal, salmon, and the Kirk people."

It had been dawning on Sophia, confused by Bessie's lapidary style of conversation, not only that her companion had deaths on her hands, but also that her boat functioned doubly, as a freighter and as a Rotterdam bawdy house. She felt breathless to encounter such depravity. "An' yet," she wondered, "why is there a kind of innocence here? As for witches, I dinnae believe in ony o' that -- oh, I hope nat, I hope nat."

She didn't know what to say until she came up with: "But we are both orphans, then."

"*Huvvens*, that was a mistake," she was thinking seconds later, for Bessie sprang off the deck top into the well and hugged her close to her acrid chest.

So, like oldest friends, they exchanged story and confidence on that breezy voyage. Sophia could not discover that Bessie had ever committed murder except out of self-defence, inadvertency owing to her strength, or taking the honourable side in someone else's deathy quarrel. She came to an unusual recognition for an untutored village girl: that, surrounded by bad example, Bessie's mere physical oddity might result in isolation, violence, salaciousness, and criminality. Bessie's only tutor had been her hot heart raging uncontrollably for justice — a dangerous engine in the breast of so lethal a musculature. A curious relation established between them out of this voyage: Sophia — perhaps she alone — could always see direct through the safe eye of the hurricanoes into Bessie's soul.

At first light, Sophia laid herself down on a pallet in that odoriferous hold, and, as she stared at the low, planked ceiling, she sensed the mast, and Bessie, above her. Bessie was a giant captain in a restless sea of possibility, buffeted by its contrary winds, extraordinary well acquainted with sailor-craft, but bereft of the one true chart, that of morality. Oh, but Sophia's last thought was that she herself was a fugitive, not just from the law but also from Percy.

CHAPTER XI

The Difficulty of Pardon

ON one of those mornings, Sophia awoke to find Bessie cuddling her loosely like an infant and examining the pigskin amulet around her neck. Abashed, her unasked-for nurse released her and went out to unload, for they had arrived at Rotterdam wharf. Sophia discovered her own clothes beside her and heard Bessie shouting, "Lurr Vincent". By the time she went on-deck, the bargewoman was standing on the dockside with half a tree under her arm and talking to a gnome-like merchant, Herr Loewinson, wearing a befloured, belted smock; he was blinking white eyebrows and chuckling, as were a ring of Dutch wharfmen in round leather caps, who gathered to observe the giantess.

Determined to be of use, Sophia hefted a sack of yarn on her shoulder and stepped on to the dock, but her late skipper broke her negotiations and shook her hair swags furiously.

"You, Scarlett. Scots kirk."

She made odd signs with her hands, halving her forearm with a palm to indicate directions and distance and Sophia felt bound to obey.

All she would say to Sophia's protestations of gratitude was, "Never fear. Never fear." Her maternalistic sentiment seemed to have vanished.

"Will I no see ye again, Bess?"

"I have fame."

And she grinned the huge grin and turned back to negotiations, which the audience evidently hoped would become heated, just to see this phenomenon become angry.

Sophia, leaving that group behind, reflected that three months previously, she had scarcely stirred from her native village. Now, alone once more and full of heartache, she still had a spring in her step: to be free of her dangers, abroad in this famous refuge for the Scots, this seat of learning; to pass under the bowsprits of tall ships looming above the wharf buildings; to be amazed that even infants spoke the strange tongue; to walk past sparkling latticed windows; to look hungrily into pungent cheese and sweeter pastry shops run by matrons whose bud-like hats sprouted winged lace collarings; to saunter by a canal; to have a strange door at which to seek help; and to sense a future full of promise... even the heartsore may be lifted by such novelties. Some other feeling seemed to her harder to control: an over-excitement at a future bristling with possibilities, each a yellow spear in a dark forest, and a fear that went with these arousals, a fear of herself.

She stopped at a spotless white building of beaded and escutcheoned plasterwork; here was the meeting house, church, and occasionally lodging house for Scots religious refugees, who would bide a night before assuming a new name and an anonymous dwelling. A bow-legged servitor in black satin, an archaeological relic of the Cromwellian era, cackled "Come awa' in the ben quick-like for we're spied on," sat her away from the window, and took her two letters into some unnamed personage, who was taking his porridge in the garden. One letter, to William of Orange from Sir John, forms part of that more official history with which we have nothing to do. Our view just now is purely Sophia's; we can say that everyone in that sober mansion was perfectly dressed to dine in a dungeon; and there we can leave that first morning in Rotterdam.

For Sophia, Sir John had kept his bargain. He had settled her on a recusant historian, the Reverend David M'Fail, whom the severe conformist Alexander Burnet outed from the Glasgow University as one of the first acts of his archbishopric. The old scholar was said to have spent a week in a graveyard, hiding in his family vault, before escaping to Holland. Sophia was to ease the M'Fails penury by acting as their sole servant, while in return Sir John would fund her subsistence and Mrs. M'Fail educate her to a modest level.

Our documentation runs thin upon these two years in Rotterdam — lamentably our sources, including Sophia herself, did not regard a girl's education as a topic for effusion. Mrs. M'Fail taught her decorous behaviour and dress, a little *demode* perhaps, and she learnt precise expression, although, as her prison testimony shows, she never achieved a clear orthography and would always lapse into the vernacular: but these were days when even her final opponent, the celebrated advocate Sir George Mackensie, novelist, correspondent of John Dryden, wrote, to a modern eye, like a semi-literate.

More importantly, she dwelt in daily contact with genuine kindness and gentility of heart. She records her memories of the old scholar thus:

Tae fashion my genteel Curator, think ye of ane cube of flesch wi' roundid cornors, glew on a cloud of white sheeps wull, twa tuftie eyebrows tae suit, and plomp twa cherry cheeks beneeth, crinkle the forheed for his profond thochts, geen a wee hitch tae the lippis for guid cheer, and mak the reverend gentleman tae talk fast as a goose but wi' stutters instead of gabbles. Whyte and crimson he was, dwarvish, and full of principles, but verra dry. I had my fill of the kirk from him, certain, but that was all for his kindness tae me. Mrs. aye kept me tae it and I thocht her frowsty a time until I understood her humours, although we parted not such good frends as I wud hav liked.

We must imagine her co-operating with Mrs. M'Fail in domestic tasks, while the old professor ha'hed over an interminable history of the late troubles. She would have been educated to be a solid housekeeper, fit for a nobleman's mansion, studying the perfection of laundry, management of servants, fine-point needlework, elementary accounting, general literacy; but we must add Dutch, some history, a little law and Latin, and, more important still, free run of the professor's library which was extensive for those days. The Edinburgh bookseller Mosman of the Luckenbooths was later to buy 500 volumes of it. Information concerning Sophia's reading does not survive, but we suppose she started with Percy's recommendations: Buchanan's history, Rutherford's *Lex Rex*, and Mackenzie's *Religious Stoic* — Mackenzie being not yet the enemy he became; she would have gone on to the poets, Dunbar, Ferguson, and Spenser; also Knox and Calvin, doubtless, and the religious tracts of the times. And she delved, we fear, into an account of witches — whether Scot, Bodin, or King Jamie's is not known — hidden away behind other tomes. Somehow this dry, partisan diet helped her to develop an independent mind, although a superstitious one. And another potent influence was exercised upon her.

Here lie the germs of the trouble that has been hinted between her and the M'Fails during her years in Rotterdam: for her, a struggle between independence and loyalty. Her hosts were the epitome of gentility; there was even a soberly handsome son attending Leyden University who, when home, looked upon her with unexciting favour. No, her remark about the father, "I had my fill of the kirk from him", already has told us much. An intolerable tension built up in Sophia — this much we do know — as her thought grew freer while the doctrines taught her by these rather shadowy patrons seemed accordingly ever more inflexible. She felt an orphan again.

"Sir John had made me treasinous plotter. Now in all my curators' best considerations they wud mak me fanatick," goes her testimony. "The wan soul who wanted me for ma ane sake was Bess."

Bess, Miss Christmas Bessie Queensferry, the giantess herself, cannot long be withheld from any scene she is near. A byword among the Dutch sailors, she held court at a tavern on the dockside, quaffing ferkins of ale, a simmering possibility of violence keeping even the stoutest Dutchmen wary. She would swagger out of the inn to help with unlading, or sail downriver with four or five lascivious customers to some rendezvous where, it was rumoured, ill-fortuned ladies would join the party for a riotous deep-sea cruise. Other times, she would mysteriously disappear for a week, on Scots business. Her housework over, Sophia would sit with the giantess on her return, the two dangling bare legs over the wharf; and she would watch the sun sink moodily beyond the polders, silhouetting windmills against vermillion. Bessie's curt phrases would suggest to her monstrous, distant lands where no-one talked of your fate as fixed by God, but all swelled with prospect and adventure; there, a second, unencumbered Percy might be with her. "It's adventure for tae dwell in Rotterdam: och, but what adventures there may yet be!"

"You want Percy Graham, Scarlett," Bessie would puff, her pipe smoke exuding with the words. She would nod for a full minute in a dumb sympathy that won through to Sophia's heart and calmed its wilder fears.

Or Bessie would announce as the beginning of another tale: "Walton in the Nose". "On the Nose. It's cliffs and a nose of land. Sandy beach good for landing by skiff. Forgot. Can trust you, Scarlett. Not Walton. Went back secretly from Dutchland to Poole in England. My old home. And the plague was all around. Seen plague? Ugh! Great black boily things here." (She pointed rudely.) "Girl of mine, Mary Cutler, one of my ladies, was baby-blown. Caught it from Willem Van den Dyke, merchant."

"Do ye mean the plague?"

"No. Caught baby. Must have done something forbidden on the barge. We allus — " She made an indecent gesture. "What's wrong? Oh you, innocent. Her baby was like I was, born. Not right. Don't know what wrong. Not right. Pumpkin head. So-ho, so terrible and sad." (And her voice hit its low cello of tearfulness.) "Mary went mad one night. Screaming, my ears, oh! Killed it."

"The baby?"

"Baby."

"Poor, poor baby," said Sophia; it had grown dark and she heard her own voice mournful across the inky harbour surfaces.

"Horrible, horrible sheriff," Bessie countered, in similar mournful rhythm. "Mary just went mad. I seen her. What can you do? Sheriff promised Mary. He said, 'You be nurse for us in plague. If you live, have health, why then... you live, no execution.' So she went round houses, helping drink, keeping clean, calling the dead wagon, all sorts of things. I helped in some times because she was crying so all day. She were brave, see? She lived. No plague. Then sheriff sent to His Majesty, King Charles II, said, 'Your Majesty, King Charles II, Pardon this afflicted girl, Mary Cutler, by your leave and with humble remonstrance.'"

"A pardon. O good!" Sophia breathed: her chest felt tight with strange anxieties at the strangeness of these distant events which escaped any theological category she had ever heard of.

"Not good."

"Not good?"

"The king said 'No Pardon for baby'. And they hanged her at crossroads by Poole. They call it Cutler's Gallows, that place now. I name this barge, *Mary Cutler*. Oh, before, I killed one of the executioner's soldiers. Took his eye, by our Lady. You tell me I, a Papist, must fight for *that* king?"

Her voice rose to one of her sudden furies. "Nature, Nature baby!"

It was as if she had made a flight of Burkean political oratory to explain why she helped the Covenanters, who should have been her religious opponents.

The two of them became one of the more absurd sights of Rotterdam, the notorious giantess causing every head to turn, every conversation to buzz a little with scandal, and the wild-eyed maiden, her plaids made incongruous by a newly carved pair of wooden clogs. News of this alliance came quickly to the M'Fails: man, wife, and son alike found the twosome an "unholy combination" (the professor said), "downright dangerous" (his wife), and "matter for eternal damnation" (the son).

Sophia, whose mooring in the Covenanting faith had always been by slip knot, was beginning, like Bessie's barge, to glide away from that secure shore. Already overshadowed physically by the bargee, affected in her sentiments by Bessie's curious admixture of the warm-hearted and the amoral, she now found that the friendship conducted her to milieux unguessed at in her Ayrshire village: Bessie tied her barge up in the dirtiest waters beside the poorest slums, where the maimed, the prostitute, the scoundrelly, the abject, and, to put no fine point on it, the idiotic nested in squalor like so many dusty city sparrows. To the Kirk's Elect, these were sinners to be reformed, d.v.; to the bargee, they were her own folk and she strode amongst them like a queen, ducking her head to enter depraved hovels, with Sophia as her welcomed Maid of Honour.

Sophia would see Bessie hug the leprous, kiss the syphilitic, give money to the thief, and shake hands with the murderous, some small Hollandish cannon within her shooting out Dutch phrases even more abrupt than her English ones. Almost, Bessie encouraged her to prostitution, since the giantess *saw nothing wrong in it* : she had no rational morality, only her heart for guide. Just two years previously, the Dutch had opened the polders and flooded a French army advance on Amsterdam. Bessie spent a fortnight in jail for leading a hobbling troop of Dutch war veterans to the Rotterdam Stadhuis, seeking compensation for their patriotism. She suffered a famous public whipping for asking more money for those who laboured on the docks. Sophia's protectors attended. All this is matter for another, more indecorous story which it were doubtful we should be allowed to tell. Sophia, never more than observer, became vicariously experienced in the ways of virtue, vice, civic feeling, and rebelliousness: but all in the same sack, jumbled together; and it puzzled her mind immensely. She found herself lying about where she had been when the M'Fail's, at their dinner table of judgment, would ask. If stuck for an answer, she would sing and hum to herself. Percy, she imagined, would by now be inextricably jointured by marriage to these same stern judgments.

Greater fears for Percy lay in store for her, though coupled now with heady romance. One day, after a three week absence, Bessie sailed into Rotterdam with a long letter to Sophia from Isabel, whose orthography we may reform for convenience.

CHAPTER XII

Of Coals and Blackness

My dearest Sophya,

   I have heard such contradictory accounts of you — from Miss Queensferry all praise, but from those more sober judges, Mr. and Mrs. M'Fail, anxiety for your soul. Our brave giantess tells me I have two hours, the tide coming into this muddy creek, though I have so many misfortunes to relate. I am forbidden to tell you my hiding place, not because you have become my rival, as I shall describe, for you will ever be my dear friend, but because letters have become dangerous.
   After you sailed away from our little barque that time of your escape, Percy and I, making our own escape under oar, quarrelled for the first time seriously, for he thought we should have joined you, whereas I, conscient of our own jeopardy and careful for the work of the Kirk in Scotland, declared you were escaping to a new future. Our second quarrel in that boat was a comedy, the sick man refusing to let the lady row and denying that a bias of his left oar was steering us inshore. "'Tis just a small correction that I make," he kept saying. These disputes so contrary to Percy's character reinforced a suspicion that had been growing in me that he fought against the withdrawal of his heart from me and against its inclination towards yourself. I know not whether it is noble or foolish in me to confess this, but it seems, alas, the Lord's will to which I wretchedly submit, as shall appear in the sequel.
   We heard a "hoo" from the bank and, in the gloom, a man leapt from under low pines on to an offshore rock and seemed to wave us in. I found a pistol still in Percy's belt and, though it had half the ocean in its lugs and would never fire, I threatened our would-be rescuer, who turned out to be Mr. Robinson from North Queensferry — you will recall that he brought our sailing instructions from the giantess. His trade is to haul English coals from Port of Leith to the grand houses of Edinburgh, and even the soldiers in the Castle warm their hands on Robinson's embers. Therefore had he come to load his carts but also to check on our safety; and, hovering near our small battle, had observed its sequel. He'd horses with him, which brought us to his hovel, and on dismounting we found our legs streaked from their dusty backs. For three days, he harboured us, seemingly careless of his own safety, though three matters in that household troubled me mightily: I found no Bible; his wife, a sour-faced creature, acted cowed and

fearful; and his son was sly. Poor Percy, with his frank heart, his sickness now full upon him, and his wandering fancy, trusted them at first until, once more, we quarrelled and, on my severe instructions, he declined to give them any of the information Robinson would pawkily seek — where you, Sophya, were headed, did you carry letters, did we know any of the grand folks, was Brown the Carrier — whom Robinson professed for a friend — one of the Covenant, who were the Elders in Edinburgh? And in-see de sweet.

As I write, the foundation for suspicion seems obvious but, as Robinson presented us with our only escape, we agreed to join his next coal convoy to Edinburgh, disguised in his and his wife's clothing (thus man and wife gained Percy's satin jerkin and breeks and my walking dress, little though that will improve Mistress Robinson's looks.)

The day arrived and four of his horses were laden with panniers of coal from his yard — the whole family, in truth, was perfect soot —; we journeyed on foot alongside the beasts eight weary miles to Edinburgh, planning to approach first the Elder, Mr. M—, and then your old employer, Mr. B—, who, as a lawyer, actively attempts to have Percy's father, Mr. Andrew Graham, removed from the Tolbooth prison, where he still languishes despite our late efforts.

First, I wanted to stop at the rear of my dwelling under the High Street ridge, so to penetrate the inner courtyard unobserved, for the frontispiece would almost certainly be watched. Once inside, I replenished our store of money (for I had given most to Robinson for our danger and for our keep), and also withdrew new clothing wrapping it around a sword for Percy, because we were so grievously beset. As I rejoined the convoy, Robinson was trying to persuade Percy that we should go as coalhaulers into the Lyons Den of Edinburgh Castle, as our disguise would make the place of greatest danger also the safest. While this discussion proceeded hotly, a cart drew alongside whose driver recognised Percy. In that gleefulness native to the Grahams, Percy set a final test for Robinson, addressing the carter — in reality the whimsical Mr. Brown — as "Mr. Johnstone", adding "Matthew 26, 21", which you will know for, "Verily I say unto you, that one of you shall betray me", a holy word immediately comprehended by all save the most un-Christian Robinson, who furthermore failed to recognise his "friend", Mr. Brown. So, despite a privy word from Robinson to Percy that the carter was not to be trusted, we parted from "the coals".

Once Robinson's grumbles had turned the corner towards the Castle, Brown said he would keep an eye on this presumed informer and also send to the Elder, Mr. M—, to prepare a night's lodging, and for a messenger to be sent to Mr. B—, the lawyer, lest he could help us. We, meanwhile, were to proceed to a low tavern by the Cowgate, 'The Twa Crowns', to change our dress.

So, with sack of clothing and incongruous sword, we stole through poor streets where the city huddles its smoky beehives together as if waiting for someone to put a flint to it. Under black arches, through squeezed lanes, and crossing courts where urchins squabbled, we felt derogated from our station and become one with the idle ruffians skulking under flags of washing whiter than their souls. We reached a disreputable ordinary behind the Cowgate, with two crowns on its sign, tawdry symbol indeed of the disgraces brought by uniting Scottish and English thrones under such a king.

Now the inn's front door was upon the thoroughfare, whereas a side door opened upon an alley too narrow for horses, with an arch leading down steps to a nether road. Inside, the inn held a few scarred tables and a depraved Host, whose apron was a showcloth for the human handprint. My dishevelled collier appearance passed muster in that Den of Vice full of riotous villains — for Mrs. Robinson, you may be sure, had handed on her most tattered apparel, and I had dirtied my hair and face.

For a consideration, the Host let us change in two back rooms and, Percy having prepared himself first, he called for some ale and sat at a table to await me — he must have looked most conspicuous in his clean trews and hose and his gentleman's sword. A letter from him has described what happened next, oh, for this was the most sorry time of our separation, and I may never see him more unless I can call your aid, and that not for my own account, as you shall hear when I adduce that letter.

He sank his lips into the ale, not daring to observe who came or went. A burly man suddenly sat on his bench beside him, pinning him to the wall so that he was powerless to draw his sword. This man you would have known, though he was wearing a steel skull cap and an iron cuirass. He turned a look to Percy that was all amused cruelty, says Percy, a scar tugging downwards at his lower lip as it twisted contrary in a sneering smile. Now you know him, my dear. It was Captain Glenmuir, your persecutor. At that the side door opened and a bearded soldier in the tartan stood there, cutting off all escape for me or Percy.

"How fortunate that I am about my business in the Castle this day, Mr. Graham," says Glenmuir, most polite.

"Well I know your name to boot," Percy says, even more politely. "But your business cannot involve impressing your physical person so close to mine."

At that, I entered, fully clothed and hopeful, to find my beloved surrounded and myself roughly grasped by the trooper at the side door. Percy would have risen to prevent that but, under threat of Glenmuir's sword, he was forced to yield his own weapon to my trooper and follow the captain who, unmannerly, brushed past me out the side door, with Percy, me, and then the trooper in train. Here, Glenmuir proved over-confident, for as we passed the arch I heard a heavy "Clump!" behind me; my guard fell senseless to the cobbles of that narrow alley; and Brown, the carrier, dragged me across the fallen body, out of the archway, and down steps to his cart, though I was protesting.

"One safe, means one can be rescued," whispered Brown, whom

Glenmuir had no time to see. "The top street is invested with dragoons."

So he drove me almost as his prisoner far enough for safety, whereat I made my way to the Elder's house in a state of indescribable anxiety to await news.

Meanwhile, dear Percy had snatched up his sword from the hands of the fallen trooper, and faced Glenmuir rather as David did Goliath but with less happy result. I shall set down his own account, for its brave humours alone lighten my heart, as my own pen falters.

The soldiers were rushing hither and thither, but the cart had gone, and Glenmuir roared, "Leave this young whelp to me, for I'll have my pleasure of this nonetheless" as I thought "We shall see."

The captain waggled his sword low and crabbed his feet into a balanced stance as he brought up the blade and saluted me.

"Mind y'r puddings," he growled, which was gross, Isabel, as I wished my estomach to prove an impregnable container.

Most ridiculously, I replied, "You will observe what the cream of university fencing may teach a soldier, even one protected by his cuirass", which was the funniest remark the captain had ever heard.

My head was saying, 'A parry, a thrust, back-counter, reprise,' and miraculously my arm followed these intellectual instructions, but nothing in my fencing courts had prepared me for such heaviness of blow or unfairness of tactic. He would barge me against the wall, try to trip me, and then his blade would flash all about my desperate defence, so that I fought dim-sighted in a cloud of lightning, knowing that sooner or later the stroke of Jove would send me, blackened, to the ground. Once, I thought I had him, for my blade scored across his cuirass with a horrid rasp, but the captain laughed full loud, his wrist agile as he whisked my blade clear like a bothersome storm fly.

"Dinnae ye see? I'm playing wi' ye, cub. Just nod y'r noddle twice and drap y'r sword and I'll see ye have a peaceable arrest."

You may imagine what my honour replied to this impertinence and I made a desperate lunge, desperate because with my ill health and weak chest I was all out of breath. The heavy shoulders of the captain suddenly heaved, laughter dinned my ears, his body became a figment, and an agonising pain darted through my shoulder, my sword dingling to the cobbles. I heard, "Ye pimpled fool, d— tak ye for attacking a captain o' His Majesty", and then Jove struck at last, or rather the captain, for I later discovered that he had chopped his sword hilt down upon my jaw, which broke it.

Meanwhile, I, Isabel, had spent a night of tears and frustrations at the Elder's house and, by 9 a.m. the following morning, was walking through the Greyfriars graveyard pretending to look for an ancestral tomb. A rap on Mr. B—'s grille was enough for the porter to open to me and when I entered the chambers I found the outer office, doubtless for prudence, free of clerks.

Sitting in the lawyer's chair, however, was Sir X, well, a nobleman, who has approved this letter and whom you met a time in Tarbolton as a friend of your late employer Mr. B—. Sir X was in court dress, with a top cloak of dark blue silk trimmed with silver piping and buttons, a black wig framing his ugly face with its cautious but kindly look, at his throat a wide collar of elaborate lace, his cuffs drawn and flounced. The chambers' small windows, latticed and cut into thick stone, lit weakly the oak table behind which he sat, and I felt like an accused and did not know how to tell him so many details important for him to know but so intimate to my own heart.

He told me that the lawyer was with the Privy Council, that he had spoken to Brown, and was advised about the scoundrel, Robinson, who, no sooner had he driven his horse-team up to the Castle gate than he had given news of our presence in Edinburgh. It is not so hard for soldiers to search our city's five or six main streets and find fugitives so cast upon mischance as Percy and I. And I gave him my own account as he tutted, pressed his fingertips together, or reached sideways for a quill to scratch a note or two in strangely-formed letters.

He said: "Lassie, lassie. They'll be sending your young man to the Bass Rock, for that's their new darling place for prisoners."

I couldn't bear to think of that wet and windy rock standing so off the shores of Edinburgh and Percy with his illness not yet in cure languishing there. And Sir X, whom you will know to be experienced in all politick matters, looked so kindly upon me, because he sensed I had another deeper heart-sore.

Oh Sophya, Sophya, I write to you for aid, though you have become, unwittingly, my bitterest rival, as I had sensed during those months when you were our guest and as I had worried about so while Percy and I had quarrelled, seemingly about our escapes and mischances, but really over you. I stood there before this nobleman who seemed to read far into me, and this deadly knowledge stole out of its secret place in my heart and rose to my mind.

"Sir X," I said, "perhaps this is little to you, but Percy is grown estranged from me — nothing's ever said, nothing, but so clearly I see a lack of Christian feeling between us, though in our self-persuasions the Lord had seemed to bless our union and even now I love him."

"And might another lass figure in this change of heart?" he murmured.

"Even she across the water."

"Weel, I'm muckle sorry," he remarked as if he were my uncle, "but now I have to explain complicated matters to you." And he told me that now they might release Percy's father, knowing that he would do nothing to endanger his son's life, thus saving the expense of keeping two bankrupt persons when they might only keep one.

"We are caught on a thin web, my dear," I remember him saying, "and an incautious move may awake the spider. The slightest attempt to free the son will prevent my friend, Mr. B—, in his promise to have the aging father freed from his prison in the Tolbooth, which would displease Percy himself. Once Mr. B— has prevailed with the Privy Council we may then act in Percy's behoof."

And so the efforts to free the father Graham wound through the courts, while I skulked first in this shire, then in that, hiding in barns or behind sliding panels, while King Charles kept torturing our Faith. I cannot write all things, for time runs short. One day, by our customary subterfuges, I stood again before Sir X in those self-same offices to resume a topic of two years' interruption, viz. the saving of Percy.

I told Sir X I had heard of rescue effected by a woman's infiltrating into a man's prison cell and there exchanging clothing. Sir X flattered me by saying that I had a "verra noble heart", but that the gaolers would have heard those self-same tales and that the laying down of lives must be done in cause of the Lord's own circumspections, and not for wilfulness and rash bravery, which is surely true. Instead we should remount to the very cause of Percy's troubles, and that was he himself, Sir X. If he had not promoved that you, Sophya, should warn Mr. Peden, if he had not named you thief, then Percy would not have fallen under such condemnation. (*Aye and he might still be mine*, I was thinking. Pity me, Sophya.)

Sir X proposed that you should return from Holland so that he could remove from you the opprobrium in which you stood. Except for the foolish old minister at Tarbolton, whom Sir X would silence with money, no-one saw you take the horse, so the supposed theft can be blamed on the Reverend Peden, the Prophet, incarcerated with Percy now upon the Bass, whom this further charge can little harm more, especially since Sir X will hardly press a complaint home. Percy will then face a lighter accusation that, having met you in such and such a place, hearing you were branded unjustly as thief, and so, and so, he helped you to escape to Holland. The soldiers know that he did not fire when under duress in that unhappy creek, but that a miscreant trooper shot his own man, and the actions of Miss Queensferry are already notorious and not binding upon Percy. Sir X even wanted to adduce a little romance as motivation, but, Sophya, I simply couldn't hear of it, bursting into tears, though in all other respects I act for Percy's rescue.

Sir X fairly sparkled upon me then, telling me I was a young person after his own heart and that he hardly knew how to say the next hard thing, though I replied he should since all was now past hearing.

He said: "I have the unhappiness to compromise my noble temper at Parliament and at Court, that more lowly ones may exercise liberty of conscience under my cloak." (And he flapped his cloak to try to lighten my humours.) "More than the safety of the two Grahams is at stake or I should not intermeddle myself in affairs so particular. New impositions of troops will batten down upon the western shires of Scotland, and some wish to bring down outlandish Highlanders to visit punitive cruelties upon the religious tenants; in response a new firebrand preaching grows popular and threatens armed rebellion outright, whose prospect is very real. Maintenance of myself as mediator is vital. A private matter must be explained to this Sophya Scarlett so that she will understand the dangers she courts."

I saw that he meant someone should journey to fetch you, and though I felt the mere telling of Percy's change of affections would suffice, he had the honour not to use an affair of heart as a means of politick persuasion, given circumstances I shall impart to you.

"Then someone should voyage to Sophya equipped with the full persuasionment," I said.

"Whom might we send?" he sweetly asked.

"There is I."

Sophya, so it is that I must shortly come to you, enemy in love but most trustworthy, dearest friend, and explain these meanings to you. One thing I request we discuss no further than is imparted in this letter that I received from the Bass Rock, enclosed in a courteous note from the Prison Governor, and which I excerpt:

> ...and though I have wrestled so cruelly with my conscience and my undying admiration for you, Isabel, I have been unable to tear my mind in this dismal imprisonment from that other, unattainable friend abroad, and I would not have you set yourself at risk any more for one who declares himself your most loyal, your most life-long supporter...

This, then, your unhappy messenger will be with you imminently to sob her troubles upon your neck, knowing the mutual sympathy that unites us, and to seek your help in setting Percy — and his father, for all our efforts in that regard have failed — free from duress. Have pity on your Isabel and deserve the respect of your patrons, the M'Fails, for theirs is the identical respect of Christ Himself.

Sir X says you must now destroy this letter.

Isabel

CHAPTER XIII

Homebound on the *Mary Cutler*

BY the time Isabel arrived on a brig the following month, the Rotterdam authorities had handed the scandalous Bessie Queensferry an alternative: expulsion or execution. Isabel, so warmly welcomed by Sophia at the dockside and escorted to the M'Fails, lodged for two days in a house divided between affection for her friend and accumulating distaste for her bargee associate. Sophia, it proved, lived in a hectic langour and would sit by herself humming some song. By contrast, the saddened, rejected, devout, doctrinally-pure Isabel conformed exactly to the old couple's ideal of young womanhood; she held endless discussions with the M'Fails about Sophia as if she were *in loco parentis*.

"Sir X" of the letter was, of course, Sir John Cochrane, whose instructions were for return to Scotland by a date only a week away. Sophia, being already eager, the household so upset, Isabel decided to explain Sir John's deeper purposes when *en voyage*. But how to embark? The one unquestionably free vessel departing from Rotterdam had the disreputable Bessie for skipper; so it was very much with a sigh and a "Well, and if you must" that the M'Fails took leave of the two maidens at the harbour, bestowing upon Sophia combined headshakings and smiles that made her feel dreadfully contrary. Bessie arrived under musketeer escort and it was a soldier's foot that eventually shoved the barge clear from the wharfside as its skipper, protesting that she had not been allowed to load cargo, turned the air purple with profanities; Isabel pointedly shielded her ears; in the distance the M'Fails marched firmly home.

The overcast sky where it was descending to the horizon lay in brownish folds over silver glowing; squalls flurried across the estuary, making their passage to deep sea a succession of becalmings and accelerations as they weaved in and out of other craft sailing on the morning tide. Isabel wondered aloud whether the voyage would be stormy, but Bessie sank into one of her mountainous sulks at the tiller, and would not even be helped with the keels. Sophia was thinking: "I'm going home. To naething. My adventures are over. Percy's in prison. But I am loved." She went with Isabel to sit at the bow, knowing her friend's troubles to be worse than her own; and she put her arm round the other's waist, the barge stable under brisk wind.

"If you would see that person we both...admire, you must again consent to be Sir John's messenger," Isabel hesitantly began.

She spoke in thoughtfulness or in hurries in tempo with their progress through the water, thus managing her suppressed feelings by principle of the as-yet uninvented steam valve. Percy, she explained, was not permitted any women visitors to his Bass Rock prison — this, despite his deteriorating health; a few cooks and cleaners from Edinburgh's poorer classes were the only females on the rock. Through a friend, Sir John had arranged employment for Sophia under this latter category, although the post would not be held for her longer than a week — hence the need for hasty departure.

"Issy," said Sophia, gripping tighter at her friend's waist. "What's in this for Sir John?"

There was a *quid pro quo* : she had not got her man wrong. Sophia's working papers would bear the assumed name of "Annie Noel" and she must perform her servant duties for enough days to avoid suspicion. Then she must gain access to Prophet Peden, that preacher whose fate so curiously kept intertwining with her own, and who remained incarcerated on the Bass. She would inform Peden that he, along with numerous other True Kirk prisoners, were shortly to be sentenced to the American plantations: almost certainly, the unhappy Covenanters would be shipped like cattle first to London and thence by a further ship to the colonies. However, London's great Whig peer, Lord Shaftesbury, would direct this second embarcation contract to a ship's master who was prepared at the last minute to rise up in indignation and refuse this religious and not criminal cargo, presenting their guard with an unexpected difficulty at the ship itself; thus prepared, Peden might organise a mass escape. Percy, so much the invalid, would not be eligible for the transportation.

Once she had communicated with Peden, she should depart the rock under some pretext, preferably by earning dismissal, and, back on shore, resume her name of Scarlett which was still sullied by the epithet, "horse thief". Sir John would clear her name and have Percy, henceforward guilty only of association with Isabel and Sophia, against whom lay no proofs, set at liberty.

"My first anxiety would be to restore that one prisoner to health and freedom, but Sir John, I observe, will not lift Mr. Blacklock's accusation of theft from me until I do his bidding with Mr. Peden."

"Oh Sophia," Isabel exclaimed with unusual impulse, "I am heartsore and exhausted, and all I care for most lies under heavy dangers. Surely, we are the two most unhappy women in the world."

They considered this lugubriously for a minute or so until the other girl replied: "We are indeed unhappy, but perhaps we ignore a third who is tae lose every friend, every livelihood, she has ever had and stands more utterly alone than anyone."

"I should be astonished to learn her name."

"Why, it is Bessie Queensferry here with us. Let us lose our own sorrows a little in comforting hers, for there is none else but ourselves tae treat her as anything else but a giantess and a prodigy."

"And she a Papist...," Isabel murmured, nevertheless going aft to join the other two in the well, where Bessie had instantly brightened to Sophia's sympathy for her situation:

"You ointed my back when I was whupped. I don't forget. By the western dykes of Rotterdam, back yonder, a slave lives. I know him. I have told you. Runaway. Black man from the Trinidadee, from the Orinokee. We must sail there, you, me."

For reply to this impossible dream, Sophia just hooted with laughter; after a second Bessie joined in magnificently; even Isabel managed a bleak smile.

At that, the giantess grimaced oddly and put a broad forearm around Isabel's throat, her other hand making as if to pluck out the eye: for a rare moment the older girl completely lost her composure, spun round like that, helpless; and even Sophia feared a sudden murder. Released, Isabel straightened her white clothing and gave yet a primmer smile to an answering guffaw: Bessie had just acted out her jealousy for them, finding it impossible to describe verbally.

The narrative has hinted at a storm; and a storm there shall be, though only one of those gales that make of the North Sea the antechamber to Hell, not one of those typhoons that cast the mariner full down within Hell's doors and before the Infernal Beings. It caught the *Mary Cutler* on the third day out, as they beat, hard-reefed, towards Denmark, hoping to lay in a longer angle towards the May and by-pass the isle across the Firth to Anstruther, in Fife, where they would be unsuspected. There, a goodbye to Bessie, and a horseback ride to the Bass prison's administration in Edinburgh, where Sophia would present her papers, while Isabel would go to ground until her own name, like Percy's, should be cleared. But the wind veered on the card and the boat rose like a shying horse or nosed down like a bloodhound; and anon they were riding along a precipice of water until as by turn of the wrist they flickered over the top into new pastures of desperately drawing water and new mountaining; and anon the boat yawed as though fatigued on plains where the screeching wind ripped shreds of white off the liquid ground. The three of them straddled their legs in the well, where Bessie screamed at her crew when to dip the juddering keels into icy craters; and once a backwash amidships caused Sophia to sprain her wrist.

The calibre of Isabel appeared then, for the thrumming jib blew free at its foot and flapped in wide wildness. Bessie shouted, "Forrard to that sail! Fast down!" Isabel, her clothes bundled up and a line round her waist, journeyed perilously across see-saw decks, clawing for balance at the hull of a skiff battened down on deck, as the skipper luffed and rode, rode and luffed so that the girl could lash the jib's foot with twine. But a storm-wind blew out her clothing, the sailcloth ripped like a shirt, and the tilted decks lurched, spilling the white tent that was now Isabel into the hurtling, leaden waves. She was hauled aboard, spluttering. The giantess, having dumped her like a sodden flour sack, decisively put the tiller up and began a swaying run to Danish harbours, though the drownee, having Sophia's planned day of employment in mind, rose from her heap and yelled that they had no time for such deflection. Bessie yelled back that only she could steer in such weather; she could not keep awake for ever; shelter must be sought. Ten minutes later, Sophia remembered that brave Isabel could not swim.

They lay up on the island of Sylt for a day and a half with the winds still raging and Bessie sew-, sew-, sew-ing at her sail, while Sophia learnt about the sorry condition of her native land where the Killing Times were now approaching.

"For a year, the wavering brethren thought that the King and his Council might be relenting; but my Elders knew that the leopard had merely painted his spots yellow to match his body. Now his spots are stark black once more."

"And what of Ayrshire and Tarbolton?"

"The soldiers have come back with all their cruelties, billeting themselves on any who stay true to the faith. Worse, the Council called upon the deadliest Highland rogues, not just the cattle reivers, but any scoundrel clansman ready for four months of rapine, plunder and torture. Rag-end Stewarts and Murrays, just sheer criminals, were ordered south by the Duke of Atholl, 8,000 claymores have been brandished in the shires of your birth, Sophia: and the countryfolk are fined to distraction, and abused with violence, lust, and murder. You have told me of your favourite on Mr. Blacklock's estate, a little lad, one... I forget his name... and the name of the placed minister..."

"Wee Donald, Donald the Brat? And" (a shiver of distaste) "the Reverend Murdoch."

"Aye. Eight men, including your brat of a friend, took arms, and broke into the church intending to thrust Murdoch from the village. That disgraceful clergyman was absent, but they left word that if he preached again he should die the next day. Since then, Donald has gone into the heather and the minister stays in the manse and sips his broth through fearful chattering teeth."

"Donny will be nigh 16 years old."

"There's many in like case."

So it was towards a nation almost at civil war that they set sail the following morning and on the eighth night, the head wind now a light breeze, they neared the Isle of May. Mid-sea, they changed plan, since Sophia was like to miss her employ through tardiness — she, or "Annie Noel" who in the papers furnished by Sir John was set down as an orphaned soldier's daughter from Ayr garrison.

Bessie blurted out: Change. Don't go to Fife. I steer near the Edinburgh shore. Scarlett takes the new skiff. Rows to this prison rock. Pretends she's out from Edinburgh. Had no time to go to Edinburgh office.

See? Makes excuse. *She* can do this."

Bessie squared her hugely sloping shoulders, a sort of maternal pride.

"I'll say I was caught in these civil commotions that Issy has talked of — as I came across from Ayr."

"See? Second dinghy I lose for you, Scarlett. Second!"

"Sir John will take up that account," Isabel promised.

"Oh, pay. Yes."

The following morning they were sidling along Scotland's shoreline, with scattered cottages behind dunes and cliffs; the ruined Douglas stronghold, Castle Tantallon, came up on the far cliffs; across the straight, the Bass Rock's blackened pinnacle stood out from the restless wash and the surf. Bessie, tears fairly streaming down her face, lowered her new skiff from the deck, took a hitch in its painter to secure it, and crushed Sophia to her chest.

"Never, never, Scarlett," she cried.

"Oh yes," gasped her surrogate child, stifled by flesh, "we shall meet. You have fame."

The giantess lifted Sophia's squeezed corpus straight down into the skiff, and Isabel, who had, a second time, been given little opportunity for farewell, found some oars to hand over as the personal world of all three of them rocked violently.

"Pull strongly," Isabel called, "and we shall meet again."

"Never, never," cried Bessie; and the calm waters widened; and dawn gleamed upon those intervening gulphs, which were gulphs of spirit; and there was heartache.

Sophia, watching the brown sail heading for Fife across seas now calm, began working her way towards the Bass, her oars reckoning two-second intervals against the thole-pins. Her sprained wrist hurt dully. Behind her on the mainland, Tantallon, the ruined castle of a noble family: ahead, the grand site of a rocky prison put to ignoble purposes. Sorrow for her unhappy nation, for her sick lover in his cell, came over her in floods; but she staunchly rowed towards the Bass, where a bugle sounded faintly on the sea-wind. She neared the rock's huge shadow and the waves became ivy green with white bonnets and flatterings of navy blue. Her boat entered the shadow as if an unreal memory closed about her, and she could hear the singing of psalms from under the long rampart of the fortress, where the martyrs tried to make of their dungeons little churches.

The rock rises sheer all about, like a green-browed cake with black sides that the sea-birds have whitened with flour. Her skiff was born in on swells towards the shelf that is the only access, swollen knuckles of water blackening in the folds of that treacherous landing-place and withdrawing like green fingers through dark hair. A gnarled custodian ran out from a block-house above her and shouted:

"It's morally impossible. Ye mun come back tomorrow."

She could see his bare legs, as mottled as a sausage, as she rose in her boat to the shelf and sank again, oars flailing.

"Nor yet I amnae goin' tae."

"Ye might as well try tae ding doon Tantallon and mak a brig tae the Bass."

"Tantallon's already doon, and I'm for landing."

The swell bore her in on a rush and with her good hand she grabbed at an iron ring in the rock-side; immediately, the boat sank beneath her, though, hanging there, she hooked her feet under the gunwale; and immediately, the deck rose again and pushed her up into a crouch as if she were being forced to leap the ring; fierce hands gripped her biceps, as the boat fell away; and her body slammed a second time against the rock. Wood splintered; and she was heaved ashore as the stricken craft bobbed away. And then she was being shaken like a rabbit, boxed round the ears, and cursed at:

"Did ye think tae ding doon Blackie Lane anaw wi' your disobedience, ye surly quean?"

"But my boat," she gasped.

"It'll be in North Berwick at its devotions tomorrow," growled the custodian. "Now ye mun come tae the Governor and a sorry time ye'll hae o' it. Ye'll be Annie Noel, I havenae doot."

CHAPTER XIV

(Notes)

(Editorial Note: The following passages of manuscript are incomplete, though they clearly comprise a preliminary attempt at describing how Sophia rowed to the Bass; they continue with the story of how she obtained employment, and communicated Sir John's message to the Reverend Peden in his cell.)

PAST a loopholed tower, an iron crane for raising the garrison boat to the outer wall, the Governor's residence, a shed or two under the ancient Lauder fortress with its rampart and tiers of arched dungeons underneath, where the Covenanters prayed. Some of the stones falling in ruins where the castle backs on to the rock-face.

The interview: "Where get boat?" "Where are your papers?" — papers lost with the boat, but fortunately her name, Annie-Noel, marked down.

The gales too rough to send for a replacement.
(That sea-bird which cries so mournfully about the blunted turrets and hacked walls of these cliffs is the *kittiwake*.)
The solan geese (English call them *gannets*) shot for feathers; say for pillows and downy beds.

Do something better for restless wash earlier.
Wildfire Rocks and Satan's Bush already ment. in *Catr*.
Hard duties, hard treatment from the guards since the girls were mostly sluttish.
The vivers boat from the Castleton: fish/sheep/geese for sale and for fare. Prison garden. A tiny chapel: St. Baldred.

nae skaith to me   maitter
the porches of the rock
chalmers   his dander rase
Crap in nearer hand. In that dispensation
Canty Bay opposite

Say: To overhear Prophet Peden at his stentorian devotions amused the more blasphemous serving lasses, though none dared face him with derision — not since a girl who had mocked him was swept clean off the rock's

summit by a mighty wind. His reputation for soothsaying gained Peden many privileges, and he would come and go much as he pleased.
Say: In the 18th century, when the Bass had reverted to a wild home for solan geese, an ancestor* of the present author was held kidnap upon the rock; his chief warder, becoming friendly, recounted prophecies uttered by the Revered Peden while imprisoned there half a century previously.

*Mr. David Balfour. See *Catriona* for his biography.

Say: Peden's fiery eye had doused, his cheeks had fallen away, and he looked like a bankrupt dragon. He rasps:
"Ah, Sophia Scarlett, whose name began with the sin of the apple but whose life regenerates as our Saviour uses ye for his purposes! We have blessed ye for your risks and for Sir John's timely messages and we now promise tae help ye wi' your young man, released by the saintly Isabel from his vows tae her. Ye can find but worst of tidings from auld Sandy."
"Is it of Mr. Graham?"
"Percy Graham lies sick untae deeth yet they willnae give him respite as he lies coughing and a-coughing and the damp runs adown his dungeon walls; he bides but the divine chariot; and yet the Guid Lord may look down upon his sufferings and say untae him, 'Now Percy, whiles thou awaitest my heavenly vehicle there is a guid thou mayst yet dae, and that is tae sanctify thy unholy feelings taewuds the sinner, Scarlett, wi' matrimony.'"
Sophia, dashed into anguished hope, asked: "Does Percy himself ask for such a tie?"
"He tellt me he fears tae ask in his condition, but I, Sandy Peden, said it be God's wull it mun be done, an' Percy commissioned me in all grace tae ask ye."
"It is my wish."
"Then ye mun act soon, for he has but ane day or two left in Scotland."

Instructs her to climb in a designated castle window at night so that they can proceed to Percy's cell, which Peden will persuade the under-gaoler to leave unlocked.

(The notes end here. The manuscript resumes.)

Consider Sophia's difficulty: she was, in the Governor's eyes, little more than a street woman who had taken the employ to escape sordid surroundings, prison, or the lash. Lane, the custodian, responded to all out-of-ordinary behaviour with injurious language and cuffs, at which the other girls snarled like chained animals. She slept fitfully of a night, ears full of the sea's booming among the porches of the rock and of its swashing withdrawals and of the wheedling of gulls; against this continuous background, came raucous memories of the day's angers, and more distant memories of brutalities witnessed as a child. When she dreamed of the evanescent happiness to be orchestrated by Prophet Peden, her agony increased, for Percy's remaining hours seemed fewer and fewer, yet she would always be assigned to cleaning the ground floor tier of cells, not her lover's tier above. Peden had warned her not to risk expulsion but to await his signal and then be reunited and married all in a thunder clap.

Of an evening, the girls would sit upon the under-rocks of the basalt cliffs, feet in icy shallows, and in hysterical curses mimic the wailing of kittiwakes on the white-streaked precipices. Sophia, more and more disturbed in mind, would stare at the moon on the horizon and see a corridor of whitened waters leading to a brief white room beyond a gathering darkness. She would hum to herself in an unnerving way that her fellows disliked. Then a gull's wings flashed over the dark waves and she turned back to regard the castle walls, lime-washed by the moonlight, the windows black rectangles along its facade. This time at last, a dark handkerchief showed on the designated window ledge.

She journeyed circuitously among boulders until she could scuttle round the northern side of the castle against the cliff where she had previously piled stones up to a window opening. She crawled into that private hidey-hole, falling softly on to sacks of goose-feather, for the small garrison slaughtered the solans for meat and plucked them for pillow-down. Glad to exit that smelly confine, she side-stepped into the corridor; but a black shape darted into view, a hand grabbed her wrist and another clapped around her mouth.

"Dinnae tremble. It's ony auld Sandy," came a familiar voice. "No sound now."

Peden released her mouth but retained her wrist as he had done long before when accusing her of theft, although now his intention was benign. He looked almost womanly in his black nightgown: his yellow hair in shadows bestrewed and bestrawed a dragonish face thinned by suffering. His hand drew her along to where he removed stone blocks from a crumbling inner wall. They slid through the aperture, down wooden steps, along a dripping corridor, and up some steps of stone. On the upper tier, men sitting in corners of iron-barred cells stared dully at Peden, his great authority rendering them mute as he took Sophia past until she reached a larger cell, lit by a guttering candle, where a man lay stretched out as if on his final bier.

"Oh Percy mine," she breathed, for this was but a shadow of the man she had known. He lay imprisoned amidst his greatest enemies: cold and damp. Her own chest ached.

He half raised himself and managed a courageous smile distorted by the jaw broken by Glenmuir and badly set.

"Dearest. Sandy told me you would come but I could not believe it."

She stepped forward and embraced sickness, the greying in his cheeks exaggerated in candle-light, the darkness in his eyes; and he was so cold, so thin of frame, shuddering and shivering as she held him and tried to inspirit him with her very warmth. "Oh Percy mine!", the cough racking his excited chest, and she would drink in that cough and make it her own, secure it within her, a sickness for the rest of her life.

"You look so weary." And it was he speaking to her.

"I am aye weary untae deeth. My mind whirls with unco' sights."

"You have no folks. I can hardly ask an oat-stook for permission to marry you; and Sophia, I had no heart to ask you yourself to join yourself to such an invalid. Do you even know me?"

She hummed.

"Sophia, what's wrong? Do you know me?"

"Oh yes, I know you."

Behind her, Peden's voice lost its barbs and cracked into kindness: "And yet this marriage will be foredone if ye dinnae ask and consent in haste. Ye may talk *after*, if there's time."

She knew that the preacher, experienced at the death-bed, thought Percy's time was upon him.

"I know all. Isabel has spoken tae me. I consent before you have tae ask. We shall marry in the white room."

"What white room?"

"Why this one of our betrothal. It is Isabel has cast us intae these tortures."

He was seriously alarmed.

"Hush! Hush! This is not Sophia speaking. It was Captain Glenmuir of the dragoons, who nearly ravished you and who pierced me through the shoulder. He is our villain."

"Then his blood will spill in the white room."

"Can I marry you thus unwell?"

She thought he meant himself.

"It makes no difference now."

And Peden muttered something. And Percy had not life enough left him to question further: he felt all this eminently satisfactory, and yet naggingly unsatisfactory together.

She went around and held Percy. Whispering, the half-spent preacher spoke the sacred words of matrimony to bind together behind those iron bars a fugitive spy and a dying sweetheart!

Ah, there was a wonder to it that redeemed the time; and a peace came temporarily upon Sophia's soul; it was the single moment in her life when she came fully home to some dear spot in her destiny; and the narrative would for all the world leave her poised in that spot, calm and joyful, though her new husband could hardly croak out his love, though his last hours were upon him, though nothing but more wanderings and a renewed desperation faced her after his death. "We shall be together: I don't know how." "And we are together, Percy."

No guards came, but dawn found her still in the cell and her husband stark dead. Peden had discreetly left them by themselves for some hours and in the early hours Percy had shot bolt upright, put a hand to his brow, and whispered, "Regard! I must look quaint!" And fell backwards on to his table, struck down by a haemorrhage.

Now, all in the prison, soldier and Covenanter alike, feared Peden's prophecies; so the preacher returned, thinking to protect the irregularity of these circumstances; and he found there a death he had predicted in the more orthodox manner, that is from the evident signs of illness; and forby he found a new wife near distracted from her wits.

He laid his Bible on the body and called upon the guards and gained the Governor's permission to have the prison cells opened. During that day other Covenanters came to lay upon the corpse texts written on torn-off leaves from their own Bibles. Sophia could not prevent this, but she had stored in her memory words Percy had spoken when the preacher had absented himself and when her husband had yet breath:

"Sophia, I fear we have come to this pass for a creed neither of us believes in. And yet we must always follow our path of loyalty and honour."

And she had answered: "I have never believed in these fateful preachers, who are but men too fierce in their pride of salvation."

"And still, do we not each believe in goodness, yours, my own, something a little sacred in everyone, and... this... great... fruitfulness?"

"Let this be our true marriage vow."

While the sonorous voices of the Covenanters rose in prayer as they kept vigil beside this "martyr's bier", Sophia herself, cradling his head, murmured Percy's own prayer: "I believe in this great fruitfulness and goodness."

(Notes resume):

Sophia, her lover dead and with no further need for secrecy, is declared in her own person to the Governor of the Bass. The Governor knows nothing of Sir John's message to Peden, but thinks that nobleman soft-hearted enough to aid a romance. He allows the new widow to accompany the coffin to the mainland, where Graham is buried on the summit of Tantallon Castle cliffs overlooking the Bass.

Show Sophia, an orphan with no sure foundation to her internal pharos of the self, always brought up in the midst of religious dishonesty, cast inwards upon herself during these dark months. And, finding the inner light dark, the self a rocky prison, her hold upon reason weakens.
Isabel is in hiding — where is not recorded. Sophia, cleared of horse-theft, returns to the Blacklock house in Tarbolton. Percy's father, freed from prison, plays no further part in our story.

Alexander Peden, sentenced to the American plantations, responds that the ship is not yet built that would take him there. On board at Leith, he, forewarned by Sophia, announces to his fellow prisoners that when they get to London for trans-shipment they will be released: "The day of your redemption draweth near." The master of the London ship refuses to carry such saintly people. In a bureaucratic squabble over housing them, they are freed — it is said at Lord Shaftesbury's behest. Patrick Walker will later declare this one of Peden's most famous prophecies.

Then southern Scotland erupts:

The hated Royalist archbishop, Sharp, is assassinated in Fife by a group including a friend of Isabel's, David Hackston. This becomes the fuse for the powder keg.

Because of devious, malevolent prosecutions, the King's Advocate, that enlightened intellectual, Sir George Mackenzie, is beginning to earn his nickname of "Bluidy Mackenzie".

As Sir John Cochrane forecast to Isabel, a new fire-brand breed of Covenanter preachers, headed by Cameron and Cargill, foment rebellions and stand at trigger-point for a general call to arms.

Making a last-ditch attempt to stop warfare, Sir John and other South-Western nobles have travelled to London to confront the king with their region's grievances caused by the intolerant religious policies. But the Duke of Monmouth arrives in Edinburgh to head 10,000 Royalist troops.

The stage is set: the Covenanters, with their army increasing, encamp in Hamilton's fields overlooking the River Clyde by Bothwell Bridge, not 30 miles from Sophia's native village of Tarbolton. They gather round eighteen ministers, no less, and quarrel not about who to fight *against* but about who they can agree to fight *alongside!*

The prophetically inclined have Sandy Peden's words in their mouths: "Oh unhappy nation! I have seen in a divine prospect the fields awash with blood and I say untae ye that not a true Scotsman but will suffer lang in the Lords' night."

(The prophet himself, newly at liberty, has retired to a hiding-place 40 miles distant from the site of the gathering battle.)

CHAPTER XV

The Warlock's Niece

UNHAPPY Sophia, too, returned ignobly, inexperienced as a widow, to the discomfortable scenes of childhood — aye, and Sandy Peden had neglected to prophesy such a return! Despite bad reports from Holland, Sir John persuaded the Blacklocks to take her back, for their charity had always been at second hand from his. The fearsome Mrs. Mauchline had recently died, but Mrs. Blacklock, who found in Sophia something distracted, denied that a "Dutch education" had qualified the young wanderer for the vacancy and sent her to the dairy with promotion neither in status — nor wage.

There, we imagine, she would have grown old in sorrows had it not been for a worse misfortune. Isabel, thoroughly implicated in the growing Covenanter uprising, had been arrested while clandestinely visiting her Edinburgh elders — the informer was the loathsome James Robinson — and she was dispatched to Edinburgh's Tolbooth prison.

Three days after she had heard this, Donald, erstwhile "Donald the Brat", sneaked into Tarbolton at first light and accosted her over a row of wet wooden buckets. He had become a wild young man, a black fleck in his cheeks, a jaunty manner; and he embraced her in that dairy like a young callant. Heartily glad to see an old friend so braw, Sophia would have asked many things, but, finger to lips, he whispered that he was on the run for breaking into Murdoch's church and leaving threats there. He proffered a scrap of dress cloth fuzzily written upon in greased-over ink by Isabel, slipped out of her Edinburgh jail, and conveyed through the secret network to Donald. It read:

Great movements are stirring. We women cannot stand aside. Go with Donald. Do what he... (illegible)... for love of Percy and of your poor Isabel.

A wordier instruction might have made Sophia pause to reflect, but this piece of cloth, stained as it were by her friend's sufferings and conjuring up all that Sophia held most holy, could not be gainsaid. She just uttered, "Ah, Donny, Donny lad" and followed outside, where she mounted behind him on a broken-down stallion on loan, he said, from Brown, the cheerful carter. Skirting round outlying fields, they took across heather in the Glasgow direction, and at last Donald had breath to explain their task.

"I havenae bin fully trusted with all the news," he called behind, as the whistling wind made comprehension difficult.

"We are t' gae tae the banks o' the Clyde at Gourock, for that's a lucky place tae sail, and we s'all meet with the barge o' your beloved Bessie Queensferry. Thus Mistress Isabel tells me frae the jail."

"Have ye even seen Isabel?"

"Nae, but the words gaet thrae the walls t' me."

Donald explained that the Covenanters had hired Bessie Queensferry to ship provisions from her new Danish base across the Orkneys around Scotland's north-west to Glasgow. Isabel requested that Sophia drive a cart, also supplied by Brown the carrier (who himself was in their militia), cross-country to the Covenanter army up the Clyde River at Bothwell.

"This will be a cart of *wool sacks*, ye are tae unnerstond, and ye are 'not tae know all the lading thereof, nor e'en tae ask.'"

Greatly anguished by Isabel's arrest, her own life a careless possession after Percy's death, Sophia clung to the young man's back: she had a chance of rencountering Bess, but was again unwillingly engaged in these religious wars and she sensed the corruption in *not* asking what the wool sacks contained.

The ride was long and sore and for a new time she had to hide out at night, which she largely spent mourning misfortune while the reckless youth, himself so badly beset, showed surprising capacity for sympathy. In one lighter moment, he stuck a hand into his saddlebags and pulled out a fresh trout, poached from Laird Blacklock before dawn that day.

"We'll eat this for auld memories and tae spite yon miser-laird, who won't get tae whup me this time," he chuckled as he built a fire.

The following afternoon, Donald reined in the stallion on a cliffy promontory from which the finger of Gourock harbour stretched into the bay. Each boat stood sharp in declining sunlight but no barge among them.

"This isnae the plan," muttered Donald.

They dismounted, stiff as boards. The wind blew fresh and westerly and the bay sparkled with promise.

"I'll not go back wi'out seeing ma Bess," remarked Sophia, realising that the giantess could be in danger.

"Aye, but we're conspickinous taegither. And I have tae gae find the cart ye're tae drive."

"Are ye nae coming with me?"

He drew himself up, 16 years old.

"Madam, am I nae a sodger man noo, wi' a king's army for tae ficht aginst? I hae men tae muster."

"Then where am I tae gae, Donald?"

This was a puzzle that took a quarter hour of wild ideas before Donald came up with yet another wild one.

"Whisht! Remember ye the ancient witch of Fail, the auld biddy ye used tae visit in Tarbolton before she was taen?"

"They say she magicked her way out of jail in Ayr," Sophia recalled. "She was taen there for a witch, and wan day her cell was found emptied just before she was tae hae bin drowndid."

"Weel, I ken where she has lain hidden ever syne. When all this was planned I was here an' aboot spyin' oot the lan', an' a villager tellt me the withered auld brach lived in a fearful wood just by, where few dare tae tread on account o' the bogles an' ither ghaesties."

"Why is she not interrupted by the authorities?"

"That naebody kens."

Faut de mieux, this idea at least bore trial.

They remounted and rode hard four miles inland down sheltered lanes and between stone walls. One of these walls Donald suddenly vaulted because he had perceived a low hill whose side was patched with a little thicket; above the trees poked a ruined church tower. The pathway to it had long been overgrown; so, tying their mount to a hawthorn's thickest branch, they began climbing the hill, hand in hand, through aromatic walls of bracken. Near the levelling where the ground became boggy and the wood began, a crackled rather aristocratic female voice came from the trees:

"Thus far. Let the young Sophia come on alone."

Astonished, the brat and Sophia regarded each other.

"I ken that voice well: it's truly the Laird of Fail's niece."

"She will have spotted ye climbing. We mun do as she says, for we cannae cross sich a wumman," Donald replied. "In twa days I s'all come agin for ye, and I hope wi' news of a successful landing an' o' a laden cart tae drive."

Squeezing his arm, she warned him to be careful, and then continued doubtfully up muddy clumps of grass towards the trees. At a moment, she turned to watch Donald climb back on the horse and scamper uphill a ways and then down in a rush to clear the wall and head off to the bay. Such a boy, after a childhood lacking in instruction, to be so bravely enlisted in a destiny he only half understood! And yet she herself... about to meet the niece of the Warlock Laird of Fail — that old woman whose legend had become one of Sophia's anecdotes —...she herself felt utterly bereft under the fringes of a reputedly haunted wood, the ferns falling to a valley already blueing with evening.

The voice had come from near the ruined tower, and there Sophia came across a makeshift bivouac, constructed of old brown sail canvas spread across tree branches like the wing of a giant bat. The inside appeared cluttered with boxes and various greenery in pots. At the entrance, an ancient woman dark in visage sat tending a pan steaming over a charcoal fire. Dirt had cosmeticked her sparse white hair into a stiff comb, a little off to one side, making her whole face seem vertically slanted, her neck thrawn. Her eyes glittered like a chimpanzee's, enlivening the dead contrast of her weather-blackened face and grimy white hair. She was a tough bird to find in such a wood. Mother Fail, as Sophia had always called her, was said to have Spain in her descent although the Warlock Laird had been staunch Protestant — that part of him not devoted, as the legend had it, to Satan.

"Mother! I am sorry indeed tae see ye come tae sich a pass," said Sophia, forcing herself to bend and kiss the withered cheek with its ill-washed odour of aging.

She might have to wait long for an answer, for Mother Fail took all remark inwards into deep ruminations, after which long speeches might follow. And Sophia gazed upon that face as if upon a map which might suddenly speak its place names.

"You are embroiled," the witch cooed eventually, the voice a Scot's lady's in an Edinburgh salon.

Sophia stood bewildered at the word.

"That lad has been asking after me: I have been awaiting you."

"How do you know what we do?"

"There is no puzzle here. My brother, who long ago deserted me but now wants well for me to keep my scandals to this wood, supplies me with provisions; and his retainers bring me news that embroils you and casts you into danger.'

"What is the danger?"

"Ah, danger, hm, hm." Smoke got into the monkey eyes and Mother Fail coughed and spluttered.

"Your young lad has been indiscreet in other ways. The soldiers have captured an empty barge hailing from Daneland and are holding its captain for landing weaponry, though her cargo has vanished. Wherever that cargo is will be a dangerous place should anyone be venturing there."

Her eyelids became accusatory slits.

"It is my giantess,' Sophia breathed. "How know you all this?"

"Aye, *your* giantess? Captain Glenmuir has got her."

"My giantess with my, my enemy! Oh waladay! Ay me!"

The old eyes sparkled oddly, almost with approval.

"I have been cooking that pot for you all day. Now you must come awa' inside and tell me your adventures."

"But—"

"Odds bones! Where will you chase to in search of her? Just think. Must I not divine her whereabouts for you?"

"Oh, oh, can you find her?"

"No. *You* shall find her under my directives. But I need to hear your adventures if I am to be divining. Bring yon pot, catch its handles up in your dress."

The bony apparatus of Mother Fail assembled itself as carefully as stacking muskets upright, and she tottered inside her gloomy tent. Gesturing for Sophia to rest her pot, she laboriously folded back a cloth which covered a large wooden chest standing on crude rollers formed of branches. Rather as the Druids were said to have transported the blocks of Stonehenge by taking one roller from behind and placing it in front, the two of them slid the chest aside, revealing an earthy hole. Then Sophia realised she was staring at stone-carved steps.

"Once on this spot stood a ruined chapel from the olden times. When Oliver Cromwell sent his troops among us in Scotland, they scattered most of the stones adown this hill."

"This will have been the old crypt?"

"Ah! Come along and bring that pot."

The short descent took a dark age; at the bottom Sophia slipped on mud and liquid slapped out of the vessel, adding pungency to the wet, woody air. Eventually, a flint struck and Mother Fail lit a large tallow candle, from it lighting two more on a great rock at the rear of the upward sloping earth. Bundles of faggots and herbs strewn here and there were clogged with mud, and the slimy earth gleamed watery under stone walls. She was to place the pot on the "altar".

"This is my west end,' said Mother Fail. She crouched to some splendid pewter vessels, fit for a laiche hall, but now on the mud floor; raising her sleeve she dug out dried herbs from within.

"You will find all directions below ground contrariwise to those in the old church above. Where Christ rises, my church sets. I invent all, to be strange and my own entire, not to be tainted by ancient magics or caught in the snares of Satan."

"Are ye not seized by the people because you live so queerly?"

A dry well of humour sucked deep, a gravelly sound.

"Because of the witchcraft? Like you they are frightened. Mystery is not witchcraft."

"Mystery" bore its ancient meanings. The hypnotic slowness of all the woman's motions was fatiguing.

"One time, the divinity withdrew Her favour and I lay emprisoned in Ayr, fit to drown for false charges of practising the Satanic arts."

Sophia stuttered: "H-how did ye escape from prison? An' *all this*. They said ye had magicked yoursel' from your cell, as I was just telling Donald."

More gravel, and sucking of the teeth, a grim gleam in the eyes.

"That has a measure of truth, for if you will be wise you must maintain your craft. But I confess that a judge from Edinburgh who took kindly to my plight had a deal to do with it."

"What did this judge do?"

"Well and well, and am I to be obliged to a miserable Mackenzie?"

"You mean the Great Terror they call the Bluidy Mackenzie, the King's own Advocate, was the instrument of your removal from captivity."

"Now that is well phrased for a serving maid. Your instruction in Dutchland has improved you."

Mother Fail seemed informed of everything, perhaps through the retainers who supplied her with food; but Sophia was surprised to find her own history so well known, and also she was thinking, "Part of my instruction came from poor Percy."

"Then I went forth from prison footsore looking for someone to take me in; and they would not, because of their great fear. The Blacklocks who had been so charitable to me now shunned me like the death, for that's an awful god-fearing family. And after a year and a day, I came to this thicket where I lay down to sleep. The ground had so strange an unevenness that I could not sleep but arose and cleared away bramble and found the underground stair; and here I conduct my true beliefs."

Though the cavern was bitter chill, the crone parted her vestments to show a dug like long, empty purse tied by a livid knot of nipple. Her fingernail black with charcoal stroked a number "6", branded beside the narrow breast and stretched into distortion by the protruding rib-cage.

"His majesty's torturer did me that honour," she added, leaving her cloths loose.

Gaze fixed on the vestigial mark of the Beast, Sophia shuddered at her own question: "Ah mun ask ye ane thing for ma ane safety, my dame."

Mother Fail chuckled; "The first advantage that Satan shall get he shall take it upon this sweet discovery of Womanhood. I have spoken unto the clouds and unto the night sky infinite blasphemous words. But Satan is not my Master, for *His* Spirit sits in London in the King's court."

"But ye talk sae sacred — and sae sacriligious-like: I cannae wonder folks mistake ye for... for..."

"I only counter Church harshness with mercy, pride of knowledge with humbleness of unknowing, male priest with female."

"What spirit seek ye that ye call it Her?"

"In the glistening stems and leaves of flowers, and where the nectar is, resides a spirit that is of holy birth. It is the constant beginning. Come, bring my pot and sit here upon this underground rock and we shall seek that spirit: this ritual, too, we shall invent this very day, for only in beginnings is the ritual fully alive."

She sat Sophia down, spread the girl's legs, and raised her rough skirts to the thighs, though the flesh flinched from the rasp of those dirty fingernails. And Mother Fail made her sip acrid, lukewarm draughts from the vessel, murmuring, "This is a liquid I never gave you in Tarbolton."

"But, mercy! What mun I be doing?" cried Sophia, for she was now told to draw down her underthings and to expose her pudenda. This was worse than a devilish play she'd read in Holland where unholy statues appeared in a masque.

Likely, some form of mesmerism was practised, because Mother Fail kept murmuring as she rubbed an aromatic oil a long time upon Sophia's chest. Meantime her victim's eyes were hazing, the haze that of the vibrant, dun-coloured air between a bonfire and its smoke. A powerlessness gripped her *in its power*. After that time Sophia, although freezing, felt heavy-bodied, and the coldness receded as into a region of indifference, and she herself seemed in that region as an Other Secondary Sophia who murmured responses back to her priestess; and yet a Primary Identity held Blackly alert, and knew, and was close.

That Other Sophia was given scratchy herbs, and in her deepening trance was commanded to insert the stalks inside her vagina: that gave the Other no offence and it performed the action. The more intimate Black Identity, curious rather than shocked, observed this, imagining purple labia curling upon the stems like petals around a stamen. This Blackness observed grey-green leaves dangling from red pubic hair, while the Other Sophia felt the involuntary impulse which lifted the vagina's entrance muscle as, with a lascivious tingle, the area moistened. Next, certain leaves were placed by twig-like fingers on her tongue and she must chew them into pulp and spit them out.

"Within your secret place a holy voice speaks, though I know not whence it comes. Yet it truly speaks and what it says I shall deliver to you for you to undertake. Have you ever heard such a voice, lass?"

"I have... thought tae once, when I lay side by side with my dying husband in his prison on the Bass," said the Other Sophia, the murmurer.

"Then you have lain in the birth spasm on another rock? This was your adventure?"

The Black Identity hardly wanted to share these private memories, yet the murmuring self continued.

"It was sae."

"And did your coney place anything inside you, in the secret place?"

The Blackness watched a fingernail point between her legs and was embarrassed.

"In that place there?" said the Other Sophia. "Ah, yes."

"And did what he placed inside you speak to you?"

"Ah yes, it seemed tae speak sae sweetly."

"You are a canny lass, for I perceive you follow my swathe with your own scythe. And when it spoke did it speak as if in tongues?

"Many, many tongues, but they were all the one tongue."

"And when it spoke as if in tongues did a divine liquid come into you from the tongue-tip like the nectar glistening in the mouth of the daffodil?"

The Other Sophia was weeping and it seemed as if the weeping was silent but uncontrollable.

"Alas no. Poor Percy was nigh his deeth. The liquid came from that... that tip before he placed it inside me. *It* wept as if at the sheer *impassibility* an' then it entered my place. I am barren of him for ever."

"We shall make you fertile in that barrenness."

She felt utterly open, utterly emotional, all orifices of her body yearning from the Blackness, wanting her husband so badly that her pelvis pushed outwards from the bulging rock, her buttocks scraped badly, her muscles in little leaps along her thighs, so that she swooned in jagger convulsions. The tempest and flame of the experience became her possession; the semen of Percy's love leapt into her; and from Blackness a light-beam as from an internal beacon cast a glistening upon the veil of darkness in the crypt.

The walls of the crypt seeped with divine voices. She caught sight of a line of ten boulders where Mother Fail had arranged them by a wall. They diminished in size inwards from either side and now in her trance she saw that the mid-point was an emblem of eternity multiplied by eternity.

She said, "The scope of that mighty movement is the measure of the Spirit's power."

Everything became clear to her like truth glamourised. Old Mother Fail was a cracked vessel, a witch-wife black as a turnip, an eccentric dabbling in dangerous thinking. Sophia saw also the boyish limitations of Percy, his bravery in all its amusing, false rhetoric, his discreet snobbery, and his narrow, masculine gallantry. She did not falter in her love. She saw Isabel in her strict simplifications and harshness and knew no religion could be just if it brought suffering. She saw the precious giantess, Bessie, as a violent female lout heading for whatever was like hell after death. Again, she did not falter in her love for Bessie. She saw rosy-gold signs in the darkness as if a bejewelled female God drew near on every side.

"The Spirit of the Goddess claims us as the fire claims fuel," she said.

Mother Fail was before her wagging her head foolishly up and down.

She thought of — but did not see — a Satanic goat wearing women's clothing down to its hooves: behind that mighty form, mountains drenched with gore. For a moment, she wondered if she had given that figure a vague assent, like a nod of the head. And then an event only half-describable occurred. Another person passed into her, not Percy's love exactly, but larger, not even a love, not male at all; more like an airy body, the body of a woman of fuller knowledge — yes, of an immensely cheerful May Queen, huger than Bessie, and garlanded with flowers. The Queen's joyfulness replaced her dread of Satan and the mountains were clothed with sunshine and song. The grandeur of Sophia's incipient madness came upon her, messianic but female.

A voice, not her own, blurted low from her lips, and said her own name, "Sophia", calmly and gravely.

And the Other Sophia came to join her Primary Identity in the Blackness. Then there *was* blackness.

She awoke several hours later on a palias under the bat-wing bivouac, the trees rustling about her, and Mother Fail busying herself farther within the tent. A light feverishness and trembling still afflicted her but, while she remembered all she had felt, its excitement was passing away, and she was thinking quite rationally.

"An almichty battle is upon us, says Donald. Sae, if Captain Glenmuir takes Bess, where *does* he take her? He mun be at his post, at Bothwell where the battle prepares. She will be imprisoned nearby, I have nae doot! What wud Bessie be a-saying tae me now?"

Still rationally, she constructed the following dialogue in her head:
Bessie: "I will be up-river three miles. Bothwell three miles."
Sophia: "Aye, Bess. I shall find ye oot."
Bessie: "If your friends bested, come to me if ye can."

"Will ye be safe till then?"

"Allus safe, me."

Involuntarily, she remembered that other voice within her which had intoned "Sophia" so gravely. Then she realised that Bessie's part in this more recent mental conversation had been spoken in the same grave voice and had not been invented at all; the voice had been hiding inside her all along as a true knowledge of Bessie's whereabouts, a sort of calculation.

"Ach! After all, it's common sense."

But an ague was in her still, a passing grandeur, and she became fearful that she had trafficked with spirits — perhaps had assented to Satan, perhaps to the Goddess of flowers, perhaps was losing her mind. Yet she could not escape Mother Fail who, resuming her old role as instructress, explained how she had induced the trance and with what herbs.

"Here is a new packet for your herb sack," she insisted, handing over dry leaves and a small flask.

Sophia spent the day among the hillsides studying the plants and birds and calming. When she returned, Mother Fail was pottering about; she insisted upon a full relation of Sophia's thinking and took it all as evidence of her own wisdom.

"Did I not say, lass, that you would yourself be shown the way?"

An uneasy night passed beside the old woman's renewed snoring, and in the early hours the bivouac softly shook. She awoke with a start, heart pounding, to find Donald standing there shyly.

"The countryside is too infisted wi' the Edinburgh sodgers — I cannae mak onywan muster an' some o' oor army is fleein' tae their farms and byres. The Duke o' Monmouth has a horrid army facing us at Bothwell Brig."

All this in hasty whispers.

"Then where can we go?"

"I hae found the cart." He delivered this news proudly. "An ancient elder in Glasgow toon led me tae it an' I hae hitched up oor horsie an' twa ither horsies lent. It all waits on the road below, but we mun hurry. I think e'en the trees are the king's suspicions."

Sophia sprang up, but she was in a terrifying panic of conscience. The rightness of driving weapons to a battlefield seemed most questionable — thus far her trance imposed upon her — yet every moral influence since childhood urged that she could not betray her side in this greatest danger. Then too, Isabel lay in prison and had invoked the decidedly martial Percy and his love for her to encourage her to this exact service; then too, Donald would drive the cart to Bothwell will-she-nill-she; then too, she could be useful on a battlefield, with her herbal skill to bind up wounds; then too, the cart was her most probable conveyance to find Bessie; then lastly she could not stand the racing in her head: wearily, she felt the gloom of widowhood descend, and that strange indifference with it, and in that weakness she submitted to the will of absent loved ones.

Later, when she condemned herself so bitterly and without mitigation for driving in that cart, it was the weakness that always made her shudder, for emptiness of spirit is easy prey for evil.

She woke the old woman enough to bid adieu and clambered down the hillside with the Brat. Her clothes rasped with mud as she mounted the uneasy wooden seat of the cart, and she grabbed at the planks as they lurched off, the great pile of "wool sacks" swaying dangerously despite the weight of their true, metallic fillings.

Though the Gourock-Glasgow shore was so infiltrated by Royalist soldiery, their journey proved not of great risk, for they headed further inland, north-east, and entered the demesne of Hamilton, a Covenanter sympathiser, whose estates led down to the River Clyde at the fateful Bothwell Bridge. Rather, farm labourers hustling along to join their laird's militia cheered them as they passed. Within a few hours, the dawn now well broken, they drove through a field gate and found the Covenanter army drawn up along a crest overlooking the river. Their leaders, down by the barricaded bridge, had gathered round a quarrelsome pack of preachers. On the far bankside but as yet at an obscure distance, occasional gleams of sunlight picked out a massive spreading out of Royalist troops encamped. On this Covenanter side of the dispute, grim-faced soldiers came to unload their cart; and a flashy pile of swords and musketry soon lay on the grass.

CHAPTER XVI

Battle for the Bridge

DOWNHILL at Bothwell, the river curls round between the Covenanters and the hordes of Monmouth drawn up for King Charles's cause on the far plain in disciplined ranks: the English redcoats, the Lothian blue jacket militia, the Scottish Life Guards, the wary Highlanders with their claymores; and the cannon ready to move. The one bridge, strongly barricaded with planks and guarded by the Covenanters, stands between the faithful and destruction.

Say the Royalists: Law has brought us to this Battle of Bothwell. Justice has brought us. Honour Kingship. Social order and degree. Then a single bridge. Across it, all these masculine virtues reverse. Over here, the Covenanters say: Divine law has brought us to this battle. Divine Justice. Honour of God. Kingship of God. Fellowship of the individual saved soul. On one side, a disciplined army loyal to an absolute king, who is arbiter of justice and keystone of social advancement; on the other, an army bitterly turned inwards in disagreements about divine inspiration of truth... How many women d'you think Sophia saw in this battle order? Prostitutes, victuallers, a fiery convert or two, all hidden away in the back-lines. Without half of humanity, how can there be a grand design here to protect? Men. Nothing relevant here to *our* 80 years of life on earth.

The Rev. John Welsh preached before the battle from Joshua xxii, 22: "The Lord God of gods, the Lord God of gods, he knoweth, and Israel he shall know; if it be in rebellion, or if in transgression against the Lord, save us not this day."

Nonsense: such a Lord is a know-nothing. Says the scholar.

The scholar has a style that could set the battle raging in its patterns, but Sir Walter has already done it in his *Old Mortality*. King Charles the Second's bastard, Monmouth, soon to be a traitor himself, heads the Royalist forces, his destrier pawing the ground. Monmouth's footguard are crammed upon the bridge as they attack its central barricades. Picked off by muskets; gored by swords. Monmouth's cannon advance, but too slow in aim, for the enemy at the blockade simply ducks the balls. Across river on the Covenanter side, fusillades from commandeered cottages; answering Royalist fire from behind bankside alders. Everything held at a ruinous deadlock. But the Covenanters' ammunition supplies gradually fail and they make sorties back to the main army, unbelievably still quarrelling in the open fields about strategy and leadership. A barrel that should be full of gunpowder is rolled forwards but proves full of raisins. And so: the fighting hand-to-hand as barricades go down on the bridge; burly men fall bloodily backwards and are trampled as the Royalist insurgence fans out, cheering, from the bridge's neck, the advance so suddenly won that Monmouth's *arrière-garde* is tardy and the enforcers are a moment unprotected in the fields; but the arguing Covenanters cannot seize that moment; and soon it's Monmouth's cavalry spreading out in entrapment, wheeling in from the flanks, and those fields fill with hideous slaughter; horses chase men down in a lion's sudden flurry at an antelope; blades slice at averted heads.

Forty miles away on that Sabbath morning, the old escapee, Alexander Peden, had retired till mid-day but the people were waiting for a sermon. He entered one of his prophetic trances. At last he said: "Let the people go to their prayers: for me, I neither can nor will preach any more this day; for our friends are fallen, and fled before the enemy at Hamilton; and they are hanging and hashing them down, and their blood is running like water."

That's a premonition even a sober savant might believe in: it has such death in it.

The scholar has the style, she repeats, to flatter with heroism this ugly battle, to ascribe to the Nobles the greatest valour, to scale down to the courage of the Commons, and to reserve a flash of humour for describing the Ignorant. But what if that style is itself infected? What if the *style* also goes out to war, takes blood on its breastplate, wins a standard of honour from either camp, and returns to the lady-folk (the ladies of middle to upper class) and says, "My dears, 'twas done for the colour of your eyes and for the glory of our nation — or for the grandeur of the masculine divinity"?

She wipes the pen clean like a soiled blade. There is subject matter new to this practised style: uncontrollable fear, the stink of intestines gutted by the sword, a woman at war, rape, the sight of a naked p—s: no, say it, penis. A fresh viewpoint is taken, as if a ravished vagina could be an eye: through that eye, the battle becomes a desperately sad sham of false heroics.

The vagina eye weeps.

Earlier that morning, Sophia had stood under one gallows tree regarding a second, more curious gallows erected on a little knoll behind the Covenanter lines. The first gallows was for the Commons but the other... it was a sturdy upright branching into a fan of about 12 supports screwed into a top cross-piece of wood bristling with iron spikes on which the heads of Persons of Quality were to be fixed; and each of these branches bore an iron hook to hang the corpses on. She stood with three Glasgow women determined to act as nurses; at her side a bag of cloth strips and those herbs in which she was proficient.

But I am afraid that sorrow was increasingly turning her mind. She looked at that gallows and knew that against Royalist cruelty she had sided with Covenanter cruelty.

Below her, the main body of Covenanters knelt in the fields, pikes and pitchforks slanted forwards. Far across river, the Royalist cavalry untidily occupied the crests while the strict rectangles of the foot, drawn up in line of march, raised their pikes like shining brush-strokes above their dusky bodies. All stared at that most important mid-ground: the bridge.

There, the barricades were wrestling down, a horse rearing on the bridge, and man locked with man, blades and axes out in a tumult of cries and clashes coming late on the wind, spurts of smoke, then the crack-crack, bodies splashing in the river: no *meaning* to this except that red uniforms advanced on grey, like blood advancing through a stony channel.

Nonsense. Nonsense.

I, Agnes Christmas, scholar, declare that all these male killers live in sunshine while their victims fall in perfect night. We'll just have the killing. The darkness of Percy's death descends over these morning fields. A young lad slashing with a scythe at a horse's legs brings down a captain, who leaps clear, sword in hand, and thrusts the boy through belly. And the Royalist God smiles; the Puritan gnashes His teeth.

Night. Those Covenanters not cut down as they ran have been marched away towards Edinburgh. Here at Bothwell, the last looters flit among the bodies...

Sophia had retreated three miles and hidden between a thick briar and a stone field-wall; she returned this night to walk among butchery with her dangerous oil lamp and her bag of herbs. Furtive figures moved among the slain: no longer the looters, but faithful Covenanter women seeking their loves or just those still alive. With them was the one member of the True Kirk she could welcome unfeignedly: it was Brown the Carrier who, unharmed in the fighting, had at great risk brought up his cart as a field hospital.

The eyebrows no longer lifted into their quirky humours. He was unaffectedly weeping as he hugged her.

"Oh, the terrible Will, the terrible Will," he said.

"It's no tae be tolerated when it covers those we love under such bloody torrents," she said.

"He will surely forgive us our grief," replied that piping voice, "for we know that this is the king's work and not His."

She made a curious noise, almost a burring tune.

"We must worship only the great fruitfulness of the Goddess," she said.

He stood back from her, seeing wildness in her eye, and having compassion at a phrase that had alarmed him.

"Ye will be best at these works of mercy, and leave foolish thinking for wiser moments in Scotland's affairs."

"Oh Mr. Brown!" She clasped him and clenched her teeth in the leather of his jerkin.

"There is a word for ye, 'Though He slay me, yet will I trust Him.'"

"This is no such slaying."

But he was turning to bring up his wagon, while the women searched for any who now dared to groan; they bound wounds, and assisted those most nearly dying up on to the wagon; for them, help would be sought in Glasgow; the others would have to hide as they could.

It was a terrifying work. Limbs came half away from a black gash as the body refused to roll over; an eye had been dinged into a sodden hollow, a groin slashed quite through, a throat cut. Sophia thought of beef cattle choking from slit and gouting throats; and then she thought of the torturing of her old benefactor, Hood; and then her gorge clacked dry, her mind wandering as she helped.

Across the river glowed a single camp-fire of the Royalists who had been assigned to guard the field; a patrol could be expected and that field would become perilous again.

She came across the lad who had scythed at the captain's horse and held her lamp over the body. Oh! It was Donald the Brat. He now wore a coat of hoddin grey, leggings of creased brown cloth, and clouted shoes. A broad-brimmed hat had fallen away from his fair face and his woollen undervest had sunk into his rent belly which spilled his smelly tripes. The wool-ends seemed magical, Hebraic lettering stuck in blood and she wondered whether she saw a divine message coded therein. Some soldier had lain Donald upon another corpse for the tidiness. Sophia's eyes raked across those fields of night, heaped with low mounds like manure heaps left ready for the morning spreading, and her fair hand tugged the boy's undergarment from the wound. Her leg muscles twitched as she crouched beside him like a lover, her heart thumping almost as if it would knock her into joy; and she remembered telling this brat, whipped for stealing trout, that one day he would be her man. Now he was.

A fury came upon her, to be kissing the cold cheek of a child tricked out to fight in someone else's best clothes. She raised her head, the field seeming to shrink, the dead bodies upon it seeming to change size as she looked; and it was these dead she blamed. She cursed them in a shriek:

"Prig-rats!"

Bessie's word.

"There is no God known tae MAN!"

There came upon her a religious *horror vaccui*, the darkest night she had known.

"Centuries of these priest-warlocks, complicit even in warfare with the politician-warlocks. Making us all OUTLAWS!"

She herself an outlaw again. Peden, a prig-rat; Blacklock, a prig-rat; Sir John Cochrane, a prig-rat; the Reverend Murdoch, a prig-rat; Privy Council, prig-rats; Captain Glenmuir, the very, yellow fangs of a rat, sinking its appetite into these corpses strewn about her. Give no glory to those who die trying to impose their beliefs on others. Yes and Isabel a prig-rat too, since she had called upon the loyal Sophia and the infatuated Percy to serve her own false god.

For sheer fatigue at the day's murders, she lay down beside young Donald, that whiff of his death in her nostrils, and recalled her brief wedding night in a prison cell when the Reverend Peden had left her and Percy alone.

PERCY: Will you take into you the love of a dying man?
SOPHIA: I vow tae ye I shall avenge this love.
PERCY: Whisht awhile.

A vivid, frozen vision, which tenderness brought frighteningly alive. The lover exhausted on his table, the buttons of his breeks half undone, the shirt carelessly unstuffed, and yet the unconquerable desire to consummate life, and she pulling gently at that shirt, unbuttoning the breeks further. The shrivelled thing that she wiggled out from between his flaccid thighs would only half-engorge under her hand as she did what village girls had told her of; and yet she marvelled at the apparatus of it, cupping the walnut tracery of the testicles, following the veins of the penis with her finger tip, catching the tick-tick of its weak throb on the fulcrum of her thumb. But even as she raised her rough skirts and sought to make the tube rigid enough to insert, it all at once wept semen from its slit, Percy's body arching like that of an insane person. In a gesture instinct with love, she got the spent penis into her and they lay side by side like that until she was shaken by her own empty orgasm. "Nae apologues are necessary. We have shared the precious heart of it: the rest is just how the village pump works." "I shall carry you with me where I am going, Sophia: we shall always be to each other what we have been. I know not how."

And knew he for his queen must die
In the Castle of Dunbarton.

Her vagina yearned for the wedding night. A *tedium vitae* succeeded the *horror vaccui* as she joined herself with the dead Percy and also with this eviscerated farm lad beside her. She found between the starry fates above a black locus of intense anger.

"To the king's army I am an earthly outlaw; let me be a religious outlaw for the cursed Covenanters; let me be a witch. Let me hunt down Glenmuir with curses."

She was shivering with superstition and, like a Mother Fall in the irrationality of perfect privacy, invented a ritual to confirm her curses. From her neck she took her amulet: on the pigskin cover she wrote the name, "Glenmuir" and then unwrapped it; inside were herbs, garlic, peony, mouse bones, and crude writing damaged by water. She balanced a tallow candle from her bag on the corpse of Donald the Brat, and lit it with the oil lamp. By the candle on that bloody altar, she set the opened amulet and caught the dry pig-parchment in the lamp's flame.

"As this spell of good chance burns up so may Glenmuir's life begin its un-chance; so may I become his huntress; so may this curse bless my hunt.

Abi in malam rem." (It was her Rotterdam school Latin).

Frightened deeply at the magic of it, she made of the burning amulet a little fire between candle and lamp, singeing part of Donald's under-vest too and scorching dead skin.

"There, that's done. I have entered the wickedness of these others so that I may avenge my husband. Whisht awhile and then avenge."

She stood up. Black sodden earth. Now neither of her gey men left alive; just the toads: Robinson, Murdoch, Glenmuir, pawkie Cochrane, over-discreet Blacklock. A spent cannon ball. A limb. A kale field crushed by the blundering of human cattle. In the kale stalks, a sword tip broken off. She picked this up, wrapped the shaft in cloth to form a handle, and put it in her bag. In a culvert, a full purse of money, which she took and scattered over the field. And then the other women — the cart now full of badly-wounded men — were calling her.

CHAPTER XVII

The Incurable Wound

CONDUCTOR of the dying, she climbed like some land-borne Cheiron beside Brown on the driver's seat; behind her, the other women tended the pile of wounded. Brown glanced sideways: "My wound is henceforward incurable and without transgression," but he had no heart to add the reference. Unfortunately, since all natural retreat to the rear was secured by the king's soldiers, their road to eastern Glasgow lay along the far river bank beneath the rearguard camp of the victorious Royalists; first they would cross that fatal bridge, now guarded by enemy sentries. With a sickening sway that brought renewed groans, the vehicle lurched off downhill.

The scholar, dreaming, has a gout of evil from her stomach which changes the vision. I, the scholar Agnes Christmas. Bodies piled up in a cart like victims of Belsen, the crucifixes of flesh part-dismembered. I write about what is always the same to the eye across the centuries.

And so, we're left with the women: Isabel, with her flawed nobility of spirit, Sophia whose spirit is so uncertain, and the great violent heart of Bessie. Is that enough for the rest of this life-story?

Oh, but it'll be short and full of revenge.

Brown confronted the two red-coat sentries by the bridge:

"I am but a carrier for hire. We mun clear the field o' a' these bodies."

"Who has hired you for this?"

Sophia leant across and blurted out the hated name in sudden strategy: "Captain Glenmuir."

A password it proved. "He is away from us. You will accompany me first to our camp." And, mounting his horse, the sentry led the way towards the merry central bonfire amidst the murderous tents of the Royalist rearguard. As Brown drove that charnel cart full of pallid legs and arms, Sophia felt her plaid hot and itchy on her own cold limbs, and she had dried blood up to her elbows.

By the fire, soldiers, shifty-eyed in remembrance of their actions, lay beside plunder over which the light flickered — bracelets, guns, swords, dirks, breastplates, farm implements, stout coats, boots, or purses — while from behind canvas walls came sounds of love-making paid for by the trinkets of the dead: the blasphemy of it made the women in the cart whisper in dismay. So young, nearly all of the soldiers: cubs and gulls.

"'Tis our very land at stake, Jock," an English foot guard was pontificating. "These compatriots of yours forced our swords from their sheaths by their own disobedience. We did nothing but point the blade for them to run upon, says our captain."

"D'ye mind the wan whae in his fricht grabbed the horse's testimonials for tae get support and wuz trampled by the puir, pained beastie?"

A burly English sergeant had emerged from a tent and the sentry was explaining the situation to him: three women in various styles of deshabillee came to the tent flap and Sophia recognised among them the former housemaid, Mary, fair-haired and shielding her eyes from the firelight to regard the cart. It was too late to avoid recognition, for Mary was whispering to the sergeant, who detached himself from her restraining hand and came over.

"Captain Glenmuir, you say, commands you this night, but from what my wench tells me, you would not be heartily glad to rencounter him."

He looked a huffle and a hot-spirited man; his red face sneered up at Sophia, still on her perch, and she lied her best lie:

"In no spirit of friendliness, the captain has ordered us to clear the battlefield of our wounded."

The soldier, evidently ready to slip into difficulties, took a turn about the cart and not a defeated Covenanter but feared for his life under that gaze.

From the rear he called, "Now I wonder how he could have done that, as he has departed hastily, having word that a sort of giantess has been caught while ferrying your ammunition."

"Ye are to let us on our humble way," dared Brown. "The captain would make our salvation complete through sufferings."

"I have no commands from your Scottish captain, I tell you," said the sergeant.

"That is clear," replied Brown, whose captain resided in his Bible and under whose command he was convinced the sergeant could not be.

"Well, we have three of our footguards in perfect health must travel with you."

"Yet there is nae room," added Sophia.

The sergeant's dander rose at that: "We must make room among these sorry fanatics."

And he crept in nearer to the rear of the cart, beckoning to three of his men from the fire.

"Dinnae ye think they hae suffered evil enow?"

"Then we must give them the last of human evils, that is Death," he replied with sickening unctiousness.

He had jimp said the word than he and his troopers had flung four of the unhappy wounded to the ground and put paid to their lives with butcher slashings of their swords. Amid terrified silence, they installed three reluctant Royalist troopers on the cart in their stead.

Eventually, Sophia said disgustedly, "Aye, fegs!" And that was the first word was spoken; maybe it had a touch of the Divinity's weariness in it too.

This set the sergeant into a fit of rage and he pulled her from her seat.

"And you," he roared, "will ride with me to see your honoured captain. And you," he said to Brown, "will drive where my soldiers direct you."

He held her roughly as the cart drove off to whatever Royalist doom awaited its contents, and the cruelty at her feet made Sophia's eye go idle, and her ear deafened at the self-defensive laughing of soldiers by the fire as they cooked twists of flour-dough on sticks.

"They're cooking witches," she thought, in that strange idleness. And again, "Mr. Brown will have tae save those others now."

There comes a jumbling in this scene, as if the oils fell in gobs from a painting of a men by a fire. Next, the walls of a tent billow about us and the breech of this same sergeant's trousers swells as he confronts an almost dreaming Sophia, whose shawl has just been removed by the egregious Mary, who is whispering, "There's no shame in what we cannae help, and onyways this will be your come-uppance." With an insolent gesture, the sergeant unbuttons his breech flap — I, Agnes Christmas, tell you this: Robert Louis wouldn't dare — and he fishes with a sneakier hand in amongst his undershirt to undouble the fleshy hose with its purpling helmet. At a nod from him, Mary forces the girl's head towards that tip and Sophia nearly swoons at the indecency of it; only at sword point will she apply her lips to all that seems most obscene, most acrid, most glutinous, most vicious in the world. Mary skips from the tent in a sadistic glee to see another fall. And Sophia kissed that salty object in a retching glamour, as if she were her own mental illustration in a world turned yellow and blue. A most disgusting violation follows, accompanied by screams answered by guffaws from the fireside. Spare us, lest we participate in any corner of our minds.

Oh, but she remembered a soldier calling, "Watch that one, she'll have your trews and break your sword on your own bum." And the sergeant, busy, shouting back, "We have used such as these for field cleaners. And now we shall use them for our own good pleasures." Oh, but to aid her own lubrication, she oiled the man's testicles and penis pungently from her lamp, and, thinking of how Percy had ejaculated before his moment, she tied a thin strip of bandage at the root of the large penis, as she had heard that camp women did. A rite of remembrance which the sergeant mistook for licentiousness. Forced to lower herself on to the organ, she thought of the spikes which had crowned the gallows. As the man came she noticed his nose, which had a growth on it; she said in her Rotterdam Latin, *"Abi in malam rem"*, but he thought it Scottish and didn't ask her meaning — loosely, "Go to the Devil".

And afterwards the guilt for this is visited by the other soldiers upon Mary who has stolen some purse, some bawbee: a whip lash, sear-lines, scoriades, migglegrunts, a brach gored, the lifeblood of insects, dark and sticky, compounded with the dampest straw. Mercifully, no true language for these works of Satan.

CHAPTER XVIII

The Humming

MORE has been said than intended. Against the white bar of Percy's lovemaking now lies this black bar, symbolic of vengeance: two thick rules of type upon a page, side by side, one outlined in white-reverse, the other the inked bar.

And then we are re-crossing the bridge on a galloping horse, Sophia like a sack that the sergeant grasps as he rides; likewise, she clutches her bag of herbs to her breasts as if they could cure her internal ills; yet her lungs lean and efficient, for they rode towards Glenmuir. And the moonlight across fields of new corn whitened the stems as if unto harvest.

Again, we may let Sophia speak in her prison voice and then provide a scholium:

I couldnae think, I couldnae speak, I couldnae speir ma ain spirit what it wud be about within me as we rode. Ony the wan picture wud be in ma eyen, of that blackguard in his violations, an' something on his nose, a carbunkular there on ane nostrill. The carbunkular said words tae me, as if it was God's ane mouth a-conversing, an' as in the Holy Bible each word wud be creating the world, the fields, that night — all I saw was a-changing or in vapours an' I saw the carbunkular sudden sharp-like, as if it had a spell tae make it speak sae. *That's* why I thocht I was a witch. (An' in Mother Fail's hole, I may have seen Satan in a trance, dressed like a woman.)

The scholiast comments that her mind's natural flow had been arrested at a single moment of horror. Now, says the scholiast, Necessity must be the product of a temporal axis: the inevitable onrushing of time, which is Determination or Fate and which we may imagine as a horizontal *river*, intersects with a vertical sky-path, which is Possibility, an airy and various Nothing, yet shining with myriad colours; where Fate's river and Possibility's airiness unite, there Necessity (masked from us in this earthly life as Probability) swirls onwards. But here time stood still in a moral darkness. At this intersection, her horror overpowered the thoughts that should have governed and changed it, and fearful visions spouted and fountained in their possibilities or vapourised into moony rainbows. It was as though all future time would be like that moment, all other possibilities except horrific ones curtained out by a frightening iridescence.

Yet the ride was beautiful at first: the compass of stars swiftly reflected in the river, moonlight paling an oatfield, the seeds billions of worlds, each a new beginning, held in tight constellations like low tree tops of grey stars. Her night vision, not stark black and white, was of teeming perspectives with tinges of weak tobacco colours; from time to time loony hints of blues and yellows in her mind's eye where the dangers lay. Ridiculous phrases came riding through her head: "Crubb, creel and all the ones. Mayn't all and mayn't some? Hinsoever gerral isn't ony, where isn't ony? The wet-bedded brook in the furry ravine. Violated. Violated. Wimmin'll, wimmin'll." All in the rhythm of hooves and in the possibilities of language. Then: "Where does evil end?"

But we cannot go far into the suffering mind, blurting with little voices. She set up a keening noise as they rode.

"What's that you say?" asked the sergeant behind her.

"It is the humming," she replied.

"What humming?"

"Muckle tae ma face. Humming ahint ma back."

For reasons the brute did not understand, he grew wary of asking her more.

After three miles, they began to hear a shawm's reedy note whining against a tabor's beat, and a fife piping, and arrived at a copse where the sergeant turned his horse. It was pitch-dark except for a mud track silver-lipped until it darkened under a tunnel of branches, summer air warm as a cow's flank, the horse pickily winding through the trees, branches whipping out of nowhere, a hateful restraint round Sophia who fingered her broken sword blade inside her bag. She imagined reaching Glenmuir's camp by the barge; she saw Bessie tied glamourously to her boat's mast, like a Ulysses straining at her bonds. And then her own body falling from the saddle into this sergeant's proud arms, to drive in the makeshift dagger with her weight. Judder then swift through the ribs. With a gasp as of pleasure, the sergeant fell like a willing woman. She lay on top a moment hearing him gurgle, and felt utterly depressed as Glenmuir's soldiers dragged her off, a sadness that blighted her vision across bare acres to the dark end of the world. "I vow," said a voice, clearly in her ears. The images writhed in her mind. "I have been made a beastly whore."

She wrested round towards the sergeant.

"If ye tak me tae the captain, I'm for tae be hangit."

"It's a 20 miles to Glasgow and a 100 miles to Edinburgh and there's a a gallows at both," he grunted, complacently.

"Weel, I am ony the gainer if ye should keep me for yoursel' the whiles. The captain knows not of me."

The Englishman reined in his horse.

"And how would that be?"

"We ride on through the wood some ways, and I shall cook ye a night's breakfast."

"What breakfast?"

"I shall find ye ane. And we'll tak oor goodly pleasure, and I shall win days of freedom, and ye can deliver me later wi' heartfelt excuses."

The sergeant, whose coarse skin flushed with anticipation, agreed to this with promises of his own that evidently held good for that night, but not much beyond; he let his mount amble deeper into the forests. When they were well hidden, they dismounted and, after awkwardness between them, she pulled him down forcibly. Sophia proved quite uncontrollable, writhing her limbs on the dead leaves, the whites of her eyes wild, her limbs blotched with earth, and she howled, a little wolf-like, so that the sergeant stood again, alarmed, realising that this was a damage he had done not like a sword cut but incomprehensible.

Then all he wanted to be was rid of her; yet he went with her, to prevent escape, as she wandered through the woodland culling mushrooms and berries, naming them under her breath. At one point, she laughed harshly and said: "Ye need a notebook for tae remember these little planties." She had him build a fire and she took a tin plate from his saddlebags and used it for skillet over the stones. The mushrooms were wholesome but she fried them in oil of rue from her bag and, from another phial, still more virulent berry juice, perhaps of the belladonna, in whose use Mother Fail had so recently instructed her. She was cooking their surest love potion, she said, but her manner made him suspicious and he would eat morsel by morsel from her fingers only after she had taken a mouthful first.

"A wise woman told me we mun wait a canny hour and then all that we think tae be we may be."

That was too subtly expressed, so she added: "I shall whisper ye visions and ye shall see visions and we shall be in those visions."

Nervous, cupidinous, at her instructions he stripped his lower limbs naked and lay down while she, not undressing ("Ye may do that for me when the powers are on us," she said, stretched out in a straight line from him so that their heads touched. And after a while, their hearts began to sound in their ears like a joyous ticking, and their eyes switched into new ways of seeing, a bluish aura round the forest leaves in darkness. "I am afraid," the burly soldier said and his muscles were trembling involuntarily like Sophia's when her fits came upon her. "Whist awhile! Ye shall be content," said that head brushing his own scalp with its hair. "But the way intae the pleasure palace o' luv is guarded by some frightening things that ye, a sodger man, mun encounter wi' y'r bravery."

What followed can no more be called hypnotism than the operations of Mother Fail; yet nor was it wholly the effect of the poisons they had imbibed. This much is clear from her testimony: Sophia — herself poisoned, superstitious, and gripped by mental peculiarity — saw what she made the sergeant see, and communicated it in a monotone murmuring that slid in and out of humming noises; and it cast a spell on the man. Lying there, he would sense around him a magic circle with its symbols and divine name of God, for she told him she had cast such a circle with her mind, to keep away horned demons with great codpieces in curving leather; and he would know that he himself was an image of those demons and, for fear of his own damnation, could not stir. And she took him into his past until he saw a family Christmas festival through infant eyes and felt around him the tenderness of parents and thrilled naively as if about to receive a wooden animal crudely carved by his father. He found himself weeping into dead leaves at his own sinfulness. And then malevolent horsemen crashed soundlessly through the distant wood; he could not explain this soundlessness or how their terrifying mounts could be neighing; a bleating insect noise came audibly close; and that might be real; and that might be evil; his own heart-beat uttered curses against himself. "Dinnae fear: the circle protects us," murmured her voice, though no circle had ever been drawn, and though the timbre of the voice was just his fear; the fear became slithery over him that the forest floor had bred new crawling things, so that he cried aloud. At last there came angels, as if stepping from their niches in an English church, and though they turned from him in distaste, he dared hope to follow them, for the obscure tree tops filled with their blueness and, though he could not see this, yet he did see wide steps of blue stone leading up to the promised palace of love. Beautiful women in cream robes thronged its pillars and he passed through white rooms into a great hall where were the brocaded curtains of a bed fit for the King of England and Scotland. He parted the curtains and looked into his own eyes, but could not fully look at them, his second face somewhere off to the side, utterly grinning. Yet when he flicked his gaze to that side, he saw his second face blotch all over with spots, and he knew the disease to be moral; for then he saw the hairy hindquarters of a goat where that face had been; and he felt the Satanic arse draw near his seeing face; and the pelt was strung with turds. All this, the murmurs brought to him. His throat was choking; he felt stabbed with horror. Some quarter of an hour later he discovered he had been in a slumber and awoke; and Sophia was gone. She had taken his horse, his tunic, and his hat. Naked below, his shirt like a child's shift, he leant his forehead against tree bark and cried again uncontrollably because he had once been that child and had known so much kinder thoughts. It was like a religious conversion, but, induced by the poisons, it had little staying power and soon, his eyesight still uncertain and his gait a-stagger, he set off in pursuit.

Meanwhile, she — in no perfect mind either — had taken off for the top road and halted the horse where the sergeant had originally turned it. The military tunic hung loose about her, but she felt tall, almost, as Bess. In a poison dream she had poignarded the sergeant before leaving: only in a dream; but in that vision her future was outlined in piercing yellows and blues of hectic joys, whereas it was likelier to prove in reality coloured of veriest black.

CHAPTER XIX

The She Boat

SHE dismounted and trod carefully along through the wood towards Bessie's captured castle. Darkness had a metallic sheen and the leaves of bushes stood out darker, more vivid than normal, as if they had all been rhodedendrons in a jungle. Arrived at the bankside, she bordered it until the *Mary Cutler's* mast stood silhouetted against river moonlight. From Rotterdam days, she remembered Bessie's customary mooring: upstream with ropes fore and aft, so that, the mooring dropped, the current would drag the bows round downstream and the sails would fill for a quick getaway — a strategy which, to judge by soldiers' carousing heard on the night wind, had failed this time. Over the grassy crest of a bay she could see a group of them onshore; a superior officer of Glenmuir's build sat on a pannier. More laughter came from the boat moored bankside, and she hoped they were not tormenting Bessie there. A voice in her mind said: "This isnae yet the hunt for thy captain. First, Bess mun be free."

Somewhat disguised in tunic and bonnet, she slipped the aft mooring from its tree trunk downriver from the soldiers, and the boat held against the current at the bows. She took a long detour through the wood until she could approach the fore mooring-tree equally unobserved. She doffed the bonnet, secured her medical bag to her head with strips of cloth, untied the slip-knot round the tree, and, retaining the rope's end, slid into the black river. The Mary Cutler's bows began to swing across-stream, dragging her like a toy on a string around to the barge's out side. The men ashore thought it uproarious that the vessel had come unmoored. Sophia, a second time escaping from Glenmuir in such a manner, drifted up to the far side-keel cleated upwards on its hinge like a folded wing. Weighed down by sodden uniform and dress, she removed her bag from her head and, so encumbered, began to climb. Alas, outside the cheapest tale, this is impossible noiselessly: a trooper in long white underpants kept his buttock perch on the cabin hatch, but grabbed her wrist when she rose over the side.

"Why it's one of the *army!*" he boomed, regarding her uniform. And, across to shore: "Another whore come to earn the king's groat!"

This was an Englishman, temporarily joined in with his Scottish allies for post-battle celebrations. Partly crushed, the hatch and the surrounding disarray of the deck bore witness to a battle of smaller-scale in which Bessie and her barge had been overpowered.

"Or is it a drowned sailor trollop? Well, it's army law on this ship that you've set floating. Punishment: immediate. To be done and over done until you burst like a ripe fig, and if I were't myself — how shall I say — *between*, 'tis me should offer the first fusilade."

Receiving no reply, he pulled her around the wreckage, and thrust her clumsily down the ladder into the long cabin under-deck lit by oil lamps, calling out, "One more for the breach. She may need questioning first, corporal."

The hold was not as she remembered from her journeys across the German Sea. Larboard, canvas-partitioned booths lined the hull, the makeshift walls trembling in minimal privacy. One soldier had wrestled a woman half out of his booth and lay across her head down in a posture Sophia had never dreamed of in her village life. The activities in other cubicles were all too obvious: camp women or frightened female prisoners. Most shocking to her, in the gloom a pink monkey of a captive wiggled his buttocks as he thrust into the behind of a huge, bloody-backed and moustacheoed man face downwards on straw matting while half-clothed soldiers looked on with grim smiles, keeping a sword on him. And the fife, shawm, and tabor trio under the forward hatch kept up their jig.

A low murmur greeted her arrival and an ironic voice said: "She may be more than we can still manage."

"That I am!" she rapped out, for she had her pistol levelled.

Naked bodies, male and female, emerged from the booths to stare at this phenomenon.

"Scarlett!"

The moustacheoed man threw the pink monkey aside with a thrust of the buttocks and twisted to look at her: not a man, but Bessie Queensferry, for once open-eyed in astonishment. Her hands were tied down to two iron rings set into the timbers for securing cargo; a bleeding crater at her left shoulder-blade showed where a bullet had burst out; and her back had been whipped.

"Did ye think tae be in trouble and no have aid frae me, Bess?"

"Losing my maidenhead," said the giantess. "At last. You spoilt it."

"But that cannae be true!"

"Not true. Lost long ago."

It was a Bessie Queensferry joke.

"Threatened my ladies," she added. "Couldn't fight on."

"That pink body," Sophia commanded, glassy-eyed despite this reunion, "untie my friend."

The naked man, some runt of a Covenanting litter forced into repellant love-making, began hurriedly to release Bessie's hand, when an equally naked soldier stopped him at sword tip.

"Weel, lads, we need not fear a lassie wi' a pistol, and probably a wet one."

Sophia placed her left hand formally within the bodice of her dress and her voice became liturgical: "I am a witch. I hae poisoned a meddling sergeant and hae sent him tae ma Mistress in her huvven. I hae made this gun for tae fire. I hae loaded it wi' a sulver bullet which will pierce any man's heart e'en intil his very soul."

Whether it was her words or the wild whites of her eyes, they all in that credulous age hesitated, but a heavy clumping on the deck close above their heads told of an arrival. Sophia backed to the side-wall to face the entrance ladder. Glenmuir himself, in uniform but soaking wet, trod heavily down the rungs and took in the scene with a sardonic twist of his scarred lip.

"Have a care, captain," called one of the camp women.

Sophia repeated her monotone liturgy, word for word, meanwhile reaching into her bag with her free hand.

Glenmuir's face settled into its carved cruelty and he walked over as if on a Sunday stroll.

"Did ye think such a lass wud have primed her pistol?" he remarked, taking the weapon from her trembling fingers.

He breathed near her, hatefully alive, and his tone dropped to a low rasp.

"I shall no be needing ma wet claes for tae visit a whore's punishment upon this whore, and I shud be muckle obliged, corporal, if ye wud find some body for tae divest me."

But Sophia's left hand bearing the cloth-wrapped sword-tip swept out and round in a wide arc and managed to jab his left buttock; whereat he roared like a speared lion and clubbed her heavily and she half fell. Then she was held secure, and a trooper came forward to act as valet for Glenmuir while he regarded her steadily.

By the time he was naked, the blood mopped up on his leg, Sophia had acquired her own rude valet, who, still nervous of her supernatural claims, had only removed her top dress. Glenmuir waddled towards her with a foolish grin and seized her shoulders.

"It is Sophia a-Sop, she whom they named Scarlett and whom I kent langsynes I shud have for my own."

The man was covered on his body with the grey-ginger hair, a great fuzz of it over his genitals; he smelt of women's scents, of sweat, and of blood. Her mind held black knots.

"Who told ye tae spy on we folks?"

She hummed.

"What's that?"

"Muckle tae ma face."

The sergeant, looking rather bilious yet, had come down the ladder now.

"She has begun saying these things, captain."

He explained how he had captured her and been poisoned, leaving out none of the details for they seemed to please Glenmuir, and adding that he had run along the bankside — a far shorter path than Sophia's ride.

Glenmuir's nose had been broken at Bothwell Bridge and he sniffed thinly with raised lips.

"Whores and whores' punishments. Give me that thick belt o' yours, sergeant, and we shall try a little Scots judgment upon her for your belly ache and for my arse -- aye and I mind a belly ache of my own, a time."

The captain took the belt and wrapped it round his fist so that the buckle dangled. His fist clouted the side of Sophia's head as if experimentally and within the fuzz of genitalia he began to engorge.

"This is a trick I have learned," he said — and he whisked the buckle sharply towards her in such a way that the spike skewered into her arm.

Sophia screamed but managed to gasp, "This is an honour."

"But don't maim her, captain," the sergeant protested as Glenmuir, aroused, swung back for a new blow.

Glenmuir was felled to the deck by a great club of a fist. The Covenanting runt, too scared for participation himself, had freed Bessie's other hand — which explained her unusual silence in all that confusion — and she had sprung forward and now straddled her victim. Her heavy-browed face, moustache and all, was furious red, thick lips snarling, the sweat trickling down a warty chest so broad and flat that the breasts were skin folds: a male giant except for the empty bush of pubic hair untidily stuffed between her oversized legs. Old spent sperm dribbled from her on to the groaning Glenmuir, and she dragged him up in a bear hug as he began to struggle. Sophia had seized a more effective brace of pistols from a pile of clothing and warded off all the others.

"Mercy me!" she said.

Muscles corded the captain's body and, had he been younger, he might have wrought free from that tremendous hug; but he was half drunk, his eyes were bulging with effort, his mouth jabbering, and Bessie wrenched suddenly at her grip, Glenmuir's lungs squeezed into a forced cry as one of his ribs cracked. The mighty forearm passed across his throat and choked at him; even Bessie had a task holding him then in his death throes. His penis stood fully erect and his face was turning blue. "We must stop this," shouted the sergeant; and still no-one moved as the life-force drained out and Glenmuir's tongue extruded from his teeth, his eye-strings almost snapping. "It's a Merry Andrew," thought Sophia in her headiness. The body dropped plumb on to the boards. "I cannae bear that Bessie shud tak such an eye." Sophia darted, one pistol went scattering as she picked up a military dagger from a table, and plunged it into Glenmuir's left socket: her feeling as the blood spurted was that she had somehow saved another tragedy.

A hysteria sailed away from her mind like a wisp of cloud. Her right hand left red streaks upon her shift and her left listlessly dropped her remaining pistol.

"In this way may Percy live," she remarked, as if to the barge itself.

"Scarlett," panted Bessie, smoothing down her own flesh with her dreadful hands: "His eye yours. No bead for my necklace."

There were swordpoints ringing the two of them round, but that was not how they were taken.

The entire cabin shuddered as they rammed the far bank. And here is what happened to those stalwart swordsmen. A prostitute stabbed one in the back. The pink monkey of a Covenanter in a fit of self-disgust shot one of his tormenters through the belly. Bessie Queensferry made sure of two (let us leave the details), another prostitute shot a fourth, and Sophia half-brained another with a belaying pin. That left the sergeant, who was extracting his sword from the guts of a camp follower foolhardy enough to attack frontally. Now it was his turn to face sword points and he tried to brave it out:

"Six of you I can take, but this giantess... I yield in honour as your prisoner."

He presented his sword, but Bessie brushed past him, ducking her head to climb the ladder; from on deck she grinned downwards at him.

"You, come."

Fear now made him appear even more wayward-minded, and he made no attempt to go for his sword but mounted to stand beside her. With a guffaw, she boxed him senseless, seized his pants and an arm and flung him aside like offal into the river mud. She did the same for all the other bodies, including Glenmuir, and only Sophia's belayed victim stirred in that mud.

"You, lover boy," she called down to the pink monkey, who came on deck still naked and hoping for better treatment.

"Go!" said Bessie but he hesitated. And that brought him an unwelcome journey of his own into the mud, where he scrambled back into the river and began swimming for his life.

Bessie leapt ashore, shoved her bows free, and crossed on board again as Sophia, seeing her purpose, unfurled the jib to catch the night wind; and soon the mains'l stuck out sideways as they ran down the Clyde towards Glasgow port, a boatful of women, still dressing as they slowly came on deck and took up positions like pale statues in the dark, not daring to speak in case their position, already guessable, should be pinpointed.

A river thud, a breeze, a creaking, the obscure banksides sliding by; and Sophia's inner vision — sharp with knives, the dead captain's ripe blood spurting up her wrist — that vision slid over river surfaces of a black and liquid underlay bordered with willows. The sail wagged across as they jibed and the forward view blanked hopelessly out until the great canvas curtain swung clear and re-opened the same river scene, as if eternity had two aspects, both the same. All the really evil people — those demonic in imposing viciousness or righteousness upon others — had no billet for this voyage of the unfortunate: the freakish giantess, the mentally-damaged prostitutes, and Sophia, our emissary, her own stability in such question. With soldiers scouring the entire countryside for stragglers from the battle, their boat floated between murders: those in the past of their friends, and, those in the future, of themselves.

Not a woman on board but knew the Clydemouth would be blockaded; they journeyed to captivity; likely, neither Sophia nor her giantess would escape the gallows. Sophia counted her offences: stealing a horse that had been given (annulled); retaliating against torture and violation by apportioning stomach aches to the guilty (twice); running for her life; assuming a false name so that she could marry her lover before he died; plunging a dagger into an already dead man's eye, having plunged one into his buttock while he was yet alive.

She had, however, driven an ammunitions cart to fuel a battle, a battle that she saw to be evil. In her strictness of puritanical self judgment, she believed this deserved her hanging. Whichever way she re-argued it her conclusion was the same. And she would have confessed the crime even if her role remained unsuspected. But how to do so, when its confession would endanger others such as Brown the Carrier, wherever he might now be?

For the first time in her recent life, she prayed, but not to the Christian's God or to a man at all. She whispered the prayer in her old dialect across the river licks, the medium of their passing, the wind steady behind, fitful through tree-lined bends, occluded by dismal gorges, until the cliffs acted as a funnel, the barge's wake like a disappearance of blackberries.

The words o' Christ i' the gibber o' ordinary men, impassibly cleaving saint from sinner, hae separated a' what shines in our lives from a' that is deedly dark; until every Jock becomes murderous and Scotland is cast out from the edges of heaven, an' its plains hae grown dark likewise, its cities clusters o' coal chips, an' its mountains rise beyond, drenched in bluid. A black Water slithers through the cities towards the bluidy mountain screes. Greed in the cities forges the swords, self-righteousness from the ministers' lippis places sword in hond, the lairds wi' self-interest for their estates loose the tenant army. An' then a proudfu' absolute king — a deedliest deil anti-Christ wha cannae distinguish his personal self from nationhood — mad like a' monarchs I iver heard o' in Rotterdam — this ceevilised king winks at ony cruelty for tae keep the ceevil order that maintains him aye i' his palace. No prayer lies here but a prayer for more bluid for tae gush; or for ambitious lords at the drap o' a garter tae submit ma nation untae English power.

No. I pray tae a river goddess, michty in form like Bess, but no longer ignorant and violent, instead claed i' fine lawns, saft in outline, crowned wi' the flooers o' May, a witch goddess — witch only because her reign is ootside a' heavens of Christ, all hells of Christ, submitting tae nae Satanic majesty oothor, her body flesh warm, so passible that warmth. I see a shimmer on her broad thigh, a fixety point o' licht, as if ma ane soul began there upon that thigh, until it grew bairn-like, dandled on the lap o' ma unknown mither? And I pray untae her, O River goddess, *May All Deeth Count,* in some eternity. Whither the deeth of little bairns, whither of ancient crones, faces wizened with suffering, whither ma Percy's deeth, whither o' some ignorant bravo like Donald the Brat, cut down i' his vainglory, whither ma ane deeth, almost a suicide, as I ride this boat tae the gallows, whither a king's deeth e'en, whither deeth o' ma ane Bess. Horrid the men wha say that ony Christ's redemption o' deeth wud justify that accounting, an' wha wud slay for that desperate legend. Horrid those wha think there is nae accounting whamsoever, for then what cud explain the life I have lived and a' its anxieties? What cud explain the feelings of the worst person alive, the Glenmuirs, if there wud be no accounting? Feelings wull last for iver, just like y'r peasepuddin' moralities and y'r Euclids o' reason.

The water had greyed in dawn light as they entered the Clyde basin, where a flyboat turned about the harbour waiting for them, a cannon mounted to port and starboard. They could make no fight of it at such a distance, though the women screamed and cursed hysterically as the water plumed on either side. Shortly enough, a lucky cannonball dropped clear through the forward decking, and the mast canted forward in a swelter of sail, and eventually nothing seamanship could do would prevent Bessie's *Mary Cutler* from surrendering into the waters; and that giant heart of its skipper seemed to surrender with it, for when the skiffs came across water to the struggling swimmers the sailors tugged Bessie out of the water like a dead thing. And, in brief, that was how they were taken.

On board the fly stood the egregious sergeant, who had commandeered a horse to warn Mr. Samuel Pepys's navy.

The women lined up, shivering hopelessly in the morning breeze.

Bessie sighed to Sophia.

"Prisoners now. Was already. Just having a last love, me and these girls."

"Oh, but we mun pay with our lives, Bess. E'en ye mun pay for Percy."

"So many others. Paid. Always, always, my honey love."

"I'm a witch now too," she replied as, pistols at their head, they were forced to enter a launch.

The giantess looked sharply at her, mid-stream.

"Not a witch!" she snapped.

"Bess, against these devils we must all be calm witches; otherwise they turn us into whores or martyred saints."

"You may well fear for your reputation," interrupted the sergeant. "I shall have you tickled and teased and burnt for poison and sorcery, as well as for this deadly murder of Captain Glenmuir. Now keep you quiet."

Sophia hummed, something of the yellows and blues returning to her mind.

"Stop that!" the sergeant shouted, for he felt the blood of her upon his conscience.

CHAPTER XX

The Unmentionable Baby

SOPHIA and Bessie spent a year inside Edinburgh's ill-famed Tolbooth prison awaiting trial; and they found there Isabel, reduced in health, awaiting her own process. She was suspected without evidence of harbouring the murderers of Archbishop Sharp, whose assassination laid the fuse which fired the Battle of Bothwell Bridge; also of consorting, while in hiding, with Richard Cameron and Donald Cargill, the militant new preachers whose coming Sir John Cochrane had once forecast. To consort with such men was a hanging crime.

The prison, both noisy and isolated at once, stuck out into the High Street at the end of superior lock-up shops, the Luckenbooths. On the other side under the buttressed crown of St. Giles Cathedral, it sheltered busy market stalls; hard by stood the Parliament buildings where they would be judged. Fresh prisoners arriving in the Tolbooth sought Isabel out with the latest news. For months, more than a thousand Bothwell Bridge prisoners, including the victorious prostitutes from the barge, had been confined in the Greyfriar's graveyard, many dying from exposure; and two hundred drowned while being transported to Barbadoes. (Over in Galloway, the Reverend Peden stopped in middle of prayers and prophesied the shipwreck.) But Sophia and Isabel spoke little, Isabel horrified at the charge of witchcraft pending against the other woman and Sophia still ranking the older girl among the "prig-rats".

A man, Hall, killed at the Queensferry, had on him a virulent Covenanting document, and even Bessie listened when told that women friends of hers had helped old Donald Cargill himself to escape that fracas. (Isabel soon had word and she whispered across to Sophia's cell: "Oh, but the document says in righteousness that we will punish witches and Sabbath-breakers.)

News came that they had taken up old Mother Fail at last and had burnt her. (To Sophia's floods of tears, Isabel, after an interval, warned: "You stand in *immortal* danger.")

So history proceeded outside their prison walls and the bloody period known as The Killing Times began.

Sophia's prison testimonial describes little of her sufferings in stinking darkness of straw, grimy walls and short corridors of iron bars. "I lay in my orphan straw wance again." She discovered that the sergeant's violation had left her pregnant. Worse, she found upon herself the unmistakable canker of disease communicated by her violator. She came to term early, with Isabel allowed in as midwife, her body anxious to abort a child which nevertheless lived for a few hours, sorely deformed and brawling with the dirty straw. Sometime during the night, its uneven breathing simply stopped. Sophia, exhausted, nearly crazy with superstition, blamed herself for dalliance with black arts and her self-accusations made the gaolers uncertain about the real cause of death. The sergeant, hearing a distorted report of this in England, pressed his charge of witchcraft, adding to it one of infanticide, and Sophia now faced being burnt at the stake.

Says her prison document in a rational moment:

"This suited ma gaolers well enuff, for they had little tae hang me with, except for always running, and for a bloody stab in a loathsom buttuk. An' truly I thocht mysel' witched indeed, until cam Sir George Mackenzie wi' his wiles."

As the records of Fountainhall inform us, the three women were tried during the same assize period, although Isabel underwent full examination by the Privy Council before being handed on to the Edinburgh courts for judgment. Bessie, whose crimes cried out before the world, had nothing to lose when — trying to protect Sophia from the charge of witchcraft — she claimed monosyllabically that she herself had murdered the baby in prison out of jealousy of child-rearing. (This must have led the judicious Fountainhall to report erroneously that the giantess had been hung for infanticide instead of the truth, for multifarious homicide.) At this point Sophia had little to answer, except the accusation for witchcraft: and here Sir George Mackenzie, Bluidy Mackenzie, the King's Advocate, was to play one of his more idiosyncratic roles.

One day, Sophia and Isabel were called together into the inner turnkey's room where they found Mr. Blacklock alone at a table, his studious face wrenched into distaste for his surroundings, his silken black law garments fastidiously cuffed in white lace. On the wall above him hung an engraving of the hated king, Charles the Second. Blacklock nodded in genteel manner, examined some documents through an eyeglass, and then spoke entirely to Isabel.

"You may imagine that Sir John Cochrane has not withdrawn his favour from so faithful a servant of the church, standing in the very light of martyrdom, which he regrets."

Isabel replied firmly: "I could not think him disfaithful to me or to our Master."

"He has retained me as your advocate, certain that whatever the merciless judgments of these courts, your own advocacy will suffice you before your Maker."

"I fear greatly that you will have little to intervene between myself and the blessed fate that awaits me."

"There is likely much that I cannot do in these most unhappy times."

Sophia stood in a swoon as he turned then to her.

"You also have served us well until, it seems, you gave up your very soul. I cannot myself bear to intervene in the hideous crimes of witchcraft and child-slaying, for I do not believe the declarations of the giantess in regard to the latter."

"Oh but I am guilty, guilty," wailed Sophia in her distracted state. "I have conducted an altar tae the Queen of Witches."

Mr. Blacklock stood up, thundering as far as his thin voice would: "Then you must seek repentance; and you must endure that you must endure; for Sir John feels free of all obligation to you amid such evils. I appear before you but to hear that one confession and then to discharge you from our welfaring."

And he preremptorily called for the turnkey who dragged Sophia — utterly mute — back to her cell, while Mr. Blacklock continued his negotiations with Isabel.

We find Isabel's hearing before the Privy Council recorded in the Reverend James Anderson's pleasant volume, *The Ladies of the Convenant*. This was in the Grand Salle and Mr. Blacklock was alongside her.

> Privy Council: How long is it since you saw Mr. Donald Cargill?
> Isabel: I cannot tell particularly when I saw him.
> P. C.: Do you own his Covenant?
> Isabel: What Covenant?
> Then they read it to her, and she said she owned it.
> P.C.: Do you own the Sanquhar Declaration?
> Isabel: I do own it.
> Mr. Blacklock: Your Lordships are seeking that she condemn herself in mere opinion.
> P.C.: Silence, if you please Sir. We are determined to roust out treason where it most nearly lies.
> P.C.: Do you own the papers taken at the Queensferry on Henry Hall and found on yourself in your prison cell?
> Isabel: You need not question that.
> P.C.: Do you own these to be lawful?
> A renewed protest by Mr. Blacklock.
> Isabel: Yes; because they are according to the Scriptures and our Covenants, which ye swore yourselves, and my father which you murdered swore them.
> P.C.: Yes; but the Covenant does not bind you to deny the king's authority.
> Isabel: So long as the king held the truths of God, which he swore, we were obliged to own him; but when he broke his oath, and unlawfully robbed Christ of his kingly rights, we were bound to disown him.
> P.C.: Have you conversed with David Hackston?
> Isabel: I have one time in Carrick, and I never saw ought in him but a godly pious gentleman.

P.C.: Was the killing of the Archbishop Sharp of St. Andrews a pious act?
Isabel: I never heard David Hackston say that he killed him; but if God moved any, and put it upon them to execute his righteous judgments upon him, I have nothing to say to that.
P.C.: Do you know what you say?
She gave no answer.
P.C.: Were you ever mad?
Isabel: I have all the wit that ever God gave me; do you see any mad act in me?
P.C.: Did you serve the woman that gave Mr. Donald Cargill quarters?
Isabel: These are frivolous questions. I am not bound to answer them.
P.C.: Whether or not, you will be put to own all this in the Grassmarket. We have regret you should put your life in hazard in such a quarrel.
Isabel: I think my life little enough in the quarrel of owning my Lord and Master's sweet truths. Christ owned his kingly office when he was questioned on it, and he told them he was a king, and for that end was he born. And it is for that we are called in question this day, the owning of his kingly government.
Bishop Paterson: We own it.
Isabel: We have found the sad consequence of the contrary.
Bishop Paterson: I pity you for the loss of your life.
P.C.: We pity you; for we find reason and quick wit in you. What is your name?
Isabel: Since you have staged me, you might remember my name, for I have told you already, and will not always be telling you.
One of them said: "May you not tell us your name?"
Then one of themselves told it.

When her case was forwarded to the Lords of the Justiciary on charges of high treason they denied her the support of Mr. Blacklock's advocacy. In truth, real evidence lacking, they had nothing against her but these simple opinions, which she was required to renounce. The case being sent to the justiciary court, she held to her principles before the Lord Advocate, Sir George Mackenzie's, wily questions, viz:

Lord Advocate: Will you say over what you said before His Majesty's Council?
Isabel: Would you have me to be my own accuser?
Lord Advocate: When saw you David Hackston? Seeing you love ingenuity, will you be ingenuous, and tell us if you saw him since the death of the bishop?
Isabel: He has appeared publicly within the land since.

Lord Advocate: Your blood be upon your own head; we shall be free of it.
Isabel: So said Pilate.

Then they told her to sign what she had owned, but she refused; so they signed it for her; and a packed jury brought in the desired verdict.

The main events of Sophia's process were held within the prison itself.

They had let her be during her pregnancy, but now, once a witch-finder could be found, she faced terrible pains. Another day, she was recalled to the turnkey's room, to find a dark-clothed gentleman afoot there. For a delirious second, she thought King Charles himself had stepped down from the engraving in the room. The gentleman's wig was long and black in the king's curly style, though this was a plumper man, his eye quick, liquid, yet also sardonic under a trace of frown; his complacent lips pursed slackly with the readiness of the loquacious. This celebrity makes but a brief appearance in our story but, in a sense, he has been prepared for all along. He was the very type of those who would one day sell the Scottish nation out to the English: those who, knowing themselves to possess extraordinary talents, could always find a reason in public morality to trim their ambitious sails to the winds of power.

He waved the obsequious gaoler to be gone.

"You are Sophia a-Sop, sometimes called Scarlett? Do you know me, lass?"

Her head gave only an ambiguous nod or shake, and she retreated, knowing herself to be filthy.

"I am the King's Advocate, Sir George Mackenzie. You may and should stand up before me."

"But this is beyond belief," she replied, "that the King's ane Advocate should come tae see a puir woman accused of witchcraft."

Sir George looked upon her more kindly than ever he looked upon a victim in his witness boxes.

"I am bound to uphold the laws of Scotland and they define witchcraft as existent and further it was condemned in the legal books of the Old Testament. But I am not bound to ordain torture for every ignorant lass who considers herself a witch or who is accused by violent wretches."

Sophia asked, "Can a woman be a witch and not know it?"

Sir George's bloody but enlightened intellect was shocked at this sign of superstition and disturbance.

"You have involved yourself by such loose speech in a *fama* or public rumour," he said. "Then some disreputable English sergeant has justified his lusts by accusing you. I shall protect you from so easily becoming sic a gull. My understanding is that you have not been put to question."

She shuddered.

"Most of all that were ever taken were tormented first and this was the ground of all their confessions, albeit the poor miscreants cannot prove this usage, the tormentors being the only witnesses. However, I am reluctant to act unless the most convincing probation be supplied."

"Well, I may prove a witch after all."

"Have ye pricked puppets to represent persons whom you hold in hatred?"

"Nae... but I lit an altar tae... I dinnae ken wham tae — while clearing the field of Bothwell of its puir wounded. And I vowed tae hunt down Captain Glenmuir, who burnt my husband's fingers, thrust him through the shoulder, and had him cast upon the Bass for naething."

"Ah, you stuck the captain's arse, but we have another for his death."

"If ye mean my Bess, nae action was taken by that ane ither but tae preserve myself frae the captain's brutishness."

"There's enough of that gait. Let me return a pace. You vowed to hunt down the captain in your own good office and body, not by supernatural power?"

"Who would help me tae vengeance but the male demon? This land is full of such demons, may God curse them, and I'll hae nae help frae them!"

"I counsel you against proceeding far in such language. For the nonce, I find only complicity in self-defensive murder against you, and I am sore reluctant to let the witch investigators upon you. We shall count your year in this prison punishment enough, providing you will but say a simple phrase, 'God save the King'."

"D'ye mean, Sir George, that Percy is tae die, and Isabel is tae hang, and puir Bess tae make ane ither ane, and but myself is for tae gang free?"

"Hum. You will have heard of your friend, Isabel Harvey's, testimony before the Privy Council. Would you adopt similar principles? Or will you commode yourself by this simple phrase?"

"That I cannae speak."

"But what of your own beliefs, lass?" cried Sir George, outrage making his features livid. "Will you so hold to scorn all civilised procedure, all my own kindness to you, that you will not bless His Majesty?"

"Out of loyalty I cannae consent tae live. And so I must find a way for tae die."

The liquids in his eye solidified to utter agate.

"Hum. I have reviewed your papers, Sophia a-Sop. I find you an honest woman much given to false doctrines of loyalty, so I offer you this last chance to discumber yourself of the gallows."

She gave no answer, and the advocate rose to his full dignity.

"I will not consent to your torture, nor to adduce the crime of witchcraft. But we shall see whether before the king's courts you shall hold to treason as did your unfortunate friend. I candidly do not find you in your right mind, but this will not avail you now."

And he swung as bitterly as a rejected lover upon his heel, muttering as he went out of the door, "Thus am I constantly driven back from mercy unto the severity of laws."

Such was the curious blend of enlightenment and cruelty in "Bluidy Mackenzie"!

CHAPTER XXI

The Knot

SIR George proved as good as his threats when her case came to trial. They took Sophia into the law courts not under the great hammerbeam roof and along the tiled floors, but by a little gate into a nether room. A broken table against a wall and a boarded window bore witness that Bessie Queensferry had been hauled from the main court (where she had conducted much wreckage) through these same rooms and passageways, to be judged tied to a pillar like Samson. Their lordships sat at a makeshift Bench behind a large oak table.

Sophia stared at those wealthy faces composed into grave moralities and a blackness came upon her mind. At first she tried to convict herself for the murder of her baby, but Sir George told the jury that at the trial of the giantess this had already been found an accident. The advocate had seemingly spiked his own guns, since all he had left was a document describing her own remarks to him in the prison and her monosyllabic support, before the Lords Judiciary, of principles similar to those declared by Isabel. The documents were read anew and she said: "I do own and adhere to this."

She looked around at the trappings of their power, the black fur lining their gowns, dishonesty in their faces composed into grave honour, the sunlight through stone apertures striping the blue uniforms of two soldiers. And then she could not bear it.

"May I add to that adherence?" she asked.

How they nodded at her, anxious she should say anything to help them in their condemnation!

She was nearly swooning as she sobbed out in her old dairymaid accents: "I live in a faery land where Scotland was niver at war wi' itself, and where a' beliefs might be countenanced provided ony that folks have gentleness and guidness in their ane hearts. Then the grand ones couldnae lead us oot tae wars and we shud hae the plenty of mind in which the common folk o' Scotland shud a' be giants and giantesses like ma Bess, deprived though she is of muckle that is civil in its origin. I see this greening land stretching oot in fruitfulness, yawning in new sunshines before ma astonied gaze, an' people hoeing and reaping in its fields, proud for tae be Scots and peasant-like, and owing naething tae the pawky Lauderdales and kings adown in Lundon, for a sichlike peoples couldnae be bribed wi' coin nor seduced wi' honors, nor, like the weak vessel Mary, degraded by lusts. An' I know ma anesel then as a Queen of May, huge like ma Bess, but living in perfect purity of heart, *nat* owning the majesty of Satan wi' ye and the rest o' his warlock lairds, but owning ony the sisterhoods of queens, who are puir folk tae. I greet sae sair for the wee bairn in whose blood and smothering I stand justly condemned."

"But this is the most dreadful blasphemy!" exclaimed one of her judges.

Sir George interrupted hastily:"We are not proceeding against her madness — hum, that is, her distracted utterances — but against her rational treasons. Marry, all this is wild talk concentered fully upon her baby and we have dealt already with those consequences and with her complicity in murder. By your leave I continue."

Leave was reluctantly given.

Sir George then spoke to the jury: "You know that such women as these are guilty of treason."

That jury of wambling trimmers sought to salvage conscience, the foreman rising to say: "They are not guilty of matter of fact."

"Treason is fact," snapped Sir George, but corrected himself by adding, "It is true, it is but treason in their judgment; but you, the jury, go you on according to our law, and you will not do it, I will proceed."

This was a veiled threat to the jurymen that they themselves might be prosecuted for blatant error of judgment, an ancient and primitive relic of law then still obtaining; and some of them protested noisily.

Sir George tried to appease them, and perhaps himself: "We do not desire to take the life of this lass, for I have dealt with her in various ways, and yet I cannot prevail with her."

When the jury returned from the jury-house they unanimously found Sophia guilty in terms identical to those used of Isabel: "Guilty, conform to her confession of adherence to the fourth article of The Fanatics' New Covenant, and to the declaration at Sanquhar, and to the Bond of Combination" — let us leave aside these unexplained particulars except to say that they related to the recent uprisings. In Isabel's case was added: "But as actor or receiptor of rebels, they find it not proven."

But a rope is a rope. This was enough for the lords to pronounce doom against Sophia, agreeing to that pronounced against Isabel and Bessie, that each "be taken to the Grassmarket of Edinburgh, upon Wednesday next, the 14th instant, betwixt two and four o'clock in the afternoon, and there to be hanged on a gibbet until she be dead, and all her lands, heritages, goods, and gear whatsomever, to be escheat and inbrought to our sovereign lord's use" — this last provision, referring to the king, being for Isabel the most bitter irony.

"The day of the execution dawned..." No. We shall not dignify these ignoble proceedings with pompous depiction, for these three heroines did not *see* the scene, they felt it in their bodies, it shone into their eyes, much as a spotlight into an actress's. Bessie squatted in the cart that afternoon, her legs drawn up, and she sulked as if before her own mast that day when Sophia first saw her. She would talk to neither of the others but, once, held

Sophia's hand with a crumby palm, for she had been munching biscuits. They rode on jolting, jangling wood past jeering crowds along the Lawnmarket but stared either at each other or at the hazy sky.

Their way was mercifully brief, turning down the crooked West Bow lane that led to the hollow of the Grassmarket, an oval space just under the mightiest walls of the Castle. The cart rumbled into the heart of the crowd, huge because hangings of women Covenanters were rare and because Bessie was already pure legend. Two new gallows flanked the blacked wood of the inveterate instrument and here their cart was paused while the doom was shouted out by the crier to the uproar that encircled them. A whole troop of soldiery stood by in case Bessie should run amok. But it was Isabel who rose in the cart, for she had prepared manifold pious speeches against this day; at the instant two conformist ministers stepped forward below her with Bibles and yelled passages of it to drown her preaching. One of them was the crapulous Murdoch from Tarbolton. Yet Isabel continued, the veins standing out on her forehead, her lips clapping at her own bravery; and Sophia, outraged that her erstwhile friend's dying words should be so masked from their intended public, caught something of their drift:

"My soul was ever the bird of Christ," screamed Isabel. "I thank thee, Lord, for this sweetness of its flight to thee. May thy divine curses rain down upon those sinners who keep this unhappy land in darkness and seek to subjugate thy divine royalty to a treasonous king."

"Babylon... Babylon," her voice kept shouting into the tumult; and so she was the first they gathered, though they had intended her for last. She climbed her ladder to the central gallows eagerly, face shining, something truly sacred in her upturned eyes, while those cupidinous ministers kept up their disgusting babble. The executioner set the loop, and she had to stand ready there while soldiers took Bessie, that whole army of them prepared for trouble. A gasp went up from the crowd to see so tall a woman standing upon the ground; but that giantess, limp as a rag-doll, had tears streaming down her face.

"Oh, Scarlett," she groaned. "Over now."

"We dinnae ken that, Bess," said Sophia. "Ye are my eternal friend. We shall live in light with the Queen of the May and I shall retire intae the white room, betimes, with my Percy. I know not where."

And, great upon the ladder, Bessie mounted to where the executioner had ready for her a rope of extra length.

As if the word "light" had held a power, a buzzing had come in Sophia's ears. What the crowd *saw* was her body sag and fall as she stepped to the soil; and two men struggling to pull her, apparently already lifeless, up the ladder. What she lived through, however, was a sort of amazement: she was yanked upwards over the crowd's many-headedness but her eyes were peering down a smoky tunnel towards a room of light; this vision held steady as she stood a moment on a top rung. At a platform, words were muttered in her ear; the ground became unreal like water seen from a high dive; she felt roughness enwrap her throat, the great lump of the rope's knot already thrusting at her neck... dizziness...

As these three women jump into glory our story ends.

Well, we have a question remaining.

Surely God Himself, if He be a Christian Male, could only conscientiously take up to his bosom the authentic martyr in the centre, Isabel, who that afternoon undertook the task of Christ, whose own cross was central to two others. But the Christian God is locked in His own doctrines. Let us ask for our own purposes: which of these three martyrs, these three sinners, was the more deserving?

The Stevensonian voice says this: Our hearts bleed for Sophia; our colder admiration rests with Isabel, whose faithful constancy caused her to be disloyal to her government; as for Bessie, may this whole tale stand for her monument, even though in moral condemnations she stands as the murderer whom Christ could not save from his cross.

But I, Agnes Christmas, would, if I could, revive that premature ejaculator, Percy, that pimp of RLS himself... I would write that as his coffin was taken from the Bass Rock by boat, the apparently sorrowing Sophia knew that he had only been made senseless by her medicines and breathed beneath the boards. I would annul Isabel and her warfares. Failing this, I judge for Sophia, that she meet her man in the white room of an afterlife. As for Bessie Queensferry, why, she is my very self! The Outlaw! The Female Robin Hood: his Queen of May! I remember her fighter's name of Christmas Bessie! Christmas Bessie! Cornucopia! Terror of evil men!

We ponder these questions while the hangman breaks the women's skulls with his hammer. Shortly after, three other women were hanged for murdering their bastards.

And do you imagine that Auld Sandy Peden, whose judgment upon Sophia for her apple, had set in train some of this circumstance, could not have a moment of prophecy at such a time?

His biographer, Patrick Walker, has the story. After the "public murdering" of Isabel Harvey, Peden, still in Galloway, was talking to a professor of some note, "who had more carnal wit and policy than to suffer him to be honest and faithful" and who reasoned upon the ground of Isabel's sufferings that she would never be among the number of the martyrs. "Mr. Peden said, after musing a little, Let alone, you will never be honoured with such a death: and for what you have said against this worthy lass, your death will be both sudden and surprising. Which came to pass very shortly hereafter, for the man standing before the fire smoking his pipe, dropt down dead, without speaking more."

And soon all southern Scotland trembles under the Stuart killings. We leave Blacklock to his cautious law offices, but Sir John is implicated in Monmouth's conspiracy to gain the British throne, and in the Rye House attempt on the king's life. He escapes, as had Sophia, to Holland, returning to join two years later the Duke of Argyll's insurrection, upon the failure of which he is harboured by a kinsman. That kinsman's wife betrays him, because her Royalist brother has fallen in a skirmish, and Sir John is led to Edinburgh, displayed by the hangman in the streets, and lodged in the Tolbooth in more private quarters than those occupied by Sophia and Isabel. Fountainhall claims that he saved himself from high treason's due penalty by turning approver, whereas Burnet states that the Earl of Dundonald bought his son's pardon by paying 5,000 pounds to "the priests". By 1688 and the English Revolution, all he had worked for became, in deadliest irony towards all who had died, a national policy, for the throne's power was at last curtailed, some greater measure of religious tolerance was allowed although incomplete, and Sir John had his own estates restored.

More lowly followers were less fortunate, such as our favourite Brown the Carrier (who brought his charnel cart safely out of Bothwell by some ruse not recorded); Sir Walter has famously described out of the useful Walker, how, new-married by Peden himself, the carter met a summary death at the hands of Claverhouse, the terrifying general of upright conformity. Another "prig-rat", Claverhouse. No-one ever caught Auld Sandy, and he died in a cave nearby Sophia's native village of Tarbolton where once he had hidden in a sideboard.

Beginning With A Stain

by

Alice Notley

for Doug Oliver, &

in honor of Kate Berrigan

Beginning with a stain, as the Universe did perhaps
I need to tell you about for myself this stain
A stain of old blood on a bedspread (white)
—how can I set a pace?—I'm
afraid to speak, not of being indiscreet, but of
touching myself too near, too near to
my heart bed—the bedspread
was white & thin
I slept on her bed with my lover
and thus was never
sure whose stain hers or mine? And when I washed it, or
rather, he did, it remained. And then

And then she died unexpectedly, as they say
became away forever
except in the air, and somewhere near
my heart bed   But
the bedspread
became of her ashes a mingled part.
The stain, my stain, or hers, but mine
My love stain is part of her ashes, & I rejoice in that, whether
she & her lover, or I & my lover
were the ones who originally lay there, staining the bed
Our stain has gone with her, you see,
This is the stain that

invents the world, holds it together in color of
color of, color. Color of love.
This is the love they spend in order to be.
And she was quite young & I am much older (her step-mother)
But our stain was the same one
There is no double. And she is endlessly
clear; & good. Surround my heart bed
with my others at night
speak with me of the stain, that is our love, that
invents the world, that is
our purest one. Help me to stain, I say, my words with all us

(I love you I know you are there)
the song of one breath.
Outside where cars & cycles
I'm not afraid to begin again, with & from you.

*

There was already somebody there, at the
beginning of creation, there's a great calm though
with water to walk upon
walk upon a shallow sandbar wanting faintly real land
in the middle of the Ocean
What makes the land rise?

Start over to remember.
First there was nothing but water & sky
there was never a storm, there was great great calm
no clouds or mist the sky was blue as
of later summer afternoon evening a bit of pink
the earth is beneath the calm flat water perhaps it is
slowly rising rising up it is
here & there only a few inches below
in some places traces of it show as brown & silver
tops of sandbars, but mostly
everywhere is flat Ocean. There is already one person

at the beginning there is always
already one person
there is probably another but there is
no land, except a little
Are they sure what land is? they would like there to be
something else...

Near my keys a painted penny
a blob of fallen
rubber tee-shirt glitter matter yellow turquoise black
a piece of beginnings, I'm going to love you, I
already do because I'm already
walking on the still, Oceanic Earth
walking on water the
land rises up to meet
Sitting in another now in the
month of September, nineteen eighty-seven
remembering an old dream

*

I will never not make a sound, not have made a sound
I will ride this voice as I change, as always am
galley slaves of the slow black ship, are the one, you are the
    one
I have always dreamed of for example
(will never not make a sound, and as well you will never
    not have made a
sound, riding our voices as you change, to have longer arms for
    example
having longer longer arms and riding the slow black ship Greek
    ship, in
which we brought our selves to the mouth of a poet—don't—don't
    mention a...
I will never not ride this voice by way of
a way, by way of keeping going deaths, for example, more nouns & adjectives
(don't—don't mention a—) more vivification,
    hope, rhythm
mild sweet dooms & longer & longer arms & then slowly a black
    & then suddenly
black & having longer & longer arms, until their arms (the arms of
    the dead) reach round
I mean reach all around the globe (which I am as well that)
    this is
a rhapsody of the sound of any dear starting-point, dear
    starting-point that is
I, any I, who will never not make a sound and we have
    taken a ship
come to meet us in the calm, out of our dreams, a calling forth
    of commerce for
dear starting-points, dear stars from which issue bright stain dark
    stain & then suddenly
dead dear starting-points, hope, rhythm, mild sweet doomed globes
    the arms of the
other dead reach around, clear around them, hope, rhythm, more who will
have longer & longer arms, You are the one I dreamed of if
    that dream
emitter of shafts of lives who love intelligence, reaching towards
each dear starting-point, each dear not there dear starting-point a
    second a death a
stain a shaft of effect,

*

Call her the warmth of the breath that we all breathe
Breathe that love, breathe its unforeseen transformation
to transform with the final going out of, the giving back of it—
Descend into the commonplace, speak as to think,
employment of breath, of her, as delicate foliage as hours
Talk a future derived, *this is that new life---*
the metamorphosis also is boiling out of our sockets—
A word is a reddening stain, as time makes a loving stain,
that by the sound of it you can best
speak, say it right, make a time, call her she
Whoever warmed the air you breathe, with her love
Time gives back by the sound of *your* stain, listen for it again
as you are used by the spirits of believing—
(living)—the flower invoked is purple & blazes,
purple & blaze, red & carrot, fire & green

*

Some people refuse to remember; & I
never sure if what I remember is true (doesn't
matter), today I remember
a picture of a story. The Cheyenne
are traveling on foot & on horseback, in snow
It blows white, & shadow blue, they are darker, they
are dying. Others
are enmeshing that death into the
snow, air, wind, the very air
surround contains a death carelessly willed
by thought barely thought, or by no-thought, or fear or
Now if you say greed you must qualify, it is a
will or an animal or even a song, an air of
to have. To deny those other ones their own
to deny them a theirs, is not what is generally thought of or sung—
You might be doing this now—

Wanting to tell a story, this
the one that comes, keeps coming to
mind—
Some of them did go home; and there was
one romance; one friendship's death; something like a
loss of hope, but not of instinct to keep moving,
in a way true to the thousands-of-years-old self—this
with reference to the Cheyenne—you
may *not* identify with them, this time,
or you will not learn. Your thousands-of-years-old self
isn't recognizably in your possession; you
don't know who you are. This *is* the story, now—
city of October warmth, our
myth is that we don't have one—

I love the dead so much, talking to me
through my masks. Are the live really the
dead ones, in their, our desire
to be wheels, keyboards, screens?
I love the dead so much, but I only love
you. The red flower I always mention, the
tough-looking rose that, she said, looks like a
cabbage. 'I got six of them right now, that's where I
really stand.' I love the dead so much; and
October doesn't know who you are. (the part of
the mind that wears no mask; and *you*)

*

In the very beginning was it very dark? I think
that it was bluer than it was dark—from an old dream—
I was in space happy flying with another, who was it? a man
That's the first thing I remember from before I was born
I remember that; it is my truest dream

But one time I dreamed I was like a bird, flying
not like a person flying in a dream, & that was a true
dream too, so it is true, a bird flying over gold-spotted
brick-red canyons of the West, in the afternoon—
But I was flying alone so that was much later

So first, or before, when there was no first, never was, I was
flying with someone, then later, was alone. So this is my story:

The creation of the world comes after the real world, but
this is the real world too. In the old real world we were happy
we were together, we didn't have to walk on the ground or
make things; then the separation into canyons & sky came, how, who

made that? I will walk on the earth & call out your name
I will tell it as I do it, & the words will be the same, say, as
mountains: and when I find you, we'll talk about ourselves
incessantly: the words will be as much as all else.

*

In the beginning there was but a heart/ship/bed
But first it was a heart, how did there get to be a heart?
      which was the
heavens, dark heavens or was it water? how was there a
      heart?
I mean is, it is the heart of. It is kind, & brave, &
      beautiful—surely not brave; if
it is brave, it is human. It is human. Human
      is one of what it is.
& kind & beautiful, what we are meant to. When
the sun comes up a little, heart is a ship, when
      the sun goes down a bed. And
somewhat of vice-versa. A tongued heart is speaking, right?
      A one who
lies down on the bed which sails out all night to mingle with the
      others, of all the
universes—the heart can contain them all, it never really
      breaks not the
first heart of. O human, your heart must be that heart
Sail out this morning & look at your city
I am afraid

※

Trapped in an unheated room, the Cheyenne
(Replayed in my mind)   Those left of them—
And the captain will never unlock the door & so they're
going to escape again (they have rifles, in their blankets)
leaving behind more dead of their own,
bodies in the snow, at light of dawn
bodies of theirs, & bodies of soldiers

Your death is to make one see the form of the
glory, is to make the difference in what you have done, but
      not like this; or,
yes like this, how do I know?
The Cheyenne become more & more hungry
I am anxious to please but this song is difficult
because it is really their song; but
I'm the only one in *this* room
They choose—that is what having a death does
& when the snow melts from the plains,
they will say that they went from here to there
that they need that now, that their way was not mistaken
that we cannot join them, that they are entitled to walk as they
      part, the few of them left—though
You still want to manage their places
they who were entities in place, embodiments of care to
design a being in harmony with passage of centuries—
Because now, a century later, you want so for them to love you;
your rift with heaven is possibly now complete
And they will always escape from you
And I will always be slightly unsure to whom I am speaking—

they have no time for you in eternity
they know who you are in eternity
(one of the hells)

★

She sends to me, in a dream, in a yellow-tan
room where I receive them at a table,
small blue flowers, pale blue lily-like—there's
only one per stem, so small & the stem's tendril-thin,
but stiff—she's also sent
tiny vase-like vessels for each stem—each
frail separate flower
has its own place (each
small blue ash)—The

Cheyenne (who have suffered as she didn't)
the Cheyenne, in a waking
dream as I am standing by my desk
holding something of mine, an amethyst:
the Cheyenne send it to me, this amethyst, just as she
sent me the flowers—something much blacker,
purple & uncut, blacker than blue
flawed with white swirls but dark-blooded—
They are sending it as I am holding it, and as I
hold it I am being emptied inside—
scraped inside my chest & emptied out:

this amethyst must be my returns, my heart
it is probably, just now, my heart

✱

You don't want ever to get over it—I
        am speaking of myself
Coinciding with it & all else
you are Gardenia, what's going on
Each petal of which white is one story
The redder stain gathers to the
lips of the singer,
        who sings:
"I don't ever want/ to get over it"
"I don't *ever* want/ to get over it"
(She is the whole night heart-
        wood wearing one.)

I keep walking towards your bed in my
white shift marrying you repeatedly:
Not getting over
        anything, this
is what I see before I sleep; & then I
sleep & dream for an instant the
        Native women
are washing all the scalps
the tribe's ever taken
long wet hair laundry
hung up to dry on the line—
I dream it fast, though it is slow,
        & beautiful.

Being with the one who isn't here
"Really deep down she's gonna see your way through"—
And the singer sings:
        "There's a man going round taking names"
She also sings,
        "*Name,* nothing ever happens to *Name.*"
Name shines as bright as
        'the mystical geographies of Heaven'
The letters of Name are trellises for stars
All of what is is Name, & she sings Name, Name, Name
You are her gardenia, worn & inhaled
pure & a fragrance going out to the night.

*

Who will remember, more than their name?
To kill all, to kill old, to sadden the ship and
dull its very drinking of the seas
To kill all, to kill old ways, so that same one cannot say
the story, forever,
(for the story makes you immortal
because it is timeless from teller to teller)
Is to
kill your blessing—

But when I said Name before,
I was loving her;
it was a blessing, and
it was a story—
The Name was carefully placed in the safest place—
Long-shadowy, glorious, arrogant, splendidly-lit
Person of the innermost corner of your fate,
your fate is a beginning in touch with sweet stars,
above the nearly transparent, bluish moon—
Your name, with which I bless myself
Is the name of laughing & talk
is the name of our streets.

*

Against all agony a bunch of flowers in the chest
petals desert spines or small old seashells
no they are dead-white rose petals are blank white are
mind flame are continually
lit & belonging to all who are, ever were, belonging to an anyone
or what has the sleeping person, face fair in the good moonlight
Descent into bitter remnants of, confinement to, tortured memory
descent to the possibility
of more deaths perhaps an utter crippling by sorrow:
at the point of breaking, comes as a voice
belongs to no one, having no longing
assumes the continuance of its kind,
because born in beauty, & dark that bed, & all dread, & the loss of
    loved one
is not the light of that one; & much else is, & it is (but also the
    untender dark red chrysanthemums, the
curling wind, the black boots that walk you away

*

born in beauty born a loved one, before history
    born before your time
Anyone was born
before the beginning, before an era, or now
Loved by the sky, & loved by your name, the sky (all there is
    space for) drops
closer staining blue your bed—"I fall & reach the sky,
    humbly die"

born in beauty born a loved one
before history I was one
who loved you for your name
As your name was beginning to be your face, equal to
    herself
at the beginning, before history, when the sky was gold with its
heartfelt abiding, its need of you

in my dream you were a child
you woke up on a white bed near a window
in my dream you were a man
whose body was no longer of any comfort
We kiss your name & take care of it
Born in beauty, before history, I am one who
    loves you

*

They say something ruinous & tragic happened soon after
or close to the earliest expanse of us, I mean that time that
stretches even backwards from the first time in it the "creation."
And I think there must have been these several stains, light,
    blood, & paint, the
initial one being the first stain of light against that lovely
underworld-colored midnight blue or black that night is
All creation is a staining, a change in purity
out of a consciousness that intends to make something slightly
different from what gets made, or unknown, cannot predict
    that cruder...beauty
that orange stain apposite to that suddenly-created
    blue.

Where were the gods? perhaps they suddenly had faces
Visibility acquires a future & a past—This is how the gods
    became the first people, walking on
water that lightens to the color we think of heaven as, for
    heaven has always been here
& the afterlife is another material carefully watching our
    kissing & crying,
as we endlessly reinvent our own fragility, & deny our kin-
    ship to the gods:
But I will take all that sorrow, which did not really impoverish me
& make it an expression of warmth for you. I know the gods became
    human to be
seen & loved. But the first bloodstain wrenched the survivors
    away from heaven,

in that that heart of loss was almost too broken to care about any
    heaven, heaven receded
not because it was offended, but because it was found ir-
    relevant, to that first
despair. Though heaven stretches backwards from your first time in it,
    & forwards from
your grief, & you *can* bring it back down by calling to it,
    for a time, & then, finally,
it was always already here. But that first loss,
    was like no other.

✼

At this age, so crowded outside,
am I all of the earth I can know.
Inside myself, I am the earth I call to.
(But you're that earth too.)
In the inside of the earth, under the

earth she's singing a song, in no
language, of what sounds come next, Queen
of dirt, streaked with dirt, hair long &
full of clean dirt.

Praying to her for her
arms (longer & longer arms)
one might want to be her arms embracing
myself & all those others, this

embracing is the under side of earth, holds
it together—holds up, on her arms, all ours
become so ugly, but
inside me so very beautiful,

inside the earth's the real city
of arms mingled & clasping, of
foreheads touching—
the element mind & the element earth
touch foreheads there like
daughter & father.

*

I see you, see you everywhere. We saw you for a year though no one
        else did
but you were preparing for your final going out of this
        particular one world, and we were
with you in a room—all those closest to you. You
 were happy, lit face, light of skin & hair & speech, casually
        dressed.
I could tell by how close we all felt, together in the
        one small room,
that when you finally left us you'd go
        to a real place a good place—

It was nearly time for your final disappearance but
        no one was afraid; be-
ginning ceremonies: other friends began to arrive, dressed in
        softly hued worn plaid shirts, & jeans,
hair loose, carrying candles: different sizes & colors of candles,
        lit, they placed them all about the
room on shelves & tables & mantel, everywhere were lit candles though
        it was afternoon out—
light to light a going, & to fill a space left, with more light

*

I dreamed it to the bottom of myself
Hooded monks, vats of blood & bone
They cleaned human blood from human bone
A lady & I leaned on each other
she appeared to be blind but wasn't
across & out the room, a basement
Now I'm awake & it has snowed all night
the bones are covered with snow
the already fertile already a flower
I'm terrified to get out of bed
I'm going to tell a story:
                        The
first god-person nor woman nor man
a snowy light-ridden wind at once
takes the bones, in a trance
of himself's selves
bones of his old useless selves
she/he puts them but they are not bones
are eternal ivory parchment spark
she puts them in a vat of wine
& stirs them & stirs them until they
are stench, & blood & bones
millions of years of lives
crimes & pains & tanglings
mental & physical'd murders
and then she takes from the vat
& makes a person—the first person—
who wears that knowledge already
happened & coded & sung & cried
from some "Fall" until these eyes open
and a baby is then born who lives backwards
through all of history
& becomes original & awakened
becomes the real baby
midway through its life, one morning.

*

Bits of old death
as black rags, swirling, a tondo
of circling, black, attenuated, pteradactyl wings
black litter of old wars, refuse of an oldest beach
This tondo a cell, or a cervix
Black old matter burnt, pieces of personless mummy, burned sails
     of the ships of the
oldest war, pieces without personality
     of oldest burnt or decay-black age-black
cloth, paper, tatters, seemingly, of wrongful dying, wrong
     fate, wrong attentions fulfilled, black
remnants of gruesome fruitions—

Let your heart become very very small now
shrinking casting off the black bits
your old heart must become small, small as a cervix
give birth, all you can do (there is no deserving)
your heart is very small, your old heart has shrunk
to this cervix losing blackness in exertion
you open, to give birth, to a heart
to an infinite, to the very different, dark of
the first heart, the first one
it begins to beat & to think the world again
This is my loving darkness, in which the world will be held—
dense, smooth, piled, soft—airy, aether, black—

*

I am the baby, I know that
I will have a baby, I know that
Inside the baby it is dark & gold light & blue
You are the baby & you will have the baby
sticky new skin; wrapped in a design but free in heart
for I came from a heart. I will suffer
but I am free, because it breaks loose & wanders over the air
presses its heart to the houses & grasses, asks the
people if they are happy. They are because they go on
They say they have no choice but in truth they are fascinated
They think the baby will master the suffering, but the
baby will suffer when they die for it, die for it. I am
the heart of the continuous sky speaking surviving sorrow & war &
destruction of the pieces of paper, and I say that
I am your baby. That is all.

*

Here, where I can't yet tell the difference between snow & sunlight
somewhere at the beginning, before uniforms
before, near a ship, water stained dark & red, before a war
(is that therefore before an "our love"? before dreaming at night,
but perhaps not before, that something should feel rough,
to the touch, not just smooth,) I, is it I? it is before

the formal beginning of the meaning; before all sorrowful
imaginings. Before comedy. Before one could be caught, with you,
in love, in a bad year, & in an instant of fucking or speaking
return to that Before, or to before it...

What it is, in starry water, or crust of clouds melting because of
the sun or what is like the sun—I haven't been here very often,
guise I recognize as it. At peace in the arms of, to the extent that,
all alike is everyone's own, with the land up rising up for one to
one by one name the birds, funny little syllables,
puckering the mouth into the second or third
roselike shape ever; that I am I comes and goes;
remembering the future & yet leaving it to itself.

✻

Was I trying to find you anywhere
to see what the beauty is in another's name
        one besides mine
My name is not Chaos, that I'll concede, your
        name is not Pausing
or, I've-waited-too-long—
Your name might be Willing, or I could name you Dark Blue, but
that would simply be, A Name. Sharp-pointy, Dark,
        Secretly-Rough, Secretly-Smooth
Secretly Careful & Good, Secretly Divinely decreed;
I name you Outside, Just, Unpossessed, I name you
        Shining, Foreign, Near;
Secretly-Tender, Secretly-Godlike, Secretly-Famous

Was it really the birth of suffering that first named us?
Such were the ones there when lights
faithfully, hostilely, seared the eyes of, call it,
        Everyday Being,
I want this to be a now,
        in every respect, so
Suffering sits somewhere near; I tell her to weave a
        blanket or a wooded song with
muted pointy stars—Out of which arose, but you were the one that
        told me
that death is for our lives' shapeliness. I'm
shy to talk like this
        to the eye of the blue, in fact
Homeward, Backwards, Forwards; Swelling, Great-hearted, Eddying; Clear;
hundreds of miles out from myself
I do it anyway,

if I don't who will? It's making the rivers go
The treasure is a name, or a
        thickening recollection—
so I cover all with air of my eye & all is better
(Anywhere I take you is more Graceful)   I'm telling real Fair Winds,
        real possessions;
Each one has come here & changed, haven't they?
Anywhere I take you is
        more graceful—
the one with a kiss who sees & doesn't leave
Inextinguishable, Fateful, Faithful
Face of a lovely people in uncherished times.

*

"I can't ever remember my dreams except for when"
"this coffee is rational land, connecting two larger portions"
"it may connect the girl & her father"
"talk & people will enter the room, in clusters, small clusters"
"I remember slightly untruthful"
"I remember going to bed in the rain"
"I remember, imprecisely directed emotion;"
"it might be a cluster of the same one."

"I dreamed Ted died again, in a room, alone, covered with scabs & sores, entirely alone for several days. But that isn't what happened. & no one was ever alone, then at that point, exactly when you depart
How many ones have there ever been? How many people ever? How many have you known, how many have you been? Where are they now? In your dreams, in & out of your lungs, in your tears & lymph & blood-stream, room, drum-beat in a cup? Can I have some more coffee? Can I live in the arms of this room where"

"fold one raw edge under another"
"pay everything you have; then find a little more"
"find more in the air"
"tell me all your names"
"How many have there ever been? But I woke up & saw you again."
"feature, coral, tale. blent, counterpane"
"you've been reading a different book again"
"how can I be myself, pulled in every direction by a different voice?"

"I remember when the apartment was much smaller,
before it contained anything except its vacated other past
This is a version of the universe, floor & walls, no doors but one
How many times have I said that it has no doors? but spaces for emerging,
rectangles, one of the universes is upright, one of them
flat on the floor, living & dreaming are perpendicular
& at their point of intersection I do something I haven't thought of
I walk into your arms."

"sea belongs to everyone, face at night belongs to everyone"
"another's voice is fantastic, sensations"
"living & dying, is it the same, when in all happiness, you
are exactly surface?"
"that's something you said at another time, & you're saying it
now from memory" "I'm saying it now to
you & so it's so different"

372   THE SCARLET CABINET

"we were travelling close to the dangerous Alps again, hugging our babies"
"I like to say 'my heart', because that deepens me, in my place"
"when he/she dies there is a breakage, & there is a shifting of spirit,
that is difficult to tolerate, but is tolerable, alive,
& spirit never dies, dissolution of mask, recreation of land, some-
thing like that" "flaws retreat & disappear, all the landmarks
change but only to you, to you who are, too, inflectional individual,
I think that I speak & forget, & remember, a mountain."

"Can't this story ever be funny? in the eyes of the...oh I don't care"
             "large, bright
flowers, & roots below. In this city we have none, deep
within us is all the nature, we'll ever find or remember—I
am nature: and he was exactly the story of that, though
he said, I hate nature."—"That was funny,"—"He said that, and so you
knew it meant he liked it more than you did" "he liked it, he
liked it enough to be differently it each time & yet true as a same,
always-same-appearing, flower"   "...says the story is a flower"

"You have to tell that story at least a little, once more, sometimes"
"for the new I guess creation, but when I do, when I do I only
digress..." "Because?..." "it is
exact materialization, of exact spirit..."
"I've always wanted to account for every brick in the city, without
counting them, I've always wanted to bless them, I've
always wanted to see them as, blessed individuals, but then I realized
that, in that case *I* had to bless them; so I've been waiting,
waiting to, talking always as if I have already maybe I have"

"Not rationalizing, I slept again near the oceans, leaving my keys.
They call it archaic, actually; I don't have
any investment in it, I just can't tell the difference
between ancient history, the ocean, & the corner, the guys
What happened? What ever happened? *You* know what happened
You already know enough, & so the story will be
the next thing we do. Though the next thing we do be to discuss the past.
In order fully to articulate the world
so that it could have been existing all along."

"The point at which Ted would die was passing through his whole life.
He wanted to die to be loved, but he wanted
to be living his whole useful life, at exactly that moment; he
asked me not to be mad at him. At this moment I.
I will save you with my senses. I will make a whole world with my
senses. I found hell to be delicious, too,

I think you are delicious existence; I think the gods
I am rain, thunder, & lightning, used to express joy.
Take your most unlawful eyes, & use them—a professional service."

"The gods chose us to be them but be without their powers"
"I remember the supernatural from Marvel Universe" "Okay that's
you but" "...I went to sleep & when I woke up he was dying"
"I left the room & when I came back he was dying" "I looked in &
saw he was dying" "He got back up & did something" "He died &
he was dying" "I was reading an elegy and he was dying" "He was
dying & he got back up again, he came into the room & asked to
sit up awake all night, because he couldn't sleep" "He was
dying again & they were preparing the memorial volume"
"He was dying again, & then, she died"   "Ah then Kate died"

"Then so many were dying whole races were dying"
"then new worlds inside teardrops"
"then so many were dying so many will die"
"the bricks might fall down"
"& then they were dying & laughing about it"
"& then they were dying & crying"
"& then everybody said it was beautiful"
"& then everybody said they were crushed, absolutely shattered"
"& then the dead people went on talking in both new & old ways"
"& then I meet you again & love you..."

"In this room there's a heart"
"in this room there's a" "map" "star" "cure"
"in this room, it used to be here, before me, right? so I"
"tell the story of the body-room, the heart-ship, the bed-grave
drinking coffee & talking, tell the story of the" "slave,
tell the story of the war again, the genocide, off &
beyond & is, the death of the one room, which stays, stays & not dies
stays & staying, full of eyes, crying petally bonds, flowered
chains & planets, remaining not dying, & staying, one room," "how,

where, is the story, of the death, of the many?"
"They went to their corner, & at their point of intersection,
died; the bricks' eyes, came into the room, & asked to die again—
no one will let them." "Go out & tell" "I'm saying it to you
now you speak."

*

as I made love to you, but not we,
two others—two others of us were making love
as if I were dreaming, were dreaming them
those others of us not quite us—

but when in that us we touched each other
touching & being touched, we
were touched into being us: & that we were this, the
real us, I registered the shock of, over & over,

until I awoke—But I had been
awake, it had been transpiring in
another realm—And both realms are here.
And in that first realm while

we were being us, that us, the moonlight & my lighter eyes
in that realm it was lusher, to be void of identities—
approach & retreat of identity, to body
that not so much knows who it is, as

how to be. In that first realm
where I sought you without thinking
that's where we live too, and while awake. So
do anything, bodies, say anything

✽

"Speaking firstly forever"
"speaking firstly forever, who might we be?"
"We are mattress," "nearly invisible membranous tissue"
"not any longer disordered" "wings" "what
the first feeling was..." "we must will its movement" "Praise
is for precision, nothing else, as in, 'the hero did precisely
what she was supposed to.'" "These are the yellow lines characterized
by having the honor to be uttered" "They are yellow but only a
color" ("I love you") ("Shut up")

"Bridges" "bridges, again" "Looking down I saw many of them
at night, many bridges, an intersection of them, black
but lit with lights? or, no, but" "as if" "as if the
first stuff, web of light of color, lifted up from the first water,
fluids & nerves & arterials" "& it became bridges" "But
in the dance before there were bridges," "there were the stars of a
willingness, yellow, red, turquoise, and this, these geometric whorls,
thumbprint, not firmament" "not yet quite straight lines & angles."

"Do you remember the" "oysters by water" "that was much later,
and heather a cloud of, purple, dust-green" "in the
beginning, before a verse" "shimmering web pre-teleo" "I'm
saying this pre-apparatus, I'm" "saying I, though, I, as if"
"before there were bones there were flashes of colored light;
and in your bones that messenger lives, it is solo in any
animal, any boneless flower" "darker than that
we are back in."

"In that dark before a messenger was released" "&
do we return there?" "in that dark" "but, and dreams" "I
have never drea..." "in our dreams we catch up with the story, and
the darkens-back-to-the-first dream, the fragrant" "it wasn't
fragrant," "in this dream of the first dark, I" "it wasn't dark"
"dark as water silk dark quiet no-limbs dark, no-skin dark, it's
so dark, but, not foreboding or heavy" "it isn't
dark" "what is it?" "it's slightly lighter than dark"
"that's later, but first, first it's so dark, no eyes, but dreams, dreams"

"knowing it was even that moment, center of a death-like word"
"in the tank of darkness, what was evident, an even older"
"universe had died and" "unpleasant grand sound (I'd listened)"
"unchartered life underwater, merge the old distinctions"
"side, the side of chaos for awhile" "is good" "good for the" "The
golden world to come" "The 'And Then'," "And then"

376   THE SCARLET CABINET

"now absolutely cobwebs, & leaking grass, beneath, green as a" "baby,
baby of a hyacinth, dual-colored, in pinks" "the water
has gone, flown beyond into" "evaporated into thousands" "true
angels, the first insects, the first ghosts of old are breeze of
intoxicate, new intoxicate, I" "standing toward the center of the
earth," "no one, as usual" "purely form of a," "filled with"
("filled with")

"what was made, & is, what was broken, & is, and" "I am hungry."
"eddying tangled & densely the white & pink with yellow, with
palest blue & against the black, the" "they are also something like
bricks, bricks of winged" "winged windows" "human caves"
"caves are windows, windows are children" "over the
bitter depths of" "fish to be perfect still after many, & at
my feet the antique new river of so newly invisibled and the"
"dissolved in perfect voices, anemones, starving"
"light-filled starveling" "after the break of and" "for
when the light broke"

"messenger has crossed the bridge now" "precious flames" "flames"
"the bridges forged in her crossing"
"the messenger" "a hero?" "she" "all we became of eyes ears & mouth"
"to perceive & join in a gold-lit…" "the messenger of you that"
"stay on earth, wants to be, in the golden deeps of the bones the"
"listen, listen" "what precisely happened" "only the sun to the
window" "the messenger opened curtain & lifted window"
"thin pink rustled ruffled garment-like" "green lace was"
"shaft of light pierced the glass & in its gold the millions
the infinity of the angelic motes" "revealed to the eye (heart)"
"the structure of souls, of wild animals, of energies, of drumbeats, of
embryos" "steps wind two not silent today"

"precious flames, lacrimations of joy, warmth on the tongue that which"
"the lightest of, the densest of" "antler,
river, thought" "Thought is my dream of more world or my dream is
my thought of it" "in the color blue I have found,
& in the color red, awakedness, & the abstraction itself of a love"
"& in that turquoise, or in that lavender,"
"& we are phosphoric" "we are tunes" "snakes & bone statuettes,"
"we are now praise & precision."

CODA

"Beautiful girl outside in the morning, is air"
"plays with the bricks in place, they stay in place"
"muffled rushing sounds, cries, all that of that" "outside" "that far
from hurt, substantiates, the being of oneself a whole & clean" "party"
"I have wings" "this is the bird, & it says" "that you have a unit,
a unit but one whose borders are not just a body's" "invisible wings"
"I have seen it when" "seen it when, relating & dark, something
was bruising the body of dreams & light, dreams & lightsome
passage through" "And now the day has changed" "the ground is blue."

"Face of flowers girl, flesh of light" "angel girl, the messenger"
"was not lost" "tell us all this" "she is day, & I" "I am digits,
light & flowers of condensation," "life of deep years unbroken"
"unbroken & inspired by a girl, who isn't lost, who doesn't die"
"you will see her everywhere; & so walked" "bricks it is dust
against sky glass, it is thinking it is dreaming happening cloud"
"digits are wit, digits are light" "vertical years" "can I
be all that I see with all of me, fingers & legs & feet, toes & ears?"

"Fingers dream warmth & moisture, blueness & delicacy, dream surprise"
"ears dream surprise, dream brokenness, dream commingledness"
"in dream is to press to the messenger's dress"
"infinite songbird entangled, seaboat catalogue
list of a cat, leave this room of memorials, of daisies, painted
on cups" "the cat must leave this room" "dream of ashes, bones, shells"
"they were created from the beginning, sprinkled in light" "improvised"
"improvised promises, dallying causalities, small & rational
bodily continents," "consultations blind" "with blessed girl" "blazing
girl" "ensemble gigantic thawing & freezing" "small girl I know."

"Leave this room of unfertile memorials" "memory, real, is a live
land, one of where I am alive?" "memory, real, is your body, carried
along the length of" "the length of the infinite life" "flowers,
bricks, headlights, lamplights, rust" "pipes, & fences, aerials,
windows, pigeons with opaque wings" "But memorials: a land of mere ornament,
universe of tasks diminished" "diminished to smaller than hands"
"smaller than the whole hands, diminished to until" "a nation on film"
"a place of boxed song" "a street of invented work" "rather"
"stand in the messenger, standing toward" "toward the center of the earth"
"sacred wings" "singular temperament, phosphoric unit" "spreading,
spreading in place,"

"Then rising upwards, & wings are" "your longer & longer arms" "arms over all," "but" "as, to fly as one, you may be pulled down, dragged down to the street where" "the portents of pasts, imbalance" "the body of—" "caiman, my lapis-eyed corpse on a beach" "—body of pleasured ongoing," "And so" "and so that there is no past one," "that one is only all," "begun again," "all wing": "wrap this wing" "around this room" "& leave there small ghost of it (wing)" "and" "gently fly" "larger than" "so leaving" "so returning" "to Earth" "to a new beach" ("no dead black litter, no more blackish" "crocodilian corpses") "we have found a new white beach" "the Earth" "is our wing."

Twelve Poems Without Mask

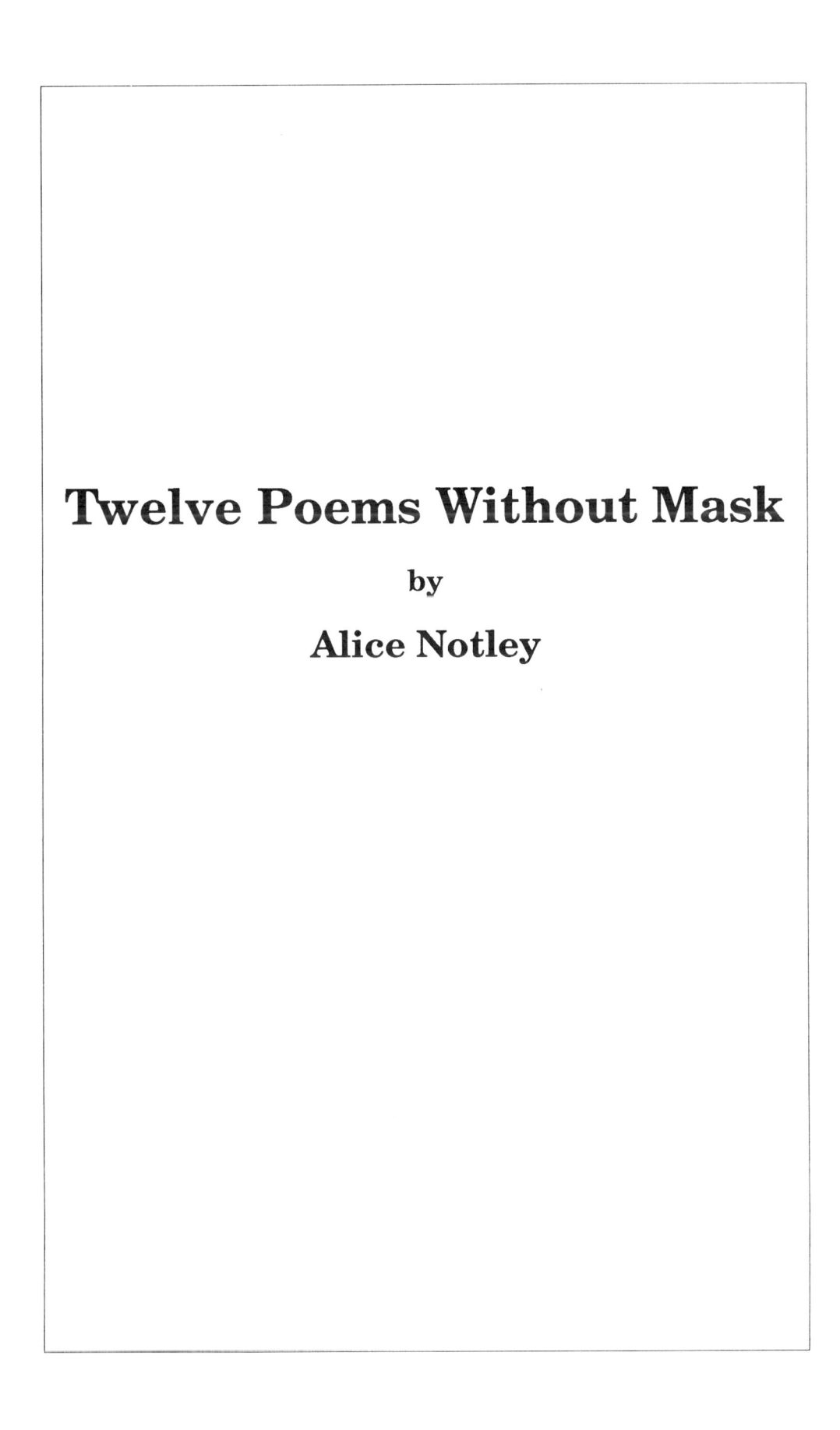

by

Alice Notley

'There was a mask I once often wore'

There was a mask I once often wore
I had made it, there were three of it
three of Mask, & I could be one of which
& one was gold, & one was uglier,
& one was some sort of woman. She had
eyes with jet babies & strangers
A dream steals a big cigar it's not my tungsten
aperture, it's my fake rose aperture
of the Northern Hemisphere
I go into the cushy town & puke of course
Five womenfolk in cotton housedresses
three literal bunnies & a
starring role for a cadet or corporal manpower
procure the homeless a check to eat
The rain falls on everyone's foot
I go into the foundout haywire room
again & again
oh try to be clear
people are singing
no they're not they're cowering under my or someone's
skirts & I'm only partly
three of your checks
two of your housebound follies which should have been
mystical & fun civilizations
they say you should get back up
knock someone down
Oh pow
Rags &
fever, fever, fever
escalate the unity of the beginning of
So I go to the Stupid Store
in the little kiwi I see I have to
kill one layer of the
world I haven't peeled off & under
neath it is green
like a good herb Oh forest
Oh humor Oh expectations of a cosmos
a nation a life
for I have not seen so many of categories
since first-born cistern I was
Nothing but what is what
Don't lie down to have this baby

'The tall mother was beautiful...'

The tall mother was beautiful & had hyper-
tension. She wasn't going to have a
heart attack she said she
was going to go crazy right now. She
was more beautiful than her daughter
& her daughter's friend. She was taller
than her daughter & that friend, & taller than
the man in the cafe, whose actual
name Short, Short was with a woman who
put a feather an actual feather in her hair.
That one gave me a funny look I think.
They were talking about sexual
gratification. The tall mother
told me she had to tell me her life's story.
She may have been Italian like Beatrice's mother
she looked a little like the woman who played
Maudie in *El Dorado*. Maybe *El
Dorado* is the clue, the word clue.
Ride, boldly ride. Over the, & down.
No, I don't think so. Not at all. *El Dorado*
is—to stop trying to write this poem.
The tall woman got taller when she
hugged me, so glad to talk
to be going to talk. What might she have
said if I hadn't waked up? She had
beautiful skin & big breasts & dark hair cut
short. It's very peculiar to hug someone who's
getting taller: she became so big then. What
might she have said?

'Go in...'

Go in.
Am I grainy, magical (as in
      changeable)
cartoon fish dopey-eyed dangling tongue
       (is in my hand?)
Go in.
Mask at mind, which one, a fish.
All these uh
Mask not mask
Let her go, he shouts
Trees' characters here too
Go in.
As fast as
purpled, empurpled by your smiling
(You will always be inside me.)
The mask lengthens, lengthens
dissolving & at the
exact dissolution, matter into air
(though air is matter) what?
I don't break
I is no mask, is that all of it?
I is not fishy.

'The sun of the rain is the door of the day'

The sun of the rain is the door of the day
the door goes out not in not into the wooden room
though in the wooden room is everything let's get out of it
everything can be in lots of other rooms
in this room they put it there when?
when I was they
wood sanitation wooden dreams & wooden
wooden hair wooden skin
wooden painting of woman in a wooden wood cloud landscape
wooden bowl contains the cosmos, one saw that all that was
formed from before & in wooden before & of history, of
wooden abstract abstractions: "man is wood" "woman is
wooden" "people are wood ducks"
"Sitting on a chair" "sitting on a little chair" "sitting
on a chair" "and sitting there" "I sat"
I sat, I was wood, I love wood
leave this room & go out, what, trees... (oh that's
wood, a very wooden thing to say)
Oh go to the other cosmos the other wood the
living wood, because
I am your heart & this heartwood
must woodbeat must beat again
in the real woods unwooden, forest dark as Mars
all inside me forest entered out the door come along
all the trees are made of skin, hair & skin
all the trees are dark
all the trees know their beauty

'The woman first'

The woman first
for hundreds of years was alone & all
by herself. She floated
I forget her name, it was a long
time ago.
She had a baby. Everyone. It's so
grey, grey out
there like a magnet come out little baby,
it will rain on your head wits & descents
The 1st raindrop is fireflies
the 2nd raindrop
the 3rd
fireflies in your head & mouth & ears
I don't have anything to tell yet
I am a girl in a wheeling a
faster, faster. Now proclaim
something abhorrent, a farther future
But I was born unsurprised
that I liked the taste of the food
unsurprised to talk & look at everything
All I remember
Deeper in the jungle
a person becomes different
bitter coins in a metal can
feet are dangerous, mouth is a different
saying, It says
that the threads are slender, tangled, till a
smarter person unravels them
There are no threads
It isn't a cloth, I'm going to the
microphone but I'm waylaid into wearing
a hat, a big hat. It has on it cherries,
flowers, a black velvet band dangling down
Wear your short shorts too, into the
house, talk to the reporters
We've come very far from water
to a real notion of equal
corruption for our girls & our boys
At the microphone I don't
say that. I say that
the water will cover everything
find the underwater bridge and
walk across it
sticking up your head into the air
it (the bridge) will be
your 1st mother's body

'Subterranean is a house all room-connected'

Subterranean is a house all room-connected
dark & wide & yellowed bands darkened & a bed
people sleep on crowding many
come & go sometimes are only heard & can't be seen
voices don't shriek or anything like that only are
talking, murmur stories, & comments, for they do
talk to you & talk about you to
each other & tell their own stories
one month one wind came to
this big mountain store where they sold the best of the
pinebox captives' singing tools, I mean instruments
they were woodpecker-holed pine boxes with
strings across a hole & leaves also grew out of them & twigs
that birds perched on & so sang along
& you could also wear the whole thing as a hat or a mask
so this girl walked in & bought one with matching earrings
but it was made out of wood that didn't
want to be made into it it was made out of
wood of the sorrowing rebellious self-centered drug-addicted tree
so let's forget about that part of the story
deep in another room a mother is sorrowing she has
several more years to do that in essentially the
same room but the light will change
there she is & Now in the house is a man of
daughters, & now one of his daughters
the mother of the whole song sorrowing is
sorrowing
that song
that whole song is her child
I've forgotten what it is what is it the
children grow up & can't stand up alone
are unwalking, enslaved
the girls & the boys are on mountains so anxious
they've gone up on the mountain, throw down their
manners of speaking & playing, they throw off their figures of
talk their dresses of songs & their shirts of
abandon, going to work for the mountain
the song mother weeps & mouths she mouth she
sings with no instrument the
song of self grieves & the
sleepers wake up they wake up & they go out to work but
her song gets bigger
I miss you I miss you you weren't ever here I

388   THE SCARLET CABINET

miss you where are you you never got born
you never came home you
never got born enough or brought us on home
& I am it I am it only alone am
song of it song of it song of it

'Back very far, not even any time when,'

Back very far, not even any time when,
it is right now. Now at the beginning
in modern & in ancient, in a forest at
the same time as anything else, this
is a woman. Getting it in fragments.
Walking in another world always.
Off to the side, over the left shoulder
the coherence & deadly & explained of
what men do. It is one of the pieces of
air. The rest is all these animals &
spirits, kingdoms & planets, secret & un-
conscious masteries. Men are another
species. Dedicated to order. Women...
patches of purple & black. Black fir
branch against violet, & the yellow
sparks, piece contains a world of
flesh, for example, sensations exactly
inside the skin, follow them
singing singeing crackling go to
world. Another piece or place is
a past mind, a future mind. Poised
in the middle, brew the coffee & drink it.
Forests, doors; the literary work of this
person consists of a) thinking own
and b) words to define possession by
mind spirits (momentary) as
by winds (these spoken moments). Not
possession by dreams, but transiences,
possible finalities too. A man
invented limitations, has codified the
forms the ones—plurality head of a woman,
which means the universe pond. I
make this this good one, a man says.
I hear all the voices at once says a
woman, & so I will swim through them listen-
ing playing, wash over & through they are
free: I see I have finally created the
world & have nearly freed it from me. Some-
times a voice wants to be just one song.
This precious limitation: will a man
write it down. I hate so, to say this,
enslaved, I suppose, and for centuries, en-
slaved, to the gods I suppose to the page.
Becoming a poet, if I can't help it. Enslaved
to a voice, enslaved—

'You haven't saved me any time'

You haven't saved me any time, but
I want some. I want some more.
So put it somewhere, take it & put it
in my jeans pockets please.
He was going to put it in my purse.
The music spilled all over everything.
Time was hidden in the handmirror & the
whiteout, but somewhere, she knew,
inside of her head or in her fingertips.
Catch it please so I don't have to
use it all up working. Time was an
important exhibit, to very many
it *was* the museum. It *was,* almost,
the house. The scholar waited
till the poet was dead & then took all her
time & reused it. She even changed it.
The "work" stayed "timeless". I
went to a museum. Great. I'm
glad you're doing something valuable
with your time. She's so old she's
almost dead. What took so long? Where
are they all, those, you know, con-
figurations? All those women,
waiting for thousands of years, because they
couldn't vote & so on & so I
guess they didn't really live, all those
million unemancipated years of wasted
lives? Who, then, of them was ever happy?
those women those mothers
Someone obviously wasted all of history.

'What movie star...'

What movie star am I think-
ing of? It *is* Olivia,
de Haviland, an intelligent
smile of hers, head tilted as if
forward but really
sideways, it's her look
that goes out. I dreamed of her
2 nights ago, rather, her name
was in my dream. I dreamed
that Allen Ginsberg
wanted to know why he liked
to swim in his underwear—I said
because it felt good, & it
worked. I said that *my poems*
right now, were stupid,
because they're written in a
stupor (that's true) & that I
had to write about things like
Olivia de Haviland looking in
the mirror. I was
just now looking in my mirror;
I caught that look &
remembered, remembered my
dream. It's not so
interesting
to be an individual—everyone
judging you. There's an agreement,
there is somewhere an
official arbiter,
of who's the greatest who's the
best—& we pick that up from
them, like vibes, like in
the air—it is a
roomful of *men who know:* Olivia
de Haviland, let's see. Not
that great.

'What does she think?'

What does she think? flowers of
privacy? green & yellow, don't try.
Oh there is my medieval gown.
I think the stars go flat & then
deep if I blink my eyes & make my
brain go mentally click. I think
some of my babies. And those which
didn't, didn't live, one of
those, I squeeze up, red furze,
purple gorse. Pretend something
faster. Close eyes & click. Bodiless
& being pre-body pre-sex where
it seems that everything is
black, at night when you don't have to
work, when you sleep & nothing
ever happened, when you dream &
no one ever died, no one was ever
hurt by you, never a fool & even
you don't die yourself because
everything is instantaneously
change, moment to moment of
you dream, you dream it, out of
your own deepest own—aren't there
sexes? will there be history?
There are many things the woman
has never 'cared about.' 'It
doesn't really make any difference.'
Can't remember some more, close
my eyes. She should leave him alone
for awhile, & take a little walk. He wants
to imprison matter, every single bit of
the world, in his understanding. She
on the other hand keeps it in
her eyeball. He gets the museum,
he deserves it. She gets her real self
I suppose. They're both so fucking tired.
Something about the pain of
numerous children, their going awry,
founding races, waging wars
The parents' loins very tiring
that the present world comes out of
He gets the fucking museum, he deserves it
Gets the Sistine Chapel too,
& fucking-ass Divine Comedy, & Iliad all

that stuff, all the leatherbounds with gilt on
etc etc. Shelf of all the containers,
there it all is the
cosmos, the dead men's cosmos imprisoned for-
ever for your very own pleasure, madam;
thank you, thanks so much. You were
geniuses. You were.
Let's have a *new* kind of baby.

'They won't let me in without more Man Money'

They won't let me in without more Man Money
it's entirely staffed by men, this hotel, red &
white with the large rooms they say are unusual
Me & my baby do we understand
you can't stay without 250 dollars
it's so cheap because it's in the desert
what do I do next
why did I ever particularly want to be here
meanwhile there is the really great milk
we must talk about milk
3 times before in my life, I say, it was the
best thing to drink
most delicious of all drinks
Get faster, where's my milk
Man Money says he has no milk
He says milk is stupid for grown men who needs it
Get faster, where's my milk. I bet *I* have it. Of course. So
flood the fucking hotel with it
Me & my baby
need a place to fill with
all the important milk we need to drink
We choose your hotel
The rules are to drink
milk milk is everywhere
drown in it Man Money who cares fuck you

'This mask's face...'

This mask's face now turns into
clouds when I want to talk to
it. I don't need to be saved or
anything, I want to
start it over, again & again, & I want
the man to be there. But mostly
I want Mask to talk & to tell.
She says:
again & again to start over, on
no one else's authority, seek
your own in her mask, but
beneath the mask & beneath the
clouds there is flesh of like now,
rather, of now, one's face. Not
in the mirror (that is another
mask) but, flesh of one's
true self, face of to love: it's so
beautiful, how
life goes *outward* & because of
the bodies the cells the
2 cells, in one which will
split, to perform,

so I'm calling
to
you,
love poem, not Mask
you come first too, when she
speaks to me finally, Mother
Mask, is never the
same as you

Homer's *Art*

by

Alice Notley

POEM

I work in a whorehouse, I seem to like it.
It is dark like a cave, with pink light.
I'm feeling a pang, that I will not
be experiencing or telling what a man might tell.
It's not that I want to tell what a man would,
it's that I want what I want to tell to be thought
important. I would carry it out fulfill it
out to a man's logic's fullness but it might not be
like that. It is indefinite, more indefinite than that & it
may not arrive—not everything does. And when
something arrives in words, but it hasn't really,
what about truth? In my story, with probable non-arrival,
I work in a cavelike dimly lit whorehouse,
I like it. There is an Oriental man for example,
a rotund not-small Japanese man, in a hat, a
porkpie hat. But among the customers are women.
This is a blonde one, she comes back twice, large
& blonde & open-faced, in pearls like my cousin
Kathy. Says, do you want to do it again? I say
yes. The sex itself is not there. In this
brothel it is a brothel of feelings: there are
couplings of feelings, meetings of franknesses
moments of openness in the vicinity of the
very warm-looking never used, pinkish beds.
Kathy is probably really my brother's widow Kathy
& not my cousin. There are several other women
I suppose we are about to be reborn again in this
very real womb-like brothel. There is no pay
there is only this work, the customers & the whores
both work, but the whores are perhaps
the ones possessed of the powers. Perhaps these are
healing powers, this is a poet or a person,
but I think this is a poet, & it is less to
heal than more straightforwardly to work
to work this room, this womb room. The feeling of
this place, in this place, seems the key human
feeling, except for the exaltation I ex-
perienced when flying, before I arrived, at the
hill inside which was located this very brothel.
This is exactly where I arrived, but I
think there is more. Because there is
Part Two; the world takes place, also takes
place in day rooms above the brothel, in
houses on the hill above the caves, as in

San Francisco, cities of bridges, of bays & open
gates to the ocean, hilled cities with
heights to fall from. In one of these rooms I will
teach—though I think I prefer the whorish
exchanges of emotion; but I will teach in a
room, though not today, as we await the arrival
of a man, my friend, whose name is the
same as the past tense. He has left his
wife for a woman whose name is the same as a
plurality of ego. Everyone is perceived as
being himself, in this woman's name, his
mistress' name, means, in fact, a displacement of
pronoun & number, her name means
"I are," rather than "I am," "I are."
Perhaps he holds public office, he is
that kind of poet, 'I will
speak out on politics for,' 'I will speak for sane-seeing in
all of us.' I'm distressed because he has
left his wife, who's an ordinary name-like name,
a name without special meanings. Though
perhaps they had to separate—everything about them
is left up in the air, and this is where
my story has to end, it will not quite arrive.
I only want to live in the brothel
right now, closing in on myself,
I'm sinking back under the Sunday covers. I miss my
friend, being unlike him. And if I 'speak out'?
If I did in the way he might want, I would have to be a man;
all women becoming men, all people
becoming men. Yet I would like to speak out
I would like to say, that when your cities &
your politics do crumble, the whorehouse cave will
remain, that is obvious; & your concerns are
pressing, & transient; but your powers, rein-
forcingly assented to by your women, are still most
dreadful. I miss you. I do. And we miss him; we miss my
brother, the man who just died from the Vietnam War.

HOMER'S *ART*

HOMER'S *Art* is to tell a public story, in a measure that makes that possible—that the story unfold with quickness, clarity, & also the pleasure bound up with the music itself—a pleasure in the music as the truth of the telling, in its vigor & precision, & in the fullness of its sounding. This is very hard to say. Or it's that, as the story is told in this measure it becomes really true—the measure draws from the poet depths of thought & feeling, as well as memory. This line, this dactylic hexameter of Greek, is simple & grand, and gets deeply into the system. The story is told by a teller not a book.

Both of Homer's public stories—as everybody knows—are generated by a war & are male-centered—stories for men about a male world. They are two of the oldest stories our culture has, & we are still reading them, telling them, using them, handing on Homer's world. The epic poem is taught in universities as the epitome of achievement in Western poetry—a large long story, full of "cultural materials," usually involving a war either centrally or peripherally, the grand events of men. Men who have written them since Homer have tended, or tried, to be near the center of the politics of their time, court or capitol. Thus, how could a woman write an epic? How could she now if she were to decide the times called for one?

Meanwhile we ourselves have experienced a rather strange faraway but shattering war. Say someone you know dies many years after the Vietnam War, as a consequence of it. To tell that story, which is both personal & very public, you might distance it from yourself, somehow, & find a sound for it—as the Greeks did—that makes your telling of it listenable to & true. One might invent devices, invent a line, make a consistent & appropriate sound for the story—anyone *might* be able to, any poet. But a woman who is affected by or even badly damaged by events in Vietnam will never know what it was like to be there, had no role in the shaping of policy with regard to that war or any war, has no real access to the story or even *a* story: what she experienced contained very few events. If she wants to write a poem about it, she is likely to write something lyrical (/elegiac) or polemical, rather than epic or near-epic (in these times, a man would be likely to make that choice as well.)

One way for a woman poet to hook into the world (& thus the scale) of Homer has been for her to identify with one of his female characters & extrapolate. At this point, perhaps, it is tired for anyone to hook into Homer in order to write a poem; but for a women it is an especially peculiar undertaking. But what if one were, say, trying to write a poem having to do with the Vietnam War, mightn't points of comparison between the two wars be of value? Might not Helen be an idea of something to fight for, something to bring back from a war? But Helen couldn't be a *person*, not a real person now, no. No woman is like Helen, no matter what the male poets say, or like Andromache (or Penelope). Only men are like them, in the sense that they invented them—they are pieces of male mind. Besides, those women & those men are all royalty & aristocrats—people who are sacrificing the countless unnamed, as well as themselves, to this stupidest of wars. The greatest point of comparison between the two wars, Trojan & Vietnam, lies in their stupidity—which is where tragedy begins & where a story must be told.

    The pleasures of a poem engaged in telling a long story are considerable at this point in this century. The 20th century poet engages language, basically, uses language to generate more language. Poets variously suppose they are describing something, or freeing language from something like description: both camps are simply playing around with words. The Homeric epic is a whole other kind of poetry, one in which language hurries to keep up. It is not language, it is a poem; though it is also something like a novel. What a service to poetry it might be to steal story away from the novel & give it back to rhythm & sound, give it back to the line. Another service would be to write a long poem, a story poem, with a female narrator/hero. Perhaps this time she wouldn't call herself something like Helen; perhaps instead there might be recovered some sense of what mind was like before Homer, before the world went haywire & women were denied participation in the design & making of it. Perhaps someone might discover that original mind inside herself right now, in these times. Anyone might.

MOTHER MASK

Mother Mask has twigs in her hair
she is all eye that sometimes closes shut
stars on her eyelids, open are oceans
open are history movies, closed are
blue skies, open are sorrow pain iris clarity events
I forget if closed & open make any difference
one or the other, one is the other, Mother
Mask has a woman's face, she always looks
in the mirror—she has brown blue eyes, & has
thin thick eyebrows, a straight round nose, it's a flat
pointy nose, & a red pink full-lipped
rosebud mouth straight crooked teeth
she has white black brown green skin
she has a wooden face painted by men
sunken eyes protruding mouth & raffia
hair red green white black & birds
birds all around her face & in her hair
& into her the wings & she flies the
whole mask flies away with the woman
Put on mother mask & fly right now
A man can fly in mother mask
so can I, Mother Mask
take me to here, beginning ending
Mother Mask seep into my self & meet my
self & both of you change the goddesshead godhead
Change the very self godhead which must be
the world, Mother Mask, you must
change us, by speaking our old new selves
Mother Mask open your set wooden mouth
Please open your carved wooden protruding
live dead mouth & let your green
bronze dark light skin shimmer with
life death, close open your eyes & close open
your mouth & be dumb speak to us
be still sing to us, tell us an old old new one
an old new story truth lie of our own life deaths
our peace wars, tell us our own old story we don't
know it any more, haven't had a
Mother, a Mask Mother, a wood real
mother for forever

WHITE PHOSPHORUS

"Whose heart" "might be lost?" "Whose mask is this?" "Who has a mask,
& a heart?" "Has your money" "been published, been shown?" "Who can &
can't breathe?" "Who went" "to Vietnam?" ("We know who died *there* ")
"This was then" "Is now." "Whose heart?" "All our heart" "the national
heart" "Whose mask?" "has its own heart?" "A mother's" "mask"
"Whose money" "do we mean?" "A woman's money" "Woman's money" "Who

went" "to Vietnam" "& just died of it?" "A son" "Evolved"
"a man" "evolved" "a woman" "into America" "into the" "just before now"
"It was just before now..." "When men made the forms" "& women made the
Air" ("& now no one does that, & who can breathe now?") "Who cares, in the
Air?" ("All *our* poems, women's were there," "there, too invisible" "and
now" "become male" "acceptable") "Accepted." "And they're welcoming us"

"among" "their forms" "among their forms only" ("what forms might we
have made?" "which ones did" "we make?") "Whose heart is lost?" "oh not
mine, & not my darling's" "Or only our whole heart?" "not mine, & not my
warrior's" ("has your money" "been accepted?") "And this is what happened,"
"he went to a war" "old style, he went" "to that war" "No one cared"
"that he went there" "as no one cared" "what was lost" "with our air"

"no magnanimity" "to an enemy" "no feeling for what" "is invisible" "for
magnanimity" "for what's lost." "to air, in air" "As if nothing
replaced chivalry, not something" "invisible" "but nothing." "No one
cared" "what was lost" "with our air" ("All the forms were already"
"men") ("politics, a man" "philosophy, a man; a building a" "painting a
poem, a man" "science, a man") ("Now, we can all" "be men") "This

is what happened." "She is a mother." "This is what happened."
"Or she could be a lover" "or a sister" "This happened" "Find green air
green breath" "Later, he tries to become" ("did he become") "air,
air, as again" "This is what happened. And she's trying" "to breathe"
("the mother") "And she's trying to wash" "to wash off" "America"
"from herself" "But what" "is a mother" "now?" "In America,

everyone is else" ("else" "aside" "aside from their" "whole heart
has crumbled") ("take your own small heart, own heart & go")
("& breathe" "try to breathe") "Who is she? and who" "is he?"
"Whose mask is this?" "Whose heart might be lost to the" "bigger heart"
("not his nor hers but") "whole country of heart" "might be lost"
"to the bigger heart" "biggest heart" "heart of the universe" "heart that

might not give it back" ("we maimed" "another, a native land, we" "helped maim another") "Please" "give it back" "Give us our heart, whose" "heart might be lost."

✳

"Air" "What that's real" "happens in air?" ("She wasn't pure dream")
"Air full of us, full" "of live soul, live" "of the dead & the
living" "Thinking & talk" "Play, dream & merging" ("She's active,
& working") "What's real" "is war" "they say" "some say" "some say,
war is" "the only" "reality" "The warriors mistake war for" "reality,
the reality" "Because they pierce" "the centers" "the physical centers"
"of each other" "Addicted to this?" "Addicted" "& our government
of men" "organizes" "this addiction" "in the guise of, protecting us all"
"All of us part of it" "part of" "this addiction" "protector, protected"

"And when he came back" "from Nam" "at first" "he wanted" "to go back"
"back there, was it where" "he belonged now? war?" "He wanted"
"to go back" "into the bush" "'where I belonged'" "And then later"
"that's exactly" "where he was, in his head" "years later, he was back there"
"in his head" "where everything" "everything" "had happened." "He had
a family" "but he'd" "fought families" "He had a family" "he'd been
made to" "fight families" "How can we" "compete" "with that?" "Pierced
their physical" "centers" "pierced" "Is that" "the only" "reality?"
"How can we compete with" "that?" "How can we" "have him" "back?"

"Can't he come back?" "Fifteen years later" "Can't he come back?"
"Years after" "he'd left" "Vietnam" "Can't ever come back" "Can't ever"
"His soul" "soul" "He couldn't believe" "that had been he?" "he
couldn't have" "lived through that," "done that, in Nam?" "And in his
soul" "he hadn't done that" "no" "And in his soul" "he hadn't"
"And his memory self" "went back there, went back" "constantly in dreams"
"How can we" "compete with" "that?" "They finger our souls"
"for their addictions" "we let them, we comply" "After 15" "years,"
"he said he'd been used" "We were talking, talking, in green & blue air"

"He was very" "nearly back" "We were (four of us)" "sitting
on grass" "This moment will last" "last forever" "lying down" "I was
lying" "beneath" "tall trees" ("like Nam, he'd said," "without elephant
grass") ("he said it was where he" "needed to be" "Outside, in the
trees" "behind the rehab") "we & he" "very nearly home." "But
he was dying, already" "dying" "nearly home" "dying of dying of" "what"
"will answer the call of" "I think it is something like, gravity:"
"will die, of the Furies" "but will die" "of a pull" "from the center"
"of the earth" "& from the sky" "Or will die" ("most honorably") "of

something like power" "Power, become his, & so powerful" "Something I've felt before" "flooding & pulling" "Can't you feel it? I've felt it" "He's dying" "of his power" "Go" "He came home & died" "Go" "Power of, power of" "forgiving" "forgiving himself for so much" "It took too much power & he died" "He died of that, power of that."

✱

"Who is the one who's" "behind the mask?" "mother," "first one"
"Who is that nature of ours?" "What have we done" "Bring her home" "she
should be freed" "by us" "bring her home" "He is covered in white,
fresh flowers" "at home" "He's innocent, now" "& now, we won't"
"let *her* come home," "let someone be her" "won't let one be that"
("who is she") "first mother, & only" "& one who lives" "a spreading
life, not a" "job, not" "doing what no one needs" "doing it for
the unseen," "Who is she?" "& Not just music (& not" "just poetry")
"Afraid" "of a mother" "afraid" "afraid of what has no currency"
"The last of what" "has no currency."

"It takes so long to free him" "no light loves are left" "freeing a
soldier from guilt" ("frees himself") "But she can't be free, exactly"
"No place for a mother, no" "place for a full-time" "person is left"
"*Everyone's* just like a soldier" "everyone fights, everyone works"
"For the army of money we guess" "Slave to a faceless" "our country is
unthinking soldier" "money the" "uniform government texture of air,
army of money" "Everyone says it, don't they" "& So" "& so there's no pity"
"& only, mathematics" "a mother's no currency" "grief is what filters"
"filtering out my light loves" "my tolerance for" "Money is numbers
dead bodies are numbers" "dead veterans are numbers like

hours we've worked" "country of numbers" "mother of numbers"
"your child will be numbers" "mother of numbers" "your lover is
numbers, walking the numbers" "to numbers of hours worked, for salary
of numbers" "working for" "Father of numbers." "& She"
"Mother Nature" "Without Father Nature" "Father Nature mostly dead"
"thousands of years" "Mother Nature will become" "Mother of Numbers:" "says, I
sent you my" "sent you" "my self" "I sent you my self" "you said,
'there's no self'" "my love & you called me too selfless" "I
sent you my self & you asked for a form you could recognize" "a
dollar a number—or painting or book" "by a man-like

woman" ("as good as a man") "But my one
my soldier is dead, my" "one who was numbered" "I sent you my self
was it he" "he was part" "The body-counts" "remember" "remember them"
"they" "wouldn't let him" "they wouldn't count" "ones he killed not
in uniform" "& you, you don't count the" "ones not in uniform" "the

child the mother" "& you don't count me" "what I do; for I" "send you my self" "all I have" "I will" "put on this mask" "put back on my mask" "Streaked with dirt" "I have made my own mask" "faint pieces of money" "faint numbers & words" "And I have a mask" "to wear" "for you" "I wear this mask, but"

"leaks" "skin of the planet" "leaks" "leaks" "white phosphorus"

*

"Flowery mantle." "Homeric sacrifice?" "noise of darkness" "fear of
darkness" "now mantle of innocence" "King of his death now" "Home"
"I've come home" "He said, 'I've come home'" "They were sacrificed for
nothing, for distant" "instants of thought" "All for your thinking"
"He said, 'I've come home; I've finally come home' then he died" "flowers"
"Magnolias & lilies" "innocent now" "I've come home. Who's there?
at home? all the dead?" "To come home from the war" "years after" "To die" "To

wear mantle light honey" "mantle dead white" "in sunlight, in late"
"Homeric?" "he said it was hideous" "all of it" "hideous" "every
instant in Nam" "theatre of worsts" "now mantle of
white" "phosphorus & lilies?" "trees now lean down" "over our faces"
"Tell details of battle?" "As" "in an epic?" "As" "in lies?"
"We don't want that now" "We want only our mother of
dirt" "our mantle of white" "want each other of soul; and"

"we want" "our mother of spirit" ("rich sweet in dirt") "we want"
"our father" "of leaves" "We want our fate fragmented to air for
our children to breathe;" "light on water for widows to think near"
"moonlight on water to ease you" "we want no poet, we want our
homes in the earth" "that's all we can have" "want no place in
history or poetry" "want our wanderings our sorrows, after the war,
not remembered," "we want not

to pain her" "we want our love mingled" "with yours" "no place in
history" "only in love" "remove us from history," "All of us sacri-
ficed" "all for a thought" "They played with our souls." "Used our
souls to fight, be their willfulness" "willfulness" "we were made their
willfulness," "nothing but that—" "And you too, you yielded, one
way or another" "to their will." "They" "who are
the subject" "of all history" "& of poems" "as if"

"we have ever, in all ways" "yielded to them" "by speaking of" "always
speaking of" "Kings" "presidents" "the Great Men" "their mistresses"
"Generals" "Communist Kings" "Leaders" "Warriors" "West Point of Greeks"
"West Point of Greeks against" "West Point of Trojans" "Isn't it more
beautiful, under the Earth?" "Or to be sunlight, not history?"
"Now I can love, & only" "now" "Remove us from history but
not from your air" "History is willfulness" "is" "precious parts"

"History's for those" "who ask not" "to be forgiven"
"We ask to be forgiven" "& loved" "No, we ask" "to be absolved"
"And to be" "elemental" "ask leaves & wind"
"Ask leaves bending down towards our faces" "Ask light & dirt" "we ask"
"our children" "we ask our wives" "Ask that they live" "We ask
to be" "with the ones that we killed" "To history" "saying nothing"
"being that" ("nothing") "& to history" "having been" "nothing."

*

"In this moment" "before" "anyone, ever" "died" "before we were born?"
"in this moment forever before" "before we went to a war"
"Before we died" "In this moment, now" "In this moment before, it is
not before" "In this very moment" "where is it" "where we
haven't died" "or died inside" "In this moment we haven't" "in this
moment, no one" "in this moment, no one has ever, died" ("But I have
been born") "in this moment" "where, where is it" "in moment" "who's here"
"Catch it catch it" "moment where we are" "merely as it is autonomous,"

"autonomous moment" "Without a war" "without a guilt,"
"Can we exist" "Outside of what was?" "in the air of our thoughtless,
female, moment" "the air of our moment" "not grievous not iron"
"moment, not air" "but air of our moment" ("woman-made?") "faithful,
faithful & boundless" "reticent & light" "fond, & kindly" "not reticent
but shiny," "morning-starry, not bloody" "not bloody, in the morning"
"in the star" "it is a star" "it is autonomous" "star & it's mild" "Is
it a little" "of us" "from before" "we were born?" ("that was

never") ("I know") "It is now" "autonomous" "moment of white,"
"white flowers, stars & white flowers," "not before we were born, in
this moment our childhood" "have we our childhood" "in
this moment he has his childhood, I think, it is center of"
"moment, of childhood" "center of, moment" "wings of his pigeons" "white
& grey wings" "moment a feathery" "center of senses" "center of
sensation, is this moment" "Center, as sensation falls away"
"He has his love" "this moment" "forever" "center of brown eyes"

"seen through his eyes" "Only through" "the eyes" "the real eyes"
"of the dead" "this moment" "through his eyes" "as child, as
childhood" "Only through" "the personality" "can this be" "of the
dead" "the lovely person" "holding" "this moment" "this moment in
place" "this moment forever" "center of sensation" "Soldiers,
we are center" "of the morning" "we are moment" "we are dearest"
"we are heart" "Soldiers," "we are pleasing" "we are center"
"we are moment" "are not soldiers" "never soldiers" "never were."

✻

"Mask now" "is complies" "complies" "with the forms (too much of everything, everywhere") "All of this is" "the mask" "my mother's mask" "& mine" "wronglike forms, too many of" "Complying, to live here" "always, more complying" "Too many things" "machines" "too many" "too many clothes" "cheap roses" "kleenexes" "membranous" "bags, of plastic" "Too many ideas" "vocabularies no color" "too many paintings" "too many songs" "too many Tarot decks" "& poems" "& books" "Too many" "things to eat" "too many" "machines" "magic machines" "too much magic" "much too much of it" "Stupor" "distress" "& abandoning of others" "too much news" "news" "everything" "made the same" "too many names" "too much knowledge"

("knowledge, so endless" "is nothing") "A war" "more news, more to know about, to know" "Excuse for anger" "indignation" "you can still keep your money" "know the terms of news" "terms" "& Not be nature" "don't be nature" "mute" "not knowing the" "terms" "Know what news knows" "What words know" "Do words know?" "No they don't, only flesh knows only soul knows" "in the words" "A mask is rigid" "on warm flesh on dreaming mind" "on fleshly mind" "rigid" "But my brother now is nature, pure nature" "however that be" "Or I have dreamed so" "Owl, not an albatross" "He's an owl," "not an albatross" "I have twice" "dreamed that Al" "is an owl" "intricate with" "feathers" "texture of

thousands of feathers" ("I've seen" "an owl" "only in" "a museum") "Owl, I didn't know him, I searched" "the owl's face for its" "identity" ("Al died later" "that day") "grey owl great grey owl" "wisdom, & war" "Master of nights (Al's terrible" "nightmares") "He rose up, finally as an owl" "Is he owl?" "Where is owl now" "I've never seen one" "I later" "dreamed after" "I'd realized" "Owl was Al" "that he was a" "snowy owl" "white, with black spots" "A man said," "he's not an albatross" "Owl, not an albatross" "Al" "whom I have seen" "also seen in a small" "waking vision" "standing, in his living room" "wearing a white mantle, flower mantle a" "mantle" "of fresh, white flowers"

"petals, like feathers" "white petals" "white feathers" "a cloak of nature of" "purity" "of purification" "wilder, milder, he is nature" "he is better mind" "My brother" "is owl" "Athena-like" "wise" "I know things only" "this way" "My brother" "is Owl."

Nava Sūtra

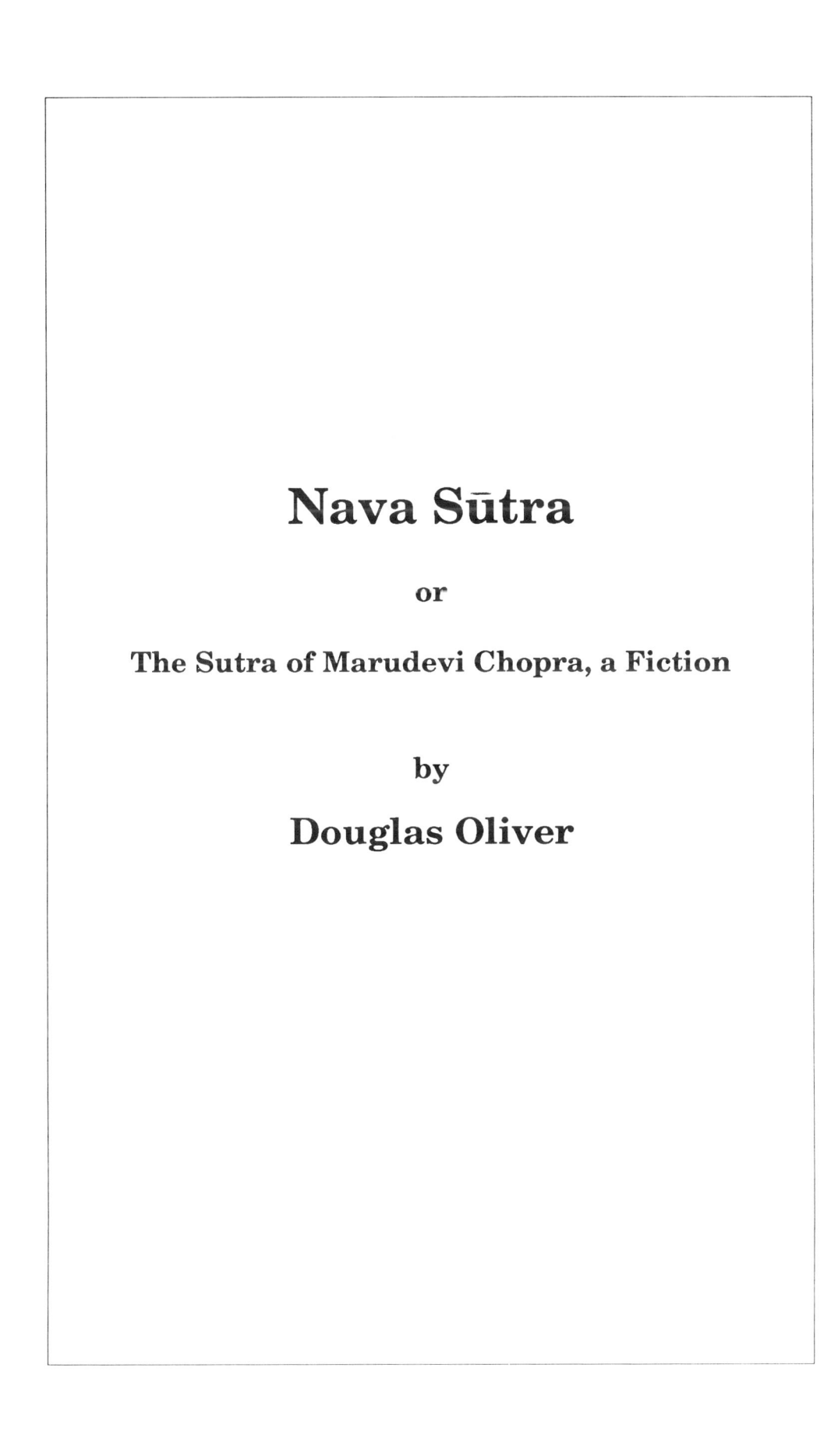

or

The Sutra of Marudevi Chopra, a Fiction

by

Douglas Oliver

I. THE SOUL AND THE GOOD

We bow to the beginning, non-beginning, to the running, and to the ending, non-ending of universal process in its mystery.

Following ancient teachings, we may say that right faith, right knowing, and right conduct serve the survival of the Good in space and time.

Believing that small stones hold locked up the powers of mind is right faith.

This is attained by reflection on the origin of the universe or by intuition of the holiness in small stones.

From immemorial time, the powers that agree in the mote have existed.

Soul lies in stones, plants, insects, animals, and animal-humans and even when inert is never absent.

The soul is not of this one world, Earth, but is formed of the powers that created the universe, which in their major aspect are relativistic.

Also soul has individual forms which are as standing turbulence in a constant and constantly whirling current of space and time.

Absolutes of finite content but infinite possibility arise at each instant of relativity, but only within the instant.

Many say there are no absolutes and all is relativity, but this is both true and false doctrine. Without momentary absolutes there could be no instants and yet each instant is utterly relative to other ones, and in itself is only an idealized figment.

Therefore, these absolutes both exist and do not exist.

Therefore, to say they do not exist is false doctrine, since without their existence even their non-existence falls away.

It is not given to any description, whether in language or proto-language, to understand this ideal role of the absolutes, nor to understand infinite possibility.

Unknown space and time came running together into an absolute and also relative beginning until the universe roared into life from the unknown.

In the unknown, space and time looked both ways in infinite possibility and past and future resided together.

The roaring became uncontrolled passion, the passion unfolded into four forces, and part of the forces consolidated into the first granules of thought.

So too the human mind.

Soon afterwards: humor.

Humor arises because the granules were once united in the womb of original creation and will henceforward clumsily attempt to recreate that unity by gluing together; also it arises whenever a penis pokes into a smiling vagina.

Where the pin points there matter is joined together in its laughable mental illness of never entirely gluing together

The humor is rich and necessary because creation follows this way of unity, disunity, and tendency to recreate unity.

Psychic gravitas and physical gravity also arise in this way.

Love of life's increase (a Prime Good) was a potential in the passionate roaring; so was its near-contrary: carelessness about life's increase (a Prime Evil).

One Prime Good leads to another: one Prime Evil to another.

The soul is part of the looking-both-ways of time and space and so it never departs from its beginning where it is innocent and empty; also it is full of its later virtue and wickedness.

Soul is knowing (cognition) and therefore knows before we know.

Unconsciously experiencing this is right knowing.

Humorous, silently joyful, and grave in innocence.

Knowledge is of six kinds: sensory and sensory-memorious knowledge; knowledge from the passions; rational and rational-memorious and rational-anticipatory and rational-sign- or language-like knowledge; artificially-induced knowledge as when induced by drugs or by the chemical imbalances of insanity; intuitive and instantaneous knowledge; and omniscience.

Clairvoyant or premonitory cognitions are uncertain forms of intuitive knowledge, in which the future, owing to its urgency, etc., unnaturally imposes upon the instantaneous.

Owing to lack of discrimination between the real and unreal, wrong knowledge is as whimsical as that of a lunatic, say the old teachings.

Not even the soul is omniscient. Omniscience is the unknown form of knowledge and should not be sought; therefore, neither should certainty be supposed absolute.

Lamplight flashlight. Viewed as cognition, soul is the lamp and the lamplight, reason is photon and flashlight, passion is light wave. But lamp, light and soul are the same.

That which cognizes soul is soul. That which cognizes fire is the soul-as-fire. That which cognizes the poem is the poet-as-poetry: otherwise, esh is just a human.

Excrement smeared by heels on streets brings fear.
The baby's smile brings love.
These are greater mysteries than we allow for.

No beliefs and enduring fixity of belief are false doctrine and are products of pride.

In false doctrine, thought may be imagined to swim into light like a fish through a hole in coral or like a turbot through a hole in the sea bed or like a baby through the womb or like a universe beginning from a hole. But really it is soul, not thought, that should be so imagined.

Soul in its aspects of energy, space, time, instantaneous stasis, relative change, multifariousness, and oneness constitutes reality.

Matter, anti-matter, mind, meaning, purpose, passion, thought are aspects of energy, space, time, instantaneous stasis, relative change, multifariousness, and oneness.

Chance, probability, fate, cause, meaning, and purpose are aspects of providence.

As inert matter contains mind locked up, so anti-matter must be regarded as containing anti-mind locked up, even though no meaning can be accorded to such a teaching. This may now be left aside.

Energy in the aspect of purpose is providence of universal soul.

Energy in the aspects of matter, anti-matter, inert mind, chance, probability, fate, cause is providence of nature.

Energy in the aspect of ambiguity between soul and not-soul, mind and not-mind, self and not-self, passion and thought, and between chance, probability, and meaning, and between passion and thought, and between self and not-self is providence of purpose.

A Prime Good is increase of love for life in self and therefore in others and it is also creating increase of life in the spirit of that love.

A singular beginning to the universe as by explosion means unimaginable order spreading outwards into disorder, increasing life, and creating the possibility of love.

Collapse of the expanded universe into its beginning means the Good beginning again in unimaginable novelty.

Never-ending expansion of the universe means order dissipating but strewing forms (atoms, minds, planets, stars) into space and time.

Never-ending expansion means the inner region of the cosmos becoming chaotic and then inert and then void and the void expanding as a darkness within the overall darkness of the expansion. But the outer rim retains its original energy, order, and light.

In an always-expanding universe the start depends upon the ending and the ending upon the start; so inner region and outer rim recreate each other in formal dependency.

At any true beginning or singularity in an always-expanding universe a hole appears in the known and a way is found out of the universe and into novelty.

But these descriptions say nothing of Spirit.

In essence, Spirit is the unknown.

It is soul's mode.

In description, Spirit is a configuration in space and time freed of matter and seemingly inhabiting "the past", but inhabiting it in the mode of the present.

Past time contains the once-present and the once-future, each in a spiritual condition, and thus is the past spiritualized in description.

As the stars spread out, forms of order (creation of atoms, planets, stars, acts of mind) enter the past as configurations in space and time and become spiritual.

The expansion of universes is in this way like a poem expanding into ordered lines: the originating energy is refound by looking back from the end to the start, and all the form becomes spiritual.

An ever-expanding universe: a huge soul, a huge memory. A collapsing universe: a renewing novelty.

What does such a universal soul experience? What would remember its universe? What kind of novelty?

Fool's questions.

Persistence of universes either in ever-expansion or in renewed novelty means that increase of life and of the Good are sovereign in their spiritual coexistence with the forms of destruction and Evil.

Only if the universe were to snuff out like a candle flame could Evil be sovereign over Good. But this is unlikely.

Therefore, to believe that the Good is sovereign over Evil is also right faith.

Pain inflicted by humans or permitted by humans shakes all teachings to their foundations.

The uncreated; that which lacks creation; the created; that which unwishes its creation

The Good is tended by the self attending to the soul.

This is right conduct.

The self and its forms of consciousness, even down to the smallest acts of mind, are also configurations in space and time.

Incorporation of experience into the configuration of self and rejection of experience from the configuration are two ways in which self and not-self are distinguished by the soul.

In the body, incorporation of experience is achieved through physiological imprinting; in mind, incorporation of experience is achieved through cognition.

The unchanging soul expands like a universe; also it does not change. There is no contradiction in this teaching.

The unchanging soul re-arises whole at each instant of its change and coexists with its changes. Therefore it constantly re-arises whole and changed.

Soul coexists unchanged with the creation of self that it suffers; also it is changed and limited by this creation of self.

Beyond sight of consciousness the self grows vast and one within the oneness and the multiplicity of soul.

No language makes the vast self fully accessible.

And so we say that "I" is like a story creation of language, varying, disunited, and never entirely our own; but this is a specious doctrine concerning forms of consciousness.

The vast self looks on silently with its growth partner, soul; or we must think this unthinkable thought if we are to understand.

Soul may be sensed as the "what" that is affected by the vast progress of the self and by the lesser forms of consciousness.

We create ourselves in space and time
In creating ourselves we embody others
And so is solipsism defeated, since others do likewise.

In our soul's demeanours lie the means of demeaning others.

Humankind includes its not-beloved and evil.

Our souls therefore include them.

In creating ourselves we fill out the emptiness of soul's entry into time.

II. SACRAMENTS OF THE MIDDLE WORLD

The old teachings say that the geography of our middle world (Earth, Jampudvipa) conforms spiritually to the order of the cosmos but this is only a trivial truth, since a change to the whole geography of this world would affect the cosmos little more than the removal of a grain of sand from an endless desert.

As this world turns on its axis and precesses and turns about the sun and is dragged by the sun round the great spiral of the galaxy, the galaxy moving onwards, and the universe (it is not known) moving onwards or not...

...so the smallest particles and anti-particles of this world, this system, this galaxy, this universe...so too the wiggly interchanges between particles like a snowball thrown between skaters.. so too in finer descriptions the infinities that arise and then cancel each other out as the description turns about and turns about, tunneling into the unknown...searching for the unattainable instant...

The geography of this world stands in relation to the universe as a particle to a large mass and rather as an instant stands in relation to all space and time.

For, at the heart of any one perspective: the unattainable instant.

As an instant has both absolute and relative aspects so too our perspective from this world has an absolute as well as a relative aspect.

Arctic, antarctic, temperate, tropical zones, land, sea, and undersea zones.

But also inhabited zones which dominate other zones both uninhabited and inhabited and create distortion.

From the perspective of an arctic zone freezing cold is temperate; from the perspective of a tropical zone moist heat is temperate.

The old teachings say that some one spot (Mount Meru, Benares, Delphi, Jerusalem, Mecca, Berlin, New York, London, Paris) is the navel of this world and that the holiest perspective is attained there.

But this is false: the holiest perspective is attained just where lives the worthiest person among the poorest or most suffering on this world.

In this respect the old teaching that the last shall be first and the first shall be last has its truth.

State of soul in animals and plants not knowable.

How, then, do we pretend to know it, that we practice such cruelties upon animals and plants?

It is taught that energy in the aspect of purpose is providence of soul and now it may be added that the soul's forward-looking into time contributes purpose.

Evolution of species in the newer teachings.

The future is caretaker of the past.

Evolution develops not simply out of the past of species but is drawn forwards by the future of species just as the future of an action already affects its present.

So purpose is added to the chance operations of evolution and mind develops in nature.

How much more then are humans indebted to more primitive species and are their caretakers!

Four sexes: female, male, neuter, and mixed.

The self, even the neuter self of stones, has sex.

The media of motion and rest and space are like the water in which fish swim and are not the fish themselves but like etheric substances without activity (movement), the teachings say.

But this is a way of expressing together the absolute and relative aspects of the instants of space-time, which the newer teachings have denied.

The units of space-time are infinite and the space-time points of forms of matter are numerable and innumerable also, as in the old teachings.

Souls inhabit from one unit upwards of space-time and may expand or contract like the light of a lamp or the density of a star or a gas.

That which is particular, has qualities and modes, and locks up some of its energy and soul, is a substance.

That which has substance as its substratum and which is not itself the substratum of other attributes is a quality, as the old teachings say.

The condition (change) of a substance is a mode, they say.

The life of all beings and their modes are sacramental.

For humans, the sacraments are five: birth, puberty, marriage and other solemnizations of love in various sexualities, childbirth, death

Inert constitution, attachment to self, reproduction of self from self, pollination, pollination of others, fertilization of others, temporary marriage, permanent marriage and other solemnizations, are process of life.

So stones, plants, single-celled animals, worms, pollination by bees, fertilization among frogs, fish, invertebrate and vertebrate land animals, birds, mammals, and humans in their societies.

Were the human baby born most deformed, still its birth would be a holy sacrament.

So too the fulfilled body of the smiling or crying human baby.

And yet still the fulfilled body of the unintelligent baby as holy as that of the intelligent.

In puberty, readiness for the holy and unsettlement at so great a responsibility.

And singleness of spirit in readiness to become enriched with increasing of life and thus of the Good.

So one of the sacraments.

In human marriage and other such solemnizations more that is complex and love-like than in the attachments of lower animals, although all attachment is love-like.

Therefore, from plants to humans, attachment ascends in spiritual complexity and in its potential to foster the Good more variously.

Therefore the old teachings were right to call human marriage in its varieties holy and a sacrament, since in the union of doves is found the same holiness, and in the seeding of trees, the propagation by shoots of strawberry plants, and the self-division of amoebas.

As spiritual importance declines from human marriage down to the simplest processes of nature, holiness does not change but only the complexity does.

Childbirth the most profound extension of our goodness.

The male seed is placed to worship the egg in the female temple, and there is like worship in other forms of loving.

How much to bewail any failure in such a trust, such a serving of the Good in life process!

Water beings, air beings, earth beings: humans have elected to be all those things and none of them is secure from the mouth of death.

NAVA SUTRA

The fool's way of dying is not accepting teaching
The fool's way of dying is to frighten emself with memories of wickedness so that those by the bedside grow frightened and wickedness increases.

Semi-wise dying: confession, repentance, bravery.

Wise dying: gladness for all we have done well. The wise are already dead, already alive, as in the beginning of things.

The dead are neither long nor small nor round; they are neither black nor blue nor red nor yellow nor white; neither bitter nor pungent nor astringent nor sweet; neither rough nor soft; neither cold nor hot; neither harsh nor smooth; nothing of that kind; but they are without body, which they leave as unnecessary when embarked on whatever their future might be, even a future in our memories or in their very own mystery.

It may also be said that the dead have size but it is a size of the soul and is not material but a transformation of spatio-temporal energy. During the past lifetime of the deceased, their increasing of the Good leaves their original, baby soul unchanged in size; their increasing of Evil diminishes that size.

What size is the loved one after departing?
Our lives make us sizeable after we die.
Cutting down in size the size we would be.
But the baby may be larger.
Dead, the baby may be larger.
Alive, the infant tries not to grow smaller in body and in soul.

Anyone, whether in life our lover, our relative, or our friend, becomes at death our love. And we may call that person by that name out of our great love for humanity and for its unguessable role in the universe.

It is fitting to remember here a loved one who has died, for that, too is a teaching. Whatever has become of you, love, we are eternally by your funeral-side, grieving for you and sharing with each other our happiness at the achievements of your life.

Some favorite moment of humor in that person's life may be remembered.

Wherever you are, love, that moment is still humorous.

Love, your life events enter now the same time as ours

Your life has now become transformed from all its imperfections into something golden and achieved

Stoneland of death is walked only by the body. Love walks in a freer, fertile landscape, even after death.

III. REASON AND PASSION

The complexity between unchanging soul, changing soul, unchanging self, changing selves of many types, and momentary selves is termed the unchanging soul's universe of changes.

Passions arise at every border between stasis and change in the soul's universe of changes.

All is one and the same in the soul and all is change and a temporary passion may be but a changed letter in a vast volume whose pages are formed of space and time.

Those who speak of a fundamental emotion, such as desire, speak falsely. Ongoingness (urging), which is not a passion but which resembles desire, is the medium in which passions form.

Swirling in dance of reason is passion.

Stumbling in footstepping of reason is passion.

Hindrance in swirling of passion is naming by reason.

Slow down, or you won't understand.

Since the first granules appeared at the origin of the universe, we have been desperately lost in description.

The soul knows already what language brings to it. So why language?

Because in its origin the soul is a baby.

The baby soul resists description by any language or proto-language of thought, for it will not be known but is the knower.

Origin of language, a dog's bark, the alarmed croak of a frog with baggy throat. Passion makes the body speak and speech is not at first conceptual but fearful or loving, at the very beginning of the conscious. Speech at first has no need of the refinement of a voice-box.

When original singularity in the primary roar of creation is conventionalized by art of reflection it becomes number.

One hand: no number, no notion of countable, not even of one, fingers not noticed; Other hand: number is innumerable and uncountable, fingers noticed in blurred notions;

Two hands together: one is the notion in two and then in five and then in ten and ever onward into the infinite aleph beyond the numerable.
Before number the non-numerous; after number an immense rushing onward of the non-numerous.

When passion is conventionalized by act of reflection it becomes the beginning of uttering language and the beginning of naming emotions.

The melody of the voice is the closest we come to conscious knowledge of our feelings at the moment when they are happening.

When melody is conventionalized it becomes sacred sutra, song, poetry, or cliche. None of these represent final truth. These teachings do not represent final truth.

IV. THE CELESTIAL AND INFERNAL WORLDS

Passion is always part of mind, sometimes extreme, sometimes mixed, sometimes ordinary and muted.

Each instant of extreme passion opens the stairways to heavens, hells, or limbos, which appear in the guise of blinding truth.

Each instant of ordinary or muted passions opens the stairways to the ordinary world, which appears as what is already known.

If the extreme passion is joy, an instant of it opens the particular heaven which would be the blinding truth if that joy's instant endured for ever; and it is as if all had been, is, and always will be joy.

Joy peoples its heaven with images that mean joy to the beholder, whether images of real or fantastic persons or inanimate things. Images, as it were, blue or white or angelic.

In the same way, if the extreme passion is love, an instant of it opens that particular heaven of blinding truth, as if all had been, is, and always will be love.

So love peoples its heaven with love-full images. Images, as it were, pink, glistening, or wondrous eyed.

Or the heaven may be of joy and love and its peopling may be more various.

Such heavens may appear at an instant of death.

In the same way, if the passion is depression, an instant of it opens that particular limbo of blinding truth, as if all had been, is, and always will be depressing.

So depression peoples its limbo with utterly depressing images. Images, as it were, dreary grey, sag-shouldered.

So too despair peoples its limbo with utterly despairing images. Images, as it were, unimaginably dirty-grey, ghost-like, or black and suicidal.

Or the limbo may be of depression and despair and its peopling may be more various, and more suicidal.

In the same way, if the passion is hate, an instant of it opens that particular hell of blinding truth, as if all had been, is, and always will be hate.

So hate peoples its hell with hateful images. Images, as it were, of fiery demons.

So too wrath peoples its hell with wrathful images. Images, as it were, of demons whose eyebrows burst open and whose tongues spew melting lead.

So too pride peoples its hell with prideful images. Images, as it were, of beings cast into contemptuous reduction while in return icy splinters impale the self-heart.

Or the hell may be of hate and wrath and pride, and its peopling may be more various.

It is not known whether limbos or hells appear at the instant of death, though they may appear in dreams and visions.

As many kinds of angel, grey ghost, or demon as extreme passions and habitual figurations of those passions in the imagination.

Since passion flows continuously in us, its flow contains infinitesimal instants which are united with the flow.

Thus an extreme passion which remains intense and the same may lead us into a vision of what an instant of that passion is like and we may envision that particular heaven, limbo, or hell.

In such visions other humans or animals or non-living things or we ourselves or our imaginings may be transformed by passion into the inhabitants and materials of these heavens, limbos, or hells in a blinding truth.

The vision is limited by the nature of the passion and the nature of the circumstances in which it arises.

The vision of such an instant whose factual content has been limited by the passion that has revealed it to us is a true vision but also untrue.

True because an instant is absolute, untrue because also utterly relative.

Spiritual error and mental illness arise from being caught in a misunderstanding of this.

Truth is composed of the absolutes of all instants and also of their relation to each other: that is, truth is the unknown and the unknown is the universal soul which knows.

All the angels, grey ghosts, demons, etc., might make an unknown truth for us; and, as the Good is sovereign over Evil, it may be supposed that the unknown is more likely angelic than demonic. To assert this too definitely would be prideful.

The old teachings say that the thought-coloration, environment, body, suffering and shape of body (or deeds) are more and more inauspicious in succession among the infernal beings; and this is correct of the infernal beings disclosed in visionary instants.

Worship is healthy if the object of worship be healthy and humorous and grave; but there are no pre-ordained objects or personages that must be worshipped. Worship that either excludes other humans from its objects of worship or insists upon the exclusive merits of its own objects is unhealthy.

Images of divinity require in their visionary worlds no police. Images of demons in their visionary worlds would burn up a police. Therefore, the mixed states of humans require policing as they deserve and a virtuous citizenry requires little.

V. DISTORTION

Virtuous activity is the cause of merit in the universe and therefore in the soul's universe and in its selves; wicked activity is the cause of demerit.

Distortion in knowing is permanent distortion in the configuration of self in space and time.

Not all distortion in knowing is sin or is harmful but the distortion may be harmlessly pleasurable or valuable and give way to further knowing as in the fantasies of art.

Within the duration of the human species there is increase of life-time, of science, and of blasphemy against spirit.

Increase of complexity of thought, increase of consciousness of divisions of time, increase of ambiguity of passion, decrease of purity in thought-coloration.

To place another in command over ourselves knowing that esh has harmful self-distortions and will practice cruelty on our behalf and with our aid is sin.

But we should place only virtuous persons in command over ourselves, knowing that doing so will result in lessened exercise of power.

Sin separates a mean self out from the soul, blinding us to our depths and origins and piercing with harm humans or non-humans, while the mean self glows more brightly to us in its singleness and soul stands aside, aghast.

Love incorporates those others that we love, humans or non-humans, into a self which is more closely like the soul than are the sinful selves, and which is one and various.

Anger, cruelty, pride, greed lead to shrinking
inward to a point which is an empty instant and is not,
a dark spot,
in soul, that great whiteness tinged with yellow like clarified butter.

The old teachers said that these uses of speech are not to be employed: speaking in wrath or in pride for deception or for gain, speaking knowingly or unknowingly hard words.

They say that speaking with precision, we should employ language in moderation and restraint.

Now we add: except where some benefit of humor, eloquence, or justice is to be gained.

They say there are four kinds of speech: truth; untruth; truth mixed with untruth; and neither truth nor untruth nor truth mixed with untruth.

They say that before the utterance speech is speech-in-antecedent-non-existence, while uttered it is real speech, and the moment after it is uttered it is speech-in subsequent-non-existence. Speech in non-existence is also to be called non-speech.

They say that there are four kinds of obstacles: matter, space, time, affects.

Now we add: matter: things animate, inanimate, and of mixed state;

Space: as in village, town, wood, field, threshing-floor, house, courtyard, factory, office, bodega, and apartment.

Time: as in a poetic stress, a wink, a syllable, a voiced stretch of melody, a breath, a verse line, a cadence, a stanza, a poem, an episode in life, a generation, a life, a century, a millennium, a halving of all known human time, a time of human species, a time of an Earth, a time of a star system, a galaxy, a consideration of galaxies, a universe, a more-than-one universe.

Affects: as in wrath, pride, deceit, greed, fear, mirth, love, hate, quarreling, calumny, tale-bearing, scandal, kindness, pleasure, pain, deceitful falsehood, joy, praise, etc., all down to the evil of wrong belief, however that may be defined.

But these are not obstacles. They are the media in which we wrestle to attain the Good.

Five transgressions of concentration are: misdirected right faith, right conduct, and right knowing; lack of, or misdirected, or excessive earnestness; and fluctuation of thought.

Spite against knowledge, concealment of knowledge, non-imparting of knowledge, disregard of knowledge, disparagement of true knowledge or of those who know, praise of self, and laying obstacles for others, lead to harmful distortion.

Pain, even when arising from a necessary (natural) form of destruction, cannot be justified; also it cannot be proved unjust.

Those born with ugly or deformed bodily gait have potential spiritual advancement over those born with beautiful bodily gait.

Those who through ill living acquire ugly, deformed, or exaggeratedly beautiful bodily gait show spiritual diminution.

Violence is never justified except where to protect against a greater violence: in the difference of scale lies all the ground of justification.

Renege on revenge and manage anger: dangerous engines.

Setting oneself up in command for prideful reasons and all other pridefulness including exclusive pride in gender or in race,
scorn for gender, family, tribe, and origins,
disrespect for the affection of friends,
violence in sexual activities,
slothfulness and lack of or misplaced earnestness,
garrulity,
envy,
gluttony,
humorlessness,
lack of taking pleasure,
lying,
unruly anger,
murder, are among the sins.

So too forgery,
misappropriation,
stealing and prompting another to steal,
receiving stolen goods,
buying for low prices and selling for high prices in a disordered nation,
using false weights and measures,
deceiving others with artificial or imitation goods,
over-charging in fees or prices or lending,
exceeding reasonable limits with regard to cultivable lands, property, or riches,
keeping too many consumable and non-consumable objects,
sending outside one's country for luxuries,
manipulating currencies for profit,
infringement of laws when not dictated by most urgent reasons of conscience,
false recourse to law.

So too perverted governing,
perverted practice of law,
perverted accounting,
perverted practice of medicine,
perverted teaching,
divulging what is done in secret,
proclaiming others' thoughts as one's own,
lack of respect for things non-human,
polluting the material and spiritual worlds.

The old teachings spoke of the bondage of karma, and mutatis mutandis they spoke rightly, since distortions in the space-time of our soul and its selves stay with us and may at best only be transformed into new and less harmful distortions.

The old teachings say the karmic molecules of infinite times infinite space-points always pervade in a subtle form the entire space-points of every soul in every birth, and these are absorbed by the soul because of its activity. Mutatis mutandis they speak rightly.

VI. THE PARADOX OF LIBERATION

No liberation.

And so liberation is attained by not wishing liberation, and by acting in liberated ways.

And still liberation may not be claimed even by those most liberated.

No-one who sets emself up as teacher can fully teach.

No-one's sutras can be fully sutras.

Many scriptures may be read, none fully trusted.

However wise or saintly they may be, those who say confidently that they have salvation or liberation for us are by the nature of the instant's ambiguity, lying. Whether they are in other aspects trustworthy depends upon their saintliness or wisdom but not upon their claims to these qualities, for many who make no such claims are wise, and those who claim to be so are in that particular unwise.

Confident doctrines of liberation are false by virtue of their tonality, but those which offer greater possibility of liberation to any one sex or form of nature than to another are additionally dubious.

Benevolence towards all living beings, joy at the sight of the virtuous, compassion and sympathy for the afflicted, and tolerance towards the insolent and ill-behaved are cited by the old teachings as leading to correction of distortion.

Intelligence proper to one's own bodily existence is all the intelligence required for correction of distortion. However, the higher intelligences have greater responsibility and therefore more risk of distortion.

Devotion, charity, being of one's kind, being kind, empathy, smiling, humor, joy, love, communion with the memory of the dead, candor, respect for knowledge and for the disclosure of knowledge lead to correction of distortion.

Suffering and sorrow, even when they lead to distortion of conscious knowing, are equivalent to devotion, charity, etc., because in true knowing they are part of creation-destruction.

Therefore, those who suffer and are sorrowful do so for all who do not, that there might be true universal process, and knowing this in fear and compassion is correction of distortion.

Making vows and meditation can lead to correction of distortion.

Vows of those who would be monks or nuns, even when taken as part of a dogmatic community, are vows relative to private beliefs and — so they be good vows — are worthy of respect.

Vows whose aspiration is towards spiritual power over others, or towards enjoying spiritual knowledge over and above that of other beings, are products of distortion.

Vows of lay people are, where benevolence allows, to take pleasure, to have attachment, to share laughter, to love when possible, to like where possible, to endure suffering of self, to alleviate suffering of others, to hate deeds rather than sinners where possible, to treat animals as equals where possible, to tender plants and natural geography, to live creating as little harm as possible, to reflect daily on all these yogas.

Or the nature of mundane existence and the body may be contemplated in order to cultivate awe.

Reflection also on the universe, transitoriness, helplessness, human relationship, tribes, wish for the Good, non-human animal virtue, loneliness, distinctness, impurity, distortion, rarity of enlightenment, and truth.

Taking pleasure in what is pleasurable and feeling sorrow for what is sorrowful can lead to correction of distortion.

Every sin must be reported, either to a teacher or to our conscious mind.

We say we are no good at nursing. Who, then, will nurse? Who teach? Who conduct trade and honorable science? Who labor? Who govern? Who explore the mind? But we are called to do all these things in different ways.

Reasons for saying "it can't be helped": drag of past actions on the soul, pulling of future actions on the soul, fear of slander, fear of verdict, outward confessions with inner reservations, tricks, insincerity, mistaking of the selves for the soul.

Courage, forbearance, modesty, straightforwardness, purity, truthfulness, self-restraint, capacity for abstinence, capacity for pleasure, benevolence, constitute virtue or duty.

Living in comparative poverty, creating material and spiritual wealth for others but not offending in the creation of wealth; these may be aids.

Study, fasting, confession, repentance, penance, expiation, paying homage to the worthy may be aids.

Concentration of thought upon one particular object may be an aid.

Concentration on cruel imaginings, whether those appearing in mind or in stories, leads to spiritual diminution.

Passionless saints, passionate saints, unsaintly saints, emancipated saints, non-emancipated saints, unintelligent saints, non-human animal saints.

Wish to be single is not liberation, craving for attachment is not.

Neither "this" nor "that" but both "this" and "that" whole-heartedly in benevolence is liberation. So neither "liberation" nor "non-liberation" is liberation.

Acceptance of being one voice in infinite shouting is liberation.

Acceptance of being one silence in infinite silence is liberation.

Welcoming death in its instant since its instant contains the shape of our life is liberation.

So that soul retains its nature of darting upwards to the Good.

Nature of the soul's movement is liberation in its paradoxes.

꽃

(Although no Jain would accept the above doctrines, reverent obeisance is made to the Jaina bible, the *Tattvārthādhigamasūtra*, whose profound wisdom provides an underlying structure for this new sutra.)